Academic Learning in Law

Academic Learning in Law

Theoretical Positions, Teaching Experiments and Learning Experiences

Edited by

Bart van Klink

Faculty of Law, Vrije Universiteit Amsterdam, the Netherlands

Ubaldus de Vries

Institute for Jurisprudence, Constitutional and Administrative Law, School of Law, Utrecht University, the Netherlands

Edward Elgar PUBLISHING

Cheltenham, UK • Northampton, MA, USA

Published by
Edward Elgar Publishing Limited
The Lypiatts
15 Lansdown Road
Cheltenham
Glos GL50 2JA
UK

Edward Elgar Publishing, Inc.
William Pratt House
9 Dewey Court
Northampton
Massachusetts 01060
USA

A catalogue record for this book is available from the British Library

Library of Congress Control Number: 2016935775

This book is available electronically in the **Elgar**online
Law subject collection
DOI 10.4337/9781784714895

MIX
Paper from responsible sources
FSC® C013604

ISBN 978 1 78471 488 8 (cased)
ISBN 978 1 78471 489 5 (eBook)

Typeset by Columns Design XML Ltd, Reading
Printed and bound by CPI Group (UK) Ltd, Croydon, CR0 4YY

Contents

List of figures vii
List of tables viii
List of contributors ix
Preface xiii

1 Introduction: re-thinking academic legal education 1
Bart van Klink and Ubaldus de Vries

PART I THEORY AND LEGAL EDUCATION

2 Knowledge and aphasia: what is the use of skeptical legal education? 15
Bart van Klink
3 Re-*Bildung*: an ideal reconsidered for legal education 35
Lyana Francot and Luigi Corrias
4 Academic education and socialization 58
Anja Böning
5 The necessary loneliness of teaching (and of being a legal academic) 79
Anthony Bradney

PART II EXPERIMENTAL COURSES

6 Teaching international law critically – critical pedagogy and *Bildung* as orientations for learning and teaching 99
Christine Schwöbel-Patel
7 Learning law differently: the importance of theory and methodology 121
Bal Sokhi-Bulley
8 Empirical methodologies knowledge and expertise: a 'necessary' skill for lawyers? 142
Terry Hutchinson
9 Visuals for a critical legal profession 160
Wibo van Rossum

10 For a new and more diverse comparative legal education 180
Sabrina Germain

PART III DIDACTIC INNOVATIONS AND LEARNING EXPERIMENTS

11 Orchestrating encounters: teaching law at a liberal arts and sciences college in the Netherlands 201
Barbara Oomen
12 Students' perception and legal education 223
Gülriz Uygur
13 Learning how to read a case: resources from the visual and dramatic arts 244
Maksymilian Del Mar
14 Law & lounge: an experiment on student self-organization and critique as skeptical reflexivity 267
Ubaldus de Vries
15 Epilogue: an overview, reflections and a student's perspective 288
Tim Bleeker
16 Conclusions: concrete proposals for change: 14 theses 314

Index 323

Figures

9.1	Photograph of Uluru, Ayers Rock	164
9.2	Randomly parked bicycles at the train station in Haarlem	167
9.3	Bike placement detail	171
9.4	Yellow lines designating new areas where bikes can be legally placed	172
13.1	Extra materials	254
13.2	'Choose your island' 1	260
13.3	'Choose your island' 2	260

Tables

7.1	Perspectives for exercise for interrogation and application	138
9.1	Relation between legal rules, legal practices and cultural values	169
13.1	Learning outcomes matched with activities for Workshop 1	252
13.2	Questions/comments linked to activities for Workshop 1	252
13.3	Learning outcomes matched with activities for Workshop 2	256
13.4	Questions/comments linked to activities for Workshop 2	257
13A.5	Feedback from activities for Workshop 1	263
13A.6	Feedback from activities for Workshop 2	265
14.1	The texts in the initial experiment	272
14.2	The texts in the experiment in its second guise	276
14.3	The texts in the experiment in its third guise	281

Contributors

Tim Bleeker is Student Research Assistant for Legal Theory and Philosophy, at the Department of Jurisprudence, Constitutional and Administrative Law at the University of Utrecht, and Supreme Court Litigation Legal Assistant at Pels Rijcken Droogleever Fortuijn. He studied law at the Utrecht Law College, and is currently enrolled on the Legal Research Master in Utrecht. He is particularly interested in legal theory, human rights and intellectual property law.

Anja Böning studied law, educational studies and sociology. She is Research Assistant at the Faculty of Law, FernUniversität in Hagen, Germany. She lectures on equalities law. In her research she addresses questions of legal education, legal academia and higher education. (Research profile available at: https://www.fernuni-hagen.de/ls_haratsch/team/anja.rudek.shtml.)

Anthony Bradney is Professor of Law at Keele University, United Kingdom. He teaches on courses on legal skills, legal systems and legal theory. He has published widely on university legal education, law and religion, and law and popular culture. He is Honorary Membership Secretary of the Society of Legal Scholars. (Research profile available at: http://www.keele.ac.uk/law/people/academicstaff/anthonybradney/.)

Luigi Corrias is an Assistant Professor of Philosophy of Law at Vrije Universiteit Amsterdam, the Netherlands. He conducts research on the (constitutional) foundations of EU law and the concept of humanity in international (criminal) law. He also has a keen interest in the relationship between time and law. He teaches several courses on legal theory, both at Bachelor and Master level. He is an Associate Editor of the *Netherlands Journal of Legal Philosophy*. (Research profile available at: https://www.rechten.vu.nl/en/about-the-faculty/faculty/faculty/legal-theory-and-legal-history/corrias-l-d-a.asp.)

Ubaldus de Vries Assistant Professor at the Department of Jurisprudence, Constitutional and Administrative Law of the Faculty of Law (JCAL), Utrecht University, the Netherlands. In his research his focus, from a legal theoretical and social theoretical perspective, is on questions pertaining to sustainability, risk and responsibility. In addition, he seeks to integrate research into teaching and experiments with new didactical ways to enhance the academic aspect of legal education. He is currently Teaching Fellow of Utrecht University. (Research profile available at: http://www.uu.nl/leg/staff/URMTdeVries.)

Maksymilian Del Mar is Reader in Legal Theory and Director of the Centre for Law and Society in a Global Context at the School of Law, Queen Mary University of London, United Kingdom. He is President of the UK IVR and an Academic Fellow of the Honourable Society of the Inner Temple. He has taught contract law and jurisprudence, as well as advanced postgraduate courses on common law reasoning. (Research profile available at: http://www.law.qmul.ac.uk/staff/delmar.html.)

Lyana Francot is Associate Professor at the Department of Legal Theory and Legal History, Faculty of Law, Vrije Universiteit Amsterdam, the Netherlands. She teaches Legal Skills (Academic Writing) and Philosophy of Law. Francot is also the Program Director of the research program 'Boundaries of Law' and the Director of the Centre for Research of Time and Law. (Research profiles available at: https://www.rechten.vu.nl/en/about-the-faculty/faculty/faculty/legal-theory-and-legal-history/francot-timmermans-l.asp and at: http://vu-nl.academia.edu/LyanaFrancot.)

Sabrina Germain is a Lecturer at the University of Surrey, United Kingdom. Her research interests lie in the many connections between law and public policy, and the importance of practical training in the realm of legal education. Previously, she volunteered as a law instructor for the Cornell Prison Education Program in a maximal security prison in Upstate New York, United States and has also lectured at universities in Europe.

Terry Hutchinson is an Associate Professor within the QUT Law School. She teaches criminal law and legal research, and has published widely in the areas of youth justice and postgraduate legal research training, including *Researching and Writing in Law* (Thomson Reuters, 3rd edn, 2010). She is a past chair and current member of the Queensland Law Society's Equalising Opportunities in the Law Committee (from 2002), and a member of the Law Council of Australia's Equalising Opportunities in the Law Committee (from 2004). She served as Editor-in-Chief and then Associate Editor of the peer-reviewed *Legal Education Review* 2004–2011.

Barbara Oomen holds a chair in the sociology of human rights at Utrecht University, the Netherlands. She is the Dean of University College Roosevelt, Utrecht University's Liberal Arts and Sciences College based in the Netherlands. Here, she teaches a range of courses in the field of law. Her research focuses on human rights implementation, and she chaired the Netherlands Platform on Human Rights Education for many years. She also holds a range of advisory functions on higher education, for instance, as a member of the Advisory Board for the National Science Agenda for the Netherlands.

Christine Schwöbel-Patel is Senior Lecturer in Law at the University of Liverpool, United Kingdom. She teaches several research-led courses at undergraduate and postgraduate level which she designed. These include 'Critical Approaches to International Criminal Law', 'International Law in Current Affairs', and a 'Marketing Global Justice' pathway on the 'Law and Social Justice' module. Christine is Co-Director of the Critical Approaches to International Criminal Law research cluster. (Research profiles available at: http://www.liv.ac.uk/law/staff/christine-schwobel/ (and at:) https://liverpool.academia.edu/ChristineSchw%C3%B6bel.)

Bal Sokhi-Bulley is a Lecturer in Law at Queen's University Belfast. She lectures in Legal Theory, Human Rights in Practice and teaches skills sessions on legal research methodologies at postgraduate level. She has previously published on 'learning theory as skill' and has co-authored a book on research methodologies in EU and International Law.

Gülriz Uygur is a Professor of law at Ankara University, Law School. She teaches Introduction to Law, Philosophy of Law, Gender and Law, Legal Ethics, Domestic Violence Clinic, Prisoner Clinic and, Gender and Ethics. She is General Secretary of the Turkish Philosophy Society and Head of the Department of Legal Philosophy (IVR Turkey Section), a member of the Executive Committee (International Association of Philosophy of Law and Social Philosophy-IVR), and Member of the UNESCO Gender Committee.

Bart van Klink is Professor of Legal Methodology at Vrije Universiteit Amsterdam, the Netherlands. He is responsible for the skills training at his Faculty of Law and gives various skills training courses, among which are Legal Skills, Methods of Legal Research, and Legal Research Lab. Moreover, he was President of the Dutch Association for Philosophy of Law (VWR) between 2010 and 2016. Currently, he is member of the board of the Dutch and Flemish Socio-Legal Studies Association VSR and, together with Sanne Taekema, Editor-in-Chief of the journal *Law* *and Method*. (Research profile available at: https://www.rechten.vu.nl/en/about-the-faculty/faculty/faculty/legal-theory-and-legal-history/bart-van-klink.asp.)

Wibo van Rossum is an Assistant Professor in Socio-Legal Studies at Utrecht University School of Law, the Netherlands. His main research interest is the empirical study of social diversity and the law. He is member of the board of the Dutch and Flemish Socio-Legal Studies Association VSR. He teaches Sociology of Law (in Dutch), Comparative Legal Cultures, and the Methodology Round Table at Utrecht University, and Anthropology of Law at Erasmus University Rotterdam. (Research profile available at: www.wibovanrossum.nl.)

Preface

The original idea of this book on academic learning in legal education resulted from a discussion meeting in Utrecht in the Spring of 2012 and at various academic conferences. What appeared to us, as editors, was that at conferences usually *research* topics are discussed, but the other main task of legal academic activity – teaching – is often neglected as a research topic.

Too often, research comes first and teaching second. However, in most law schools, we believe, teaching is essentially the core business as each year we 'raise' a new generation of lawyers that will shape tomorrow's laws and, thereby, the whole political and legal system. Therefore, we believe that we should reflect more on our role as teachers, what it means to create an academic legal curriculum and design courses, how we should and could teach law, what type of lawyers we want to raise and about the nature of academic legal education.

The initial step was to dedicate a special issue of the journal *Law and Method* to academic learning in legal education, which was published in the Spring of 2013. It consisted of five contributions and it seemed to have hit a note.

Hence, we decided to draft a book proposal in which we could extend and expand upon the themes addressed in the journal's special issue. The result is this book, published by Edward Elgar, in which theoretical perspectives about the nature of academic legal education is complemented by contributions about innovative courses and innovative teaching and learning experiments beyond the traditional 'black-letter law' education, each of which can be read in its own right.

Nevertheless, to guide the reader through this book, we suggest to not only read the introductory Chapter 1 (which focuses upon the general theme of academic legal education) but also the Epilogue (Chapter 15) in which Tim Bleeker, a graduate student and our Assistant Editor, provides an overview of the contributions, shows the interconnections between the themes and topics, and concludes with a student perspective on legal education.

A book like this depends on the assistance of many others. In particular we would like to thank the contributors whose professionalism and scholarly high quality made our work as editors easy. We also thank the external reviewers for their timely feedback, that was full of constructive comments and suggestions. A special thanks also goes to Tim Bleeker, who joined as an Assistant Editor, for being meticulous in his editing work, and in the end also proved to be a valuable contributor in his own right.

Finally, we would like to thank Edward Elgar for taking on board this project and the trust given to us, a particular warm thanks to Ben Booth, Tori Nicols, Karen Jones and Iram Satti.

Bart van Klink and Ubaldus de Vries
June, 2016

1. Introduction: re-thinking academic legal education

Bart van Klink and Ubaldus de Vries

In many countries across the world, the nature of the university and the purpose and function of academic education are subject to intense academic, social and political debate. The protests in cities such as Amsterdam, Hong Kong, London and Melbourne, in Spring 2015 have created a momentum to re-evaluate what the university is about and, in particular, what we want to achieve with academic education.

Both students and lecturers call for a fundamental re-evaluation of the Academia. A common thread in the protests is the resistance against the managerial culture (or 'managerialism') prevailing at universities. According to RethinkUvA (an Amsterdam based protest movement consisting of both lecturers and students), '[o]utput-focused management has severely compromised the quality of both university education and research. [...] What is called for, are 'structural reforms in education and research.'[1] RethinkUU (based in Utrecht) argues that the ideals of the academic community are under pressure and warns that the 'trend toward efficiency and standardization threaten the depth and versatility of academic learning and expand bureaucracy on paper and between individuals'.[2] At the London School of Economics (LSE) in London, students and lecturers oppose the current trend of neoliberalism in the academic world: 'LSE is the epitome of the neoliberal university. It is managed and organised around corporate interests, which promote

---

[1] Available at: http://rethinkuva.org/about-rethink-uva/ (accessed 7 July 2015, our translation).

[2] Available at: http://www.rethinkuu.nl/wp-content/uploads/RethinkUU.Open_Letter.English.pdf. For the original letter in Dutch, see: http://www.rethinkuu.nl/open-letter/ (both accessed 7 July 2015, our translation).

elitism and perpetuate inequality.'[3] OccupyLSE has started a project called the 'Free University of London', proposing that students, lecturers and workers run the university together. As *The Guardian* notes, the protests are directed towards the threats of 'commercialisation' and, additionally, at the threats of: efficiency, short-term interests, and at the instrumentalization of teaching and learning.[4] In Quebec, students have protested in particular against funding cuts and fee increases.[5,6]

Politicians, policymakers and university administrators seem, finally, to have heard the wake-up call. For instance, the Dutch Minister of Education, Jet Bussemakers, responded to the recent protests by confirming that academic education is 'of course' about *Bildung*. Moreover, Bussemakers argued that 'what is at stake is that the university enables the education of young adults to become the future driving force in our society, both nationally and internationally.'[7] Bussemakers' strategic vision resembles Nussbaum's idea of global citizenship (as discussed below):[8]

> A democracy [...] exists by virtue of people who think about what kind of community we wish to be. People who give guidance as to how we want to live together in our society, what we find important and which choices follow from this. Higher education should not only educate to be able to make these choices but also to be able to lead the discussion and sharpen the debate.

Statements such as this suggest that there is a shared desire, both in the academic world and in society at large to change the course the

---

[3] Available at: http://www.theguardian.com/higher-education-network/2015/mar/25/university-protests-around-the-world-a-fight-against-commercialisation (accessed 7 July 2015).

[4] Ibid.

[5] Available at: http://theindependent.ca/2015/03/27/quebec-students-are-fighting-for-you/ (accessed 20 July 2015).

[6] Similar protests, about a variety of issues, took place in Melbourne, Mexico, Honduras and Hong Kong. See, respectively: http://www.theage.com.au/victoria/thousands-of-university-students-protest-in-melbourne-against-federal-budget-20140521-38ofu.html; http://www.interaksyon.com/article/107783/mexicans-mark-6th-month-since-43-students-vanished-with-protests; http://www.telesurtv.net/english/news/Assassination-of-4-Student-Leaders-in-Honduras-Prompts-Protests-20150327-0001.html; http://blogs.wsj.com/chinarealtime/2015/03/23/in-wake-of-protests-hong-kong-student-group-changes-leader/ (all accessed 20 July 2015).

[7] In an interview with *Science Guide*, 13 March 2015; see: http://www.scienceguide.nl/201503/waar-het-echt-om-gaat.aspx (accessed 14 June 2015).

[8] Available at: http://magazines.rijksoverheid.nl/ocw/ho2025/2015/01/voorwoord-minister-bussemaker (accessed 7 July 2015, our translation).

university is taking nowadays, and to rethink the true vocation of academic learning.

ACADEMIC DEBATE

In the academic world there is a lively debate going on as well. Many scholars have criticized the marketization of higher education and the reduction of the student to the role of consumer.[9] Generally, academic education is perceived to be too instrumental and specialized. As many scholars observe, too much emphasis is placed on economic and career interests.[10] Henry A. Giroux speaks alarmingly of 'neoliberalism's war on higher education'.[11] Academic education has become skills-driven.[12] According to Frank Furedi, education in general is turned into a tool of social-engineering, teaching students how to cope with the challenges of modernity by providing them with practical skills training and obligatory IT courses.[13] Against the influence of so-called curriculum experts and social engineers, he advocates a pluralist approach that gives more freedom to schools and teachers to develop their own educational programs and pedagogical methods.[14] Increasingly, students are put under pressure to finish their academic career fast. There is no time for students to make mistakes and detours, to grow and develop as a person and to prepare themselves to fulfil a meaningful role in society.

---

[9] See, for instance, M Molesworth, E Nixon and R Scullion (eds), *The Marketization of Higher Education and the Student as Consumer* (Routledge 2011) and R Brown, *Everything for Sale? The Marketization of UK Higher Education* (Routledge 2013).

[10] Lyana Francot & Bald de Vries, 'Adieu Von Humboldt? Over Domme Organisaties en Slimme mensen', in: LJ Dorsman & PJ Knegtmans (eds), *Het Universitaire Bedrijf. Over Professionalisering van Onderzoek, Bestuur en Beheer* (Verloren 2010) 73.

[11] Henry A Giroux, *Neoliberalism's War on Higher Education* (Haymarket Books 2014).

[12] The hype of twenty-first century skills is an example of this tendency and is illustrative of the unreflective instrumentalization of higher education. For a glossary of the notion, see: J Bellanca & R Brandt, *21st Century Skills: Rethinking How Students Learn* (Solution Tree Press 2010).

[13] Frank Furedi, *Wasted. Why Education Isn't Educating* (Continuum 2011).

[14] In the volume *Waartoe is de universiteit op aarde?*, edited by Ad Verbrugge and Jelle van Baardewijk (Boom 2014), with contributions from both lecturers and students, the autonomy of the university is also promoted against the demands of the New Public Management.

Opposing this trend of instrumentalization, scholars such as Anthony T Kronman and Martha Nussbaum, each in their own way, call for a fundamental re-evaluation of the idea of academic education. Kronman appeals to the intrinsic value of academic education, when he observes that the 'question about life's meaning [has lost] its status as a subject of organized academic instruction and [is] pushed to the margins of professional respectability […].'[15] Due to the contemporary culture of political correctness and the modern research ideal, we can no longer, according to Kronman, speak meaningfully about the meaning of life. In order to revive this lost tradition, he advocates the reading of classical works in literature and philosophy. Whereas Kronman conceives of education as the quest for knowledge for its own sake (that is, for understanding life), Nussbaum emphasizes the social and ethical aspirations of academic education. According to her, education is needed to make students aware of ethical problems and to prepare them for global citizenship. Inspired by Kant and Stoic cosmopolitanism, Nussbaum stresses the importance of using 'the faculties of thought and imagination that make us human and make our relations rich human relations rather than relations of mere use and manipulation.'[16]

LEGAL EDUCATION

As the direction, function and nature of academic education are subject to intense debate inside and outside the university, this is also true for academic *legal* education. The debates confront law schools with fundamental questions about the nature of legal education. For what purpose(s) do we educate law students? Is legal education primarily vocational in the tradition of the American law schools? Or does it (also) have an academic mission, as it used to have in continental Europe where faculties (rather than schools) provide an academic programme at both undergraduate and graduate level?

In an extensive study of the modern law school, Carel Stolker notes that, from the perspective of other disciplines, the study of law is not taken too seriously and the law school (or law faculty) is considered to be

---

15 AT Kronman, *Education's End: Why Our Colleges and Universities Have Given Up on the Meaning of Life* (Yale University Press 2007) 7.

16 Martha Nussbaum, *Not for Profit. Why Democracy Needs the Humanities* (Princeton University Press 2010) 6.

'the odd man out'.[17] Why does this negative perception exist? Stolker gives several reasons, including legal education's vocational characteristic, the 'massification' of student enrolment, the normative character of legal research, as well as its implicit methodology and fluid line between research, consultancy and legal practice in which many academics are involved.

These reasons may be correct, but the same may be said about education in other disciplines, such as medicine and veterinary medicine. Possibly, this negative perception is fed by the huge emphasis on methodology and empirical-based science that dominates our thinking about the university in general. However, this should not be the only yardstick against which a discipline is measured as being more or less academic. This is, in our view, too narrow a focus. It implies a schism between the humanities on the one hand and the social and natural sciences on the other, whereas these three form the trinity of thought upon which the university is based. Moreover, it ignores the hermeneutic character of the legal discipline, and the argumentative way in which knowledge is justified and debated in the study of law, as in other disciplines of the humanities.[18]

As Stolker points out, there are other good reasons for considering law to be an academic discipline. These reasons have to do with the function of law. Law affects us in our daily lives and responds to social developments. Law is becoming increasingly complex and, therefore, strong analytical skills are needed to understand it in order to construe a consistent body of legal norms. In its application, it requires a constant supply of future academics (not only practitioners) to reflect upon law's (just) application and to guarantee its continued existence. Hence, Stolker concludes that 'law is a condition for civilised living [and] is far too important to be left to the profession or to the workplace only.'[19] In other words, law is more than a vocational enterprise but must be studied, criticized and debated by academics who teach students not only the 'black-letter law', but also how to reflect on the nature of law and its actual functioning in society.

This is also the point of departure of this book: legal education is and should be academic. The point is, however, how to *guarantee and*

---

17 Carel Stolker, *Rethinking the Law School. Education, Research, Outreach and Governance* (CUP 2014) 88.

18 See Sanne Taekema, 'Relative Autonomy. A Characterisation of the Discipline of Law', in: Bart van Klink & Sanne Taekema (eds), *Law and Method. Interdisciplinary Research into Law* (Mohr Siebeck 2011) 33–52.

19 Stolker *op cit*, 96.

strengthen the academic character and quality of legal education on the one hand, and how to avoid that legal education and its curriculum become too much practice-oriented on the other hand: the study of black-letter law (legislation and case law) has to be firmly embedded in a social and theoretical context that opens up the possibility of developing a critical outlook on law – of 'thinking about the law'.[20]

This is, of course, not to say that the study of black-letter law is unwarranted. The point is rather that the preferred case study method is in itself not sufficient to meet all the requirements of what can count as an academic legal education. As James Boyd White states:[21]

> The case method [was] a method of exploration and dialectic, a technique for discovering what is problematic in the law or in life, [but is now seen] as a way of distancing oneself from all that – a way of reducing experience to the level of summaries and outlines. The implied contract between the student and teacher shifts focus: our insistence to the student that 'You are responsible for these texts as you have never been responsible for anything in your life', all too frequently entails the acceptance of a correlative as well: 'and responsible for nothing else in the world'.

Any discipline contains 'ready knowledge', consisting of its basic concepts and theoretical assumptions, and methods. However, this knowledge of the legal system and its norms as it is, has to be questioned and problematized from both internal and external perspectives. Students have to be stimulated, encouraged and challenged in order to develop their faculty of judgment, that is, their ability to assess critically knowledge claims on their merits. A critical attitude provides insights and, hence, new knowledge. In academic legal education, this is no different: students acquire knowledge about the law and should reflect upon this knowledge to gain insight into law's operations. To become truly academic, legal education has to offer more than the traditional hermeneutic methods of interpreting the law, such as the case study method.

One thing that law students have to learn, thus, is that the law is no fixed entity and can be questioned from many perspectives. In an e-mail

---

[20] See also: Lyana Francot & Bald de Vries, 'Legal Education Re-Enchanted', [2006] 3(1) *European Journal of Legal Education* 3 (actually published in April 2007).

[21] James Boyd White, 'Doctrine in a Vacuum: Reflections on What a Law School Ought (and Ought Not) to Be', [1986] 36(2) *Journal of Legal Education* 155 at 156.

exchange, our student assistant Tim Bleeker, who helped us with editing this volume, reports about his experience as a freshman:

> When I started studying law, I expected law to dictate answers to legal problems in some kind of syllogistic manner. After all, law organizes power and wealth, and it even has the potential to take away individual freedom. Far-reaching as the law is, my assumption was that the rules provide legal certainty and dictate a set outcome in a particular case. This illusion I had as a freshman resulted in a particular focus on finding a 'right answer', rather than understanding the law as such.

After a while, Bleeker's motivation to learn diminished:

> The pursuit of a 'single right answer' haunted me for quite some time. Eventually, my hopes on the syllogistic potential of law faded, as I could not – based on the rules and facts in 'hard cases' – consistently arrive at the same answer as the lecturer or textbook provided. At some point, frustrated, I found that my curiosity lessened as my focus shifted from understanding to memorizing.

Starting from our email exchange, Bleeker has developed his own position in the ongoing debate on academic legal education and will present his views more extensively in the concluding chapter of this book in which he also summarizes the other contributions and shows the connections between them. We believe it is important, considering the central theme of the book – academic learning – to give voice to a student. In his contribution, Bleeker gives his view on how legal education can be strengthened, building on his own experiences as a law student at Utrecht University.

OUTLINE OF THE BOOK: THEORY, DIDACTIC INNOVATIONS AND LEARNING EXPERIMENTS

In order to stimulate reflection and critical thinking, and the student's desire to learn, the teacher has a responsibility to confront students with alternative views and perspectives, with different ways of learning and being taught. This may require the teacher to experiment with different didactic avenues. Some of these avenues are introduced in this book.

A key question is to what purpose we – as law teachers – teach law and how we can achieve our educational goals. How does our teaching contribute to the students' intellectual development and their faculty of judgment? Within this broader question, the issue can be raised whether, for example, legal education has to be practice-orientated (in the sense that legal education consists of the study of what happens in practice, with the judge as a role model). Is there a tension between practice and academic learning that cannot be overcome? Or do they supplement each other and, if so, in what ways? What is needed for an integrated approach? In this book, we investigate the nature of academic legal education. How does the legal curriculum contribute to academic learning, both in terms of content, pedagogy and didactics? What skills are necessary for academic learning? What does a critical attitude consist of, and how can this attitude be promoted?

The contributions in this volume address these questions and, by implication, go beyond the dogmatic, black-letter law approach, which is still prevalent in many law curriculums in Europe and beyond. A brief examination of the programmes of study is illustrative to this end.

The book is divided into three parts.

Part I introduces theoretical positions of academic learning in the context of legal education. Acquiring knowledge of the existing legal norms in itself is not enough. The authors in this part address the question on the goal and purpose of academic legal education. What exactly can be required, and how this can be achieved, depends on the perspective one takes as a point of departure. Van Klink introduces the concept of skeptical legal education (SLE). Inspired by Oakeshott's ideal of liberal learning, Van Klink advocates the value of legal education for its own sake; as an introduction to established ways of understanding, evaluating and discussing the law. Building on the ancient skeptical notion of *aphasia*, he stresses the importance of interruptions in the learning process which temporarily halt the creation of knowledge. Francot & Corrias excavate and reconsider the idea of *Bildung* as a means to effectively counter the hegemony of economic rationality. Academia needs to rebuild its core: *Re*-Bildung. In addition to these positions, Böning addresses, from a sociological point of view, the socializing (or institutionalizing) processes of legal training and assessment with which students are confronted and what this means for their critical potential. Bradney, on the other hand, focuses on the teacher, addressing how his or her autonomy is eroded by external forces, resulting in legal education becoming uniform and instrumentalized.

Part II includes contributions about how to teach law beyond the traditional approach focusing on conveying the law 'as it is'. The common denominator in this part is that these types, of course, open up new ways of looking at and thinking about the law. It includes contributions that report on how courses are designed with an aim to open up different perspectives as to how law can be studied and taught. Schwöbel-Patel teaches international law from a critical perspective (in the tradition of the Critical Legal Studies movement) with an aim to expose the hegemonic character of international law. Schwöbel-Patel asks whether the current focus on the technical practice-oriented teaching of international law should be questioned or even disrupted. She suggests a counter-hegemonic approach, employing critical pedagogy and *Bildung* as orientations for learning and teaching. Sokhi-Bulley has a similar aim, but intends to achieve this by teaching students to look at law from different theoretical perspectives ('camouflaged' as methodologies). She gives examples of classroom scenarios in which the *interrogation and application* formula is used in an attempt to make 'methodology' a less scary, and more accessible part of legal education, in order to allow students to be curious and inquisitive. Hutchinson shows the worth of empirical methodologies and knowledge. She argues that the emphasis on rules in legal education obscures the importance of facts in the determination of the law and suggests a move towards an 'evidence-based' practice of law. Van Rossum stresses the importance to enhance critical reflection on the exclusivity of legal systems. He shows how he does this in three socio-legal courses by using visuals (documentaries and images) to support the written word. Germain, finally, takes comparative law to its extreme, both in what is compared and where it is compared – in prison. It allows her to hear the voices of diversity that come out of untraditional environments and populate the law schools.

Part III includes contributions about innovations in teaching and learning experiments. The contributions in this part are meant to confront us, as readers and teachers, to think about and re-evaluate the ways in which we teach law by providing concrete examples of didactic experiments. The contributions offer a variety of practices of academic learning and teaching that seek to apply theoretical conceptions and instil the possibility of a critical attitude in students. Oomen stresses the importance of narratives by orchestrating encounters between students and teacher, using the didactic tools a liberal arts and science programme offers. Uygur emphasizes the importance of ethical awareness and the need for students to see injustices, which she achieves by creating a learning environment that confront students with prejudices about, for example, suspects and prisoners, using Foucault's mirror metaphor. Del Mar teaches students how to read case law using techniques from the visual and performing arts to show students that what is written might not always be enough to understand a case. De Vries experiments with student self-organization and the reading of fundamental texts, with an aim to open up his students' critical potential. In doing so, he urges for a critical attitude that is reflexive, in the sense that there is a task to uncover the self-evident assumptions in how we understand law, in order to judge whether society demands a reconsideration of law's foundational principles.

All contributions are in the concluding chapter summarized in more detail by Bleeker. He also opens up the various connections between the book's three parts and among the contributions and, subsequently, presents his view on academic legal education from a student's perspective.

The book concludes with concrete proposals for change, formulated in 14 theses. Each contributor has drafted a concrete proposal in the form of a thesis that might serve as a stepping-stone for actual change in the ways we teach law, both at course level and curriculum level.

THE FUTURE OF LEGAL EDUCATION

The main theme of the book is how the academic nature of legal education could be both guaranteed and strengthened. It also shows how lecturers, as Bradney argues, can 'use' their professional autonomy in being innovative and experimental.

The book is timely in the sense that there exists a momentum in how we want to view the university and how we reconsider the value of a university education. We hope that this momentum persists and will lead to the necessary changes of the university system in terms of finance, management, organizational structures and co-decision procedures, pedagogic visions, academic content, collegiality and career perspectives, the integration of teaching and research, and so on.

Roughly two positions on the purpose of academic legal education can be distinguished in this book: on the one side, higher education as an intrinsically academic activity – learning for the sake of learning, as espoused by Kronman – and, on the other side, higher education that instils a particular ethical and social responsibility, as argued, for instance, by Nussbaum – creating responsible democratic citizens that can shape tomorrow's world by addressing contemporary social problems. These two visions are mirrored in this book in the contributions in all three parts.

The contributions in this book offer different perspectives, ideas and theories about how to learn and teach the law. As Bleeker points out above, and will elaborate on, it is important to recognize the open texture of law and to question the case-study method aimed at discovering the 'one-right answer'.[22] The same is true for how to teach and learn the law – there is not one single best way.

What the contributions do have in common, is a focus on the so-called meta-perspectives on law: not only the traditional reflective disciplines such as legal theory, jurisprudence and ethics, and empirical disciplines such as the sociology of law and the psychology of law, but also other kinds of 'law and …' perspectives which, for instance, integrate social theory and theories about power, communication and media.[23]

To be truly academic, the study of the black-letter law should, in our view, be put in a theoretical and social context that allows for reflection, skeptical detachment, critique and reflexivity. In addition, the way in which we teach law should be pluriform and innovative (however, not experimental for its own sake). This is how, in our view, the future of *academic* legal education can be guaranteed and strengthened.

---

22 Not to be confused with the Dworkian perspective on law's (in)determinacy; see: Ronald Dworkin, *Law's Empire* (Harvard University Press 1986). Dworkin considers the law to be determinate, consisting of an integrated whole of rules, norms and principles, in the sense that it provides the right answer to a legal question. The task is to *find* the right answer.

23 As discussed in Bart van Klink & Sanne Taekema (eds), *Law and Method. Interdisciplinary Research into Law* (Mohr Siebeck 2011).

PART I

Theory and legal education

2. Knowledge and aphasia: what is the use of skeptical legal education?

Bart van Klink

1 CRITICAL THINKING

If one were to ask law teachers at the university what distinguishes academic legal education from professional and vocational training, they probably will refer to the capacity of critical thinking. As academics, we are not satisfied that students are able to reproduce faithfully what they have learnt but we want them to develop a critical attitude towards the things we have told them and the texts we have given them to read. However, what exactly does it mean to be critical and why is it important to be critical? How can a critical attitude be promoted and developed? At the core of our modern self-understanding lies the notion of critique. Kant defined Enlightenment famously as 'man's emergence from his self-incurred immaturity' or, more properly, 'speechlessness' (*Unmündigkeit*).[1] In the *Critiques* that Kant developed he sought to liberate thinking by means of reason from the *idées recues* handed down by tradition.

In contemporary legal theory, the notion of critical thinking seems to be annexed by the critical legal studies (CLS) movement. By wearing the banner of 'critical', 'crits' such as Duncan Kennedy, Allan Hunt and Peter Goodrich, suggest that they have acquired the monopoly of being critical; other, mainstream liberal or conservative approaches have to be dismissed as hopelessly uncritical.[2] 'Critical' in this understanding is connected to a left-wing political agenda that aims at exposing and subverting existing power structures in society. What is needed, in Kennedy's view, is nothing less than the 'total dismantling of the

---

[1] Immanuel Kant, 'What Is Enlightenment?' in HS Reiss (ed), *Political Writings* (CUP 2003) 54.

[2] Kelman offers an introduction to the 'first wave' of CLS; see: Mark Kelman, *A Guide to Critical Legal Studies* (Harvard University Press 1987).

system'.[3] American society should be transformed radically, which requires the 'building of a left bourgeois intelligentsia that might one day join with a mass movement'.[4]

However, as I have tried to demonstrate earlier,[5] there are other and less politically biased ways in which critical thinking can be understood, and promoted in legal education that do more credit to the academic ideal of disseminating and generating knowledge for its own sake. This other sense of being critical I intend to capture in my notion of skeptical legal education (SLE) – SLE offers a critical-hermeneutic understanding of legal education. It departs, to begin with, from the Kantian tradition that attempts to strengthen people's autonomy by freeing them from their traditional beliefs and prejudices,[6] because it holds that there is no escape from tradition, except by taking one's cue from particular traditions. Subsequently, it dismisses the politicized, neo-Marxist notion of critical legal education, as advocated by CLS, since it considers teaching to be something else than a preparation for political activism. Though it deems political reflection in the study of law to be valuable, it does not promote concrete political goals. As Max Weber stated: 'politics has no place in the lecture-room'.[7]

Skeptical legal education is inspired by Oakeshott's notion of liberal learning. Michael Oakeshott belongs to the tradition of secular humanism that aims at initiating students in a 'great conversation' which shapes

---

[3] Duncan Kennedy, 'Legal Education and the Reproduction of Hierarchy', in Duncan Kennedy, *Legal Education and the Reproduction of Hierarchy. A Polemic against the System* (New York University Press 2004) 9–144. Schwöbel-Patel's contribution to this edited volume is written in this spirit.

[4] Ibid 117. For a critical discussion of Kennedy's view of legal education, see Bart van Klink, 'The Role of Hierarchy, Example, and Language in Learning. A Confrontation between a Liberal and a "Critical" Understanding of Legal Education', [2013] 1 *Law & Method*, 26–47.

[5] Van Klink (2013), op cit; and Bart van Klink & Bald de Vries, 'Skeptical Legal Education. How to Develop a Critical Attitude?', [2013] 2 *Law & Method*, 37–52.

[6] A Kantian view of autonomy in educational theory is defended, for instance, by Paul Carrington, 'Reproducing the Right Sort of Hierarchy', in Duncan Kennedy (ed), *Legal Education and the Reproduction of Hierarchy. A Polemic against the System* (New York University Press 2004) 145–153 and Martha C Nussbaum, 'Cultivating Humanity in Legal Education', [2003] *The University of Chicago Law Review*, 265–279 – that I will discuss briefly later in section 3.

[7] Max Weber, 'Science as a Vocation' (translated by Michael John) in Peter Lassman, Irving Velody & Herminio Martins (eds), *Max Weber's Science as a Vocation* (Unwin Hyman 1989) 19.

them intellectually as well as morally.[8] In *The Voice of Liberal Learning* (a collection of essays published in 2001) Oakeshott characterizes learning as a strictly non-instrumental activity.[9] Learning does not follow a pre-established plan and has no final destination. It is an adventure with an uncertain and unpredictable outcome: 'This engagement is an adventure in a precise sense. It has no preordained course to follow: with every thought and action a human being lets go a mooring and puts out to sea a self-chosen but largely unforeseen course.'[10]

In this chapter, I want to show how critical thinking is promoted in SLE, how it differs from Kantian and 'critical' approaches to critical thinking, and what scientific and practical purposes it may serve. First, I will describe Oakeshott's view of education, characterized as liberal learning (section 2). Second, I will present the notion of SLE, which builds on the idea of liberal learning but which relativizes its insistence on the non-instrumentality of learning and reinforces its critical potential (section 3).[11] In addition, some skeptical methods and techniques within the study of law will be discussed. Third, I will address three kinds of critical questions that may be raised against it: can everything be questioned? Should everything be questioned? And why need law students to be encouraged to be critical? (section 4). Finally, I will show what the (individual, scientific and social) relevance may be of the suspension of judgment that SLE intends to bring about, both for the practice and the science of law (section 5).

2 OAKESHOTT'S NOTION OF LIBERAL LEARNING

According to Oakeshott, the human world is essentially a 'place of learning'.[12] Throughout his whole life man is engaged in learning. Within this *education permanente* schools and universities occupy a privileged position. Characteristic for these educational organizations is, to begin with, that those involved are recognized and recognize themselves as

---

[8] Anthony T Kronman, *Education's End. Why Our Colleges Have Given Up on the Meaning of Life* (Yale University Press 2007) 86–87.

[9] Michael Oakeshott, *The Voice of Liberal Learning* (Liberty Fund 2001).

[10] Ibid 11.

[11] Sections 2 and 3 are partly derived from Van Klink (2013), op cit and Van Klink & De Vries (2013) op cit. I have expanded my characterization of SLE and added some concrete examples of skeptical methods and techniques.

[12] Oakeshott, op cit 10.

learners, besides possible other roles they may fulfill in society. Subsequently, learning in educational organizations is focused on the learning of *something specific*. It does not aim at promoting intellectual development, spiritual growth or the broadening of one's horizon in general, but at acquiring knowledge about a particular subject, within a particular discipline, with the help of the methods and conceptual tools typical for the discipline at hand. Finally, in schools and universities learning is not an instrumental activity, but *a goal in itself*. Knowledge is acquired not only, or not predominantly, for external purposes. Learning takes place in a separated sphere, far away from our daily cares and concerns. Therefore, Oakeshott characterizes learning as liberal, not in the political sense but in the existential sense of 'liberated' or 'freed': at least for a couple of years, learners do not have to worry too much about 'satisfying contingent wants'.[13] What the university offers, is 'the gift of an interval'.[14]

Oakeshott describes education as a transaction between generations, which aims at introducing newcomers to an 'intellectual, imaginative, moral and emotional inheritance'.[15] The inheritance is shaped and reshaped in an ongoing conversation in which people are engaged in understanding themselves and their world. In order to be able to participate in this conversation, learners have to learn first to speak the language and to recognize the different voices that can be discerned within this language. Every academic discipline constitutes a language of its own, with its own rules, by means of which certain aspects of the world and human existence can be expressed. It is the task of the teacher to teach the students the rules of the language, and to show how one can make one's own contribution to the ongoing conversation. Liberal learning is an initiation in this art of conversation.

According to Oakeshott, the 'free' conversation that takes place at universities was threatened by various developments within the British educational system in the 1950s and 1960s of the last century and modern society in general. In ordinary life, he argues, mainly one language is spoken – the 'language of appetite'.[16] It is a language full of clichés by means of which superficial impressions and emotions can be expressed in general terms that are recognizable and repeatable for everyone. Its sole purpose is to satisfy immediate needs in the quickest, easiest and cheapest way possible. Increasingly, learning is transformed

13 Ibid 15.
14 Ibid 114.
15 Ibid 69.
16 Ibid 33.

into some form of *applied education*. That means that education is used for socializing students and preparing them for certain tasks in society. Instrumental learning replaces liberal learning and, as a consequence, teaching is reduced to the training of a series of technical functions.[17] Nowadays, education is more and more subjected to the logic of economic reason that requires universities to apply business models, based on output, efficiency and economic utility as benchmarks of quality.[18] Due to these developments, schools and universities are no longer free spaces of learning, where learners acquire knowledge mainly for its own sake.

In modern universities there is an increasing tendency to reduce learning to skills training. Oakeshott argues that education never coincides with the training of specific techniques, not even in vocational education. In order to know *how* to do something, one has to understand: first, *what* one is doing. In Oakeshott's view, knowledge contains two components: information and judgment. Information consists of both facts (for instance, about what statutes are and where they can be found) and rules that prescribe how a specific skill (such as the interpretation of a certain statute) has to be carried out. Judgment is the knowledge that makes it possible to interpret information and to assess its relevance and, moreover, to determine which rule has to be applied in a given case and which actions are required by this rule. Without knowledge of this kind one would not be able to learn a skill: 'Before any concrete skill or ability can appear, information must be partnered by "judgment", "knowing *how*" must be added to the "knowing *what*" of information.'[19] A lawyer, for instance, needs to know more than the content of the legal norms; s/he also must know when in a given case which norm s/he has to apply and how that norm has to be interpreted in the case at hand. This kind of knowledge cannot be expressed in rules or, in other words, be translated into information. It gives us guidance in situations where there are no specific rules or methods available, or where we do not know which rule or method to apply. Generally speaking, when we learn a language – whether it is English or Spanish, or the language of

---

[17] Cf. Oakeshott, ibid 13.

[18] See: Lyana Francot & Bald de Vries, 'Adieu Von Humboldt? Over Domme Organisaties en Slimme mensen' ('Adieu Von Humboldt? About Ignorant Organizations and Smart People') in *Het Universitaire Bedrijf. Over Professionalisering van Onderzoek, Bestuur en Beheer (The University Enterprise. About Professionalization of Research, Governance and Management)* LJ Dorsman & PJ Knegtmans (eds) (Verloren 2010) 73–86.

[19] Oakeshott, op cit 49.

philosophy or the law's language – it does not suffice to learn the rules only. A competent speaker is someone who is able to express himself or herself in a way that is not prescribed explicitly by the rules. Judgment cannot be learned, because it cannot be made an independent object of study. The teacher transmits it implicitly when giving information: 'It is implanted unobtrusively in the manner in which information is conveyed, in a tone of voice, in the gesture which accompanies instruction, in aside and oblique utterances, and by example'.[20] Students develop their judgment by recognizing and appreciating the individual intelligence at work in the way in which the teacher thinks and speaks, in her or his personal style and mode of expression.

In the past, nobody gave lessons in the art of conversation, but it had to be learnt by listening to competent speakers engaged in conversation. There are no shortcuts for learning by way of simple techniques or 'easy methods'.[21] Only by 'submerging' oneself in the practice of scholarship one can become a fully-fledged participant in this practice.

3 SKEPTICAL LEGAL EDUCATION

Following Oakeshott, I conceive of education as an initiation in the art of conversation in which scholars of a certain discipline are engaged. This does not imply that students have to be trained to be their master's voice; on the contrary, they have to develop their own voice. For that purpose, it is important to encourage students to reflect critically and to develop their faculty of judgment. What matters is that students learn to make their own assessment of the information that they receive from teachers whilst reading the literature, listening to lectures and engaging in discussions. Students cannot and do not invent the standards of evaluation from nowhere, but they have to build hermeneutically and critically on the values that are already accepted within the community of legal scholars. Whereas Carrington conceives of 'moral and intellectual autonomy' as the ultimate goal of education.[22] I would prefer to speak of the moral and intellectual *integrity* to use one's 'own' faculty of judgment. The student's autonomy is always related and relative to the intellectual environment in which s/he is raised. So it is a critical attitude that has to be developed starting from an 'uncritical' (or self-evident) background of shared opinions and beliefs. One can never get rid of the

---

[20] Ibid 60.
[21] Ibid 179.
[22] Carrington, op cit 149.

background of accepted ideas from which one perceives reality, that is, in terms of Gadamer, the prejudices that make up one's horizon.[23] However, through reflection and discussion one may get a better understanding of this background or horizon, and one may put some shared opinions and beliefs into question by confronting them with other accepted ideas and replace them by other ideas that then will pre-structure one's perception of reality.

It is exactly in this hermeneutic sense that SLE intends to contribute to critical thinking: knowledge claims should never be taken for granted, but questioned and discussed from within the context of accepted ideas handed down through particular traditions. Contrary to the Enlightenment project, it does not conceive of education as a liberation from one's prejudices by the force of reason alone, but as a constant questioning (or 'playing-off') of prejudices on the basis of other prejudices in order to preserve the ones that seem to be, for the time being, the best-fitting. According to Martha C. Nussbaum, the 'examined life' Socrates advocated consists of a life 'that accepts no belief as authoritative simply because it has been handed down by tradition or become familiar through habit, a life that questions all beliefs and accepts only those that survive reason's demand for consistency and justification.'[24] However, as follows from Oakeshott's characterization of liberal learning as an initiation in an ongoing scholarly conversation, reason can never stand on its own but has to build on habit, tradition and authority.[25]

Against 'critical' approaches, SLE puts forward that being critical is not the same as understanding society according to some pre-established political scheme. The 'critique' exercised by Duncan Kennedy and others is *one* way of being critical, because it can make students aware of power structures in law and society at large. Legal education may engage in political analysis; it should, however, refrain from political engagement. Academic education teaches students not to embrace any kind of political ideology (either of a conservative or a progressive strand) but instead to question and debunk it. The general aim of education is to raise

---

23 Hans-Georg Gadamer, *Truth and Method* (translation revised by Joel Weinsheimer and Donald G Marschall), (Bloomsbury Academic 2013) 313–315.

24 Nussbaum (2003), op cit 269.

25 For a more detailed analysis of the role of authority and hierarchy in legal education, see Van Klink 2013, op cit.

intellectual, rather than political awareness, by feeding epistemological doubt and uncertainty, so that students learn to assess knowledge claims critically.[26]

In order to promote reflection and develop the faculty of judgment within SLE, in particular, three conditions have to be met. These conditions which I will discuss below concern:

(1) the student's activity inside and outside the classroom;
(2) the manner in which the teacher transfers knowledge; and
(3) the institutional context of the faculty management respectively.

I have derived them partially from Oakeshott's notion of liberal learning as described above, but I have added some points in order to make the learning process more (or more explicitly) critical and challenging.

Ad (1) Student's Activity

To begin with, legal education should give more room for student participation in courses. According to Oakeshott, students have to learn the language of a specific discipline, so that one day they are able to generate new utterances in this language. For that purpose, it is essential that students participate more actively in class than Oakeshott acknowledges. One may learn a lot from reading texts and listening to competent speakers, but in order to master a language fully, one must be given regularly the opportunity to speak for oneself. This may be accomplished by means of group discussions, presentations, moot courts and so on, and solely in classes of limited size.[27] The cases discussed in law courses should give a representative overview of the law as it is understood in legal doctrine and should encourage students to make their own assessment of it (without 'politicizing' the classroom as advocated by Kennedy).[28] Furthermore, students should be encouraged to continue their learning process outside the classroom through various kinds of study-related extracurricular activities: such as reading groups, online blogs, and student seminars.

---

[26] For a detailed critique on Kennedy's view on critical legal education, see Van Klink (2013), op cit.

[27] So I agree with Nussbaum (2003), op cit 273, that in legal education, classes have to be much smaller.

[28] Duncan Kennedy, 'Politicizing the Classroom', [1995] 4 *Review of Law and Women's Studies*, 81–88; Kennedy (2004), op cit.

Ad (2) Mode of Teaching

What is required, furthermore, is that law teachers convey information from a detached point of view. That is, they should present the law as it is, as much as possible independently from their own ethical and political preferences.[29] This descriptive, seemingly 'neutral' account of the law does not presuppose that understanding law is in itself a neutral or value-free activity. On the contrary, law teachers are required to present the law as it is and to expose the legal, moral and political values on which the law (and their understanding of it) is based, however without identifying themselves with these values. If they evaluate the current law and give recommendations to amend it, they have to make clear that they are not describing the law as it is at a certain moment in time but are expressing their personal opinion about how the law ought to be in the future. Value judgments are controversial in science, because their validity depends on the acceptance of certain values and ultimately of a worldview (or an ideology in 'critical' terms) whose truth can never be established by scientific means. So when teachers are evaluating the law, they should make clear the basis of which values they are reasoning, how they understand these values in the given situation, and how their evaluation is connected to their general worldview. As Weber (1989: 25–26) argues, teachers may offer examples of hypothetical reasoning: if one accepts a specific value (for instance, democracy) one has to acknowledge certain rights as well (such as the freedom of speech) without committing themselves (nor the students) to the acceptance of this value. In addition, the pros and cons of the means suggested to reach a certain end can be discussed scientifically (which, in Weber's view, will discourage an uncritical acceptance of certain values).[30] Reasoning in such a way gives students the opportunity to arrive at a different assessment, building on different values, on a different understanding of the same values, or on a different worldview. Similarly, law teachers

---

[29] This requires what Raz calls 'non-committed detached statements': 'Since one may know what the law is without knowing if it is justified, there must be a possibility of making legal statements not involving commitment to its justification'; Joseph Raz, *The Authority of Law. Essays on Law and Morality* (Clarendon Press 1979), 158.

[30] Weber states as follows: 'Anybody who is a reasonable teacher has as his first duty to teach his students to acknowledge "inconvenient" facts, I mean facts which are inconvenient for their party opinion'; Weber, op cit 22.

should explain and justify the basis of what theoretical assumptions and what sources they derive and make factual assertions about the content of the law.

Knowledge is always fallible and disputable, when it comes to both normative and factual statements. In order to give students a feeling for the fragility of knowledge, it is important that teachers, in group discussions with students, take a counter position against the *communis opinio* in the group at hand, question it, and demonstrate its ultimate groundlessness, as in Socratic dialogues.[31] Inspired by Socrates, Ancient Greek skeptics such as Sextus Empiricus developed practices of argumentative inquiry that are meant to expose internal contradictions within a given position. As a result, the dispute remains undecided and one has to suspend one's judgment (*epoche*).[32] *Skepsis* means an inquiry or an examination guided by reason and in search for truth, however in vain perhaps, this search may be. In the interim that the university offers, interrupts have to be built in, that halt temporarily the creation of knowledge. Learning also involves the experience that one does not know, or does not know enough of. In Ancient Skepticism, the suspension of judgment served to attain a peaceful state of mind (*ataraxia*) so that one no longer worries about truth and falsity anymore. Being unable to speak, one enters a tranquil phase of *aphasia*. In my view, the ultimate goal of the infinite questioning is not tranquility or peace of mind but, on the contrary, an increased awareness that knowledge is always a temporary and a fallible construction.

Ad (3) Institutional Context

Finally, on the institutional level, the faculty management has to provide for a mixture of teachers with different political, cultural, and religious backgrounds. If they are exposed to a variety of opinions, students will soon discover that truth in science is always a matter of debate. As Oakeshott argues, education is an introduction to a shared heritage. However, the heritage that is handed over from one generation to the

---

[31] For an introduction to the Socratic method in legal education, see Phillip E Areeda, 'The Socratic Method' [1996] 109(5) *Harvard Law Review*, 911–922.

[32] Burnyeat gives an insightful description of the skeptical practice of inquiry; MF Burnyeat, 'Can the Skeptic Live His Skepticism?', in: Myles Burnyeat (ed), *The Skeptical Tradition*, (University of California Press 1983) 117–148.

other is not a fixed entity, but is changed in every transmission.[33] Each teacher will give his/her own version of the canonical texts, depending on the theoretical perspective and worldview s/he has adopted. Not one dominant voice should be heard, but a plurality of voices. This plurality of voices will inevitably be a *limited* plurality, because not everyone will be allowed to speak. In the selection of teachers not only academic requirements are applied (teachers have to have the right qualifications) but also standards of civility (teachers have to meet some standard of decency and political correctness).[34] Kennedy is undoubtedly right that the mainstream in law schools is quite moderate.[35] Generally speaking, law teachers are conservative in the sense that they want to protect what they deem to be valuable in the law as it is. They tend to resist radical change because they believe – for good reasons[36] – that a legal system can only function properly if the law is more or less stable and predictable. However, within this mainstream many different (e.g. liberal, republican, conservative, communitarian, feminist, and other) positions can be discerned and, if one listens carefully, one may even hear some radical and 'critical' tones. In order to set the stage for a (by necessity limited) plurality of voices, the curriculum should not only consist of courses where the 'black-letter law' is taught, but also of courses in which the law's efficacy and legitimacy, and its historical development can be discussed on a more principled and theoretical level: in particular, legal sociology, legal philosophy, law and politics, law and ethics, and legal history. Although these so-called meta-juridical and historical courses are doomed to remain in the periphery, as Kennedy notices, they are central for critical reflection on the law as it is, and how the law ought to be according to mainstream law teachers who teach 'black-letter law'.[37]

In working groups, various techniques and methods can be used in order to encourage the kind of questioning that SLE calls for. I already referred to Socratic dialogues, skeptical argumentation techniques and Weber's idea of hypothetical reasoning. A contemporary practice of questioning is offered by deconstruction which, through close reading, aims at exposing binary oppositions in texts (for instance, between man

---

33 This follows from Gadamer's characterization of understanding as application; Gadamer, op cit at 36–38ff.

34 Universities will not be inclined to give voice to teachers who, for instance, have overtly fascist sympathies or engage in criminal activities.

35 Kennedy (2004), op cit 15.

36 See next section, point (ii).

37 Kennedy (2004), op cit 36.

and woman, black and white, nature and culture) and subverting the hierarchical relation between the terms involved. Deconstruction is a never-ending activity, because every reading can itself be deconstructed, *ad infinitum*:[38]

> The end-point of deconstructive thought, as Derrida insists, is to recognize that there is no end to the interrogative play between text and text. Deconstruction can never have the final word because its insights are inevitably couched in a rhetoric which lies itself open to further deconstructive reading.

Moreover, Bal Sokhi-Bulley has applied Edward De Bono's thinking hat-method to legal education in the Legal Research workshops that she teaches at Queen's University, Belfast.[39] Following this method, students are asked, first, to identify the key issues regarding a particular topic – e.g. the London riots in 2011 – and, subsequently, to write a paper on this topic from a specific perspective, either a legal positivist, or a critical race theory (CRT), or a feminist, or a Foucauldian perspective. By doing so, students experience that the same story can be told in different ways, depending on the perspective one takes, and that 'alternative truths' are possible.[40] Finally, in the so-called Law & Lounge experiment carried out by Bald de Vries at Utrecht University,[41] the student's activity is maximized, and the teacher's involvement is reduced to a minimum. Students are exposed to difficult classical texts in the field of legal philosophy (such as Hobbes' *Leviathan* and Mill's *On Liberty*) and they have to read and discuss them in the way they think is appropriate. The teacher is present as an observer and can only be consulted on organizational matters; the teacher abstains from giving the 'right' answer to the questions raised.

4 QUESTIONING THE QUESTIONING

Several kinds of questions can be put forward against the practices of questioning that SLE promotes. First, one can ask, from an

---

[38] Christopher Norris, *Deconstruction. Theory and Practice* (Routledge 2002) 84.

[39] Bal Sokhi-Bulley, 'Alternative Methodologies. Learning Critique as a Skill', [2013] 1 *Law & Method* 2013, 6–23.

[40] Ibid 18.

[41] Described in Van Klink & De Vries (2013), op cit 45–49, and expanded upon in De Vries' contribution to this volume.

epistemological point of view, whether it is possible to question everything. How to question current opinions if the ground one stands on is itself unstable and shaky? Second, from a moral point of view, the question is whether everything should be questioned. Why should we as teachers give up all the things we believe in so dearly, if only by way of make-believe and for the sake of argument? According to Nussbaum, skeptical detachment is not so much a help but a hindrance to ethical and legal reasoning.[42] Third, practically and politically speaking, what is the point of making law students more critical? One could argue, on the one hand, that law students do not need to be critical because they have to be educated (in Kennedy's words) to serve 'the system'. After their graduation, they will probably occupy important positions in society – as law makers, judges, attorneys, legal advisors to the court, the administration or the legislature, and so on – and for that purpose they should accept, by and large, the things as they are, including the existing power relations.[43] On the other hand, it can be maintained that law students are already critical enough, since they are trained to examine cases very carefully in order to find clever arguments to support their position and to refute the opponent's arguments.[44]

(i) Can Everything be Questioned?

It is a hermeneutic truism, but therefore no less true, that one can only question some convictions on the basis of other convictions that one does not question – either for argument's sake, as Socrates did – or for real, because one believes in them. If one, for instance, argues that the parliamentary system nowadays fails to represent the voter's interests, one has to presuppose some idea of representation. Ludwig Wittgenstein also argues that the practice of doubting is only possible in a context where some things are excluded from doubt.[45] In his view, radical skepticism is not possible, because all doubt is embedded in underlying

---

42 Martha C Nussbaum, 'Skepticism about Practical Reason in Literature and the Law' [1999] *Harvard Law Review*, 714–744, at 742.

43 According to Kennedy legal education in the US is aimed at 'the reproduction of hierarchy'; Kennedy (2004), op cit.

44 These two, seemingly contradictory questions were raised to me by two students at the symposium on 'Ancient Skepticism', organized by the Faculty Association of Utrecht Philosophy Students (FUF), on 31 October 2013 in Utrecht, The Netherlands.

45 Ludwig Wittgenstein, *On Certainty* (translated by D Paul and GEM Anscombe) (Blackwell 1977).

beliefs. As a consequence, not everything can be questioned at the same time. However, building on some accepted ideas, which are part of conventional or traditional knowledge, one may criticize other ideas: if one believes that political representation is a matter of serving the voter's interests, one can criticize the idea that political parties are a valuable intermediary between state and society. As Odo Marquard argues, the skeptic is not someone who knows nothing; he only knows nothing *for sure*.[46] The skeptic may accept certain beliefs, not because s/he is certain about them, but out of habit, or for the sake of convenience.[47]

So what SLE offers, by acknowledging the inevitability of prejudices in understanding, is not radical epistemological skepticism, but a modest and mild variety of skepticism that rejects any claim to absolute truth or ultimate foundations. It values questions over answers and doubt over certainty. Therefore, SLE does not aim at questioning everything simultaneously, but only those ideas that seem to have a weak position in the existing network of ideas (according to the criterion of coherence) or do not seem to fit our perception of reality (following the criterion of correspondence). The teacher may, for educational purposes, question some mainstream beliefs, not so much to refute them – because that would only mean a transfer of certainty from one belief to another – but to heighten the burden of proof on those who hold these beliefs to be self-evident. Thus, the suspension of judgment that SLE intends to bring about, is never complete but partial and temporary, and the questioning takes place from within a context in which some beliefs are not questioned (for the time being).

(ii) Should Everything be Questioned?

In her critique of Ancient skepticism (Sextus Empiricus) and postmodern skepticism (Derrida and Fish), Nussbaum argues that skeptical detachment is detrimental to ethical and legal reasoning: 'by depriving us of commitments to the importance of things outside ourselves, skepticism has even deprived us of the information we need to make sense of social ills and to respond to them in a humanly appropriate way'.[48] However, skepticism does not equal nihilism or radical value relativism, because both the denial and the equalization of values presuppose a certainty of

---

[46] Odo Marquard, '[D]er pyrrhonische Skeptiker weiss also beilebe nicht nichts, er weiss nur nichts Absolutes. Der Skeptiker zersetzt nicht, er mässigt'; *Skepsis in der Moderne* (Philipp Reclam Jun. 2007) 77.

[47] Marquard (2007), op cit 78: 'Skepsis is Usualismus'.

[48] Nussbaum (1999), op cit 742.

belief that skepticism abstains from. What skepticism intends to bring about is a suspension of judgment, so that we no longer worry about the truth or falsity of our opinions. It does not necessarily deprive us of our commitments, as long as we do not conceive of our opinions as absolute, invariable and eternal truths.

Skeptical legal education does not require that teachers give up their ethical convictions and emotional responses entirely. They are solely asked to present their value judgments for what they are: fallible opinions which are debatable and have to be debated within the community of both teachers and learners. By presenting their opinions with some distance and stressing their provisional character, they leave room for other opinions. This does not mean that 'anything goes'. To begin with, teachers are allowed to favour one position over another as long as they do not rule out the possibility of other positions and discuss them in a fair and balanced way. Subsequently, they cannot be required to pay the same amount of respect to every kind of opinion: opinions that are commonly perceived as inappropriate or indecent can be dismissed. The playfield of scholarly conversation is determined by the range of acceptable and accepted values within a certain academic community, that is, by current standards of civility.[49] Finally, for didactic reasons, teachers may choose not to take sides within a discussion, or to take a counter-position against the mainstream, in order to make students think for themselves. So skeptical detachment serves an educational and ethical purpose: by confusing or even 'paralyzing' reason,[50] opinions are questioned that are too easily taken for granted.

(iii) Why Should Law Students be Critical?

It may be argued that law students do not have to be encouraged to think critically, either because they are expected to serve 'the system', or because they are already critical enough, clever as they are in discovering arguments in difficult cases. In its academic ambition, the study of law is no vocational training, although many law students will afterwards occupy jobs in legal and political practice. It is aimed at understanding

---

49 These standards should not be taken too strictly, in order to prevent what Kronman (2007), op cit 90, calls a 'culture of political correctness' which, in his view, has dominated the humanities since the 1960s and has undermined his ideal of secular humanism. I do believe, however, that some notion of civility is needed, since one cannot expect scholars to take seriously opinions that are generally considered to be morally unacceptable or wrong.

50 This expression is used in Burnyeat (1983), op cit 133.

the existing law in a given field and in a particular time and place (e.g. contemporary environmental law in the Member States of the European Union) evaluating the law as it is and making suggestions for how it ought to be. For these purposes, it is necessary that students are trained to reflect critically on how things are arranged legally because, on a factual level, current descriptions of the law may not be adequate and, on a normative level, the law may be in need of improvement. Innovative analysis and assessment can only be carried out if one looks with some distance at the legal system at hand and one does not identify oneself fully with the present arrangements. From a political perspective, it can be objected that, by describing a certain collection of norms as law and thereby, in Kelsenian terms, accepting the basic norm of a given legal order, one endorses and supports the existing political system. That is no doubt true. If you want to make a revolution, the law is usually not your ally. The law only allows for small and incremental change, although these changes can be in the long run quite substantial. According to Bruno Latour, slowness is a fundamental quality of the law. Unlike science, law aims at stabilizing its system of rules: 'A premium is put on legal stability but there is no such thing as scientific stability'.[51] Therefore, law resists radical change, according to Latour:[52]

> Although one might speak admiringly of 'revolutionary science', 'revolutionary laws' have always been as terrifying as courts with emergency powers. All those aspects of law that common sense finds so irritating – its tardiness, its taste for tradition, its occasionally reactionary attitudes – are essential to law's functioning.

You may regret law's resistance to radical change (as the 'crits' do) or you may welcome law's propensity to stability (as I do). However, these political and pre-scientific preferences do not affect the academic ambition of law as a scientific discipline. As generally in science, the point is not merely to change the world, but first and foremost to understand it. So, given its focus on knowledge dissemination and creation, legal education does not aim at producing servile civil servants, but at providing an inspiring intellectual environment for critical minds to flourish.

---

[51] Bruno Latour, *The Making of Law. An Ethnography of the Conseil d'Etat* (translated by Marina Brilman and Alain Pottage; revised by the author) (Polity Press 2013) 242.

[52] Ibid 242–243.

Whether law students are already critical enough, can be questioned. In mainstream law courses, students do learn to analyze cases and to construe arguments supporting their own position and undermining their opponent's position. However, critical thinking is more than an exercise in skillful legal reasoning. According to Nussbaum, 'legal education all too often blurs the distinction between sophistry and philosophy, clever argument and argument that tracks the truth.'[53] In order to promote critical thinking, it is important, as I already argued (see section 3) that the curriculum – next to courses where the 'black-letter law' is taught – also provides for courses in which the law's efficacy and legitimacy, and its historical development are discussed on a more fundamental level. In courses such as legal sociology, legal philosophy, law and politics, law and ethics, and legal history, students learn that the law can be approached from many different perspectives and cannot be reduced to a mere 'set of technical maneuvers', as Nussbaum puts it.[54] In Nussbaum's view, legal education serves an ethical mission: law schools have to prepare students for global citizenship by cultivating their humanity. Whatever one may think of this ambitious ideal, and its desirability and attainability, it cannot determine the scientific virtue of education. I prefer to conceive of legal education's end primarily in scientific terms as a matter of moral and intellectual integrity, that is, the ability to assess knowledge claims critically drawing from the reservoir of accepted ideas. Exposed to different perspectives and approaches, law students will acquire a feeling for the fragility of knowledge, its uncertainty and open-endedness. Moreover, they will experience that scientific knowledge is a matter of permanent debate and does not generate ready-made answers or quick solutions.

5 THE METAPHYSICS OF QUESTIONING

Skeptical legal education is an attempt to enhance critical thinking in legal education. In this sense, it is indebted to what may be called the modern metaphysics of questioning. As with Kantian and 'critical' approaches to education, it believes that reflection, discussion and criticism will move humankind forward in its search for perfection. However, in contrast to the Enlightenment project, it does not presume that this questioning starts from nowhere and is carried out by an 'empty' mind, deprived of traditional and conventional knowledge. It also departs

53 Nussbaum (2003), op cit 272.
54 Ibid 271.

from the 'ethics of supersession' that, according to Kronman, characterizes the contemporary ideal of scholarly research, inspired by the ideal of *Bildung*, which requires scholars to be 'original' and to break with their predecessors.[55] Instead, SLE accepts the hermeneutic presupposition that some ideas can only be questioned when other ideas are taken for granted – ideas that belong to the intellectual inheritance that is handed down through education. There is no escape from tradition, except by exploring and exploiting the critical resources available in the various scientific traditions developed within different academic disciplines. As Oakeshott indicates, education is a transaction between generations, which aims at introducing newcomers to an 'intellectual, imaginative, moral and emotional inheritance'.[56] Each discipline constitutes a language of its own by which certain aspects of our existence are revealed. Students have to learn the language first, before they are able to make new utterances that are not prescribed explicitly by the rules. Against CLS, SLE does not conceive of education as an activist enterprise. A skeptical attitude entails that knowledge claims and value judgments are questioned from a detached point of view rather than from a particular political ideology. If one wants to engage oneself politically, there is a world outside academia.

As indicated in section 3, SLE intends to promote critical thinking in three ways. First, it stresses that learning not only consists of a passive reception of texts and lectures, as Oakeshott assumes, but also requires an active involvement of students. By means of group discussions, presentations, moot courts and extracurricular activities such as reading groups, students can develop their own voice in the ongoing conversation. In terms of examination, papers and open questions are much better suited for promoting reflection and critical thinking than multiple-choice questions, which teachers often resort to nowadays for convenience's sake.[57] Second, teachers have to adopt in their mode of teaching a detached point of view. This means that they are asked to disengage themselves from their strong beliefs and present their knowledge claims and value judgments as fallible opinions which are to be discussed within the community of both teachers and students. Moreover, teachers have to

---

55 Kronman (2007), op cit 118, states as follows: 'A scholar does not aim to stand where his ancestors did. He seeks originality, but accepts the transience of his own original achievements' (ibid) On the ideal of *Bildung*, see also the contribution of Francot-Timmermans & Corrias to this edited volume.

56 Oakeshott, op cit 69.

57 Nussbaum (2003), op cit 273, also stresses the importance of paper-writing in basic courses.

incorporate interrupts in the learning process by using skeptical methods and techniques that hamper the process of knowledge acquisition temporarily. Confronted with alternative truths (as in the thinking hat method), inconvenient truths (through hypothetical reasoning in Weber's proposal) or incompatible truths (as in deconstructive reading practices), students are compelled to suspend their judgment. A transient phase of *aphasia* is crucial to the creation of knowledge: it give students the opportunity to reflect and to discover new insights and expressions in order to find a way out of the aporia they are stuck in. Speechlessness, from which the Enlightenment sought to save us, thus appears to be a condition for speech. Finally, the faculty management has to take care that in the curriculum a plurality of voices can be heard by selecting teachers from different social and intellectual backgrounds. Moreover, next to the regular law courses, philosophical, empirical and historical courses have to be provided that promote reflection on the foundation and the functioning of law, now and in the past.

A last question that is perhaps still not answered satisfactorily: What is the use of SLE? All this questioning, what is it good for? I want to answer this question on three levels: an individual, scientific and social level. On an individual level, questioning can make people very insecure. In the face of truth, one cannot but fail. Every knowledge claim or value judgment may be criticized from some perspective or other. At the same time, it can be a liberating experience to discover that there is not one truth or dominant perspective that one is forced to accept. According to Marquard, skepsis is not the 'cultivation of helplessness' (*Pflege der Ratlosigkeit*) but the 'sense for the division of powers' (*Sinn für Gewaltenteilung*).[58] This means that, in the collision of different opinions, the subject can free him/herself – not from opinion itself – but from the oppressive force of one particular (viz. scientific, political, social, moral, religious or other) opinion.

On a scientific level, questions are more important than answers. As Gadamer argues, scientific inquiry always starts with a question.[59] Every answer is provisional and gives rise to new questions, and so the endless search for truth continues. Progress in science is achieved, not by abandoning everything that was accepted before, but by critically building on the ideas of earlier generations of scholars. In contrast, Weber states that '[e]very scientific "fulfilment" means new "questions"; it asks

---

[58] Marquard (2007), op cit 18.

[59] Gadamer (2013), op cit 370ff. He calls this the hermeneutic 'priority of the question' (*Vorrang der Frage*). On the relation between question and answer, see also Bernard Waldenfels, *Antwortregister* (Suhrkamp 1994) 125–133.

to be "surpassed" and made obsolete.'[60] In his view, the hope of being superseded is what drives every scholar: 'To be overtaken in science is [...] not only the fate of every one of us, but our common goal. We cannot work without hoping that others will get further than we do'.[61] However, old and already accepted scientific ideas will continue to influence and inspire new ideas, which are never created *ex nihilo*. In that sense, SLE departs from the modern Weberian ethics of supersession and replaces it with the hermeneutic ethics of 'effective history'.[62]

On a social level, finally, SLE provides law students with a critical and detached perspective on law and society in general. Equipped with a healthy dose of skepticism, they won't take everything for granted in the present legal and political order (nor will they reject everything out of hand) but raise critical and uneasy questions in order to improve it, starting from the values that this order intends to serve. Since they are well aware of the fallibility and fragility of knowledge, they won't be inclined to embrace any political ideology or to follow political leaders uncritically. Skepticism does not necessarily make life easier, but it at least makes it easier to endure.

---

60 Weber, op cit 12.

61 Ibid.

62 See Gadamer (2013), op cit 312ff (in German: *Wirkungsgeschichte*).

3. Re-*Bildung*: an ideal reconsidered for legal education

Lyana Francot and Luigi Corrias*

'I look at my environment
And wonder where the fire went
What happened to everything we used to be'

(*The Miseducation of Lauryn Hill*)[1]

1 INTRODUCTION

Over the last decades there has been an ongoing debate on the changing nature and functions of academic education.[2] Central to the debate is the clear and present tendency to let the market dictate both the nature and the functions of academic education. This results in an increasing emphasis on teaching students practical legal skills with evident economic value. This development concurs with an erosion of the appreciation of general knowledge and of an attitude, both critical and academic. This lack of appreciation results in steadily decreasing time, space and funding for the transfer of fundamental knowledge and of an academic attitude. While Academia seems to be united in its disapproval of this tendency, it has yet to find a way to effectively counter the hegemony of economic rationality.[3] Hence, Academia needs to rebuild its core.

---

* The authors are grateful to Bart van Klink for his valuable remarks on earlier versions of this chapter and to Irina Leichenko for checking the English. We are responsible for all remaining errors.

1 Label: Ruffhouse, 1998.

2 Illustrative in this regard is: G Lock and C Lorenz, 'Revisiting the University Front' [2007] 26 *Studies of Philosophical Education*, 405. See also: W Cornelissen, 'Verdwijnt de vrijheid van de universiteit?' [2011] 68(7/8) S&D, 66.

3 See CEJ Schwöbel-Patel, '"I'd Like to Learn what Hegemony Means" Teaching International Law from a Critical Angle' [2013] 3 *Law and Method*, 67.

One way to voice the academic discontent is to reconsider the ideal of *Bildung* against the backdrop of the contemporary situation of Academia. We argue that contemporary developments, such as the ongoing economization (reducing everything to its economic value) and instrumentalization (reducing everything to a means for attaining a certain end) of both society and education, necessitate a reinterpretation of the traditional concept of *Bildung*. In the history of education, *Bildung* reflects in its own and unrivalled way: the non-economic value of education.[4] The ideal of *Bildung* has a rather protean quality, evading a clear and univocal definition. Yet it is exactly this protean nature that renders it also a palimpsest of interpretations. Even so, the heart and soul of *Bildung* concerns the desirable self-formation of students with the aim of making them into citizens, who are able and willing to take their responsibilities in an ever more complex world. The ongoing confrontation with a multitude of options and possibilities requires citizens to make choices and to make them responsibly. Even though *Bildung* is not confined to the exclusive domain of Academia, universities are (or rather: were) traditionally deemed to be the places *par excellence* to breed responsible citizens with a critical attitude. In this light, we will reconsider the ideal of *Bildung* with the aim to arm Academia against the proliferation of economic rationality.

This contribution will start with a broad outline of the historical background of the ideal of *Bildung*. For this purpose, we will take our cue from the work of Wilhelm von Humboldt who famously developed the concept in the nineteenth-century. While the Humboldtian concept of *Bildung* inspires this contribution, an exegesis of his work lies beyond its scope. In the next move, we will analyse the contemporary predicament of academic education and address the issue of *Bildung* in these changing circumstances. To illustrate these circumstances, we turn to the work of contemporaries, such as Lock and Lorenz who analyze the increasing influence of economic rationality on Academia. This development hits Academia at its very core, shifting its focus from being an end in itself to merely an instrument to satisfy the demands of the market. We will argue that this calls for a reconceptualization of *Bildung*. This reconsideration we will call Re-*Bildung*. To this end, we will address some aspects of the thought of Hans-Georg Gadamer and Hannah Arendt in order to conceptualize Re-*Bildung*. In our understanding, Re-*Bildung* – as a contemporary reconceptualization of the Humboldtian ideal – shifts the focus back

[4] While *Bildung* has traditionally been at the forefront of the German debate, in the Netherlands it is more present in the undercurrent.

to what is fundamental to Academia. Finally, we will inquire into the potential consequences this reconceptualization has for legal education.

2 THE HISTORY OF AN IDEAL

The concept of *Bildung* has a long and meandering history.[5] It is a child of many fathers and its most commonly known parent is Wilhelm von Humboldt.[6] It is also for this reason that the Humboldtian notion of *Bildung* constitutes our point of departure. Notwithstanding, the fact that it is probably one of the most successful German export products in education, *Bildung* does not come with a univocal conceptualization. On the contrary, it is subject to many interpretations and reformulations. Oelkers traces the origin of this ambivalence back to the three sources *Bildung* springs from. First, is the medieval *Imago Dei*. Second, concerns the post-medieval *Bildung* through science. Third, is modern *Bildung* understood as individual self-formation.[7] This background renders *Bildung* a hybrid harbouring at the same time both a religious dimension (that is nevertheless pivotal to the modern, disenchanted academic culture) and a focus on subjectivity. However, so says Oelkers, it is this lack of theoretical unity that enables a remarkable discourse, because *Bildung* is a 'Assoziationsfeld' (a field of association) that magically overcomes possible paradoxes.[8] Or, in the more down to earth approach of Prange: *Bildung* resists a clear definition but facilitates many descriptions.[9] It is not our aim to depict a complete genealogy of the concept but

---

[5] See R Horlacher, 'Bildung: A Construction of a History of Philosophy of Education' [2004] 23 *Studies in Philosophy and Education*, 409. This part of our contribution is an elaborated translation of the section 'Het Humboldiaanse Bildungsideaal' in: L Francot and B de Vries, 'Adieu von Humboldt? Over domme organisaties en slimme mensen' in LJ Dorsman and PJ Knegtmans (eds), *Over Professionalisering van onderzoek, bestuur en beheer* (Verloren 2010) 73–77.

[6] Just to name a few other famous parents: Herder, Schlegel, Schiller, Goethe, Fichte, Schleiermacher, Hegel. See J Ruhloff, 'Bildung heute' (1997) 10(21) *Pädagogische Korrespondenz* 23.

[7] J Oelkers, '"Bildung"; Ein Schutz vor "Standards"?' (Vortrag im Institut für Erziehungswissenschaft der Universität Zürich, 17 December 2013) 1 and 2. Available at: <http://www.ife.uzh.ch/research/emeriti/oelkersjuergen/vortraege profoelkers/vortraege2013/Bildung_IfE.pdf> (accessed 29 April 2015).

[8] Ibid 2 (paraphrased).

[9] K Prange 'Bildung: a paradigm regained?' [2004] 3 *European Education Research Journal* 501–502.

a brief excursion in the history of *Bildung* illustrates both its allure and versatility.[10] It is precisely this versatility that will allow us, in section 4, to reconsider the notion of *Bildung* and show the value of this ideal for contemporary Academia.

The notion originates in the Pietistic theology of the sixteenth century and refers to a divine mission: Christians should unfold their possibilities and qualities in accordance with the image of God (*Imago Dei*). Moving towards the eighteenth century, Leibniz employed *Bildung* to describe the development or the unfolding of certain possibilities within an organism. His work on the concept turned out to be fundamental to Humboldt's interpretation of *Bildung*.[11] Leibniz' input enables the transition of an essentially spiritual conceptualization towards a more philosophical and perhaps even political formulation of *Bildung* that addresses the emancipation of human beings, and as such it plays a crucial role in the (German) Enlightenment. Typical of the German Enlightenment is not only the liberation from tradition and superstition but also the emancipation of the German nation into a pre-modern political system, constituted by small feudal states. Within this context, *Bildung* does not only formulate an instruction at the level of the individual, but also at the level of the cultivation of the people. It also bestows a specific task upon philosophy. Its function is now the production of a specific result, i.e. human self-formation. To put it somewhat differently: philosophy should transform and educate people into autonomous individuals but, at the same time, should have an impact in a broad social sense, that is to say: be of use for an entire nation.

By the end of the eighteenth century, the notion makes its entrance in pedagogy through the work of Johann Gottfried von Herder. He, in his turn, draws upon Shaftesbury whose conceptualization of 'Inner' or 'inward form' was translated by Herder into *Bildung*.[12] Especially in Germany, *Bildung* then evolves into an essentially non-political concept,

---

[10] See Horlacher, *op cit* 410.

[11] D Sorkin, 'Wilhelm Von Humboldt: The Theory and Practice of Self-Formation (Bildung), 1791–1810' (1983) 44(1) *Journal of the History of Ideas* 55, 58.

[12] Horlacher, *op cit* 419 and further. Also see: J Oelkers, 'Das Konzept der Bildung in Deutschland im 18. Jahrhundert' in: *Zeitschrift für Pädagogik – 38. Beiheft: Bildung, Öffentlichkeit und Demokratie,* 1998 (J Oelkers, F Osterwalder & H Rhyn eds) 45, 56–57.

that is to say that it is entirely directed towards the individual process of self-formation.[13]

Despite or maybe even due to its dispersed and rich history, in hindsight there is a basic consensus on the ideal of *Bildung*, or so says Horlacher:

> *Bildung* is more than knowledge and [...] has something to do with holistic development; it is used in connection with the name of Humboldt just as it is linked with very broad expectations of a better society (economically, morally, politically).[14]

Education in the broadest sense is without a doubt fundamental to the realization of this ideal but this holds in particular for academic education. Consequently, universities play a key role in the process of self-formation. The most important function of the university, according to Humboldt, is bringing students together in a community that is dedicated to science as well as to safeguarding their freedom of exchange of knowledge and insights. Furthermore, the university should be a safe haven that facilitates students to develop and flourish in an environment permeated with science, free from force and not limited by instrumental goals or direct ends. Direct ends refer to education with an aim to serve purposes of either the state, the church, or the economy.[15] The unity of research and education should constitute such a setting within the university.

The above depicts the type of university Humboldt envisioned during his educational reforms in the period of 1790–1810. In this period, as the Minister of Education (or: *Sektionschef für Kultus und Unterricht im Ministerium des Innern)* Humboldt left a permanent mark on the German interpretation of the concept of *Bildung*. Its single most important point of departure is, as indicated above, the possibility of self-formation, free from state intervention.[16] Humboldt elaborates this principle in 'The

---

[13] Beiser discusses a possible explanation of this development: FC Beiser, *The Romantic Imperative: The Concept of Early German Romanticism* (Harvard University Press 2003) 88 and further. Ever since the introduction of the notion of *Bildung* in education and pedagogy, there has been a recurring (predominantly German) debate on *Bildung*. A fairly recent example is a conference held in Bielefeld (2009) titled: *Hat die Zukunft eine Universität*? Wissenschaftliche Tagung 18–19 November 2009, Universität Bielefeld, Bielefeld. See D Schwanitz, *Bildung: Alles was man wissen muss* (Eichborn 1999). J Krautz, *Ware Bildung: Schule und Universität unter dem Diktat der Ökonomie* (Diederichs 2007).

[14] Horlacher, *op cit* 410.

[15] Krautz, *op cit* 14, 21.

[16] Sorkin, *op cit* 55.

Limits of State Action'.[17] Here, he draws upon Rousseau's distinction between the inward development of men and the outward action of citizens.[18] The first condition regards the internal or inward dimension of *Bildung*. Only in liberty, free from state intervention, are individuals able to act upon the realization and unfolding of their potential and qualities. The second condition pertains to the outward aspect of *Bildung*, i.e. the possibility for social interaction. Through the exchange of experiences, of knowledge with others, the unfolding of one's own individuality can be brought about. Consequently, *Bildung* calls for social bounds, a community.[19]

As we have argued before, the requirement of liberty pertains to the relationship with the state and this relationship is historically determined. In this case, the requirement of liberty entails the limitation of the powers of the absolutist (Frederican) state to the bare minimum, i.e. to the extent that the state is necessary to guarantee the internal and external security and safety of its citizens.[20] From a somewhat different perspective it could be denoted as a Humboldtian resistance to colonization by the state. That is to say: resistance against the instrumentalization of research and education by the state with the direct aim to groom obedient citizens. It follows that the second condition regarding the necessity of social bonds does not only refer to a reformation of the absolutist state but also to a fundamental reconsideration of the relation between state and individual, and hence between individuals.[21] Here, there is also something else at stake besides the limitation of state intervention and the transformation of the relationship state-individual. Humboldt was confronted with the requirement which follows from his own theoretical approach. If individual liberty and individuals *per se* are the point of departure, then the question arises how these 'monads' (cf. Leibniz) can bring about fruitful interaction and build a harmonious unity. This harmony is, according to Humboldt, not an assumption or an *a priori* in

17 Translation of: *Wilhelm von Humboldt, Ideen zu einem Versuch, die Grenzen der Wirksamkeit des Staats zu bestimmen*). Available at: <http://docs.mises.de/Humboldt/Humboldt_Grenzen_des_Staates.pdf> (accessed 29 April 2015). This work was probably written in 1791–1792, but first published after Humboldt's death in 1835. We use the digitally printed translation: J Coulthard (tr), *The Sphere and Duties of Government* (John Chapman 1854). Available at: <http://lf-oll.s3.amazonaws.com/titles/589/0053_Bk.pdf> (accessed 29 April 2015).

18 Sorkin, *op cit* 58.

19 Ibid 58 and 59. Also see: Krautz, *op cit* 15 and Ruhloff, *op cit* 23.

20 Sorkin, *op cit* 60.

21 Ibid 59.

a transcendent sense, but a factual political and social condition produced *within* the state. It limits the intervention of the state in the sense that the state is only allowed to provide the external conditions to safeguard liberty and development.[22] The second condition, of social bounds, confronted Humboldt with a problem: What institutions – other than the state – could contribute to the free interchange necessary for social cohesion? Whereas, according to Sorkin, Humboldt could not answer this question in a first instance, he later sought to meet the second requirement via his own educational reform centering on *Bildung*.[23] Exemplary was the founding of the University of Berlin in 1809, dedicated to the realization of the ideal.

There is an inherent tension between the two conditions, individual liberty and a fruitful community within the confines of the state. It is a tension that also surfaces in the person of Humboldt himself: as Minister of Education, and thus a representative of the state, Humboldt aimed at a reform of the Prussian education system that bade farewell to intervention of the state in education.[24] Humboldt circumvents this tension by disconnecting the second condition – of sociality – from the state and subsequently reconnecting it to the concept of nation. In his work, Humboldt also seems to shift his focus more and more towards the internal dimension.[25] In Humboldt's conceptualization, the nation mediates between the individual and humanity and is a substitute for the relationship between the individual and the state:[26]

> If the nation were made responsible for education, and if freedom prevailed within the educational institutions themselves, he (Humboldt, LF&LC) thought, then the nation would develop an associational life in and around the educational system that would foster the interchange requisite to *Bildung*.

---

22 See, for example, Humboldt, *op cit* Chapter IV.

23 Sorkin, *op cit* 60–61.

24 Sorkin addresses the issue of consistency of a practical educational reform by the state and a theory advocating self-cultivation without state intervention. He raises the question in a wider context, that is the relationship between the intelligentsia and the Prussian State. Sorkin states that Humboldt's theory of *Bildung* was employed to legitimize 'the alliance of the intelligentsia and the state through the university'. Sorkin (n 10) 56. If this was indeed the case, the ideal of *Bildung* could even be deemed propaganda. Something similar is suggested by Prange: 'Historical analysis is inclined to show *Bildung* as the educational ideology of the leisured classes, as a by-product of a sociopolitical situation which is definitely over and gone.' Prange, *op cit* 503.

25 Sorkin, *op cit* 61.

26 Ibid.

Furthermore, the nation should carry the financial burden of education in order to ensure independence of the state in that sense as well. Education should address the person and not the citizen – citizens being the category linked to the state. In addition, this reveals Humboldt's intellectual equality: persons communicate at the same level with each other, which was not necessarily the case for citizens within a Prussian state.[27] Finally, Humboldt geared his reform towards a *general* education that was meant to do justice to individual development, before entering the path of specialization. In all this, the function of the university 'was to congregate students in a community devoted to learning (*Wissenschaft*), and to vouchsafe their total freedom to interact with their peers'.[28]

This principally semantic move from Humboldt wherein sociality was not connected to the state but to the nation cannot divert from the fact that *Bildung* undeniably has a strong political aspect: each individual's self-formation that takes place within a political community (thus meeting the requirement of social bounds) can never be entirely free from the state. In his analysis, Sorkin observes that this implies a civic conception of *Bildung* which is addressed in Humboldt's *The Limits of State Action*:

> The civic conception of *Bildung* appears in those passages in which man is to consummate and activate his powers developed through self-cultivation. The civic conception is therefore the necessary completion of the social bounds necessary for *Bildung*.[29]

Bildung appears as a delicate interplay wherein sociality is the precondition for self-formation and this successful self-formation, in its turn, bears upon that sociality, reordering it in conformity with the findings and reflections of that preceding self-formation. However, what remains pivotal is the self-formation *per se*: it is the highest goal for all mankind. This process is deeply political because the self-cultivated man must again act within his political community, now as a citizen – deliberating and evaluating the state by his self-achieved reflections.[30] In fact, this process renders *Bildung* fundamental to politics.[31]

However, the political dimension of *Bildung* – its importance notwithstanding – seems to lose its theoretical prominence in Humboldt's own

[27] See G Kutscha, 'Zum Verhältnis von allgemeiner und beruflicher Bildung im Kontext bildungstheoretische Reformkonzepte: Rückblick und Perspektiven' [2003] 99(3) *Zeitschrift für Berufs- und Wirtschaftspädagogik* 328.

[28] Sorkin, *op cit* 63.

[29] Sorkin, *op cit* 68.

[30] Ruhloff, *op cit* 24–25.

[31] Humboldt, *op cit* 185ff.

work later on. The focus becomes entirely directed towards the inward part of the process, on the *self* of self-formation. We can only conjecture that the political dimension got somehow lost along the way in Humboldt's theorizing and conveniently so: the praxis of *Bildung* could then never be conceived and perceived as a threat towards the state. It left the notion of *Bildung* disarmed.[32]

Nevertheless, Humboldt's point of departure – individual development as a human and not only as a citizen, in freedom and within a community framed by the unity of research and education – is still an attractive and a relevant one. And this is so even now because:[33]

> *Bildung* has high demands and expectations; *Bildung* contains a promise of salvation, and *Bildung* cannot be reduced to mechanics, and certainly not to economics. *Bildung* is the haven for "Good" and "Whole".

In the next section, we will sketch the changed academic and societal environment which make the original Humboldtian ideal of *Bildung* both of the utmost importance to and evermore difficult to realize in contemporary Academia.

3 THE CHANGING CIRCUMSTANCES OF ACADEMIC EDUCATION

It goes almost without saying that ever since the founding of the University of Berlin in 1809 and Humboldt's conceptualization of *Bildung*, society and the circumstances of Academia have been subject to fundamental changes. In our post-industrial, technology-driven society, neo-liberalism reigns supreme in an ever-increasing number of societal domains. In this regard, Lock and Lorenz point out the general tendency to understand the university in purely economic terms, i.e. as a 'business'.[34] As an important chain in the 'knowledge economy', universities should serve 'their clients' (i.e. the students) in an 'efficient' way by

[32] Of course, this does not mean that Bildung could not be re-armed and even take a turn for the worst if and when utilized for political reasons. Illustrative is the work of Alfred Bäumler, best known for his nazification of Nietzsche's work. Bäumler employed the work of Fichte on *Bildung* to link *Bildung* with *Nationalerziehung*. See: D Pan, *Sacrifice in the Modern World: On the Particularity and Generality of Nazi Myth* (Northwestern University Press 2012) 127ff.

[33] Horlacher, *op cit* 410.

[34] Lock and Lorenz, *op cit* 406–409, 412.

'textbook transmission' responding to the social demands of the market.[35] This also has immediate consequences for the way in which universities are organized. The key concept in this regard is managerialism.[36] The culture of control comes to the fore in an ongoing circus of 'audit, assessment, accreditation and accountability'. Note that also these concepts need to be understood in economic terms.[37] Although seldom addressed in public, this neo-liberal approach to Academia has a detrimental effect on individual scholars, too.[38] Echoing Humboldt, Lock and Lorenz hold that:[39]

> the role of a university is to provide a sphere in which genuinely critical thinking, investigation and debate can take place, it would follow that university research cannot take the form of a mere response to "societal demand", nor university teaching that of "textbook transmission". The integration of university teaching with research, as well as the demarcation line between university education and professional education, thus become more relevant than ever. Yet this critical function seems now to be structurally threatened.

To be clear, this instrumentalization and economization of education does not as such constitute a threat to the right to education. As is well-known, this right is enshrined in basically all modern constitutions and human right treaties (e.g. in Article 26 of the Universal Declaration of Human Rights and in Articles 13–14 of the International Covenant on Economic, Social and Cultural Rights). However, we hold that market rationality has a parasitic effect on the right of education by casting education in purely economic terms, that is: education is reduced to an instrument geared to achieve direct – profitable – results. In this way, it might leave the right *senso strictu* unaffected, yet it erodes the underlying interest which this right protects. In this regard, it is telling that both the UDHR (art. 26 section 2) and the ICESCR (art. 13 section 1) mention that 'education shall be directed to the full development of the human personality'. This underlying interest cannot be valued in (purely) economic terms. Indeed, where market rationality is called upon under conditions of scarcity and

---

35 See R Abma, 'De kennisindustrie en de teloorgang van academische waarden' [2008] 4(32) Waterstof.

36 Lock and Lorenz, *op cit* 408.

37 Ibid 415–416.

38 See R Gill, 'Breaking the Silence: The Hidden Injuries of the Neoliberal University' in R Flood and R Gill (eds), *Secrecy and Silence in the Research Process: Feminist Reflections* (Routledge 2009) 228–244.

39 Lock and Lorenz, *op cit* 413.

goods need to be redistributed, non-market goods (e.g. education) are always in a worse position. Furthermore, this relates to another contemporary problem. In late modernity, due to technological innovations information has been democratized resulting in a situation in which it is available for many more people at much lower costs. What is often forgotten in this respect is that information does not yet constitute knowledge. The latter concept presupposes the ability to identify and select the relevant context for information in order to be able to assess it.

Reinvigorating the unity of research and education should, however, not become a plea for simply transposing old ideas to a new environment. As Baggen and Weijers also argue, it rather means giving central place to a critical reflection on specialized knowledge and skills.[40] Academic education aims at teaching an 'investigative attitude', or 'reflective stance'. Hence, the good university professor is not simply the one with most knowledge of a specific field, but rather she who can actually teach her students this stance. This will create 'the good academic', someone who 'does not only know her trade, but who has also obtained knowledge of the backgrounds, history and uncertainties of her field. This insight should enable him or her to autonomously pass her own critical judgment and to act with "the uncertainty of the professional"'.[41]

Note how this formulation – the *un*certainty of the professional – is negative. We believe that this is important because teaching substantive values through academic education is no longer an easy, or a desirable function in a pluralist society. Furthermore, *academic* education should not serve ready-to-consume truths to its students. The negativity which forms the core of the 'reflective stance' is a certain hesitation or restraint concerning one's own professional opinion, and a sensitivity regarding situations on the border of one's professional knowledge, situations where the power of judgment is truly called upon (i.e. situations where there is no rule to rely on).[42] In short, this is what education in Academia should be about: the courage to hesitate and question even the most basic assumptions of one's field, and the sensitivity to recognize when an independent judgment is needed as well as the power to actually pass it. Hence, we argue that a reinvigoration of the ideal of *Bildung* today should embrace the unity of research and education, thus not succumbing to the demands of the market but focusing on a broad formation of

---

40 P Baggen and I Weijers, 'De toekomst van de universiteit' (1993) 13(53) *Krisis* 64, 67.

41 Ibid 68.

42 Also see B van Klink, 'Knowledge and Aphasia: What is the Use of Skeptical Legal Education?' in this volume.

students. The outcomes of research flowing into the everyday practice of legal education would ideally result in lawyers not simply being trained in 'thinking like a lawyer',[43] and in the possession of a set of legal skills. It would train *academics* through the 'negative' reflective stance or investigative attitude. It would moreover breed citizens able to take responsibility and aptly equipped to judge complex situations. In the next section, we will elaborate on this idea drawing upon the work of Gadamer and Arendt.

4 TOWARDS RE-*BILDUNG*

In the previous sections, we have described the broad outlines of the historical development of the ideal of *Bildung* and the current debate on the future of academic education. Here, we will start mapping the outlines of what it could mean for university today. For this purpose, we will draw on the work of Hans-Georg Gadamer and Hannah Arendt. The former provides us with the rough idea of the content of a current reinterpretation of *Bildung*. Thus, Gadamer's ideas will be used to fine-tune the inward dimension, i.e. the self-formation of the individual. Some of Arendt's ideas can help us to grasp the outward or social dimension in terms of the specific place and the responsibility of institutions of education within society.

Hans-Georg Gadamer is one of the authors who have tried to breathe new life in to the ideal of *Bildung*. In his *magnum opus*, he places himself and his project explicitly in the tradition of *Bildung*.[44] In dialogue with Hegel, Gadamer works towards a hermeneutic reinterpretation of the ideal.[45] In his version, Gadamer stresses the dialogical aspect of learning and the ability to take the viewpoint of one's interlocutor:[46]

> That is what, following Hegel, we emphasized as the general characteristic of *Bildung*: keeping oneself open to what is other – to other, more universal points of view. It embraces a sense of proportion and distance in relation to

---

[43] See F Schauer, *Thinking Like a Lawyer: A New Introduction to Legal Reasoning* (reprint, Harvard 2012).

[44] H-G Gadamer, *Truth and Method* (trs. revd. by J Weinsheimer and DG Marshall, 2nd edn, Continuum 2011) 8–17.

[45] For a comparison of Hegel and Gadamer on *Bildung*, see A Odenstedt, 'Hegel and Gadamer on Bildung' [2008] 46 *The Southern Journal of Philosophy* 559.

[46] Gadamer, *op cit* 15.

> itself, and hence consists in rising above itself to universality. To distance oneself from oneself and from one's private purposes means to look at these in the way that others see them.

Important in this respect is to call to mind that according to Gadamer understanding always takes place within a specific situation and accompanying horizon, comprised of the whole of prejudices through which we can make sense of something in the first place.[47] In dialogue with the other (a person or a text) interpretation aims at understanding through an unending mediation between the other's and my own point of view, a 'fusion of horizons'.[48] It is crucial to understand the transformative nature of this process in which the interpreter as a subject changes. In short, it requires a sort of openness to the other consisting in 'recognizing that I myself must accept some things that are against me, even though no one else forces me to do so'.[49] The (ethical) consequences of this formula might, among other things, point to a duty to question oneself and one's own views. Henrik Bohlin argues exactly that, here there is an interesting parallel between Humboldt and Gadamer regarding a 'negative' didactic method.[50] Later, we will return to this 'negative' aspect of

---

47 Gadamer, *op cit* 301–302:

> We define the concept of "situation" by saying that it represents a standpoint that limits the possibility of vision. Hence essential part of the concept of situation is the concept of "horizon." The horizon is the range of vision that includes everything that can be seen from a particular vantage point … . A person who has no horizon is a man who does not see far enough and hence overvalues what is nearest to him. On the other hand, "to have an horizon" means not being limited to what is nearby, but to being able to see beyond it … [W]orking out of the hermeneutical situation means the achievement of the right horizon of inquiry for the questions evoked by the encounter with tradition.

48 Gadamer, *op cit* 305.

49 Gadamer, *op cit* 355.

50 H Bohlin, '*Bildung* and Moral Self-Cultivation in Higher Education: What Does it Mean and How Can it be Achieved?' [2008] *Forum on Public Policy: A Journal of the Oxford Round Table*, 6. Available at: <http://forumonpublicpolicy.com/summer08papers/archivesummer08/bohlin.pdf> (accessed 29 April 2015):

> Note how well the analysis fits in with Humboldt's idea of the "negative" didactic method of presenting "all possible solutions of the problem in question, so that the citizen may select, according to his own judgment, the course which seems to him the most appropriate" … . In the process of *Bildung*, as Gadamer explicates it, the student or participant in the process is (i) made to reflect on a certain problem, (ii) presented with more than one

Bildung. First, however, we want to address the political stakes of the concept. Education, and certainly academic education, is not something we can simply separate completely from politics because what is also always at stake in education is the future of individuals and the community they are part of. To elucidate this point, we will briefly turn to the work of Hannah Arendt.

In her article on the crisis in education, Arendt immediately frames this crisis as a political one.[51] She explains how this crisis is connected to a greater crisis of authority and tradition within society.[52] Education can simply not do without authority, she argues. This is not the only way in which institutions of education differ from other places. Indeed, Arendt stresses the special place institutions of education occupy in the space between the private sphere of the family and the public sphere of the world. Especially their distance with regard to the public sphere is relevant here. Arendt argues that childhood benefits from a certain amount of darkness, i.e. a place protected from the light of the public sphere.[53] Institutions of education offer such places: transitional spaces where children (and young adults) can be prepared for their role in the world:

> possible solution without being told that this solution or the other is the right one, and thereby (iii) provoked or stimulated to think independently on the problem. … The *Bildung* process as described by Gadamer could be called doubly negative; neither the solutions nor the problems are pre-defined, or at least they need not be so.

[51] H Arendt, 'The Crisis in Education', in H Arendt, *Between Past and Future* (Penguin 1961) 173:

> The general crisis that has overtaken the modern world everywhere and in almost every sphere of life manifests itself differently in each country, involving different areas and taking on different forms. In America, one of its most characteristic and suggestive aspects is the recurring crisis in education that, during the last decade at least, has become a political problem of the first magnitude, reported on almost daily in the newspapers.

[52] Ibid 195.

[53] Ibid 186:

> Wherever the latter [i.e. childhood] is consistently exposed to the world without the protection of privacy and security its vital quality is destroyed. In the public world, common to all, persons count, and so does work, that is, the work of our hands that each of us contributes to our common world; but life *qua* life does not matter there. The world cannot be regardful of it, and it has to be hidden and protected from the world. Everything that lives, not vegetative life alone, emerges from darkness and, however strong its natural tendency to thrust itself into the light, it nevertheless needs the security of darkness to grow at all.

> Normally the child is first introduced to the world in school. Now school is by no means the world and must not pretend to be; it is rather the institution that we interpose between the private domain of home and the world in order to make the transition from the family to the world possible at all.'[54]

Arendt thus (also) gives *political* reasons for the separation of the schools, and one might say education in general, from the world (i.e. the public sphere, the political sphere).[55]

In order to grasp the exact relationship between education and authority, one must first call to mind how Arendt understands authority. Drawing on the Roman origins of the concept, she holds that '[t]he word *auctoritas* derives from the verb *augere*, "augment", and what authority or those in authority constantly augment is the foundation.'[56] Authority always includes a reference to *the past*: it presents what is new as born from a time-honoured origin. At the same time, what is once founded, needs to be taken up and act as a fruitful soil for future acts. Hence, the reference to the *future* is crucial to grasp: i.e. *why* authority is so important to Arendt. Authority makes things in the world last, it concerns 'the permanence and durability which human beings need precisely because they are mortals – the most unstable and futile beings we know of.'[57] It should thus not be confused with force and whereas it is hierarchical in nature, it 'implies an obedience in which men retain their freedom.'[58] While she does warn against simply transposing a political concept of authority to the realm of education, Arendt firmly states that education cannot do without authority. This need for authority in education is untimely: already in Arendt's time authority was in decline and this development has only continued in the decades which separate us from her. And yet, the responsibility for the world, so dear to Arendt

---

54 Ibid 188.

55 See Ibid 196, the beautiful lines with which she ends the article:

> Education is the point at which we decide whether we love the world enough to assume responsibility for it and by the same token save it from that ruin which, except for renewal, except for the coming of the new and young, would be inevitable. And education, too, is where we decide whether we love our children enough not to expel them from our world and leave them to their own devices, nor to strike from their hands their chance of undertaking something new, something unforeseen by us, but to prepare them in advance for the task of renewing a common world.

56 H Arendt, 'What is Authority?' in H Arendt, *Between Past and Future* (Penguin 1961) 91, 121–122.

57 Ibid 95.

58 Ibid 106.

in politics, also applies in the realm of education in the sense that '[i]n education this responsibility for the world takes the form of authority.'[59] Children, Arendt explains, are new in a double sense: both new in the world (a *new* human being) and in the process of becoming (a *becoming* human being).[60] They need someone who, himself having taken responsibility for the world, can teach them to do the same.[61] Since the world depends on the new for its durability, education should, exactly for the sake of what is new, refrain from controlling it. Paradoxically, education should preserve the new. In other words, in this specific sense education must be conservative in nature.[62]

5 RE-*BILDUNG* AS AN IDEAL FOR LEGAL EDUCATION

The process of instrumentalization and of gearing academic education towards the market discussed above seems to hold true for Academia in general. However, it raises special concerns for the humanities in a broad sense, including legal education. The particular threat stems from the fact that legal studies are traditionally close to and directed towards the legal practice that is subject to the demands of the market. Legal education centers on the problem-solving potential of law and is casuistical in

---

[59] Arendt, *op cit* 189.

[60] Ibid 185.

[61] Ibid 189: 'The teacher's qualification consists in knowing the world and being able to instruct others about it, but his authority rests on his assumption of responsibility for that world. *Vis-à-vis* the child it is as though he were a representative of all adult inhabitants, pointing out the details and saying to the child: This is our world.'

[62] Ibid 192–193:

> Because the world is made by mortals it wears out; and because it continuously changes its inhabitants it runs the risk of becoming as mortal as they. To preserve the world against the mortality of its creators and inhabitants it must be constantly set right anew. The problem is simply to educate in such a way that a setting–right remains actually possible, even though it can, of course, never be assured. Our hope always hangs on the new which every generation brings; but precisely because we can base our hope only on this, we destroy everything if we so try to control the new that we, the old, can dictate how it will look. Exactly for the sake of what is new and revolutionary in every child, education must be conservative; it must preserve this newness and introduce it as a new thing into an old world, which, however revolutionary its actions may be, is always, from the standpoint of the next generation, superannuated and close to destruction.

nature, taking the judge as its role model. It confines the study of solutions to existing law, i.e. legislation and case law.[63] In sum, legal education's aim seems to train legal practitioners, ready to enter a well-established profession of judges, public prosecutors, corporate lawyers and so on. While legal education is traditionally joined at the hip with legal practice, it nevertheless belongs within the walls of Academia ever since the birth of the *alma mater studiorum* of Bologna.

Besides this pedigree, the academic value of legal education is established and safeguarded by courses which in the Dutch Academia are referred to as '*meta-juridica*', meaning legal philosophy, legal theory, legal sociology, legal history, methodology, etc. What these subjects contribute to the curriculum is that they specifically contextualize law, and excavate its foundations and normative assumptions. This allows students to develop a critical perspective on law.[64] This perspective involves being able to question the function law fulfills or claims to fulfill on behalf of society, the way it does this and what this means in a society which becomes increasingly complex, also due to technological developments and globalization.

This academic core of legal education is, however, under siege.[65] As we have discussed in one of the previous sections, the demands of the market and increasing political pressure entail that legal education is pushed towards more efficiency. This comes to the fore in an increasing emphasis on the teaching of positive law and skills. Furthermore, a more general trend is that students and university staff are pressed to make the whole endeavour of following an academic education as efficient as possible, that is to say to generate as much 'output' (i.e. diplomas) in as short a time as possible.[66] This strikes academic legal education at the heart and what remains, bleak a perspective as it may seem, is a

---

63 L Francot and B de Vries, 'Legal Education Re-Enchanted?' [2006] 3 *European Journal of Legal Education* 3, 9.

64 See B van Klink, 'Knowledge and Aphasia: What Is the Use of Skeptical Legal Education' in this volume.

65 D Baecker, *Studien zur nächsten Gesellschaft* (Suhrkamp 2007) here especially his essay 'Die nächste Universität' 98–115. Baecker states that universities change in the course of time and unavoidably so. What is remarkable according to him is 'wie sich Leitdisziplinen oder Leitwissenschaften etablieren und wieder verschwinden, die die Aufgabe haben, für das Universelle, das Übergreifende und damit auch dem politischen und wirtschaftlichen Zugriff Entzogene Sorgen zu tragen und geradezustehen' (ibid 100). Examples are philosophy, theology and nowadays the humanities (ibid 101).

66 See Lock and Lorenz, *op cit* 408, where they explain that nowadays students are first and foremost seen as 'clients'.

vocational training conditioning students for the market. However, while academics reject reducing the study of law to a form of vocational training, one could argue that it fits the *Zeitgeist*, as economic rationality reigns supreme. Still, we hold that it behooves academics to question this economic supremacy and to counter-balance developments that seem to erode quality for the sake of efficiency and profit, as there is a discrepancy between what the market demands and what constitutes a good lawyer. The latter is not simply trained in selecting and applying the right rules to the case at hand, but rather someone who possesses the analytical skills to think about law (and its boundaries) on an academic level. When practicing law, lawyers acquire the necessary knowledge about the actual application of rules. However, the good lawyer is not a shop worker as Nietzsche would call him.[67] The good lawyer is able to frame law within the proper historical, cultural, social, ethical and political context and hence appreciates the value and the limits of law in general, and legal solutions in particular cases. Exactly because of this understanding, he or she is able to take responsibility.

Still, the 'ideal' of the shop worker frames academic education in terms of functionality and instrumentality, and more so of economic rationality. As we have argued above, this leads to academic education growing scantier, specifically in terms of community, the autonomy of the individual, authority, responsibility and its ability to act as a counter-force against the all-encompassing grasp of economic rationality. The question now is how this notion of the good lawyer relates to the notion of *Bildung* in our times. First and foremost, we would like to emphasize that we do understand *Bildung* to be an ideal. As such, it should not be thought of in terms of a factual and organizational output, but rather as a directive that may guide Academia. Since social circumstances now differ

---

67 Friedrich Nietzsche, 'Über die Zukunft unserer Bildungs-Anstalten', Sechs, im Auftrag der *Academischen Gesellschaft*, in Basel gehaltene, öffentliche Reden in F Nietzsche, *Kritische Studienausgabe* (Bd. 1, 2nd edn, De Gruyter 1999) 669–670:

> In his specialization, he might stand over the *Vulgus*, and yet he belongs to it in every other respect, that is in all important aspects. Such a specialized scholar resembles the shop worker who devotes his life to nothing but making a certain screw or handle for a precise tool or machine, a task in which he, evidently, reaches a certain degree of virtuosity … . For centuries, it has been self-evident that thinking of the cultivated man [*Gebildeten*], one thought of the scholar and the scholar only. Yet, contemporary experience does not allow us such a naive identification. The exploitation of a man for the sake of his science is now a generally accepted principle: who still questions the value of a science which uses its servants as would a vampire?

vastly from those in Humboldt's time, we think that even though it concerns an ideal, its reach and meaning are not static but should be reconsidered against the backdrop of our era. To mark the difference between the Humboldtian concept of *Bildung* and our re-interpretation, we refer to it as Re-*Bildung*. From Humboldt we readily accept the inheritance of the two aspects of the inward self-formation (the individual level) and the outward action. As we argued above, Humboldt connected this outward aspect to the state and later it somehow vanished in favour of an emphasis on the inward aspect of *Bildung*. There is, unequivocally, a tension between the inward and the outward dimension that was evaded by Humboldt. This lacuna needs to be addressed, even though this tension cannot be solved. Nevertheless, we will seek to relieve it through rethinking the connection between the two dimensions.

There are, we believe, three relationships constitutive to this connection: the relation of the student to herself, the relationship between the student and the teacher, and the relationship between Academia and society. The first relationship can be understood with the help of Gadamer. His hermeneutic take on *Bildung* casts the process of self-formation in terms of an ongoing process in which understanding is only obtained through the interplay of myself and the other (person or text). In this dialogue, one learns to question oneself and one's own knowledge, and to open oneself to new insights. From a slightly different perspective, one could say that the relationship of the student to herself is constituted by an ongoing external reference contributing to a critical attitude. Openness in the private realm represents the normative aspect and thus the foundation of individual responsibility.

We want to elicit the point that Re-*Bildung* is also always self-formation, in this respect it does not differ from *Bildung*.[68] What is different is the individual as such. Whereas Humboldt sought to contribute to the realization of Enlightenment ideals such as the emancipation of the individual, Re-*Bildung* clearly seeks to address the self-formation of the late-modern autonomous, articulate individual. Nowadays, we are considered – for better or worse – to be emancipated from religion and God, and face a different set of problems, first and foremost the uncertainty contemporary social complexity brings along. One source of social complexity, and hence uncertainty, is vast and widely available information that is communicated through the (social) media. However, whereas the access to and the availability of information is generally

---

68 Krautz, *op cit* 14: 'Bildung meint eigentlich *Selbstbildung*. Man wird nicht gebildet, sondern man bildet sich'.

deemed an achievement, it also confronts us with the necessity of adequate selection and evaluation. It is at this point that self-formation within the walls of Academia regains momentum, in the enduring confrontation of the individual with contemporary uncertainty: self-formation here does not aim at the complete reduction of uncertainty but refers to rendering it manageable, by acquiring tools and knowledge to select, and (re-)order information.

In the second relationship, the one between teacher and student, the concept of authority in the vein of Arendt takes the meaning of the teacher's responsibility for the student as a new inhabitant of the world, or public realm. In an ever more complex society, teachers should help their students to obtain the ability to select and value information. Valuing is never a neutral act, it always involves separating essentials from side issues. It thus asks for a critical and hence normative assessment of the information at hand. This assessment is crucial, for it forms the precondition of entering into the Gadamerian dialogue with the text. It is at this point that Arendt's claim that education cannot do without authority also gains weight.

Finally, the third relationship is that between Academia and society. Note, that this relationship has two aspects. First, Academia should be understood as a transitional space between the private sphere and the public sphere, in the sense of Arendt. In order to grasp what this might entail, one should take into account the state of society at the beginning of the twenty-first century. As sociologists such as Beck have argued, the process of modernization has led to a society which is hyper-individualized.[69] He detects the withering away of traditional frames of meaning, for example, religion. As a result, people write their own life stories and are thus forced to choose how to lead their life. At the same time, the domination of the market renders that others appear as competitors. Arendt's concept of transitional spaces helps us to steer away from the university as a market-driven place by focusing on the role of institutions of education in society. As such, they also bear a clear responsibility for their students. Re-*Bildung* thus points to the fact that Academia should be aware that both students and universities are always also *part of* society. At some point, students will start to contribute professionally to society, understood in a broad sense.

What does this mean for legal education? As law is increasingly becoming a European and international affair, lawyers can no longer be

---

[69] U Beck, *Risikogesellschaft: Auf dem Weg in eine andere Moderne* (Suhrkamp 1986) 161ff, also 205ff.

trained in only one legal system. The curriculum should devote ample time to the study of European, international and comparative law.[70] Furthermore, law should also be studied in its proper historical, cultural, social, ethical and political context in such courses as legal philosophy, legal history, legal sociology, etc.[71]

Universities are not simply schools where individuals come for their own benefits and diplomas only. A university is indeed a place where everyone, students, lecturers and researchers, share the common goal of the highest possible quality of education and research. By focussing on this common goal, it also becomes clear why the core of *Bildung*, the unity of education and research, has lost nothing of its value. Good *academic* education, we argue, takes into account, discusses and, where appropriate, questions the latest developments of research. Here the negativity, the *un*certainty of the professional may be called to mind: a university is a place in which students, lecturers and researchers share this uncertainty regarding the truth and foster it, so that they may take it as a starting point for new questions in the vein of the hermeneutic circle of Gadamer. Dirk Baecker even goes so far as to argue that the function of today's university is to develop both students *and* professionals' proficiency to deal with *nicht-Wissen*, the absence of knowledge, in a complex society. According to Baecker this requires method, theory and practice. And the orientation to practice here equals an orientation towards to the complexity of our society.[72]

Re-*Bildung*, finally, encompasses the idea of re-gaining authority of Academia. This aspect is closely connected to other aspects of a re-evaluation of the societal role of Academia. One characteristic of contemporary society which we have not yet mentioned should be taken into account here: we live in times of acceleration.[73] Authority, however, far from seeking novelty, has to do with what is time-honoured. In this sense, it also asks for a different time, another rhythm. Universities are

---

70 See JM Smits, 'European Legal Education, Or: How to Prepare Students for Global Citizenship' [2011] 45 *The Law Teacher* 163 and BF Fauvarque-Cosson, 'Restructuring Legal Education in Europe: The Necessity of Comparative and European Law' [2014] 63 *Ars Aequi* 867.

71 CEJ Schwöbel-Patel, '"I'd Like to Learn what Hegemony Means" Teaching International Law from a Critical Angle' [2013] 3 *Law and Method* 67, 79: 'Translating a political, social, organic notion of *Bildung* to the law classroom involves, above all, the contextualization of norms'.

72 D Baecker, *Studien zur nächsten Gesellschaft* (Suhrkamp 2007) 108–109.

73 H Rosa, *Beschleunigung: Die Veränderungen der Zeitstrukturen in der Moderne* (Suhrkamp 2005).

places which thrive on a slower, more contemplative pace.[74] The contrast with the fast world of the market could not be greater. The university is also an institution in the specific sense of something which lasts. In times of acceleration, institutions are under strain. However, the understanding of universities as places of authority, places where tradition is valued, highlights the crucial role of these institutions for society: in the line of Arendt, one could argue that institutions connect our world both with the world of our ancestors and with the world of our children. They thus fulfil the role of binding the generations and making the world into a *common* world.[75]

Re-gaining authority for Academia entails being aware of this role of institutions in general and of the university in particular, as the place where the knowledge of centuries is stored for new generations. Hence, the core task of the university, to provide a place where scientific research can be done and an academic education can be followed, needs to be seen as a value in itself. Academia can ultimately only derive its authority from this value. Fundamental research and an education which teaches students a reflective stance and an investigative attitude are not important primarily because they benefit the growth of the economy, or because society becomes a better place but, first and foremost (even if not only) because the pursuit of the truth has value *per se*.[76] Precisely because the pursuit of truth has value in itself and beyond education, a plea for Re-*Bildung* is never a plea to reduce education to an instrument for society. However, this does not preclude the possibility of institutions of education having an important function in and, indeed, a responsibility towards the society they are part of. Here, Arendt's idea of a common world may prove illuminating. The proper 'place' of academic education is then in-between, in the specific sense Arendt gives to this term:

---

[74] Cornelissen (n 1) 71: 'The university wants to create time and space for what can only be deemed valuable when we are not busy with what is directly useful.'

[75] H Arendt, *The Human Condition* (2nd edn, Chicago University Press 1958) 55: 'If the world is to contain a public space, it cannot be erected for one generation and planned for the living one; it must transcend the life-span of mortal men'.

[76] Cornelissen (n 1) 69: 'The greatest danger is that, if universities only legitimize themselves by reference to an external, secondary goal (like economic growth or democratic citizenship), they run the risk that as soon as these goals are brought into disrepute, the universities themselves may become discredited and have no own values to fall back upon'.

> To live together in the world means essentially that a world of things is between those who have it in common, as a table is located between those who sit around if, the world, like every in-between, relates and separates men at the same time.[77]

6 CONCLUSION

Drawing inspiration from the original Humboldtian ideal, we have contended a reconceptualization of *Bildung* as an ideal which can take up some of the major challenges with which universities struggle today. We have argued that Re-*Bildung* can act as a powerful counter-narrative addressing several aspects resulting from the dominance of market rationality and managerialism in Academia. In fact, we have sought to rearm Academia against the market. This project of rearming may only prove successful if universities dare to question the dominant discourse of the market and firmly argue that their value cannot be understood primarily in economic terms. This entails rupture with the prevailing narrative of the knowledge economy and the role universities play herein, so popular among (some) politicians. It also requires the state to step back and not act as a mediator between the economy and academic education, thus giving Academia space to re-build its autonomy. It is in this sense, we believe, that Re-*Bildung* contributes to a much needed second emancipation of the individual, this time from the iron cage of economic rationality.

For legal education, this means resisting the demands of professional practice and reinvigorating legal education as *academic* education. As we have argued, we believe that this can only be done by breathing new life into the core of *Bildung*, i.e. the unity of research and education. Practically, this means maintaining and fortifying the academic core of the curriculum by giving due place to such courses as legal philosophy, legal sociology, legal history, methodology, etc. Only through these subjects, Academia will remain a place where not just any lawyer but the *good* lawyer is educated, the Re-*gebildete* lawyer.

---

[77] H Arendt, *The Human Condition* (2nd edn, Chicago University Press 1958) 52.

4. Academic education and socialization[1]

Anja Böning

1 INTRODUCTION TO THE PROBLEM AREA

The discussion on legal educational matters reveals an odd discrepancy: On the one side it represents a 'long runner' regarding legal and education policy matters, whilst on the other side it could hardly have attracted scientific interest in the past. So, up to this point, law students' socialization still describes a rather poorly illuminated subject matter.[2] Topics such as socialization and discipline within educational institutions are regarded as subjects classically attributed to educational science or sociology.[3] According to Brun-Otto Bryde the timidity to look (or to let someone look) closer at legal education's very own formation praxis can

[1] This contribution appeared in a modified version in Judith Brockmann and Arne Pilniok, *Prüfen auf dem Prüfstand: Prüfungskultur in der Rechtswissenschaft* (Nomos 2014) 159.

[2] For example, Wolfgang Kaupen, *Die Hüter von Recht und Ordnung* (Luchterhand 1971); Andreas Heldrich and Gerhard Schmidtchen, *Gerechtigkeit als Beruf: Repräsentativumfrage unter jungen Juristen* (Beck 1982); Wolfgang Schütte, *Die Einübung des juristischen Denkens: Juristenausbildung als Sozialisationsprozess* (Campus-Verlag 1982); Tino Bargel, Frank Multrus and Michael Ramm, *Das Studium der Rechtswissenschaft: Eine Fachmonographie aus studentischer Sicht* (BMBF 1996); Lena Damm, 'Sozialisation durch Prüfungsangst und Leistungsdruck' [2006] *Forum Recht*, 60; Elisabeth Mertz, *The Language of Law School: Learning to Think Like a Lawyer* (OUP 2007); Ulrike Schultz, 'Legal Education in Germany – An Ever (Never?) Ending Story of Resistance to Change' in Vittorio Olgiati (eds), *Higher Legal Culture and Postgraduate Legal Education in Europe* (Edizioni scientifiche italiane 2007) 125, 131ff.

[3] Cf. Michael Wrase, 'Recht und soziale Praxis – Überlegungen für eine soziologische Rechtstheorie' in Michelle Cottier, Josef Estermann and Michael Wrase (eds), *Wie wirkt Recht? Ausgewählte Beiträge zum ersten gemeinsamen Kongress der deutschsprachigen Rechtssoziologie-Vereinigungen an der Universität Luzern 2008* (Nomos 2010) 113, 136ff.

be attributed to its refusal to deal with the factual status quo of law studies, in order to protect it from a possible delegitimation.[4] In Hans-Werner Prahl's research papers, which deal with university examinations, this point is argued in a similar way. According to Prahl, examinations represent rule and authority and sciences stabilize them by tabooing academic exams themselves.[5] The current state of research regarding educational, learning and socialization processes in law studies is also unsatisfactory, because university socialization still is a relatively unexplored research area.[6] This particularly regards the university daily routine and examination practices of various study subjects. Questions such as how to characterize the social formation program in law, how students deal with the legal habitus, and in what kind of appropriation processes it amalgamates with individual biographies and dispositions remain most widely unexplained.[7]

This contribution, which can to be understood as an experimental workshop report, intends to focus upon the inside of law studies. This will be done by reconstructing institutionalized exam practices specific to law studies in Germany. The reconstruction is based on publicized empirical material which will be analysed from the socialization research's perspective. This brings out complex social modes of action that are specific to the legal examination culture, which shall be discussed as socialization and disciplining effects. The law students' life-worldly experiences and adventures, which in terms of 'lived experience' may shed light on difficult mechanisms within law's subject socialization, provide the basis.

This 'interpretative and discovering' approach is quite new to the legal education area.[8] The selection of the interview sequences results from the

---

[4] Brun-Otto Bryde, 'Rechtssoziologische Anmerkungen zur Diskussion über die Reform der Juristenausbildung' in Dieter Strempel (eds), *Empirische Rechtssoziologie* (Nomos 2002) 213 (218).

[5] Hans-Werner Prahl, *Hochschulprüfungen: Sinn oder Unsinn? Sozialgeschichte und Ideologiekritik der akademischen Initiationskultur* (Kösel 1976) 8ff.

[6] Marianne Horstkemper and Klaus-Jürgen Tillmann, 'Sozialisation in Schule und Hochschule' in Klaus-Jürgen Tillmann, Matthias Grundmann and Sabine Walper (eds), *Handbuch Sozialisationsforschung* (7th edn, Beltz 2008) 290–291.

[7] To this Desideratum also refers Arne Pilniok, 'Rechtswissenschaftliche Fachdidaktik als Reflexion der Rechtswissenschaft' in Jörn Griebel and Florian Gröblinghoff (eds), *Von der juristischen Lehre: Erfahrungen und Denkanstöße* (Nomos 2012) 17, 19.

[8] Available subject-related comparative research papers, which consider law, provide a proper insight into different subject cultures. Anyway, conceptually

desire to explore different aspects of student's experiences and to identify the various facets of socializing and disciplinary power in legal education. The analysis is based on the method of qualitative content analysis.[9] The empirical material being used here is extracted from the interview volume 'Examiniertes Examen', which was published by Nell Bickel et al. in 2004.[10] The underlying idea of the interview collection was to survey the experiences and adventures law students have gained through legal examinations in order to examine psychological and social-psychological effects of legal testing. The project's aim was to point out the strategies to cope with stress during the examination phase. The worth of this project – given the scarcely satisfying state of research (you could also attribute a pioneer status to it) – lies in the presentation of an (although analytically and theoretically abstinent) attempt to describe what happens to students when studying law. When studying law, what does the social reality look like and how do students react when experiencing challenges and conflicts? Furthermore, the project expresses an academic attention and sensitivity for the students' needs, which is remarkable for the German legal discourse. Within educational studies or sociology, the students' perspective plays a recognized role for gaining valid insights into the social reality in legal education. Within law, the students have not attracted academic (and/or university-political) attention as research subjects yet. This omission does actually allow inferences as to the construction of law students: Their 'aphonia' corresponds to an inferior position within the institutional structure,

---

they rather present the differences between particular subjects, in order to dissociate them from one another. E G Margret Bülow-Schramm and Karsten Gerlof, 'Lebensweltliche Konstruktionen von Studierenden – Brücken zum Habitus?' in Steffani Engler und Beate Krais (eds), *Das kulturelle Kapital und die Macht der Klassenstrukturen: sozialstrukturelle Verschiebungen und Wandlungsprozesses des Habitus* (Juventa 2004) 141; Barbara Friebertshäuser, *Übergangsphase Studienbeginn: eine Feldstudie über Riten der Initiation in eine studentische Fachkultur* (Juventa 1992); Steffani Engler, *Fachkultur, Geschlecht und soziale Reproduktion: eine Untersuchung über Studentinnen und Studenten der Erziehungswissenschaft, Rechtswissenschaft, Elektrotechnik und des Maschinenbaus* (Deutscher Studien Verlag 1993); Regula Julia Leemann, *Chancenungleichheiten im Wissenschaftssystem: wie Geschlecht und soziale Herkunft Karrieren beeinflussen* (Rüegger 2002).

[9] Mayring Philipp, *Qualitative Inhaltsanalyse: Grundlage und Techniken* (Beltz 2015).

[10] Nell Bickel et al, *Examiniertes Examen. Das Erste Juristische Staatsexamen – Interviews mit Prüflingen durch einen Prüfer und andere Texte* (BOD 2004).

which is more hierarchical and authoritative than in other disciplines. To me, this marginalization seems to be related to law's social status and the nature of the legal habitus.[11]

The research papers of the critical social theorist Pierre Bourdieu, who examined the French elite institutions in his last educational-sociological study, serve as a frame of reference to this explorative analysis.[12] The central concepts in the research papers of Bourdieu, who dealt with social relationships and reproduction mechanisms of society, educational system and socialization, are the social space and the habitus. In the sense of a social cartography, the more-dimensional social space is designed as a graphically converted coordinate system in which individuals and classes take up social positions in accordance with different types of capital (economic, cultural and social capital), volume of capital and – corresponding to this – different lifestyles (taste, cultural preferences, etc.).

As Bourdieu stated in an interview: 'Imagine a kind of axes of coordinates – the vertical axes contains "up" and "down", the horizontal

---

[11] It shall at least be suggested that the consideration of the students' perspectives is also to be regarded a democratic act. Asking or not asking particular academic questions always includes, even if done so unconsciously, a political implication. To read the students' reports with equal attention as, to stay in the legal field, a sentence of the Federal Constitutional Court is associated with symbolic recognition, which requires the critical examination of possible discipline-internal biases.

[12] Pierre Bourdieu, *Der Staatsadel* (UVK 2004); Pierre Bourdieu and Jean Claude Passeron, *Die Illusion der Chancengleichheit: Untersuchungen zur Soziologie des Bildungswesens am Beispiel Frankreichs* (Klett-Cotta 1971); Pierre Bourdieu, *Entwurf einer Theorie der Praxis auf der ethnologischen Grundlage der kabylischen Gesellschaft* (Suhrkamp 1979); Pierre Bourdieu, *Die feinen Unterschiede: Kritik der gesellschaftlichen Urteilskraft* (Suhrkamp 1982); Pierre Bourdieu, *Die verborgenen Mechanismen der Macht* (VSA 1992); Pierre Bourdieu, *Sozialer Sinn: Kritik der theoretischen Vernunft* (Suhrkamp 1987); Pierre Bourdieu et al, *Das Elend der Welt: Zeugnisse und Diagnosen alltäglichen Leidens an der Gesellschaft* (UVK 1997). Legal education in terms of elite recruitment has only been discussed occasionally. For example, Ralf Dahrendorf, *Gesellschaft und Demokratie in Deutschland* (Piper 1965); Michael Hartmann, *Der Mythos von den Leistungseliten: Spitzenkarrieren und soziale Herkunft in Wirtschaft, Politik, Justiz und Wissenschaft* (Campus 2002); Michael Hartmann, *Elitesoziologie* (2nd edn, Campus 2008). A proper overview of the current elite research is offered by Heinz-Hermann Krüger et al, 'Mechanismus der Elitebildung im deutschen Bildungssystem – Ausgangslage, Theoriediskurse, Forschungsstand' [2012] *ZfE* 327. The more traditional elite education in law faculties is not mentioned here.

one contains an intellectual and an economical pole'.[13] The mechanism of social (re-)production can be illustrated by the following succinct formula:[14]

> Via socialization, the *structure* (the individuals' positions within the "space of life situations"/"social space") characterizes particular dispositions, perception, interpretation and action patterns, the *habitus* as an incorporated social structure; the habitus on the other hand creates – mostly unconsciously – specific social structured practice patterns, actions and lifestyles; the *practice* (re)generates the objective structures.

The different modes of the habitus must always be regarded in relation to the different social areas, which organize the space into relatively definable social partial areas and produce genuine social logics and practices. According to Bourdieu, university socialization can be perceived as a dynamic habitualizing process. These habitualizing processes are at one time produced and reproduced by the subject cultures and their different practices. In order to illuminate the socialization and disciplining mechanisms, which may enable students to self-activate and react, Michel Foucault's power-analytical studies will be consulted here,[15] as they discuss behaviour regulation and regimen within modern society. According to Foucault, the regulation of individuals and collectives is realized by a governmental functional model of invisible power, which differs essentially from the political government. *Gouvernmentality* means: 'the leadership of people in the sense of them being guided, controlled and led. This contains the governance of oneself as well as of others'.[16] In this way, law studies can be decoded as a productive disciplinary power which intends particular normalization effects.[17]

---

[13] Hans Dieter Zimmermann, 'Pierre Bourdieu im Gespräch', reprinted in Franzjörg Baumgart (eds), *Theorien der Sozialisation* (3rd edn, Klinkhardt 2004) 206, 210 (author's translation).

[14] Hildegard Schaeper, *Lehrkulturen, Lehrhabitus und die Struktur der Universität: eine empirische Untersuchung fach- und geschlechtsspezifischer Lehrkulturen* (Deutscher Studien Verlag 1997) 36f (author's translation).

[15] Michel Foucault, *Überwachen und Strafen: Die Geburt des Gefängnisses* (Suhrkamp 1976).

[16] Susanne Weber and Susanne Maria Maurer, 'Die Kunst, nicht dermaßen regiert zu werden. Gouvernementalität als Perspektive für die Erziehungswissenschaft' in Susanne Weber and Susanne Maria Maurer (eds), *Gouvernementalität und Erziehungswissenschaft: Wissen – Macht – Transformation* (VS 2006) 9–10 (author's translation).

[17] Cf. Sonja Buckel, 'Die Mechanik der Macht in der juristischen Ausbildung' [2002] *KJ* 111.

In essence, this contribution analyses legal education from a point of educational sociology to illustrate what's happening inside German legal education. In this sense academic learning is modulated as a socializing process embedded in a specific learning setting. This approach allows connecting factors in the learning environment with subjective learning experiences.

2 CRAMMING, CRAMMING, CRAMMING – EXAMINATION TECHNOLOGY AND ITS EFFECTS

The interview scripts presented in the interview section are various and rich. The biographic texts tell of daily learning and examination situations when studying law – of hope, frustration and success. They open the door to the examinees' microcosm and enable a first, cautious probing of the structures and social mechanics represented in these narratives. These publicized narratives form the empirical reference point of this contribution, since they allow the analysis of the habitus forming law-specific structures as if under a microscope. This research-economical procedure may be criticized from a methodical perspective. Nevertheless, this may be countered by – the more so, as this one-person-research-establishment cannot collect new material – an alternative that does not promise really new insights as it normally takes normative positions into account or systematizes previous evidence coming from university research, law and profession sociology in order to study them anew from a law-specific socialization's point of view. Law's education praxis would remain a widely white spot in the research map. Since in this contribution, the experience narratives will not only be recited but also interpreted and related to institutional backgrounds, the analysis level by Bickel et al. will be developed further and the focus will be modified. This procedure corresponds to the research program of Bourdieu who looks for a synthesis out of action and structure-theoretical dimensions. As a result, underlying structures of meaning and effects that are hidden behind the smoke screen of formal and neutral regulations of legal education become visible. In order to sketch some structuring moments of law studies generically, excerpts from various interviews will be presented below, followed by interpretation proposals along the lines of Bourdieu and Foucault.[18]

[18] The orthography and interpunction in the interview passages has been smoothed somewhat. To aid in concise appreciation textual interview omissions

Organized Psychological Pressure

> M: […] I gave myself so much a fright, I hadn't known myself this way. I was foreign to myself. I panicked, I shouldn't go to university, "Have you learnt this yet, have you learnt that yet, did you read this?" I was completely uneasy and powerless. I didn't have any clear thoughts anymore. I was like in fog. […] And out of this fog I didn't come but now on vacation. When I read the letter which contained the first three grades for the essay and the written task, I was aware that I performed really poorly in the exams and that the essay will be, well, so-so, perhaps even poorly, too, that I probably failed. Well! The result came, I saw the essay: Nice – deep breath – cried. Then came the difference to the exams. I was in panic. I was so very afraid, because I knew exactly that the examiners had already formed a certain view on me without having known me before. […]
>
> L: You get overly crazy. I received my grades and everything was bad, accompanied by the feeling that you have to take this oral exam. And they know your grades and think you don't know anything at all; and then you've got the feeling that you take this exam and prove on top that you don't know anything at all. From the first, I had the feeling they think I'm dumb, I also think I'm dumb and that's it. After all this time, you get so wasted, that you're not able to uplift yourself.
>
> M: It was a really testing point in life, of which you can say […] here your personality will either be cut down or developed further.
>
> *(Interviews with L and M*[19]*)*

L and M report in this interview passage their massive psychological pressure that was established during the examination phase, starting whilst preparing for the examinations and remaining up to graduation. There is talk of a 'fog' which did not disappear until on vacation and thereby enabled the student to recall her/his own person, of a powerlessness and a kind of spiritual 'testing point in life', because 'after all this time, you get so wasted, that you're not able to uplift' yourself.

In order to not be put under additional pressure by fellow students, L in the end avoided going to university. The university is a public place, at which you have to present yourself and to produce, but not a place to

are indicated by […]. Direct quotes from the interviews, which are recited in the interpretation, are marked by '/'. The abbreviation 'I' indicates the interviewer. He takes two roles in the discourse: on the one hand the role of an examinee and on the other hand the one of an examiner. Due to his field knowledge, he shares the various experiences of the narrators and provides, due to his context knowledge so-called expertise.

[19] Bickel et al, *op cit* 55ff.

articulate and talk about fears and uncertainties. It is a place at which you deal with higher principles such as law and, like a court, it is not an environment wherein to exchange views on personal states. The topics the students usually talk about – at least during current examination phases – seem to be determined by study contents. In this way, the examinees are being maneuovered into solitude and a state of 'must-rely-on-myself', which individualizes conflict situations and increases their stress caused by a possibly deficient social integration. Self-estrangement caused due to uncertainties may be understood as a psychological strategy to irritate identities and subsequently reshape them. The language used by the interviewees' points out how powerful and effective these processes are. The phrasings 'panic', 'fear', 'crazy' represent an existential quality.

Since the commission at the oral exam mostly consists of practitioners the students do not know, and due to the high number of students, the professorate usually does not know every individual student, the examination is linked not only to special challenges regarding 'impression management'. The examiners form a particular view on the candidates, based on their grades. The students are indeed aware of this circumstance, which even intensifies the examination situation and the self-doubts, and fears that are evoked by the organization of the examination: 'And they know your grades and think you don't know anything at all; and then you've got the feeling that you take this exam and prove on top that you don't know anything at all. From the first, I had the feeling they think I'm dumb, I also think I'm dumb and that's it.' As a result of the power asymmetry between examiners and examinees, the students' anticipated estimations get reflexively elevated, perceived as not to be controlled – and eventually internalized. As the examinees' grades are provided to the examination commission beforehand, their estimation of being able to personally influence the examination outcome turns out to be rather low. This is important for the examinees' perception of self-efficacy, which could substantially become damaged. The assessment of third parties poses a crucial feature to the nature of examinations. Performance is being determined by an unreflective evaluation mechanism. What counts is not to be personally content with the result or the intrinsic motivation to deal with the subject matter; it is rather the external assessment by the examining body, which essentially decides the realization of individual future plans.

Anonymized Examination Apparatus

L: […] As a law student you don't associate anything positive with the judicial examination office, you just need to go there in case of examinations or inconvenient occasions. Written exams, oral exams […] not a beautiful building, too. You only hear of people who took the examination, went into the judicial examination office – and the written exams. And that was horrible. You already have this idea of the judicial examination office.

M: Awful [… .] The government tests you […], not the teacher anymore. Not the professor but the government. You are in awe of it. […] It puts even more pressure on you. It doesn't come from my home. I chose this way on my own. And everything worked fine. But then came this invitation, to the written exams, […] that's the room and it was foreseeable, but suddenly everything was horrible und it said "Please bring your ID card". This mode, this form, that was suddenly so very alien to me. I even forgot my legal text, because I was addled. I wasn't anymore, I couldn't remember which way I came, I didn't dare drive the car during the whole examination phase. Because I thought, […] either you might damage the car or you hurt yourself or both. I was apathetic, I've never known myself this way. While I wrote the essay, this state relaxed a bit. It was this "The government will test you and your whole life is liable to it, it will be the same in the future and suddenly he wants to know something from you" and this will not be only one person but a sphere of control which I can't grasp and which I can't visualize. And I don't know who's behind it. This provoked fear which I've never known before, never! […]

L: There are people who stay the course easily […]

M: Yes, yes.

L: […] So, what's the problem? The problem lies in […]

M: In you, of course […]

L: Exactly, you can't say that the trappings wears everyone out, it's somehow also on you. But where exactly this problem lies, I still don't know. You get overly crazy or it drives you crazy. You put yourself under pressure, I just don't know.

I: Such a situation, such a system attacks the weak points that are presented by the individuals. The starting points are different but the construction of the examination procedure causes each individual weakness. Many report similar things, on situations in which they couldn't demonstrate what they know.

L: But isn't this similar in other disciplines, that some cope better with examinations than others?

I: I think that there are a lot of specific elements, as this construction with the judicial examination office, duration, formality, it differs from diploma programs, for example. Due to the missing control on the part of the examinees that they don't get the expert report, that they struggle to look at the records and that the grades are being withheld for quite a long time, that are all aspects which are different in other subjects. If you write a diploma thesis, you receive supervision.

L: So why isn't it this way with us?

I: Well, [… laughs]

M: Uptight, that's what I'm saying. The government is conservative and that's the way everything revolving around is constructed! Law is conservative. I already sensed this when I started my studies. That it will await me, the examination, but in this mode! In such a stiff way that it doesn't seem to be human at all.

I: One of my hypotheses has something to do with the key word civil servant. If you need servants you need to teach them how to serve. To do so, a procedure is well-suited that upsets the individual. You just described it, this creation of dependence, so that you eventually control whether you're properly dressed.

M: If you observe the proprieties.

(Interviews with L and M[20]*)*

This extract from the interview points out how the situation regarding the state examination is arranged symbolically and spatially. The judicial examination offices, which are not entirely coincidentally located off-campus but at High Court and in the Justice Ministries, are part of the system they represent and which the students want to join after they have finished their legal education. Function, symbolism and aesthetics intertwine efficiently. 'As a law student you don't associate anything positive with judicial examination office, you just need to go there in case of examinations or inconvenient occasions.' It remains unexplained what exactly is meant by 'inconvenient occasions'. L possibly refers to the examination enrollment or the subsequent post-exam review. Certainly, the occasions are negatively connoted.

Final examinations are no longer being conducted at the examinee's home university and in familiar rooms but in a foreign place with an unfamiliar journey. Compared to exams set alongside the studies, this performance situation is topographically modified. The examinees must spend more energy and individual initiative, in order to 'be allowed' to get examined. Considering the pressure caused by the upcoming examination, M did not feel able to drive a car during the examination phase and

---

20 Ibid 57–62.

does not even remember to having walked the way to the judicial examination office, and, on top, forgot her legal text.

The examinations take place in a rather unattractive building which has a specific atmosphere, a sensible quality that evokes anxiety and discomfort. The access to this secured building, characterized by passing security doors and the doorman's box which is occupied by persons in uniform, tells the entry to a higher, powerful area that is separated from other societal divisions. This access is prepared by a formal invitation to the examination, with the note to bring the ID card for identification reasons. The examinee's individuality gets hereby reduced to an identity number which is – according to bureaucratic logic – a warrant to equal treatment. The mode the classification system 'incorporates' in the student's bodies and garb, is patently identified by the carefully chosen and obviously very important wardrobe the examinees wear at the examination.

This technology of smartly-composed symbolic and structural-spatial examination framework conditions evokes both surprise and fear. Behind it hides the anonymized examination apparatus, which is – due to its apersonality – hardly vulnerable. Particularly interesting is that M names this mechanism and thereby unmasks it. This knowledge does not seem to have acted as relieving or unburdening, as it nevertheless took hold of her at full tilt. It is possible that M evolved this insight not until after the examinations or during the interview situation. However, we do not know this for sure.

There are stories and myths of examinations going around that build the scenario of final exams already during studies and are thereby fixed in the examinees' minds. Although the students are prepared for the imminent event and they also have the opportunity to deal with it beforehand, they get caught by the machinery's engine, and subsequently join the line of ancestors of those who exposed themselves to and survived the examination procedure. The 'beforehand', which is used to design the examination as a frightening abstraction, turns into the 'afterwards', which labels the metamorphosis. The intensity and sharpness of the precise experience seems to even surmount the imagined frightening situation, as L reports: 'I already sensed this when I started my studies. That it will await me, the examination, but in this mode! In such a stiff way that it doesn't seem to be human at all'.

It is striking that both M and L do not know where to refer the enormous examination pressure to. Both struggle for explanation patterns and for concretization. M determines that, in her case, the pressure is not put on her by her parents, since she 'chose this way on [her, AB] own'. Although M realizes that the problem must lie in the examination situation and examination mode, 'the government tests you', this knowledge does not seem to be really understood and is thereby able to explain the experienced 'sharpness'. The thicket revolving legal examination seems to be too complex and confusing. By contrast, in L's opinion, the experienced pressure caused by the examination interacts with individual dispositions, that there are persons 'who stay the course easily'. Eventually, M and L agree that the problem 'of course' lies in themselves. This self-conception refers to a deficient-inferior construction of identity, in which the power structures are reflected.

Learning as Practicing against Non-transparency

> L: […] You don't learn for yourself, in terms of that it means something to you, but pigheadedly, because you have to and "Hopefully, this is enough, hopefully someone will ask me this". Suddenly, you learn for others. It wasn't this way at the beginning of my studies. Then, you are interested in topics and you look for those topics that you're interested in. Later you must cover a huge array of topics and you just learn towards day X.
>
> (*Interviews with L and M*[21])

This 'huge array of topics' L mentions aims at the state examination's ample examination topics.[22] These comprehensive study matters form the setting for the permanent and formal practicing which does not satisfy any personal interests, but trains routine, regularity, endurance and self-discipline instead.[23] The enormous scope of examination matters results from the formal educational objective to qualify for judgeship. In order to qualify the students for authority through law, legislation first needs to advance into the students. Thereby, students and legislation fuse and correspond: 'Legislation holds me and I also hold legislation'.[24]

The non-transparency of the examinations, which accompanies the examination scope, leads to a strong burden for the students which can be identified as efficient education strategies and selection strategies. Non-transparency not least favours the examinees who are habitually able to

---

21 Ibid 62.

22 For example, the catalogue in § 11 JAG NRW.

23 Cf. French elite schools: Pierre Bourdieu (2004), *op cit* 137.

24 'Pascal expressed it this way: *Le monde me comprend, mais je le comprends* – like: The world holds me and I also hold it. So to speak, the social reality exists twice, within the objects and within the minds, in the fields and in the habitus, inside and outside the agents' (Pierre Bourdieu and Loïc J D Wacquant, *Reflexive Anthropologie* (Suhrkamp 1996) (author's translation).)

cope more confidently with diffuse requirements. This is getting especially virulent when you consider the social background of law students. After the eleventh survey on students at universities and universities of applied sciences the amount of educational climbers regarding law, rose significantly, i.e. the number of students with an academic background decreased.[25]

The collective belief in the efficiency of the pedagogical method not to limit the study matters, or better: the fear of educating 'narrow-gauge lawyers' otherwise, as well as the established praxis of distributing positions and resources based on the investments, provides the reputation and plausibility of this kind of principles of teaching. Referring to this, Bourdieu explains:[26]

> The graduates […] play an essential part in this mechanism of circular reinforcement of belief. Because they have to justify the means and aims of a pedagogical action their excellence is bound to (according to the following argumentation pattern: We are excellent, because the education, whose product we are, is excellent, and besides, the education form we result from is excellent, because we are excellent).

'Eliticization'

> L: But what's different to other study subjects is, that when you're new to university, there's an implicitness "Come along, I show you this and that, that's over there" and then you're going to talk a bit "Did you just start?" With us it's: "There they come along, the stupid beginners".
>
> M: Yes, […] sitting on one's high horse […].
>
> L: At least, those who advanced a bit more in their studies, they think they were oh so great.
>
> M: It was the same for me at the beginning. I didn't know where green, blue and yellow were. Nobody wanted to explain it to me, because they looked down at you. Lawyers try to contrast from others. For whatever reasons.
>
> I: An exciting question.
>
> L: Yes, this is what is being taught. I remember vividly, when I started my studies, a professor of some sort told us in a lecture, law was the royal

---

25 Michael Ramm, Frank Multrus and Tino Bargel, *Studiensituation und studentische Orientierungen: 11. Studierendensurvey an Universitäten und Fachhochschulen* (BMBF 2011) 12. However, the percentage of 'subject descent' caused by the parental home in law is, comparable to medicine, particularly distinct (ibid 27).

26 Bourdieu (2004), *op cit* 138 (author's translation).

science. And if you finish the studies, you belong to the *crème de la crème*. And I thought by myself, oh, well, he seems to have a screw loose.

(*Interviews (5) with L and M*[27])

L and M mention in this interview passage their experience of the social climate within legal studies. They report on an insufficient helpfulness and cooperativeness and an invisible barrier between those who are already acclimatized and who already arrived and those who are new, who are smiled at: 'Lawyers try to contrast from others'. This urge for distinction is connected to the traditional elite educational mission, which is communicated straightforwardly to the students and is meant to incentivize proper performance: Those who invest and get educated in the 'royal discipline' called law will be awarded extraordinarily and rewarded with a privileged perspective in life.

Before the newcomer will be integrated and allowed to join the game, he must conform to this milieu. The fellow students' smile at the beginners can be deciphered as a subtle strategy to evoke uncertainty, and convey the idea that only those are regarded as adequate for the system are able to adapt to it.[28] This also illustrates differences in status as the appreciation seems to be distributed unequally depending on the semesters that are already completed. This mechanism leads to an acceptance and internalization of these group norms: 'The desire to be loved [...] is a powerful stimulus for conformity'.[29]

As can be seen from L's reaction, socialization and the processes of discipline are not realized in a mechanic and linear mode. Socializing persons deals with their environment, they do not let them get reduced to educational dolls who shall incorporate the subject's habitus. L seems to be rather skeptical towards and also seems to distance from these processes, when he states, 'this is what is being taught'. He distances from the completely integrated persons who, caused by the intended membership, define themselves as 'best of the best' and thereby create their normative and social orientation. Here, it becomes apparent that socialization always takes place within an area of tension between the conflicting priorities of individualization and enculturation.

---

27 Bickel et al, *op cit* 63ff.

28 Cf. Horst Bosetzky and Peter Heinrich, *Mensch und Organisation* (Kohlhammer 1980) 112.

29 Robert Vance Presthus, *Individuum und Organisation: Typologie der Anpassung* (S Fischer 1966) 169.

'Grade nobility'

> F: […] I know it this way, too, that actually the grade is the decisive motive to learn anything for the examination. In our team, this really escalated and turned into an envious atmosphere. Lots of my friends went to oral examinations, too, and witnessed the examinations of the other team members and afterwards, there was almost only evil talk. It was very remarkable that everything was focused on the grade. The whole person […]
>
> G: […] focuses on grade, that's unbelievable. […] Due to the fact that you permanently have to job alongside studying, the concentration on the studies is possibly not as high as it should be, but to be able to rely on yourself is really important, to know that there are other things you're good at. This leads to the growth of the ability to prove yourself in other fields in any form. […]
>
> (*Interviews (8) with F and G*[30])

The grade achieved in the examination sets the course for the professional future in the legal branch. Graduation with honours is comparable to an accolade which allows the examinees to become civil servants. The legal education, which is still tailormade for judgeship, selects in respect of grade, along with the consequence that there is a line drawn between those who achieved the grade and those who cannot adorn themselves with it. If grades provide access to privileges or prevent it permanently, it can be called 'grade nobility'. It is the grades that lead the examinees after passing the examination and the second state examination to the individual subprofessions. As Buckel states:[31]

> It would be most obvious that it is not acceptable that more than 80% of all law students only obtain average or mostly below-average performances, however, but actually it is far from it. Instead, it feels like this particular subject is outstandingly demanding and the crowd is not able to cope with it.

Grades allow for ranking, a hierarchical arrangement of examinees. By abstracting, scaling and ciphering performances, they become a 'code of disciplinary individuality'.[32] They specify the expectation towards the examinees as very handy: it is all about achieving graduation with honours. The technical involvement does not take place alongside one's interests but is stimulated by the desire for a certain grade which is prescribed by the environment and thus extrinsically stimulates learning.

---

[30] Bickel et al, *op cit* 116.
[31] Buckel, *op cit* 112 (author's translation).
[32] Foucault (1976), *op cit* 244.

This explains why 'the whole person focuses on grade', as F and G describe. In terms of legal education, grades become an identity-establishing substrate which strengthens the students' backbones after the gruelling examination procedure. G realizes the dangerous effects caused by this 'focus on grades' as she states that a job alongside one's studies allows one 'to know that there are other things you're good at'. The studies are possibly construed as something that you are not 'good at'. It faces other areas of life in which 'proving oneself' is not equally important but stabilizes the personality and affects it positively. Thereby, G somehow crosses the mechanism Bourdieu paraphrases as symbolic embedment[33] because of the pressure caused by the examination and the significance of the examination grade, the examinees hide themselves away in order to be able to fully concentrate on their studies. In this shielded cosmos, stimulations and opportunities to experience something else get artificially reduced and life-worldly connections get rearranged. The examinees arrange themselves for a mental test which factually and practically prescribes impacts. Of particular interest, are the aspects that are connected to the examinations. Old things, different things, unknown things become – as they are not relevant to the examinations – uninteresting and thereby obscure.

Collegiate Social Controlling Network

> N: Me and my friends pursued different learning goals, that's why they couldn't hear what I was doing, because they might have got a bad conscience. "Oh my god, N is doing this now, do we have to do this, too?" That's how it happened to me. As soon as I learned that M and O dealt with property law, I panicked and dealt with property law, too. That means, we weren't able to communicate in a normal way, because we thought the other one may outface the other one! We weren't even able to look at each other's desks, because we were afraid to spot something we knew we all had to deal with.
>
> (*Interview (9) with N*[34])

The volume of material and the competition for good grades evokes, as can be learnt from N's narrative, a social atmosphere that is characterized by distance and mistrust. That means, the circumstances create a community that is always threatened by the danger to burst out on the examination's framework conditions. The study situation turns out to be a

33 Bourdieu (2004), *op cit* 110.

34 Bickel et al, *op cit* 127.

competition on knowledge resources and the respective stakes to the game: for excellent grades.

Caused by the circumstance that the examinees hardly have the opportunity to set personal key subjects and to individualize the examination procedure, they *nolens volens* control each other. Within this mechanism they push each other; the learning catalogue of the one becomes a painful pointer to the other's lack of preparation, and causes a *quasi*-ubiquitous monitoring. The constant comparison to the others' state of knowledge, which was already induced by a hasty look at each other's desks, has a normalizing and discipline-internalizing effect. Reversely, this automatism results in students whose individual value has been withdrawn. Now, this becomes, fulfilled by the companions of fate themselves, a value which is prescribed by the institution. Bourdieu explains it as follows:[35]

> This kind of scholastic struggle for survival turns everyone into the enemy of everyone else and determines and constrains exorbitant investments, regarding the contents of teaching as well as learning methods, at the examinations, with the teachers and the competitors, briefly, a total agreement to the game and all its values which, as they are the products of the game, obviously establish and justify its value.

Organized Uncertainty

> P: After the complete academic studies and praxis: no strategic judgment, whether you made it or not. That's insane. You won't find this in any other subject.
>
> O: Also the grades which sometimes are extremely poor, I don't want to deny this, we all are, we: the graduates perform poorly. […]
>
> P: I thought I was in the services. […] Self-disciplining times ten and I got really lessoned. In the first five civil law exams I achieved zero points. Yes, 'author doesn't get anything' [laughing] was written below gruesomely. And then, slowly, it improved.
>
> (*Interviews (13) with O and P*[36])

Law studies' teaching and learning settings coordinate and administer the students' self-image and self-confidence. It seems to force this uncertainty with the aid of organizational amplifiers, in order to socialize and discipline the students efficiently. The constant attempt while studying to assess one's own performance ability, 'whether you made it or not',

35 Bourdieu (2004), *op cit* 136 (author's translation).
36 Bickel et al, 189ff.

evolves to an exhausting ride on the rollercoaster and may eventually even condense into a negative (performance-related) self-image, that 'we: the graduates' just 'perform poorly'.

The socializing persons react to this uncertainty and self-image difficulty strategically with activation and mobilization. The rejection conveying culture of performance feedback keeps the students inline and pushes them to be fully devoted to their studies. The 'self-disciplining times ten' and the regulations from without, as P mentions, led to the fact that the students are very willing to make an effort. This results from the desire to be acknowledged by the system, which claims a radical agreement in this approval authority.[37] Up to the completion of all examinations the institutionalized distance between examination system and examinee is significantly marked. The anonymous examination procedure reinforces and perpetuates this gap. The severity (which resembles the social behaviours in the military) seems to be an element of a particular pedagogical concept. This aims at evoking a humble attitude and acquiescence, which are fed on the idea and gratitude that the examinees are admitted to and accepted by the system, even though they were – in most different constellations during their education – faced with their human and personal weaknesses and imperfectness again and again.

3 RÉSUMÉ

The structural marginalization of the students' personal needs indicates that the social function of legal examination is to encourage enculturation and disciplining as well as to inhibit the individualization processes. At the close of the examinations, a new social identity awaits the examinees; one which gets one prepared to be part of the '*crème de la crème*' as a specific collective that walked the way of the cross up to graduation, at the same time together and on its own. From this point of view, similarities to monastic Jesuit education aiming at the birth of the ascetic monk flare-up. Bourdieu speaks of a 'threnodical ritual, directed to kill

---

[37] The fact that P meanwhile is able to laugh about his failure at the first civil law exams indicates that the *habitus* has already been modified. The subject-related conventions and standards do not appear disconcerting or violating anymore. The first exams accompanied by harsh comments cannot any longer be regarded as critical experiences which initiated transformation processes. As the grades slowly improved a gradual familiarization and the adjustment to performance requirements becomes visible.

old people which in this case means young people, along with his passions, desires, in a word, his nature'.[38]

The formal exam regulations deeply intrude upon the students' daily life and control it. This effect intensifies the subject socialization. Because 'transitions need to be [...] *provided*; they wouldn't arise out of pure irritations. Something must change, something that is ponderous enough to make every single person capable of acting in any unfamiliar contexts'.[39] It can be presumed that due to the permanent imagined meanings that are attributed to examinations, law studies turn into a specific students' praxis, whose tough expectations are gladly addressed to the students: capability optimization and strategic self-regulation to carry oneself to extremes, and at the same time to ensure traction: in order not to fall. The self and other disciplining legal examination processes are characterized by a merging into a superior identity policy which prescribes ideationally how a legal being has to be like, and which offers the students an identity draft.

However, the education structures commemorate an intensive boot camp and leave little to the handling with important psychological development tasks in the post-adolescent phase whilst studying, e.g. cutting the cord from the parental home, autonomy and individuality identity developments, or the development of long-term relationships, which seem to get forced back by the subject-related development, that has priority. These status inconsistencies characteristic for this phase of study even increase the uncertainties which are evoked by the education system. Against this background, the legal socialization programme can be understood as an intended 'selective destruction of "successful socialization"'[40], as it is characteristic for total institutions (e.g. the military, monasteries, prisons, etc). Regarding the stimulated inner self-work, these interferences are not only destructive but highly productive. However, it must be considered that a successful development of an extra-subject-specific identity is the condition to be able to successfully stand

---

[38] Bourdieu (2004), *op cit* 136 (author's translation).

[39] Jürgen Wittpoth, *Rahmungen und Spielräume des Selbst: ein Beitrag zur Theorie der Erwachsenensozialisation im Anschluss an George H. Mead und Pierre Bourdieu* (Diesterweg 1994) 113 (author's translation).

[40] Maja Apelt, 'Sozialisation in "totalen Institutionen"' in KJ Tillmann, M Grundmannand S Walper (eds), *Handbuch Sozialisationsforschung* (7th edn, Beltz 2008) 372.

intensive university-related examination phases, and to develop professional subject-specific identities: 'Lawyers believe', as can be summarized according to Sonja Buckel:[41]

> To be the exact opposite to the inmates they deal with. Whereas in Foucault's terms, prison does not – and this will surely provoke your protest – differ too much from universities. It is much more the ideal type of a study subject to examine with an analytical clarity a power technology that is quite characteristic for modern societies.

Legal studies do not only convey expert knowledge but do also take up an unwritten societal educational mission. As the contribution refers to German legal education it is certainly to ask as to which extent this analysis is able to claim generalization and whether it is transferable to other countries. Nonetheless, I mean its critical direction of impact is able to increase a law teacher's awareness of the subtle socializing processes in law schools and the importance of looking at learning law from the student's point of view. Concerning the effects of learning factors this perspective is quite enlightening. Stress, feelings of anxiety and excessive demands influence a student's motivation and self-efficacy in a negative way and can hinder academic maturation.[42]

Beyond that, demands for a student's inner self-work can also be regarded in a context of actual developments in higher education. In the last 15 years there has been a shift from teaching to learning, which was in Europe mainly forced by the Bologna Process and its educational program. Learning and testing environments have changed from testing methods to new forms of assessment.[43] In fact the learning-setting described in this contribution refers rather to bygone and old-fashioned practices. However, the idea of a student's empowerment which became more and more popular in the last decade played traditionally an important role in the German elitist legal education and was a central element of its hidden curriculum. If learning conditions are experienced as diffuse and nontransparent, students are stimulated to develop practices of empowerment to 'survive'. In face of the material to be studied

---

41 Buckel, *op cit* 114.

42 Also Barbara Glesner, 'Fear and Loathing in the Law Schools' [1991] *Connecticut Law Review* 627; Kennon M Sheldon and Lawrence S Krieger, 'Understanding the Negative Effects of Legal Education on Law Students: A Longitudinal Test of Self-Determination Theory' [2007] PSPB 883.

43 Filip Dochy, Mien Segers and Dominique Sluijsmans, 'The Use of Self-, Peer and Co-assessment in Higher Education: A Review' [1999] *Studies in Higher Education* 331.

there is little space left for reflexivity. At present, it seems that contemporary demands for a student's empowerment make a fatal deal with the radical neoliberal changes in higher education: students are addressed as self-regulated and self-controlled subjects who have to improve and control their learning performance. They become objects of their learning processes in the new testing era again.

In this case they have to improve their self-management qualities to fulfill formal academic requirements. For Australia, New Zealand, the UK and Canada Margaret Thornton has observed that the ideology of the market has changed law schools, their academics and students.[44] These reforms lead an economy of knowledge whose idea seems to contradict reflexivity as a constituent of academic thinking once more. Reflexive thinking permits discussions on the interdisciplinary: namely, the political, the ethical or the economical topics of law and accompanying it the development of a professional role characterized by critical distance to legal positivism and legal practice. Given this situation academic practices are faced with new challenges and have to remember their founding mandate: the education of responsible and critical members of society.

44 Margaret Thornton, *Privatising the Public University: The Case of Law* (Routledge 2012).

5. The necessary loneliness of teaching (and of being a legal academic)

Anthony Bradney

1 INTRODUCTION

Legal academics will usually find themselves involved in research and administration as well as teaching. For reasons of space the focus of this essay is on teaching. This essay will also draw mainly on examples taken from the United Kingdom and usually from the jurisdiction of England and Wales. Drawing comparisons between the situations in university law schools in different jurisdictions is possible but it is also difficult and would demand more space than is available here.[1] Nevertheless in other jurisdictions, the arguments put forward here will have a resonance, albeit with variations in detail and emphasis.

Academics in university law schools work not just as individuals but as members of institutions. Their research will commonly be pursued on a purely individual basis; this latter point being true not just for legal academics but for most academics who are not in laboratory sciences.[2] When involved in administration academics will work with others. When teaching they frequently work as members of teams. These teams can now include both other academics and also non-academics.[3] At the same

[1] Stolker correctly observes that some people will think his 454-page comparative analysis of university law schools too short for its purpose (C Stolker, *Rethinking the Law School: Education, Research, Outreach and Governance* (CUP 2014) 12. See further A Bradney, 'Can There Be Commensurability in Comparative Legal Education?' [2007] 1 *Canadian Legal Education Annual Review* 67.

[2] R Deem, 'The Knowledge Worker, the Manager-Academic and the Contemporary UK University: New and Old Forms of Public Management?' [2004] 20 *Financial Accountability & Management* 107, 111.

[3] T Evans and D Nation, 'Introduction' in T Evans and D Nation (eds), *Changing University Teaching: Reflections on Creating Educational Technologies* (Routledge 2005) 3.

time academic work is regulated in many ways. Assessments of their work are often made both by their institutions and by external bodies.[4] This means they are, in these ways, not independent. Yet, at the same time, academics are said to possess academic freedom. In some jurisdictions this academic freedom receives legal recognition.[5] Academic freedom reflects the fact that, amongst other things, academics are professionals and that autonomy is one of the hallmarks of professional work.[6]

These two things, membership of a regulated institution where individuals sometimes work in teams and the pursuit of professional work involving autonomy and academic freedom, seem, prima facie, to contradict each other. In this essay I will look at this contradiction and suggest how, in relation to an academic's work as a teacher, it should be resolved.

2 PROFESSIONALISM

Perkins has argued that '[u]niversity teaching is the key profession of the twentieth century'.[7] Perkins' argument rests on the proposition that other professions begin their process of education within universities.[8] The example of law schools within the United Kingdom illustrates Perkins'

---

[4] In England the quality of teaching was first assessed by an external body, the Higher Education Funding Council for England, in 1993. On the external assessment of teaching in English university law schools see A Bradney, *Conversations, Chances and Choices: The Liberal Law School in the Twenty-First Century* (Hart Publishing 2003) 176–182. On the external assessment of teaching in British universities generally see M Shattock, *Making Policy in British Higher Education 1945–2011* (Open University Press 2012) 199–204.

[5] Thus, for example, in the UK the Education Reform Act 1988, which applies to England and Northern Ireland, says that 'academic staff have freedom within the law to question and test received wisdom, and to put forward new ideas and controversial or unpopular opinions, without placing themselves in jeopardy of losing their jobs or privileges they may have at their institutions' (s 202(2)(a)). On this provision see E Barendt, *Academic Freedom and the Law: A Comparative Study* (Hart Publishing 2010) 92–95. See also C Russell, *Academic Freedom* (Routledge 1993) 19–20.

[6] E Freidson, *Professionalism: The Third Logic* (Polity Press 2001) 221. See further below.

[7] H Perkins, *Key Profession: The History of the Association of University Teachers* (August M Kelley 1969) 1.

[8] Perkins, *op cit* 1. Friedson, however, sees academics as the 'ideal model' of professionalism simply because of the nature of their job; E Friedson, *Professionalism Reborn: Theory, Prophecy and Policy* (Polity Press 1991) 177.

point. Attaining a law degree in any of the jurisdictions within the United Kingdom does not give a person the right to practice law in the various legal professions that there are. Indeed it is not even necessary to obtain a law degree before taking any of the professional qualifying examinations that do give this right to practice. However, as for example the Law Society of England and Wales notes on a regular basis, the majority of those going on to qualify to practice do in fact begin by taking a law degree.[9] Academics teaching on undergraduate law degrees in the United Kingdom do not generally see themselves as preparing students for the practice of law, instead seeing the degree as a liberal education.[10] Nevertheless, in the United Kingdom, university law schools are the usual starting place for acculturation into the legal professions.[11] If academics are themselves professionals who begin a process of professionalization for so many of their students this puts a particular stress, for these academics, on what it means to be a professional.

The primary question about the nature of professionalism for the purposes of this essay is what is it that makes professional life different from life in other occupations?[12] Whilst answers to this question vary widely in their detail, one pervasive theme focusses on the relationship that the professional has as an individual with the nature of their work. Friedson writes that: '[t]here is a long tradition of observers who claim

---

[9] See, for example, *Trends in the Solicitors' Profession: Annual Statistical Report 2011* (2012) The Law Society, London 123. The second biggest group of those going on to practice as solicitors are people who have first obtained a degree in some subject other than law (*Trends in the Solicitors' Profession: Annual Statistical Report 2011*, *op cit*). The number going in to practice as solicitors who are not graduates is now negligible.

[10] F Cownie, *Legal Academics: Culture and Identities* (Hart Publishing 2004) 67. Cownie's study is of academics in English universities. However, given the widespread movement of academics between law schools in the different jurisdictions within the United Kingdom it is unlikely that there would be any significant difference in opinion elsewhere. On the concept of a liberal education in a law school see Bradney (2003), *op cit*.

[11] F Cownie, A Bradney and M Burton, *English Legal System in Context* (6th edn, OUP 2013) ch 7.

[12] There is also a longstanding argument that professions are simply yet another example of the fact that when '[p]eople of the same trade seldom meet together, even for merriment and diversion, but the conversation ends in a conspiracy against the public, or in some contrivance to raise prices' (A Smith, *The Wealth of Nations* (Dent 1910), Vol. 1, 117); that professions are wholly or largely there to ensure market closure for the benefit of those within them (see, for example, M Friedman, *Capitalism and Freedom* (University of Chicago Press 1982), ch IX).

that professionals place the good of their client, the public, or the development of a discipline over their own economic interest […]'.[13] This comment encompasses two arguments. First, is the idea that the work is, at least in part, altruistic in its nature; second, is the idea that the individual has a personal responsibility for ensuring that this is so. Whether this ideal has ever been reflected in practice is not critical to this essay because it is normative in its intentions. However in the case of the United Kingdom it is possible that the ideal is central to patterns of thinking that first arose in the nineteenth century.[14]

3 ACADEMIC FREEDOM

The special character of academic work is engrained into its history. Western universities in the medieval period garnered a series of privileges from both secular and religious authorities. Some of these privileges, although valuable for the academic communities concerned, were essentially mundane in character. Thus, for example, by 1355 the University of Oxford had the rights to, inter alia, 'control of the market, control of the price and quality of bread and ale and wine and of weights and measures'.[15] Other privileges, however, related to the universities duty to pursue scholarship.[16] These particular privileges took on a heightened importance with the changes in German universities from the eighteenth century onwards. As Paulsen notes, in these universities it became 'the

---

13 Freidson (2001), *op cit* 214.

14 A Bradney, 'How to Live: Aristocratic Values, the Liberal University Law Degree and the Modern Lawyer' [2011] 2 *Web Journal of Current Legal Issues*; see <http://www.bailii.org/uk/other/journals/WebJCLI/2011/issue2/index.html> accessed 7 August 2015. For an argument that the existence of the professional ideal in itself gives an economic reason for appearing to live up to the professional ideal see T Haskell, 'Professionalism *versus* Capitalism: RH Tawney, Emile Durkheim, and CS Pierce on "The Disinterestedness of Professional Communities"' in T Haskell (ed), *The Authority of Experts* (Indiana University Press 1984) 217.

15 W Pantin, *Oxford Life in Oxford Archives* (Clarendon Press 1972) 101. Pantin describes the university at this time as acting 'as a gild of masters, using trade-union tactics […]' (Pantin, *op cit* 69). On the university as a guild see E Krause, *Death of the Guilds: Professions, States, and the Advance of Capitalism, 1930 to the Present* (Yale University Press 1996) 9–14.

16 O Kivinch and P Poikus, 'Privileges of *Universitas Magistrorum et Scolarium* and their justification in charters of foundation from the 13th to the 21st centuries' [2006] 52 *Higher Education* 185, 203–204.

function of the university teacher [...] to search after scientific knowledge by investigation and to teach his hearers to do the same'.[17] Since the pursuit of knowledge by the individual had become central to the function of the university, academic freedom to do this also became central. For the German universities at this time academic freedom referred not just to *Lehrfreiheit*, broadly an academic's freedom to pursue their own teaching and research in the way that they thought appropriate, but also *Lernfreiheit* and *Freiheit der Wissenschaft*, the freedom of students to pursue their studies and the right of academic self-governance.[18] For the purposes of this essay it is *Lehrfreiheit* that is crucial although it is important to note that for the Humboldtian ideal of the university at the time the unity of all three was vital.[19] In the modern era it is *Lehrfreiheit* that is the academic freedom that, for many, is at 'the core of the mission of the university'.[20]

Discussion about academic freedom has tended to focus on the protection that it does or does not give academics to pursue their professional lives. In this sense whilst discourse about academic freedom is about academics but the discourse is directly addressed to those who would impinge on the work of academics, setting out the limitations to what they might legitimately do in this respect. This tendency in the literature is particularly noticeable in those works which attempt to describe and analyse situations where, in the opinion of the author, academic freedom has been denied or ignored.[21]

For the purposes of this essay I would like to focus on a different aspect of academic freedom, the obligations that it creates for academics.[22] Russell observes that 'an academic who listens to pleas of convenience before publishing his research risks calling in doubt the whole of his determination to find truth' and later in the same book suggests that '[t]he moment one suggestive quotation is tailored for fear Professor So-and-so may not like it, the quality of the whole undertaking

---

[17] F Paulsen, *The German Universities and University Study* (Longmans, Green and Co. 1906) 228.

[18] W Metzger, 'Profession and Constitution' [1987] 66 *Texas Law Review* 1265, 1269–1271 and W Metzger, *Academic Freedom in the Age of the University* (Columbia University Press 1955) 109–133.

[19] T Karran, 'Academic Freedom: In Justification of a Universal Ideal' [2009] 34 *Studies in Higher Education* 263, 268.

[20] P Altbach, 'Academic Freedom: International Realities and Challenges' [2001] 41 *Higher Education* 205.

[21] See, for example, A Arblaster, *Academic Freedom* (Penguin Books 1974).

[22] For a more general account of the obligations of academics see D Kennedy, *Academic Duty* (Harvard University Press 1997).

[of research] is called in question'.[23] In a similar fashion Dworkin connects academic freedom with the concept of ethical individualism. For Dworkin this idea rests on the proposition that 'we each have responsibility for making as much of a success of our lives as we can, and that this responsibility is personal, a matter of felt personal conviction, about what a successful life for us would be'.[24] This in turn leads to the notion that we are all responsible for not saying what we believe to be false and 'speaking out' about that which we think is true.[25] For Dworkin some occupations and roles have a heightened form of this general obligation that exists for everyone. 'Professors and others who teach in universities have an even more general and uncompromising responsibility. They have a paradigmatic duty to discover and teach what *they* find important and true [...]'.[26] This position is not unique to Dworkin nor is it necessarily grounded in ethical individualism. Thus, for example, Jones argues that '[a]cademics [...] have obligations to teach and publish what they honestly believe to be true'.[27] The obligations created are absolute. 'If academic research is not devoted to finding the truth, it is a form of propaganda, and not necessarily to be preferred to other forms [of research], much cheaper and perhaps more persuasive'.[28] As with research, so with teaching. Academic freedom, when it is successfully implemented, provides protection for academics. However, for those who believe in academic freedom, it also gives academics obligations and responsibilities which remain the same whether or not it is successfully implemented.

Russell, in his analysis of academic freedom speculates that academics pursuit of knowledge for its own sake in their teaching and their research will lead students to value the same thing, and thus they will be unwilling as graduates to tell their employers things that are not true, even if their employers would wish them to do so.[29] There are clear links between such an argument and both Perkins' notion of the place of the university's role in professionalization, and the concept of the professional ideal discussed above even though Russell does not

---

23 Russell, *op cit* 19 and 28.

24 R Dworkin 'A New Interpretation of Academic Freedom' in L Menard (ed), *The Future of Academic Freedom* (University of Chicago Press 1996) 187.

25 Dworkin, *op cit* 188.

26 Ibid 189 (emphasis added).

27 H Jones, 'Academic Freedom as a Moral Right' in E Pincoffs (ed), *The Concept of Academic Freedom* (University of Texas Press 1972) 48.

28 Russell, *op cit* 19.

29 Russell, *op cit* 27–28.

advert to this. Academic freedom, a heightened form of personal responsibility for Dworkin, can thus also be seen as a heightened form of professionalism.[30]

4 INSTITUTIONS AND GOVERNANCE

There is nothing new in the fact that academics now work in institutions. Universities in a variety of traditions have existed for many centuries.[31] Socrates taught as an independent scholar.[32] This phenomenon largely disappeared long ago.[33] However this is not to say that there have not been important changes since scholars first banded together in institutions.

The massification of higher education has been a widespread trend.[34] In many places including the United Kingdom ever larger student numbers are now being taught in ever bigger institutions. Universities in the thirteenth centuries were institutions as are universities in the twenty-first century but, in many respects, there is little comparison between the natures of these institutions. The ways in which they are now financed and organized are radically different to what they once were. For many the modern university seems to be more a bureaucracy or a

---

[30] Important connections can also be made with a number of other ideas including the aristocratic ideal (on this concept see H Perkins, *The Origins of Modern English Society* (2nd edn Routledge 2002) 237–252); the mandarin tradition (see, for example, F Ringer, *The Decline of the German Mandarins: The German Academic Community, 1890–1933* (Harvard University Press 1969) ch 2); and Sennett's notion of the craftsman (R Sennett, *The Craftsman* (Allen Lane 2008)).

[31] See, for example, H Rashdall, *The Universities of Europe in the Middle Ages* (OUP 1936) and M Nakosteen, *History of Islamic Origins of Western Education AD 800–1350 with an Introduction to Medieval Muslim Education* (University of Colorado Press 1964).

[32] Plato, *The Apology* in H Tredennick (ed), *The Last Days of Socrates* (Penguin Books 1954).

[33] Largely but not entirely. See, for example, L Mumford, 'Telling My Story: the Narrative Problems of Being and Independent Scholar' [1994] 2 *Narrative* 53. More broadly on the phenomenon of the public intellectuals, who may or may not be academics, see R Posner, *Public Intellectuals: A Study of Decline* (Harvard University Press 2003).

[34] See, for example, M Kogan and S Hanney, *Reforming Higher Education* (Jessica Kingsley 2000) 66–68.

corporation than the collegial environment of past times.[35] Along with this have come changes to the relationship that there is between the individual academic and the institution in which they work.

The life depicted in novels about academia such as CP Snow's *The Masters*, set in 1937, or Kingsley Amis' *Lucky Jim*, set in the postwar period in the United Kingdom, would have little resonance for a contemporary British academic.[36] *The Masters* is about the academic politics involved in the Fellows decision as to who will next be in charge of their College whilst *Lucky Jim* is about the first year of a new lecturer in history at an unnamed university college. Unsurprisingly, given that both authors held academic positions in the type of institution that they were writing about, the novels are an accurate portrayal of their times. Both the University of Cambridge college in *The Masters* and the university college in *Lucky Jim* are, by contemporary British standards, very small. In his memoir L Neville Brown notes that there were just four other full-time academics when he joined the Law Faculty at the University of Sheffield in 1953.[37] A little over a decade later in the academic year 1965/66 there were only 5,238 undergraduate students in United Kingdom university law schools.[38] By comparison 17,495 students graduated in law from United Kingdom university law schools in 2013.[39] Such changes in size bring changes in modes of governance. In both *The Masters* and *Lucky Jim* the academics feel assured of their control of their institutions and their lives. Aitken's description of the administration of the University of Birmingham in the mid-1960s sees academics as 'each teaching and investigating in his own subject in his

---

[35] See, for example, B Readings, *The University in Ruins* (Harvard University Press 1996) 3. See also F Furedi, 'The Bureaucratization of the British University' in D Haynes and R Wynyard (eds), *The McDonaldization of the British University* (Bergin & Garvey 2002).

[36] On these two novels see A Vogel, 'The Academic World of C.P. Snow' [1963] 9 *Twentieth Century Literature* 143 and R Fallis, '*Lucky Jim* and Academic Wishful Thinking' [1977] *Studies in the Novel* 65.

[37] L Neville Brown, *Law Without Frontiers: Memoirs of a Comparatist* (L Neville Brown 2004) 65. The first survey of legal education in the United Kingdom recorded that there were 391 full-time legal academics in law schools in the United Kingdom in the academic year 1965/66 (J Wilson, 'A Survey of Legal Education in the United Kingdom' [1966] *IX Journal of the Society of Public Teachers of Law* 1, 26).

[38] Wilson, *op cit* 13. Law students typically spend three years in an undergraduate programme.

[39] Higher Education Statistics Agency *Statistical First Release 197*. Available at: https://www.hesa.ac.uk/stats (accessed 7 August 2015).

own way'.[40] In the United Kingdom now for many the notion of such academic control over their places of work are a distant memory; instead academics have long ago been seen as being 'suppressed, side-lined, divided and [are] ineffective'.[41]

Changes in university governance have meant that for many those teaching and researching in British universities are no longer just academics but are now 'managed academics'; that there has been a move from collegiality in universities to 'managerialism' 'and it is difficult to see this trend changing in the foreseeable future'.[42] One thing that is important for the analysis in this essay is the fact that reports of managerialism in United Kingdom universities are not new but instead go back several decades.

Managerialism as a term of art refers not to the fact that the modern university is managed but to specific new management practices imported into universities, usually from the private sector. There is no universal definition of managerialism.[43] One specific example illustrates the approach. Between 2001 and 2004 the Higher Education Funding Council for England and Wales (HEFCE) made an extra £330 million available for universities to enhance their approach to human resource management.[44] One result of this was that 57 per cent of universities increased the number of people in their human resource management departments.[45] The HEFCE initiative was part of a process of making human resource management central to the governance of universities.[46] One of the two major concerns of human resource management has been seen as being ensuring commitment by employees to goals of the employing

---

40 R Aitken, *Administration of a University* (University of London Press 1966) 74.

41 I McNay, 'Changing Cultures in UK Higher Education' in D Braun and F Merrien (eds), *Towards a New Model of University Governance for Universities?* (Jessica Kingsley 1999) 40.

42 J Fanghanel, *Being an Academic* (Routledge 2012) ch 1; M Tight, *The Development of Higher Education in the United Kingdom since 1945* (Open University Press 2009) 154.

43 J Dearlove, 'The academic labour process: from collegiality and professionalism to managerialism and proletarianisation' [1997] 30(1) *Higher Education Review* 56, 61.

44 KPMG LLP, *Evaluation of Rewarding and Developing Staff in HE initiative 2001-02 to 2003–04*. Available at: http://dera.ioe.ac.uk/5856/1/rd14_05.pdf (accessed 7 August 2015).

45 KPMG LLP, *op cit* 58.

46 D Guest and M Clinton, *Human Resource Management and University Performance* (*Leadership Foundation for Higher Education* 2007) 4.

organization.[47] Enhancing human resource management was thus about attempting to transform the university.[48] Autonomous professionals, with academic freedom and their academic discipline as their focus, were to become managed employees concentrating on the needs that non-academics saw their institutions as having.

One thing associated with managerialism has been the introduction of a regular, formal appraisal of the work of individual academics. Introducing annual assessments of academic performance was first suggested by the Jarratt Committee in 1985.[49] As with managerialism in general such assessments were intended to bring universities into line with management within the private sector. United Kingdom universities were slow to respond to this recommendation but faced increasing pressure to do so.[50] In 2001 HEFCE heightened this pressure.[51] By 2007 74.6 per cent of universities had schemes for the regular appraisal of academics.[52] Outside of universities the purpose of appraisal is quite clear; it is a performance management tool where performance management is seen as being about making sure that employees meet targets set by their employing organization.[53] Similarly, within universities appraisal was about increasing control over the work of individual academics.[54] Both individuals teaching performance and the quality of their research would be measured against criteria determined by the university rather than by the individual being appraised. Appraisal provides the clearest and most concrete

---

47 K Legge, *Human Resource Management: Rhetoric and Realities* (Macmillan 2005) 209.

48 KPMG LLP, *op cit* 75.

49 *Report of the Steering Committee for Efficiency Studies in Universities* (1985) Committee of Vice-Chancellors and Principals: London, 29.

50 See, for example, *Independent Review of Higher Education Pay and Conditions* (The Bett Report) (1999) Stationary Office: London, 91 and National Committee of Inquiry into Higher Education, *Higher Education in the Learning Society* (The Dearing Report) (1997) NCIHE, London, 222.

51 HEFCE, *Rewarding and Developing Staff HEFCE 01/16* (2001) HEFCE, London 9.

52 Guest and Clinton, *op cit* 21.

53 Chartered Institute of Personnel and Development (CIPD), *Performance Appraisal* (2011). Available at: http://www.cipd.co.uk/hr-resources/factsheets/performance-appraisal.aspx (accessed 7 August 2015); A McDonnell and P Gunnigle, 'Performance Management' in D Collings and G Wood (eds), *Human Resource Management: A Critical Approach* (Routledge 2009) 190.

54 F Wilson 'Dilemmas of Appraisal' [2002] 20 *European Management Journal* 620, 622. See also J Beesley, P Guilford, R Nestor and S Rex, *Emerging Practice in Staff Appraisal and Review* (Higher Education Staff Development Agency 2004) 21.

example of the degree to which managerialism now pervades British universities. Murphy comments that "[t]hese days I find that I am supposed to have a 'career' which is something to be 'developed' through a bilateral process of 'appraisal'."[55]

5 THE PUBLIC AND PRIVATE LIVES OF UNIVERSITIES

Two things seem clear from the sections above. First, academics have an obligation to take personal responsibility for their work both because of the nature of academic freedom seen as an obligation as well as a right and because of what the professional ideal says about how they should work. However, secondly, managerialism and things that have arisen as a consequence of managerialism are intended to make it impossible for academics to work in this way. To managerialism one could add a variety of other mechanisms that have been introduced into British universities in the past few decades that have also sought to decrease or even remove autonomy from academic lives.[56] Thus, for example, Halsey sees the introduction of the external assessment of the quality of research in individual university departments as being "a dramatic moment in the decline of donnish dominion".[57] Some commentators certainly would seem to think that there has been a significant change in academic life. Thornton writes of legal academics as "auditable performers".[58] Similarly Collier writes of a "university education … transformed into an industry preoccupied with economic rationalism, efficiency and the generation of income".[59] In the final section of this essay I will discuss what follows if these observations are correct. However, first I will look at whether suggestions about legal academics total loss of autonomy are wholly sustainable.

---

[55] W Murphy 'Reference Without Reality: A Comment on a Commentary on Codifications of Practice' [1990] 1 *Law and Critique* 61, 75. On the notion of the academic career see further below.

[56] On these innovations see Bradney (2003), *op cit* ch 7.

[57] A Halsey, *The Decline of Donnish Dominion* (Clarendon Press 1992) 189.

[58] M Thornton, *Privatising the Public University* (Routledge 2012) 211.

[59] R Collier, 'The changing university and the (legal) academic career – rethinking the relationship between women, men and the 'private life' of the law school' [2002] 222 *Legal Studies* 1, 16.

In his work on universities Trow has distinguished the public life of universities from its private life.[60] The public life of universities is to be seen in things such as university mission statements or governance structures whilst its private life is to be found in, inter alia, what actually happens in seminars and lectures. Trow's argument is that account has to be taken of both things if a university is to be properly understood. Knight and Trowler however differ, seeming to give priority to the private life of universities by arguing that:[61]

> The diversity and dynamism of a university's cultural configuration derives from smaller units within it. These are the cultural powerhouses of university life, places where culture is both enacted and constructed and where personal identity coalesces, is shaped and re-shaped.

The discussion in the section of this essay above is a discussion of the public life of British universities. In this realm there can be no doubt that new audit structures have been introduced and that management regimes have radically changed. However, to conclude that because of this there has been a resultant loss of academic autonomy is to conflate the private and public lives of the university without examining what in fact has happened in the former. The fact that a new audit procedure or form of governance has been introduced does not necessarily mean that it has had any impact on the private lives of academics; still less does it follow that new structures and procedures have had the impact that they were intended to have. One simple example will illustrate this. In 2000 a Law Benchmark was issued setting out what employers and others might expect from a law graduate.[62] The chair of the group that wrote the Benchmark, John Bell, suggested that the Benchmark was simply a matter of 'articulating standards at a national level".[63] However in

---

[60] M Trow, 'The Public and Private Lives of Higher Education' [1975] 104 *Daedalus* 113.

[61] P Trowler and P Knight, 'Coming to Know in Higher education: Theorising Faculty Entry to New Work Contexts' in M Tight (ed), *The RoutledgeFalmer Reader in Higher Education* (Routledge/Falmer 2004) 158.

[62] All subjects in British universities now have a benchmark which is periodically revised, the process being managed by the Quality Assurance Agency. For information on the Law Benchmark see: http://www.qaa.ac.uk/en/Publications/Documents/Subject-benchmark-statement-law.pdf (accessed 7 August 2015).

[63] J Bell, 'Benchmarking: A Pedagogically Valuable Process?' [1999] 2 *Web Journal of Current Legal Issues*. Available at: http://www.bailii.org/uk/other/journals/WebJCLI/1999/issue2/index.html (accessed 7 August 2015).

articulating standards the Benchmark necessarily still set limits on what law schools could and could not do.[64] It thus became a new audit procedure that law schools seemingly had to comply with and as such is part of the process of change in universities described above. The Law Benchmark is clearly now part of the public life of British university law schools. However, in her account of academic life in English university law schools, based on a series of interviews with academics, Cownie, whilst discussing the result of various kinds of audit, never refers to the Law Benchmark.[65] This is because whilst her respondents talked about and complained about other forms of audit no-one mentioned the Law Benchmark.[66] It has not become part of the private life of law schools. There is no mechanism for systematically enforcing compliance with the Benchmark. Thus there is a need to ask the question, given the changes to the public life of the university how far has the private life of law schools changed?

Having noted the literature on the pervasive presence of manageralism in English universities and its deleterious effects Kolsaker goes on to observe that:[67]

> [a] casual visitor to an English university may be surprised, therefore, to encounter an environment where academics seemingly come and go as they please, have a relatively free hand in course design, and disappear to do 'real work' (research) for days on end.

Similarly, in her study of English legal academics Cownie notes that, when she asked her respondents what they liked about being an academic, the factor that was reported most often was the autonomy that academics had.[68] How can autonomy continue to be so widely valued in law schools when universities, and their academic members are subject to the kind of regimes noted in the sections above?

The new disciplinary technologies such as appraisal and audit are a real presence in United Kingdom university law schools, they are

---

64 A Bradney 'Benchmarking: A Pedagogically Valuable Process? An Alternative View' [1999] 2 *Web Journal of Current Legal Issues*. Available at: http://www.bailii.org/uk/other/journals/WebJCLI/1999/issue2/index.html (accessed 7 August 2015).

65 Cownie, *op cit*.

66 Personal communication with author.

67 A Kolsaker, 'Academic Professionalism in the Managerialist Era: A Study of English Universities' [2008] 33 *Studies in Higher Education* 513, 516.

68 Cownie, *op cit* 104.

resented and are thought to be oppressive.[69] However, it is important to note that the response on the part of academics to such technologies has not necessarily been passive or acquiescent; resistance is regularly reported in the literature that analyses contemporary university life.[70] Indeed Kolsaker, using the work of Foucault, argues that power should be seen as a process which involves interdependency in a relationship between people rather than simply being something which one person possesses and applies to another; on this view power involves resistance. Characterizing academics as just the subjects of power will therefore always be inaccurate.[71] The picture is further complicated by the fact that those who are responsible for the implementation of managerialism in universities, the academic managers, are not always themselves in favour of such an approach, some instead preferring an academic identity or attempting to meld academic and managerial values.[72] Finally account needs to be taken of the fact that even in the places from which the new control mechanisms have been imported, largely the private sector, widespread scepticism about the efficacy of such procedures exists.[73] The private life of universities and their law schools has been affected by

---

[69] On appraisal as a disciplinary technology see Wilson (2002), *op cit* 622; on academic resentment of appraisal see L Elton, *Teaching in Higher Education: Appraisal and Training* (Kogan Page 1987) 12; on the academic view of research audit as being oppressive see D Vick, A Murray, G Little and K Campbell, 'The Perceptions of Academic Lawyers Concerning the Effects of the United Kingdom's Research Assessment Exercise' [1998] 25 *Journal of Law and Society* 536.

[70] See, for example, M Cheng, 'Audit Cultures and Quality Assurance Mechanism in England: A Study of their Perceived Impact on the Work of Academics' [2010] 15 *Teaching in Higher Education* 259, 269 and Guest and Clinton, *op cit*. Such resistance is also reported in other jurisdictions. Thus, for example, in Australia see G Anderson, 'Mapping Academic Resistance in the Managerial University' [2008] 15 *Organization* 251 and N James, 'Power-Knowledge in Australia's Legal Education: Corporatism's Reign' [2004] 26 *Sydney Law Review* 587, 609–611.

[71] Kolsaker, *op cit* 523.

[72] M Henkel, *Academic Identities and Policy Change in Higher Education* (Jessica Kingsley 2000) ch 11. See also Deem on feminist academic managers (R Deem, 'New Managerialism and Higher Education: Management of Performances and Cultures in Universities in the United Kingdom' [1998] 8 *International Studies in Sociology of Education* 47, 37–61.

[73] For example, in the case of appraisal see, amongst others, S Bach, 'New Directions in Performance Management' in S Bach (ed), *Managing Human Resources: Personal Management in Transition* (Blackwell Publishing 2005) 305; T Newton and P Findlay, 'Playing God? The Performance of Appraisal' [1996] 6(3) *Human Resource Management Journal* 42, 56 and Legge, *op cit* 235.

matters such as appraisal and audit. However, what that effect has been is not entirely clear.

6 CONCLUSION

Academic employment is not like life elsewhere. The cues that there are for appropriate behaviour in most other areas of employment are not cues for academics. Jackall observes that for corporate managers what matters most is 'not what a person is but how closely his many personae mesh with the organizational ideal'.[74] Careers made by doing this, chart the success of the worker.[75] In the modern era the ability to be part of a team, to submerge one's individuality, is often central to this process.[76] For academics the position is different. Academics do have careers in the sense that most seek increases in salaries and to move up a hierarchical employment structure.[77] Yet many academics' attitude to academic careers is ambivalent. Halsey suggests that getting to become a professor is the 'high point of an academic career'.[78] However, few of the respondents in Cownie's study of legal academics thought that having a chair was important in terms of academic success and a nearly equivalent number thought that it was not relevant.[79] For those outside universities a successful career is a guarantee of the value of what they have done.[80] For academics it is their own sense of the worth of what they have done that matters more and it is easy to find academic lives where individuals

---

74 R Jackall, 'Moral Mazes: The World of Corporate Managers' (OUP 1988) 193.

75 H Newell, 'Managing Careers' in S Bach and K Sisson (eds), *Personnel management: a comprehensive guide to theory and practice* (Blackwell Publishers 2000) 218.

76 J Barker, 'Tightening the Iron Cage: Concertive Control in Self-Managing Teams' [1993] 38 *Administrative Science Quarterly* 408, 412–413, Jackall, *op cit* 51–53, R Sennett, *The Corrosion of Character* (Norton 1998) 99. Maister argues that teamwork is also central to the ethos of professional service firms (D Maister, *Managing the Professional Service Firm* (The Free Press 1993) 306.

77 T Becher and P Trowler, *Academic Tribes and Territories* (2nd edn, Open University Press 2001) ch 7.

78 Halsey, *op cit* 200.

79 Cownie, *op cit* 94.

80 Although even here Sennett suggests that there are worries about the possibility that 'qualities of good work are not qualities of good character' (R Sennett, *op cit* 21).

have pursued what they thought was important even at the expense of personal preferment.[81]

Anderson writes that it is academics 'perceived *responsibility*' that leads them to resist managerialism.[82] In the main, academics, even though they work in large institutions with many other people in them, are as Dworkin above demands, *par excellence*, individuals.[83] The obligation that comes from their academic freedom and professionalism makes them take individual responsibility for the truth and the value of what they are teaching irrespective of any pressures from audit or managerialism and irrespective of the institutional fact that in the modern era they must work with other people. The literature of resistance cited above suggests that the space to do this continues to exist in universities. However, even if those who take a more sceptical view about the present situation for academics are correct, the nature of academic obligations and responsibilities are not changed. If academics cannot meet the challenge of Dworkin's 'heightened responsibility' in their teaching as well as in their research then they have to accept that, whatever the form of words on their contracts of employment, they cannot be academics.

In the field of large law firms Hanlon has described the emergence of the phenomenon of 'commercialised professionalism' where commercial imperatives take precedence over traditional professional ideals.[84] More broadly, Evetts has suggested that a 'new professionalism' or an 'organizational professionalism' is emerging in some areas of the economy where the employer determines what professionalism entails.[85] Whether 'commercialised professionalism', 'new professionalism' or 'organizational professionalism' are legitimate descriptions of new forms of

---

[81] See further: A Bradney, 'Instead of a Career: Work, Love and Art in University Law Schools' in P Maharg and C Maughan (eds), *Affect and Legal Education: Emotion in Learning and Teaching the Law* (Ashgate 2011).

[82] Anderson, *op cit* 256 (emphasis in original).

[83] Katzenbach and Smith note that academics can be amongst those who work best on their own (J Katzenbach and D Smith, *The Wisdom of Teams: Creating the High-performance Organization* (Harvard Business School Press 1993) 22). The degree to which it is common for academics to pursue their work as individuals does depend to some extent on the discipline that they are working in (Henkel, *op cit* 189–200).

[84] G Hanlon, *Lawyers, the State and the Market* (Macmillan Business 1999) ch 4. See also R Greenwood, 'Your Ethics: Redefining Professionalism? The Impact of Management Change' in L Empson (ed), *Managing the Modern Law Firm* (OUP 2007) 194.

[85] See, for example, J Evetts 'A New Professionalism? Challenges and Opportunities' [2011] 59 *Current Sociology* 406.

professionalism or something more akin to Orwell's newspeak in his novel *1984* is a matter for debate.[86] What is clear is that for academics professionalism and academic freedom mean that individual responsibility take precedence over all else in teaching; the new forms of professionalism, if they are professionalism, have no place in universities. This is not to deny that academics, especially when they are involved in teaching large student intakes, inevitably work in groups. Such work necessarily involves mutual accommodation by those in the groups. Nonetheless, it is important to remember that such accommodation can only be successful if it allows every member of the group when they teach to say what they believe to be true and important. More than this, in the final analysis it remains the individual responsibility of the academic to make sure that this is so both for themselves and for their fellow academics. The fact that they work with other people does not make them as individuals any less lonely when they come to the matter of reaching personal decisions about what they do in their teaching.

[86] 'Newspeak was designed not to extend but to *diminish* the range of thought …' (G Orwell, *Nineteen Eighty-Four* (Penguin Books 1989) 313).

PART II

Experimental courses

6. Teaching international law critically – critical pedagogy and *Bildung* as orientations for learning and teaching

Christine Schwöbel-Patel[1]

1 INTRODUCTION

International law is largely taught in a way which aims to inculcate a language of expertise employed in international legal organizations. Such training is causing the reproduction of a cultural hegemony in the classroom, in the law school, and society at large. In the following, I investigate whether there is a possibility (and an obligation) for teachers of international law to disrupt this reproduction, to be counter-hegemonic in their teaching. In particular, I am interested in the relationship between critical theory in teaching and the demands of teaching law as a profession. Teachers of (international) law often feel that theory is something that needs to be 'slipped into' a more practice-oriented syllabus. They feel market pressures demand a doctrinal mode of teaching rather than one which looks at law in context. Market pressures may be exerted by student numbers signing up to courses, by the way in

---

[1] An earlier form of this chapter was published as '"I'd Like to Know What Hegemony Means". Teaching International Law from a Critical Angle' [2013] 2 Law & Method, 67–84. For this revised version I have benefited from discussions at two teaching workshops, namely at the 'Critical Approaches to International Criminal Law Conference' in Liverpool and from the workshop 'Teaching International Criminal Law: Between Fragmentation and Constitutionalisation'. In particular, I would like to thank Sara Kendall, Rob Knox and Tor Krever for discussions in and around these workshops. I would also like to thank the editors, anonymous reviewers and Mike Gordon and Dave McGrogan for their comments. Finally, a piece on teaching would not be complete without acknowledging my students in the past years, from whom I have learnt a great deal. All errors remain my own.

which courses are marketed to prospective students, and by the students' potential employers. These market pressures may lead to a feeling of compulsion to teach 'doctrine' as opposed to, or instead of, 'theory'. The defining features of the former would be that it concerns a rather technical debate about what the law is or should be in a given situation; the latter concerns questions of contextualization, asking, for example, whether lawmaking processes are biased, for example, in favour of a particular class, race, or gender.

The practice- and doctrine-oriented forms of teaching are seemingly reproducing a cultural hegemony of dominance of a particular class of lawyers who privilege and represent individualism, the global North, males, whites, and neoliberalism. The term 'cultural hegemony' was coined by Antonio Gramsci to denote the actions of a ruling class which constructs particular cultural norms, sustaining and endorsing them as natural and inevitable, for the purposes of domination. There is an emphasis on ruling by consent, rather than simply through force.[2] Gramsci dedicated his writing, particularly in *The Prison Notebooks*, to exposing the accepted cultural norms as artificial social constructs, put into place and sustained through institutions, practices, and beliefs.[3] In Gramsci's view, education is central to understanding hegemony, signalling 'every relationship of "hegemony" is necessarily an educational relationship [...]'.[4]

In the following, I apply this analytical frame to the practices involved in teaching international law and ask what the relevant cultural norms are, and whether they are presented and perceived as natural and inevitable.

There are several reasons why international law presents an interesting lens for discussing issues of cultural hegemony and legal hierarchy through education. First, it is a discipline largely determined and influenced by lawyers in the global North, although it claims to concern the interests of all people. Institutions such as the United Nations (UN), the World Trade Organisation (WTO) and the International Court of Justice

---

2 Antonio Gramsci, Selections from the Prison Notebooks, Quentin (Hoare & Geoffrey Nowell Smith (trs eds)), (first published 1971, Lawrence and Wishart 2007).

3 Michael A Peters explains hegemony in Gramsci's sense as 'an essential part of the sociology of capitalist society enabling an understanding of the manufacture of consent by the powerful through the institution of cultural values'; Michael A Peters, 'Foreword' in Peter Mayo (ed), Gramscian Educational Thought (Wiley-Blackwell 2010) ix.

4 Gramsci (2007), op cit 350.

(ICJ) are largely based around the New York City-Geneva-The Hague-triangle of influence. The influential academic institutions moreover are overwhelmingly situated in the global North. While these institutions are not exclusively populated by lawyers from the global North, there are nevertheless biases manifested through location. Second, relative to the fairly small number of institutions concerned with international law as such there is a disproportionate number of students studying international law. While there may be many law jobs, international law jobs which correspond to the way in which the subject is taught are fairly rare. Regardless, international law as a discipline of international institutions is still imparted on students as though the expertise in the practices of these institutions were a realistic career perspective. Third, despite its political nature, international law is overwhelmingly claimed to be a mechanism to keep a check on politics, implying the neutral nature of law that stands in opposition to the biased nature of politics. The most traditional form of lawmaking in international law is the treaty, which is constituted through the consent of state representatives. Such a political and politicized instrument is nevertheless regarded by many students of international law to offer a space for unbiased law.

I have explored these themes in a previous piece, commissioned by the editors of this collection.[5] In this chapter I aim to build on the recent article by adding some practical considerations of how to teach in a counter-hegemonic fashion to complement the theoretical observations already explored. I will be drawing from my own teaching experience, in particular two courses I teach, namely International Law in Current Affairs and Critical Approaches to International Criminal Law. I will reflect on some of the experiences I have had; some of the opportunities and some of the limitations I have encountered while teaching these courses. In addition, I will be drawing on literature and discussions from two teaching workshops I co-organized in the frame of the critical approaches to international criminal law research network.[6] The object of these workshops was to bring together researchers and educators who adopt a critical approach to international law in their research and to discuss if and how this critical approach translates to teaching.

In the following, I first consider Duncan Kennedy's piece on 'Legal Education and the Reproduction of Hierarchy'. I place this seminal piece

[5] Christine Schwöbel-Patel, 'I'd Like to Know What Hegemony Means. Teaching International Law from a Critical Angle' [2013] 2 Law & Method, 67–84.

[6] Available at: www.caicl.net (accessed 5 May 2015).

within today's higher education systems. From this emerges that Kennedy's key concerns are still as salient today as they were 30 years ago. I then turn to international law by drawing on a piece by Anne Orford in which she interrogates the depoliticization of international lawyers, achieved through their *disciplining*. From these two sections I take that legal education in its focus on training is causing the cementing of an existing hegemony, meaning that the interests of the most powerful social groups are constantly reaffirmed.[7] Against this background of hierarchy and hegemony, I then consider the possibility of a counter-hegemonic approach to teaching international law. I first explore some of the thoughts associated with the field of critical pedagogy and then consider opportunities which may lie in *Bildung*. Critical pedagogy and *Bildung* foreground a reflexive notion of education, viewing education as a social and a political process. Finally, I explore some of the ways in which critical pedagogy and *Bildung* may be used as orientations in international law syllabi: Do these enable social and political engagement in a field of study which is largely individualistic and (supposedly) apolitical?

2 TEACHING LAW

In 1982, Duncan Kennedy published 'Legal Education and the Reproduction of Hierarchy'. In this piece, Kennedy interrogates the US law school as a site in which hierarchies are both manifested and reproduced.[8]

He begins with a description of a typical first-year law school experience. His examination spans the classroom experience ('the teachers are overwhelmingly white, male, and deadeningly straight and middle class in manner'[9]) the pressures of performance ('performance is on one's mind, adrenalin flows, success has a nightly and daily meaning in terms of the material suggested'[10]) and the intellectual experience. The intellectual experience includes the revelation that there is no purchase for left or even for committed liberal thinking: 'The basic experience is

---

[7] Peter Mayo, 'Antonio Gramsci and his Relevance to the Education of Adults' in Peter Mayo (ed), Gramscian Educational Thought (Wiley-Blackwell 2010) 22.

[8] Duncan Kennedy, 'Legal Education and the Reproduction of Hierarchy' [1982] 32 Journal of Legal Education, 591.

[9] Ibid 593.

[10] Ibid.

of double surrender: to a passivizing classroom experience and to a passive attitude toward the content of the legal system.'[11]

Much of this approach to law and legal teaching, according to Kennedy, comes about through an artificial distinction between law and policy. Such a distinction lies at the intellectual core of the ideological content of legal education.[12] Lecturers teach law in a way which presumes that legal reasoning exists, moreover that it exists as a rational neutral practice, and that it is different from policy analysis. Policy analysis is presented as the only outlet for uncovering indeterminacy, and as the only space for biased decisions. Public policy, as opposed to law, offers an entry-point into discussions on the indeterminacy and manipulability of ideas and institutions.[13] Contract law, tort law, land law, criminal law, are all taught as though they had an inner logic. Against this assumption, Kennedy argues that these subjects are not random subjects built on the foundation of neutral reasoning, but are rather 'the ground-rules of late nineteenth-century laissez-faire capitalism'.[14] The primacy of property and restrictions on interference with the market are foregrounded as central values. The relevant rights are those reflecting the interests of private property owners, businesses, multinational corporations and financial capital. Through the idea of the 'inner logic', law does not only naturalise these interests, but also appears to have an almost magical, and certainly mysterious, authority. The authority of the law is mirrored in the classroom by the authority of the lecturer who imparts knowledge. Students mimic such authority, both of the law and of the individual who has the knowledge to impart the law. Ultimately, students learn to embody established hierarchies without questioning them.

Kennedy's description of a US law school in the 1980s is an equally accurate description of many law schools in the world today. Certainly, it seems particularly familiar to the law schools in the UK, where the three-year law course is heavily influenced by the professions. The subjects required by the legal profession are compulsory subjects on the degree programme so that completion of the degree will also satisfy the requirements of the professional bodies. There is a tacit understanding of the distinction between 'hard' and 'soft' modules. The former include the core modules of contract law, tort law, criminal law, law of trusts, commercial law; the latter include modules such as family law,

---

[11] Ibid 594.
[12] Ibid 596.
[13] Ibid.
[14] Ibid 597.

human rights law and legal theory. Soft subjects are often feminized and infantilized.[15] Syllabi are increasingly skills-focused, emphasizing communication skills, teamwork and critical analysis.[16] Notwithstanding the importance of such skills, understanding and analysing the role of law in society, even regarding law as a social language, have largely disappeared (if they ever were present) and have given way to the training of professionals who will fit in well with a market-focused legal practice.[17]

Kennedy was also concerned about the neglected left programme in law schools in the 1980s, claiming that it is often reduced to a triumph of human rights.[18] This has the effect of marginalizing political engagement and agendas. Kennedy observed that the (human) rights discourse presupposes, or takes for granted, that the world is and should be divided between the public and the private sphere. The state sector, the public, enforces rights; and the private world of 'civil society' is one in which atomized individuals pursue their diverse goals. The site of the political then exists exclusively in the public sphere. Individuals are distanced, even alienated, from this sphere. Relying purely on the language of rights possibly subjects the left to complicity in the construction of a distinction between law and politics; and with this, the seeming neutrality of the law. Kennedy's conclusion is that the 'rights discourse is a trap'.[19] Regardless of whether one agrees with his conclusions, the left programme as a meaningful discourse of structural problems, which includes a consideration of the complicities of law in such structural problems, certainly is a neglected site in law schools then and now.

---

15 Anne Orford, 'Embodying Internationalism: The Making of International Lawyers' [1998] 19 Australian Yearbook of International Law 1–34, 18.

16 It should be noted that critical analysis does, on the whole, not refer to an understanding of the underlying assumptions of the law or its place within society at large, rather it refers to the ability of students to make pro and contra arguments. Critical analysis encompasses the skill of identifying the conflicting principles – usually two or three (one conservative, one liberal, one in the middle). At the end, these conflicting principles are simply 'balanced away', Duncan Kennedy, 'How the Law School Fails: A Polemic' [1970–1971] 1 Yale Review of Law and Social Action 71–90.

17 Campaign for the Public University. Available at: http://publicuniversity.org.uk/ (accessed 5 May 2015).

18 Kennedy, op cit 598.

19 Ibid.

3 TEACHING INTERNATIONAL LAW

The artificial distinction between law and policy in foundational law modules can be mapped onto the artificial distinction between law and politics in the vast majority of international law modules. The following may serve as an example: Most international law modules, and certainly all modules specifically dealing with the *jus ad bellum* (the right to war), will consider the legal arguments pertaining to the 2003 Iraq invasion of both the US and UK. In the dominant narrative, the Iraq war is deemed 'illegal' under international law because there were no provisions or recognized interpretations under the UN Charter which could have suggested either self-defence or a Security Council resolution authorizing the use of force. The topic is mostly taught as a historical moment when politics managed to override law. The US invaded for political reasons *despite* illegality under international law. International law is thus taught as the voice of reason and neutrality which (more or less successfully) reigns in, excesses of politics. It is the so-called liberal perspective on international law.

In such rhetoric, both the law and the student are depoliticized. Law is portrayed as the rational, neutral voice. The complicity of law in its commitment to a particular liberal ideology is obscured. How law enables inequality, unfairness and bias is left out of the picture. This in itself is a politically motivated move: The depoliticization of law is political.

Anne Orford refers to this process as 'disciplining', drawing both on Michel Foucault's work of 'technologies of the self' and feminist theorist Terry Threadgold.[20] Foucault's idea of technologies of the self is that the self exists as an effect of power relations, making individuals into 'subjects'.[21] Threadgold's work highlights how the process of being trained in a discipline involves the belief, reproduction, guarding and passing on of the narratives at the heart of the discipline.[22] Orford begins her analysis of 'disciplining' with legal education – as the primary site in

---

20 Orford, op cit 1–34.

21 Michel Foucault in Luther H Martin, Huck Gutman and Patrick H Hutton (eds), Technologies of the Self: A Seminar with Michel Foucault (University of Massachusetts Press 1988).

22 Terry Threadgold, 'Everyday Life in the Academy: Postmodern Feminisms, Generic Seductions, Rewriting and Being Heard' in Carmen Luke (ed), Feminisms and Pedagogies of Everyday Life (State University of New York Press 1996) 280–314, 281.

which the self-image of international lawyers is produced and reproduced.[23] She is particularly interested in the writing, reading and performing of narratives of intervention by international lawyers. She singles out four aspects of intervention narratives, which 'in particular shape the sense of self of international lawyers'.[24] First, *New world order professionals*, a role attributed to international lawyers as managerialists, 'pragmatic, problem-solving professionals, striding the corridors of power and being involved in history-making events'.[25] Second, *Agents of humanitarianism*, those international lawyers who are 'humanitarians, saving victims of oppression and human rights abuses'.[26] Third, *Gentle civilizers*, an image of 'international lawyers as humane, professional, elite advisers to real decision-makers'.[27] Fourth, *Men of action,* professionals who 'do something' in a difficult and torn world which requires decision-making, not dithering. In sum, and regardless of the specific intervention narrative adopted, 'international lawyers come to understand themselves as the embodiment of heroic internationalism, and of the values and myths that underlie international law'.[28] And who is this disciplined 'subject' of law according to Orford? 'The "subject" of law is an aggressive, capitalist, heterosexual, white man'.[29] In this disciplining and in this technology of the self, legal education is political; it is an exercise of reproduction of power relations, at the same time as being declared non-political. In Gramsci's sense, an elite class of international lawyers has manipulated the system of values within international law in order to establish its own *Weltanschauung* as the dominant one.

The regionalism of international law is worth highlighting as a particular feature, particularly as the discipline claims to concern universal values and global interests, and its advocates repeatedly claim to adopt an unbiased and non-political view on global issues. Although it has shifted away from *exclusive* Eurocentrism, the discipline of international law unarguably originated in Eurocentric enlightenment ideas, which continue to shape the discipline today. The centres and clusters of international law teaching (all in the global North) reproduce these Eurocentric enlightenment ideas and present them as global. In an international law syllabus, the Eurocentric idea of international law will

---

23 Orford, op cit 15.
24 Ibid 5.
25 Ibid.
26 Ibid 8.
27 Ibid 11.
28 Ibid 16.
29 Ibid 17.

generally be entrenched in the first few classes, either with a section on history or a section on statehood and sovereignty. The history of international law is often taught as beginning with the Dutch so-called 'father of international law', Hugo Grotius. Statehood and sovereignty are mostly pinpointed as first devised in the Treaty of Westphalia 1648. This method of teaching, with its familiar origins story, privileges the place of origin, namely Western Europe. The Third World Approaches to the International Law movement has done some significant work in highlighting and decentering this bias.[30]

Future international lawyers who are taught today will enter international legal organizations, or other legal outfits (law firms, governments) with a certain influence and a particular notion of 'how the world works'. Teachers of international law students are teaching a global elite, a global class, which carries ideas of the law into their work and private lives. International lawyers of tomorrow therefore sustain and reproduce the *status quo* by viewing this domination as natural and the paradigms as neutral and universal.[31]

It should be mentioned that not all students buy into this depoliticization of course – the student 'body' is by no means homogenous and students are not to be understood as simply passive recipients. There are some who are suspicious of the role of the law. Yet, often, what this minority of students learn to do with this suspicion is to package it away into their private lives – it is seen as having no place in the professional, legal, sphere.[32] Learning how to use the law is regarded as exam- and job-relevant; learning about how law works in society is not deemed relevant. So even those students who do have a political sensitivity which would tie into a questioning of how law works in society save this for a space outside of law.

Is it therefore the role of the educator to expose these politics and shift the (self-)understanding of the role of lawyers? If one takes the demands of the market into account, this seems an almost impossible task.

---

30 See for example, BS Chimni, 'An Outline of a Marxist Course on Public International Law' in Susan Marks (ed), International Law on the Left (CUP 2008).

31 This is in reference to Marx and Engels in Die Deutsche Ideologie. Karl Marx, Friedrich Engels, Die Deutsche Ideologie (Jazzybee Verlag Jürgen Beck 2012).

32 Kennedy, op cit 608. Kennedy already mentioned this in a piece he wrote as a student at Yale Law School: '[T]he division of life into hermetically sealed "private" (emotional) and "public" (effectiveness) compartments must lead to deformations in both areas'. Kennedy, op cit 77–78.

Educators are working in a neoliberal world to which the education system is largely committed; legal education will, therefore, privilege the cardinal features of neoliberalism: individualism, competition, growth, and an idea of the guaranteeing of freedom through free markets and trade.

4 CONSTRAINTS ON EDUCATORS

The constraints on educators in regard to counter-hegemonic teaching are wide-ranging. Lecturers submit to and re-entrench the cultural hegemony of international law due to: first, their own education of international law, and, second, because they are disciplined to teach in this way. The disciplining of international lawyers relates to the combination of subjection to the discipline,[33] as well as a culture of accountability imposed on them.[34] Despite good intentions, institutional restraints (which stand alongside historical, social and societal restraints) are likely to be felt with the most intensity. Student surveys on teaching performance, university league tables, decisions on promotions, are all means by which the notorious 'academic freedom' may at times appear farcical. Cris Shore and Susan Wright have described the audit culture in higher education as 'coercive accountability'.[35] They observe how processes of auditing have been transferred from the financial domain to the public sector. This includes the incorporation of terms of the new managerialism, a vocabulary of audit, such as 'performance', 'quality assurance', 'quality control', 'accountability' etc.[36] Gramsci notably wrote in his essay *On Education*:[37] 'The problem was not one of model curricula but of men, and not just of the men who are actually teachers themselves but of the entire social complex which they express'.

The 'entire social complex' which teachers express today is perhaps best described as neoliberalism. Neoliberalism has assumed worldwide scope. The reach of neoliberalism has sharpened further since the financial crisis and the consequent funding cuts across the public sector.

---

[33] Threadgold, op cit.

[34] Cris Shore and Susan Wright, 'Coercive Accountability – The Rise of Audit Culture in Higher Education' in Marilyn Strathern (ed), Audit Cultures – Anthropological Studies in Accountability, Ethics and the Academy (Routledge 2000) 57–89.

[35] Ibid.

[36] Ibid 60.

[37] Gramsci, op cit 26.

Meanwhile, the limitations of free market capitalism have also become more evident, with Eurozone sovereign debt crises being a case in point. David Harvey's work on neoliberalism is instructive for pinning down some of its central themes. In particular, Harvey states that a cardinal feature of neoliberal thinking is 'the assumption that individual freedoms are guaranteed by freedom of the market and of trade'.[38] Commitments to neoliberalism are becoming more evident in higher education – prompting a move away from educations' former place in the public sphere. Students are largely viewed as consumers; universities are viewed as competing in a global marketplace, with franchised universities becoming more common, particularly in the so-called emerging markets; education is being 'sold' as a financial investment in the future; universities are trying to meet customer demand by changing their syllabi and training foci. In the UK, the commitment to neoliberalism became sharpened with the Conservative-Liberal Democrat coalition government of 2010 and the attendant rise in university fees. All in all, higher education has become commodified and marketized.[39] It appears that this is not only the case in the free-market centres of Europe and Northern America, but also in the global South.[40]

Symptomatic of the influences of market forces on education is that law schools are increasingly steered by the professions. This manifests itself in the law syllabus (which subjects are 'core' subjects) and in terms of requirements of employability skills. The more this is so, the more a tradition of training rather than teaching, of technical expertise rather than critical thought, is established. In how far this is an issue of being steered by supply (the law school as supplying legal training) or demand (the students demanding training for the purpose of securing a job) is difficult to disentangle. Certainly, it can be stated that students come to law school to be trained, expecting the inculcation of a particular

---

38 David Harvey, A Brief History of Neoliberalism (OUP 2007) 7.

39 Joyce E Canaan, Wes Shumar, 'Introduction' in Joyce E Canaan and Wes Shumar (eds), Structure and Agency in the Neoliberal University (Routledge 2008).

40 See for example Rajani Naidoo, 'Entrenching International Inequality: The Impact of the Global Commodification of Higher Education on Developing Countries' in Joyce E Canaan and Wes Shumar (eds), Structure and Agency in the Neoliberal University (Routledge 2008) 84–100; Sarah Amsler, 'Higher Education Reform in Post-Soviet Kyrgystan: The Politics of Neoliberal Agendas in Theory and Practice' in ibid 101–130; Mahmood Mamdani, Scholars in the Marketplace: The Dilemmas of Neo-Liberal Reform at Makerere University, 1989–2005 (Codesria 2007).

expertise; they largely do not come to law school to understand the underlying social structures of the law.

For international law this means that an understanding of international law's own hegemonic tendencies, as well as its possible counter-hegemonic properties, are left un(der)explored. An example from teaching concerns the selection of teaching materials – there is a clear bias in favour of work by academics and practitioners from the global North. This perpetuates the prevailing notion of authoritative voices and materials as stemming from male, white scholars from elite Western universities. Themes such as statehood, interventionism, and human rights are therefore often prioritized over concerns of, say, solidarity, resistance, and socio-economic equality.

At stake is the understanding of the university as a place outside of a market logic, in which knowledge can be more than simply a means to acquire particular skills for securing a particular profession.

5 CRITICAL PEDAGOGY AND *BILDUNG*

It appears then that the problem at the teaching level is one of focusing excessively on training students. Education is instrumentalized for the individual. Training is part of the reproduction of cultural hegemony since it does not encourage reflection. In subscribing to training our students, we are ultimately subscribing to a particular exercise of power: one that emanates from viewing students as consumers within a context of a submission to neoliberalism. We are furthering an individualized – rather than a social – idea of teaching, treating knowledge as a means to a particular individual end.

Critical pedagogy and a reorientation towards *Bildung* aim to address these problems. Paolo Freire is considered one of the chief pioneers of the critical pedagogy movement, particularly through his seminal work *Pedagogy of the Oppressed.* In this book, Freire brings structures of oppression to the fore, in particular the dialectical relationship between the oppressor and oppressed. In order to address this oppression, Freire suggests 'a humanizing pedagogy in which the revolutionary leadership establishes a permanent relationship of dialogue with the oppressed'.[41] Dialogical teaching involves a process of both learning *and* knowing. It is, he states, a pedagogy which must be forged '*with,* not *for* the

---

[41] Paolo Freire, MB Ramons (tr), Pedagogy of the Oppressed. 30th Anniversary Edition (Continuum 2000) 68.

oppressed'.[42] Dialogical teaching provides the tools to access the critical discourses that deconstruct colonial and hegemonic paradigms. Dialogue is in this understanding not an end in itself but a means to develop a better understanding about the object of knowledge.[43] Freire's pedagogical proposals clearly go beyond the classroom boundaries with the aim of having an impact on society at large. Freire himself used this theoretical frame to address some of the issues which he found pressing in terms of education and emancipation from oppression, namely teaching peasants from his native Brazil to read and write.[44] Dialogical teaching then means a constant reflexive attitude towards the roles of the educator and the educated.

Joyce Canaan emphasises the importance of critical pedagogy for the neoliberal university. The restructuring of universities is in her view down to the neoliberal forces of marketing and branding. How a university markets itself *vis-à-vis* its competitors has become key.[45] She considers critical pedagogy as a left counter to the process of neoliberalization. Canaan believes critical pedagogues aiming to resist the process of neoliberalization and the structures of hegemony should work together with students in this endeavour. Drawing on Freire, Canaan notes that the assumption of critical pedagogy is that of students as 'knowers guiding teaching'; students and teachers are 'co-investigators in dialogue'.[46]

The notion of *Bildung* is perhaps useful in this context since it captures a wide understanding of education.[47] It is a word which implies activity rather than passivity. Dörpinghaus *et al* note two interconnected attributes which are central to the understanding of *Bildung*: First, *Bildung* relates to a complex relationship of self, the other, and the world. Second, it relates to 'critical reflexivity'. By this they mean that the relationships of self, the other, and the world are no neutral formulae, that they are thought and language processes (reflexive) which are differentiated and questioned (critique). Their understanding of *Bildung* is a discourse,

---

[42] Ibid 48.

[43] Paolo Freire and Donaldo Macedo, 'A Dialogue: Culture, Language, and Race' [1995] 65 Harvard Educational Review 379.

[44] Ibid 12.

[45] Joyce E Canaan, 'Resisting the English neoliberalising university: what critical pedagogy can offer' [2013] 11 Journal for Critical Education Policy Studies 16–56, 17.

[46] Ibid 36.

[47] See for a different view on Bildung; the contribution of Francot & Corrias in this book.

mediated through differentiation, thought, and language, of the individual with oneself, with others, and the world.[48] Such an idea of *Bildung* can be attributed to Hegel who believed in an organic understanding of education.[49] Education according to Hegel is the developmental formation of an individuals' unique potential through participation in society. Norms, beliefs, and values, constantly growing, are reflected back through immanent critique and active reconstruction of such cultural norms, beliefs, and values, affecting others and their *Bildung*.[50] *Bildung*, then, is to be understood as a social activity.[51]

There is something distinctly appealing about such an idea of *Bildung* – it is a social as well as a political notion. Harmut von Hentig wrote a notable essay in 1996 in which he places *Bildung* in the context of politics from antiquity.[52] Von Hentig explains that a privileged education in antiquity brought with it a responsibility to engage in the Greek *polis* as well as in the Roman *res publica*. As Dörpinghaus *et al* comment, such an approach to *Bildung* may appear alien to us: In today's world, we have replaced social engagement and common responsibility with our individual needs and our 'self'.[53] For such an idea of *Bildung* to take hold, we must aim to rethink the deeply entrenched (liberal) notions of individualism.

However, some caution is also necessary. The German etymology of the word, according to Schilling, reveals that *Bildung* derives from *Bildnis* which can best be translated as 'image' or 'effigy'. *Bildung* has, so Schilling claims, theological roots in that it was first conceived of as 'living in the image of God', *zum Eben*bilde *Gottes*.[54] With this in mind, *Bildung* concerns not only the relationship of an individual towards knowledge and society, but a relationship towards God, an entity embodying universal knowledge. A strict and unbreachable hierarchy is

48 Andreas Dörpinghaus et al, Einführung in die Theorie der Bildung (Wissenschaftliche Buchgesellschaft 2012) 10. A somewhat different view on reflexivity is addressed in De Vries' contribution in this book.

49 Georg Wilhelm Friedrich Hegel in AV Miller (tr), Phenomenology of Spirit (first published 1807, OUP 1977).

50 James A Good, A Search for Unity in Diversity: The 'Permanent Hegelian Deposit' in the Philosophy of John Dewey (Lexington Books 2006) xix.

51 See also Gramsci 'On Education' in Selections from the Prison Notebooks, who claims that the aim should be to 'insert young men and women into social activity'. Gramsci, op cit 29.

52 Hartmut von Hentig, Bildung – Ein Essay (Beltz Verlag 2009) 205–210.

53 Dörpinghaus et al, op cit 39.

54 Hans Schilling, Bildung als Gottesbildlichkeit. Exegetische und Motivgeschichtliche Studie zum Bildungsbegriff (Lambertus-Verlag 1961).

implied. Since secular displacements of God nearly always mean re-entrenchments of hierarchies elsewhere, *Bildung* must, if it is to serve as a useful interpretative tool, be dislodged from a sense of hierarchy, certainly from an idea of a locus of universal knowledge. Yet, how to address the inherent hierarchy of teacher to student?

John Dewey's work may provide some rudimentary points of departure. Dewey, often referred to as a scholar of the philosophy of education,[55] was particularly critical of the idea of vocational education as job training.[56] He was wary of the instrumentalism of knowledge, suggesting that this fostered an alienation from larger societal issues. According to Dewey, learning was an intensely social process, and it was paramount for him to put that into practice.[57] In 1896, Dewey and his wife set up a school, the University Elementary School, in Chicago which foregrounded learning through experience. The aim was to discover 'how a school could become a cooperative community'. Children learned through experimenting in a learning environment composed of materials, workshops, library and school gardens; they learned about themselves cooperating in and with their environment. The teacher was not viewed in the role of the domineering instructor, but rather as a co-worker.

How can a counter-hegemonic approach through *Bildung* be translated into higher education? Kennedy suggests 'building a left bourgeois intelligentsia that might one day join together with a mass movement for the radical transformation of American society'.[58] Although it would be subscribing to a myth to claim that intellectuals (students and educators) are independent of class,[59] a notion of *Bildung* at least enables flexibility within this class, makes it more sensitized to the inequalities it creates and reproduces.

A further myth is that there is no element of training in *Bildung*. It would be erroneous to claim that training and *Bildung* are polar opposites; rather, *Bildung* complements training. Gramsci warned against an

---

[55] Jim Garrison, Stefan Neubert, Kersten Reich, John Dewey's Philosophy of Education: An Introduction and Recontextualization of Our Times (Palgrave Macmillan 2012).

[56] John Dewey, 'Education vs. Trade-Training: Reply to David Sneddon', [1915] New Republic 411ff.

[57] Available at: www.ucls.uchicago.edu/data/files/gallery/HistoryBookDownloadsGallery/-chapter1_3.pdf (accessed 5 May 2015).

[58] Kennedy, op cit 610.

[59] Gramsci, op cit 1–23.

excessive emphasis on the distinction between 'instruction' and 'education', which can be mapped onto 'training' and '*Bildung*' respectively:[60] 'For instruction to be wholly distinct from education, the pupil would have to be pure passivity, a "mechanical receiver" of abstract notions – which is absurd'.

Both critical pedagogy and *Bildung* presume a life-story behind the student and educator. Students come with a certain 'baggage', as Gramsci calls it, of previous education acquired, but also crucially from the sector of civil society in which they participate, within the social relations of their family, neighbourhood. And it is this 'baggage' which needs to be brought to the fore (not repressed) in the engagement with self, the other, and the world. The same applies to the educator.

6 CRITICAL PEDAGOGY AND *BILDUNG* IN PRACTICE

The following suggestions are by no means a blue-print for counter-hegemonic teaching. Some of the suggestions come simply from reflecting on the given restrictions and possibilities mentioned above, others from discussions with fellow teachers, lecturers, educators, and others still have been tested in the classroom. I have ordered the below along the lines of 'how'? and 'what'? *How* to create the conditions in a classroom which are counter-hegemonic? And *what* would one teach in (international) law?

The first suggestion for a more reflexive form of teaching would be a suggestion for an engagement with pedagogy, including critical pedagogy, of all who teach. Problematically, those who teach at university level do not, generally, have any knowledge of pedagogy. In terms of teaching, they are simply expected to 'get on with it'. This often leads to emulation of the way in which the teacher was taught. Even if there is some form of required educational development focused on teaching, critical pedagogy is a neglected area. In the Introduction to the 30th anniversary edition of *Pedagogy of the Oppressed,* Donaldo Macedo writes:[61]

> Whereas students in the Third World and other nations struggling with totalitarian regimes would risk their freedom, if not their lives, to read Paulo

---

[60] Ibid 36.

[61] Donaldo Macedo 'Introduction' in Freire (2000), op cit 16.

> Freire, in our so-called open societies his work suffers from a more sophisticated form of censorship: omission.

At most universities across the UK, the curriculum for the required pedagogical course, what is known as the Certificate in Professional Studies in Learning & Teaching in Higher Education at the University of Liverpool, is entirely silent on critical pedagogy or any form of considering the privileged position of the lecturer in the classroom. Indeed, the Higher Education Academy, the UK's national body for enhancing learning and teaching in higher education, has no mention of critical pedagogy on its website and affiliated documents.[62]

Questioning the power relations in the classroom or lecture theatre can bring with it some practical changes to the way lectures and seminars are held. A rather obvious exercise would be one where the lecturer does not employ the frontal teaching method but rather sits among the students, for example, in a circle. These small adjustments to space will already feel empowering to students. Paul Rabinow and some students in the Department of Anthropology at the University of California at Berkley devised the so-called *labinar* – an amalgamation of lab-meeting and seminar – as an experiment in venue construction.[63] In the *labinar*, a radically anti-authoritarian and egalitarian form were aimed for, set against the assumption that no space is actually free of social constraints or power hierarchies.[64] At the forefront was the question which pedagogy fosters thinking. In the *labinar*, various attempts were made to destabilize the regular balance of power. This included the lecturer moving to a chair placed outside the circle of students to the back of the room as well as separating out the procedural tasks of running a classroom. In addition, the students were split into groups of facilitating and monitoring the learning process. Overall, the student's evaluation is that the form adopted is unsustainable. 'It simply requires too much willpower, or what the French call *voluntarisme.*'[65] Some of the observations include that the lecturer will always retain a privileged position. Although the new seat of the lecturer effectively shifted the balance of attention, 'it also elicited

---

62 Available at: https://www.heacademy.ac.uk/ (accessed 15 May 2015).

63 Paul Rabinow, 'Venues: The Labinar and the Anthropology of the Contemporary Research Collaboratory' in Paul Rabinow (ed), The Accompaniment. Assembling the Contemporary (University of Chicago Press 2011) 127–153. Many thanks to Sara Kendall for drawing my attention to the labinar.

64 Ibid 131.

65 Meg Stalcup (student protocol) ibid 140.

humorous student contortions in the effort to glimpse his facial expressions during the discussion'.[66] The separating of procedural tasks (timekeeping, etc.) meant that too many student contributions were lost. However, according to the student's account, there were also notable successes. Differentiating between clarifying and expository questions proved particularly useful for the discussion. Students signalled whether their question was one of clarification on the point previously addressed or whether they intended to state an opinion or address broader issues.[67] Breakout sessions with a designated notetaker in small groups also facilitated discussion. The notes were posted online and were read out at the beginning of the class in order to put everyone on the same page.

Such attempts, albeit small, are useful to negate the conventional assumption that the teacher is the all-knowing sage of the stage of the classroom to whom students passively listen.[68] More radical attempts to destabilize this relationship may, given institutional restraints, not be practical.

Reflecting on the privileged position of the lecturer imparting knowledge should lead to the conclusion that there is no such thing as a neutral educational process. It is either about teaching conformity or transformation.[69] This leads to the question of 'what?'. Particularly in a traditional subject such as law, there are certain expectations which must be fulfilled in regard to the syllabus. A specific language must be learned, concepts explained, and cases discussed. The primary question, then, is the relationship between doctrine and theory.

Seemingly, teaching in a critical manner can be approached from one of two ways. One approach is to teach the doctrine and then 'slip in the theory'. Kennedy asserts that politicizing the classroom must begin with black letter law: 'I see myself as having a major responsibility to teach doctrine'.[70] He fears otherwise that he may 'lose the students'. Annelise Riles has written about teaching property law from the perspective of an anthropologist, viewing the relevant case as a cultural text to be interpreted discursively for their cultural meanings.[71] She attempted to teach a case by unpacking wider political and cultural issues, but soon sensed her

---

66 Ibid 137.

67 Ibid 138.

68 Canaan, op cit 36.

69 Freire (2000), op cit 34.

70 Duncan Kennedy, 'Politicizing the Classroom' [1994–1995] 4 University of Southern California Review of Law and Women's Studies 81–88, 81.

71 Annelise Riles, 'Property as Legal Knowledge: Means and Ends' [2004] 10(4) Journal of the Royal Anthropological Institute 775–795, 779.

control over the classroom slipping away.[72] On asking a colleague, he advised to 'slip the theory in'; students would not accept a 'theoretical orientation'. She reflects that 'it was doctrine that needed to emerge from the cases, not relations of ownership and their meanings'.[73]

The problem with this kind of 'slipping in' of theory means that complex theoretical issues are often presented in a simplistic, thin, way. In international law, this kind of foregrounding of doctrine frequently leads to an oscillation between legalism and realism. The rule will be presented (legalism) and then the relevant power relations will be opposed to this (realism). In regard to above-mentioned example of the 2003 US invasion of Iraq, the structure would be something like the following: Military intervention would be discussed as part of an analysis of the prohibition of the use of force under the UN regime (Art. 2 (4) UNC). This would first be presented as an important norm in international law, perhaps even a norm of *jus cogens* (binding law). Then the possible legal justifications for intervention would be set out (Art. 51 UN Charter) to determine whether the US invasion in Iraq was legal. Given that neither self-defence in accordance with the UN regime nor a UN Security Council authorization were given, the intervention is deemed illegal. The US' actions would then be explained with reference to its military and economic interests; perhaps its status as a super-power and a hegemonic power would be referenced in this context. The latter consideration of hegemony would, most likely, be the site of the 'slipping in' of the theory. Theory is in this manner reduced to crude categorizations, and rather than creating a more nuanced idea, an even larger distance between the academic observer (student/teacher) and the event could be created. A further, perhaps more pressing, problem with the prioritization of doctrine is that before slipping in the theory, one has already presented the doctrine (the law) as opposed to politics; law has taken on a neutral voice of reason. In our example of international law, the UN Charter is presented as encapsulating neutral non-political rules.

It is important to note that an over-emphasis on theory also risks a distancing from practice, and possibly reality. Freire is adamant that the centrality of theory does not mean an 'over-celebration of theory'.[74] Theory's connection with practice and to the lived experience is to be highlighted.

---

[72] Ibid 780.
[73] Ibid 782.
[74] Freire and Macedo (1995), op cit 382.

In my experience in teaching international law, a case study approach goes some way in addressing the supposed neutrality of law. One of my undergraduate courses 'International Law in Current Affairs' is organized around particular events in current affairs, some of them ongoing conflicts, some of them new developments. Around these events, I unravel international law. Sticking with the example of the Iraq war, I set out some of the general facts: That the US invaded Iraq in 2003 with the assistance of the UK; that the governments employed legal terminology to explain and defend the intervention; but that the intervention was generally perceived as 'illegal' under international law. This focus on the event allows an introduction whereby international law is *one* of the available languages to make sense of these events. One could also adopt a geo-political approach (why was it opportune from the perspective of territory and power for the US to invade Iraq at this time?), a political-economy approach (whose economic interests was the invasion serving?), a cultural-religious approach (what was the significance of tensions between the different strands of Islam and who was supporting whom?) and so on. This allows for the doctrine to be taught: What constitutes an 'illegal' intervention under international law? – However, it also highlights that the binary of legal/illegal is not employed in a neutral space. Conflicts do not fall from the sky.[75] They occur in a complicated cultural, historical, socio-economic, religious, and political context.

Importantly, I find that teaching international law in this way opens up the possibility of revealing indeterminacy, bias and manipulability in law. For example, linguistic distortions within the accepted terminology of international law can more easily be revealed and discussed. International law, particularly the law of armed conflict, is awash with such linguistic distortions: What is 'humanitarian' behind the warfare coined 'humanitarian intervention'? What is 'smart' about drones which kill from an automated high-altitude bomber? Why can the killing of civilians in warfare simply be deemed 'collateral damage'? Why is the cute sounding 'responsibility to protect', or even cuter 'R2P', used as a term to denote *further bombing*? Highlighting such distortions sensitizes students to the fact that they are dealing with dominant social constructions of images that are treated as largely unproblematic and clear.[76]

---

75 Freire (2000), op cit 21.
76 Ibid.

Gerry Simpson has warned of the pitfalls of teaching with case studies, expounding on the importance of navigating between too broad a 'theory of everything' and the narrow legalistic focus which will 'founder on a lack of explanatory power': 'The solution lies in a severe, probably traumatic, narrowing of focus followed by a broadening of perspective'.[77] The severe narrowing of focus is indeed problematic. Contextualization means a sweeping and broad-brush overview of complicated discourses from other disciplines outside of law, including anthropology, sociology, international relations, philosophy, and more. It is only possible to give a taster of these debates and one has to make the decision to foreground one particular concern.

This form of teaching presupposes and acknowledges that teaching is a political process and not nondirective and neutral. When it comes to international law, the discipline itself is highly political. Teaching, then, is always a form of politicizing students; an intervention. The question is therefore: What kind of politics am I teaching?

7 CONCLUSION

In 1982, Duncan Kennedy wrote about the reproduction of hierarchy within law schools. Over 30 years later this seems more pressing than ever. In the predominance of neoliberalism, training has become the key objective in law schools. Law is taught as a neutral apolitical discipline. Such training employs a very narrow understanding of education as well as viewing education as a means to an end. The outcome is the reproduction of hierarchies within law and within society. In international law, the reproduction of hierarchy has a global scope. The relevant hierarchies are ones which privilege the global North over the global South, men over women, heterosexual over LGBT, white over non-white.

Yet, critical pedagogy and an orientation towards *Bildung* in education may present some initial tools for counter-hegemony. Bertold Brecht's poem *In Praise of Learning* signals the potential for emancipation through learning particularly powerfully:[78]

---

[77] Gerry Simpson, 'On the Magic Mountain: Teaching Public International Law' [1999] 10 European Journal of International Law 70–92, 89.

[78] This is an excerpt from the poem in Bertold Brecht's, Die Mutter (1932, 2011) (author's translation).

Learn, man in the asylum!
Learn, man in prison!
Learn, woman in the kitchen!
Learn, sixty-year-old!
You must take the lead.
Find a school, homeless person!
Acquire knowledge, you who are freezing!
You who are hungry, grab for a book: It is a weapon.
You must take the lead.

The poem is addressed to the weak in society, those who are disadvantaged. Notably, this poem was regarded as so radical in the postwar United States, that it was the central piece Brecht was questioned on by the 'House of Un-American Activities Committee'.[79] In 1947, Brecht's anti-Nazi activities (which he had previously been celebrated for) looked to the Americans to be communist and revolutionary activities. Such suspicion illustrates particularly well how the neoliberal system, albeit then in an earlier pre-globalisation guise, is opposed to empowering those who are disempowered.

Law schools should sit at the centre of empowerment of the disenfranchised rather than reproduce disempowerment of the weak. And, in the end, this is arguably the message educators want their students to take away with them. Orford has summarized this in regard to international law as educating 'ethically aware global citizens'.[80]

Knowledge is not only a tool, or a weapon, for successfully attaining a profession. One may take from this that knowledge is not just about instrumentalism; however, I think the message is that knowledge is not about instrumentalism in a narrow sense, simply concerning the possibilities of the individual. Knowledge can also be instrumental in a wider sense, concerning the possibilities of addressing the pressing concerns of society at large.

---

[79] Entire transcript available at: http://doktorgee.worldzonepro.com/BrechtProject/HUAC.htm (accessed 17 August 2015).

[80] Anne Orford, 'Citizenship, Sovereignty and Globalisation: Teaching International Law in the Post-Soviet Era' [1995] 6 Legal Education Review 251–261.

7. Learning law differently: the importance of theory and methodology

Bal Sokhi-Bulley*

1 INTRODUCTION

> I like the word [curiosity] … . It evokes "care"; it evokes the care one takes of what exists and what might exist; a sharpened sense of reality, but one that is never immobilised before it; a readiness to find what surrounds us strange and odd; a certain determination to throw off familiar ways of thought and to look at the same things in a different way; a passion for seizing what is happening now and what is disappearing; a lack of respect for the traditional hierarchies of what is important and fundamental.[1]

I recently gave a paper where, explaining that I was adopting a 'Foucauldian perspective', I mentioned rather flippantly that my *methodology* was 'governmentality'. I took for granted that my audience would know what I meant – govern/mentality is,[2] as it says in the word itself after all, a mentality of government and hence a way of thinking about the processes of governing. I have always understood this *process of thinking* as a methodology. However, I was challenged on this and pushed to explain my viewpoint. Surely governmentality is not a methodology but a 'theory'? I do not agree but it made me think more deeply about what a methodology is, how if at all it differs from theory and also

* I would like to thank the editors for their invitation to contribute to this valuable work. I would also like to thank my colleagues at QUB for their influence on and inspiration for this piece – in particular my *Legal Theory* team of Dr Dug Cubie and Dr Natasa Mavronicola.

1 Michel Foucault, 'The Masked Philosopher' in M Foucault, *Ethics: Vol. 1: Subjectivity and Truth: Essential Works of Foucault 1954–1984* (P Rabinow (ed) R Hurley (trs)) (Penguin 2000) 321, 325. My emphasis.

2 Anne Barron, 'Foucault and Law' in J Penner et al (eds), *Jurisprudence and Legal Theory: Commentary and Materials* (OUP 2005) 955, 984.

how – given I was in a room full of non-lawyers – it is relevant to the study of law.[3] How can we teach our students to think, or learn, law differently – by making use of a variety of methodological perspectives that 'throw off familiar ways of thought and to look at the same things in a different way'?

I aim to tackle these questions in this chapter and begin with an attempt to differentiate 'theory' from 'methodology'. I then go on to focus, in Part II, on what I call 'alternative methodologies', so-called because they take a break from the dominant and traditional approach of legal positivism. In Part III, I attempt to outline how we might adopt ways of learning/teaching law differently; I describe some exercises that promote the skills of *interrogation* (curiosity) and *application* (putting the curiosity into practice) that could form part of a wider pedagogical project to encourage students and researchers to *be curious* about the law; to look at it in a different way, to challenge its traditional hierarchies, all in a bid to be less governed (as students, teachers and researchers) by its supposed neutrality and apolitical character.

2 THEORY *v* METHODOLOGY

'Why do I have to study *theory* when I am doing a law degree?' is a common question articulated by law students. The word 'theory' (used in the context of a *Legal Theory* course, for instance) connotes 'high theory' or 'philosophy' – an area alien to and surely outside the appropriate realm of a law degree. The term frightens not only law students but staff (or what I will now call 'educators') also. However, 'methodology' is not much better. Most students do not know what the term means and educators usually associate methodology with theory or with research *methods*.[4] I understand 'methodology' as having theoretical foundations but not being *about theory*; it is instead about understanding how to *use theoretical tools* (hence I use the terms perspective, approach, way of thinking and lens in this chapter to describe 'methodology').

---

3 For more on govermentality as a methodology, see Bal Sokhi-Bulley 'Governmentality: Notes on the Thought of Michel Foucault', on *Critical Legal Thinking: Key Concepts*. Available at: http://criticallegalthinking.com/2014/12/02/governmentality-notes-thought-michel-foucault/ (accessed 10 January 2015).

4 For further comment on this and the distinction between 'methodology' and 'method', see Bal Sokhi-Bulley 'Alternative Methodologies' (2013) 2 *Law and Method* 6–23.

'Methodology' is technically defined as 'a system of ways of doing, teaching or studying something'.[5] What is not typically highlighted is that it is also a system, or way of thinking, about how to do the study or activity. Academic teaching and learning requires us to think *critically* – indeed 'critical thinking' is a key factor of assessment. Methodological awareness is thus highly significant as it informs *how* we think critically. Are you interested in questions concerning the rule of law and the 'what is law' question? You are most likely coming from a positivist methodology. Are you interested in questions concerning gendered power relations in society? You are perhaps coming from a feminist perspective. The point is that it is important to be aware of your perspective, or way of thinking, since this *is your* methodology. A methodology is a way of approaching the law, or a research project; it is your perspective, your approach, your *system of methods for thinking*. It is also highly significant because it influences the research questions that you ask, which in turn influences the narrative and then the outcome of your project, and indeed the way in which you interpret 'law'. Methodology is, moreover, personal – at least to one's own project. The way in which we research, or think our projects or think the law, is an attitude – more precisely a 'critical attitude'.[6] However, the individualization is only important as researchers. As educators we are responsible for allowing our students to develop their own critical attitudes by exposing them to something of a canon, or at least a range, of legal research methodologies.

Whether borrowing the way of thinking from positivism, feminism(s), international relations or indeed any other approach, the key is that you are thinking about how you are thinking! I have elsewhere described methodology as a *skill*.[7] It is a skill to be able to think differently about the law. Whilst questions concerning the nature of the law, why we obey the law and its relation to morality are integral to an understanding of the discipline, so are questions concerning the claim of the law to neutrality (as to gender, class, race, culture, etc.) and autonomy (is the law about politics? About society? About power? How then can it ignore the influence of the disciplines of political theory, sociology, anthropology

---

[5] Cambridge Dictionaries Online. Available at: http://dictionary.cambridge.org/dictionary/british/methodology (accessed 10 January 2015).

[6] Michel Foucault, 'What is Critique?', in Michel Foucault, *The Politics of Truth* (S Lotringer and L Hochroth (eds)) (Semiotext(e) 1997) 24. See also Panu Minkkinen on 'critical legal method' in 'Critical Legal "Method" as Attitude', in Dawn Watkins and Mandy Burton (eds), *Research Methods in Law* (Routledge 2013) 119.

[7] See Sokhi-Bulley (2013), *op cit*.

and philosophy, for instance?). The 'integral' questions are the concern of the traditional legal perspectives – namely legal positivism and natural law theory. The skills associated with these or indeed *any* methodology are twofold: they are the skills of *interrogation* and *application*. That is, *interrogation* as the skill of being able to ask different questions about the same issue or project (whether based on the rule of law, or gender, or race, for instance) and *application* as the skill of being able to apply a range of different methodologies to the problem to thereby arrive at different outcomes through telling different narratives. Think of the 'methodologies' then as *not* 'theories' but as 'tools' that can be *used* to work through the problem; or as 'lenses' that magnify certain themes and not others (rule of law, gender, race, power, etc.).

3 A CANON OF LEGAL METHODOLOGIES?

The Absence of a Canon

There are now a number of texts available on legal research methods and/or methodologies of legal research. Notable recent texts include Mike McConville and Wing Hong Chui's *Research Methods for Law* – which interestingly uses the language of 'method' and 'methodology' interchangeably and refers to the possibility of a method being theoretical; the book aims to make 'available methods of research – legalistic, empirical, comparative and *theoretical*' accessible to law students. *Research Methods in Law*, edited by Dawn Watkins and Mandy Burton, tackles the semantics of method *versus* methodology directly, highlighting that there is not agreement on a single, canonical definition of these terms. What is important, the editors assert, is that of the contributors to the volume 'all of them agree that establishing an appropriate theoretical basis for a research project is as important as determining the appropriate method/s for carrying out the research'.[8] And this is the point of my chapter – to assert that awareness of methodology is important for teaching *and doing* law. The Watkins and Burton collection also presents a 'challenge [to] readers who are intending to take a pure, doctrinal approach to their research to provide a justification for the reason for doing so'.[9] Mark Van Hoecke's *Methodologies of Legal Research: What Kind of Discipline for What Kind of Method* offers an interesting and contrasting perspective to my own – Van Hoecke suggests that law

[8] Watkins & Burton (2013), *op cit* 2–3.
[9] Ibid 4.

should not try to integrate itself with other disciplines in the social sciences (this goes against my proposing, as you will see in particular below, that we do indeed borrow the theoretical way of thinking that is a more inherent part of other social science disciplines such as International Relations and Political Theory); such integration, he suggests, would lead to problems of epistemology, of methodology and of research skills.[10] Yet, can we borrow the *theoretical character* of other disciplines, so as adopt a more conscious and educated *critical attitude*?

There are also, of course, a range of textbooks on *legal theory* or *jurisprudence*, which suggest the importance of theorising in law. Those that are more 'traditional' in style – such as Hilaire McCoubrey and Nigel White's *Textbook on Jurisprudence*[11] – and those that adopt a deliberately alternative style which reflects a rejection of the traditional style of academic writing, such as Costas Douzinas and Adam Geary's *Critical Jurisprudence*.[12] The more traditional style favours 'legal positivism' as 'the "properly" legal perspective',[13] focusing on this (and on natural law theories). There are usually subsequent chapters on 'postmodern legal theory', or 'feminism and law' for example – these being examples of what I call 'alternative methodologies'.[14] The traditional approaches represent the activity of 'jurisprudence' (i.e. interrogating the conscience of the law)[15] as an *internal* task; these internal perspectives (of positivism and natural law) rely on the position of the judge or lawyer.[16] The external theories (and these are what I call 'alternative' approaches) search for a broader socio-logical, socio-legal and non-legal context for the 'facts' expounded by the judges and lawyers. These external theories, as Douzinas and Gearey also argue, have been

---

[10] Mark Van Hoecke, *Methodologies of Legal Research. Which Kind of Method for Which Kind of Discipline?* (Hart 2013) xiii.

[11] Hilaire McCoubrey and Nigel White, *Textbook on Jurisprudence* (Blackstone Press 1999).

[12] Costas Douzinas and Adam Gearey, *Critical Jurisprudence: The Political Philosophy of Justice* (Hart 2005).

[13] Minkkinen (2013), *op cit* 119. Minkkinen takes this from HLA Hart, *The Concept of Law* (OUP 2012).

[14] See for example and also James E Penner et al, *Introduction to Jurisprudence and Legal Theory* (OUP 2005) and Suri Ratnapala, *Jurisprudence* (second edition, OUP 2013).

[15] This is a definition of jurisprudence to which I refer below and which is taken from Douzinas and Gearey (2005) *op cit* 1.

[16] This distinction between internal and external theories is made by Douzinas and Gearey (2005), *op cit* 5.

'demoted' in the traditional law school curriculum where 'legal positivism has been the dominant and typically modernist internal approach'.[17] This has led, they argue, to the 'moral poverty of the jurisprudence of the twentieth century'.[18] I argue that the external approaches, or what I am calling 'alternative' (i.e., to legal positivism) approaches to law are necessary so that we, and our students, might discover alterative truths about the law and about society. I have already made this point elsewhere.[19] What I want to stress in this chapter is that aside from/as well as this discrepancy in the law school curriculum between internal and external theories,[20] there is a *lack of awareness* and a resultant *lack of curiosity* amongst students and educators on both the variety of legal perspectives, and on their value to an objective and interrogative study of law. This interrogative element is crucial to a (legal) education, since 'the very process of theorizing itself becomes a vital object of inquiry'.[21]

There is thus no set 'canon of legal theories', or legal methodologies or perspectives. A typical range of perspectives is easier to identify in other 'theoretical discipline[s]' such as International Relations[22] – although even here there is a great diversity of conceptions of theory, making IR a 'discipline of theoretical disagreements; a "divided discipline"'.[23] We attempted something of a 'canon' in the *Research Methodologies in EU and International Law* book.[24] The non-exhaustive list of perspectives that are presented in this book are split into two sections: the internal, or traditional, approaches – or what we called the 'Main Jurisprudential Approaches' – that is, legal positivism and natural law perspectives. The second section consists of the external or alternative approaches – labelled 'Extensions and Negations'. This latter section is then split further into 'Modern and Critical Approaches' and the 'Law And'

---

17 Ibid.

18 Ibid.

19 Sokhi-Bulley (2013), *op cit.*

20 Elsewhere, a distinction is made between explanatory (theories that test hypotheses and propose causal explanations with the intention of identifying trends and patterns) and constitutive theories (theories that examine *lenses* through which to view the world – language, culture, religion, ethnicity, class and gender, for example) – see Scott Burchill and Andrew Linklater 'Introduction', in Scott Burchill et al, *Theories of International Relations* (Palgrave Macmillan 2009) 16–18.

21 Ibid 3.

22 Ibid 1.

23 Ibid 5. Burchill is quoting Holsti here.

24 Rob Cryer, Tamara Hervey and Bal Sokhi-Bulley, *Research Methodologies in EU and International Law* (Hart 2011), *op cit.*

approaches. The former includes governance, Marxism, critical theory, feminist perspectives and postcolonial theory, and the latter includes law and geography, law and international relations, and law and economics. These categorizations attempt to cover a range of theoretical perspectives that pay respect to the dominant traditions within law but which also nod to interdisciplinarity and learning techniques of interrogation and application from disciplines such as IR, politics and philosophy, and also to other and specific areas of law, such as international law which has a more obvious and accepted theoretical basis.[25] Crucially for the law student (it is for this genre that the book is primarily written) each perspective is illustrated using examples of writings in EU and international law that take this particular approach – so, for example, the section on 'queer theory' refers to Nico Beger's re-reading of the *Grant* and *P v S* cases (re sex discrimination in the employment of transsexuals) heard by the Court of Justice of the European Union.[26] What we highlight in particular is the types of questions that each perspective allows you to ask; it is as if each perspective is a lens bringing into magnified focus certain themes and issues. A queer perspective is thus interested in *heteronormativity* and the issues of gender and sexuality – Beger's article, for instance, provides a critique of 'sex', 'gender' and 'identity' as the foundations for rights battles. The 'queer theory looking glass'[27] allows her to make the wider observation that the Court made intelligible a homosexual identity and then excluded it as deviant through maintaining a 'heteronormative binary gender system'[28] in its reasoning. In the book we also provide materials that were used in either or both of the workshops that preceded and informed the book. There are two types of activities listed here – activities designed to promote awareness in the postgraduate research student of various possible approaches (such as those included in the 'canon' according to the book); and, activities intended to help the student identify and articulate her own approach.[29]

---

[25] Some of the inspiration for 'the list' of methodologies in the book is taken from Steven Ratner and Anne-Marie Slaughter's *The Methods of International Law* (ASIL/Hein 2004).

[26] Nico J Beger, 'Queer Readings of Europe: Gender Identity, Sexual Orientation and the (Im)potency of Rights Politics at the European Court of Justice' (2000) 9 *Social and Legal Studies* 249.

[27] Ibid 258.

[28] Ibid 264.

[29] For example, activities promoting reflection on the latter (the student's own approach) include: The Dunleavy 'dinner party test'; 'imagining your

4 WHAT A CANON MIGHT LOOK LIKE

Given that there *is no* canon, then, of legal methodologies/theories/perspectives, what ought a canon of legal theories to look like? I believe it would and should encompass traditional and alternative perspectives – but also that it provide guidelines on *how to apply* these. It thus needs to emphasize theory not only as a methodological perspective but also as a skill. The course on *Legal Theory* that I run and teach with two other colleagues attempts to do this. The module starts by asking the questions of 'what is law' and 'why do we obey the law', before moving on to how to look at the law differently – i.e. from different critical perspectives. There is a strong focus on *how to apply* these different theoretical perspectives to current legal issues and problems – and we use case studies to look at critical perspectives on rights, on judgment writing and on the unproblematic giving of foreign aid, for instance. The course itself is structured in four parts: (1) Introduction and Legal Theory as Skill; (2) Traditional Legal Theory (Why do we Obey the Law & What is Law?); (3) Critical Legal Perspectives & Law Today; and (4) Essay Writing Skills and Feedback. The skills sessions focus on presenting *theory as a skill* to the students (so, for instance, we replace the well-known ILAC formulation for how to solve a legal problem question with the ITAC formulation – I explain this further in Part III, below). They learn to read current situations and legal problems through different lenses – for instance, I covered Foucault on poststructuralism and power using the illustration of the recent Ferguson Riots of August 2014; this lens allows us to see and interrogate the type of conducting power at play (police power) and to question forms of resistance, or counter-conduct, to that power.[30] It is a different type of interrogation and application to the internal or descriptive (i.e. positivist), which might focus on the rule of law, on statute and on criminalization.

Exposure to theory as methodology, or skill, should really happen in the early stages of the student's life – so, ideally in the first year of the degree. This would ensure that not only are students exposed to the essential elements of black-letter law, but that they learn to interrogate the assumptions made therein and to thereby see black-letter law (or what I have above called legal positivism) as *a* single perspective (as opposed to *the* 'properly' legal perspective). Collaboration between other (core)

---

research as a picture' and 'the Thinking Hats exercise' – Cryer et al (2011), *op cit* Appendix A.

30 Bal Sokhi-Bulley, 'Performing Struggle: *Parrhēsia* in Ferguson' (2015) 26(1) *Law and Critique* 7–10.

modules taught would also be ideal – can contract law be studied from a Foucauldian perspective? Can property law be studied from a feminist perspective? Should students know, and question why, the dominant teaching technique favours legal positivism? These are important and challenging questions for critical legal education. It would be a fascinating project to take on to examine how interrogation (and then exercises in application) can be integrated into the core law modules – and one that the scope of this chapter, which is to challenge the current legal pedagogical attitude, does not allow (but proposes).

5 LEARNING LAW DIFFERENTLY

Teaching Methods *v* Teaching of Methodologies

When you use the language of 'skill', it is easier to market methodology as useful – both as a teaching and research tool. But talking about methodology as 'skill' is not falsely selling it. Methodology is not only theory and does not need to involve 'high theory' – I, for instance, would say I *do* critical theory in that I use Foucauldian tools to interrogate discourses of rights and governance but I would not call myself a 'theorist'. And by 'doing theory' here I mean using a set of (methodological) tools to interrogate the assumed autonomy and apolitical nature of the law. These semantic subtleties are also important because there is an aversion to 'theory' within the discipline. Having taught *Legal Theory* for the last three years, I see that students do not (initially at least) see the point of being asked to read Plato, Socrates and Hobbes, for instance. In my institution at least, *Legal Theory* is not a compulsory module – and although this compulsory element differs between institutions, 'legal theory' or 'jurisprudence' is always taught as one module in any one year of study (i.e. it does not inform all modules or indeed all years of education) and is usually not taught in Year 1 as an integral and upfront element of learning law.[31]

---

[31] Taking a random sample out of the top 100 universities (according to the Times Higher Education World University Rankings 2014–15: Europe) the LLB at the following institutions features Legal Theory in the following forms: London School of Economics – no compulsory module in Legal Theory or Jurisprudence (ranked thirty-fourth); King's College London – *Jurisprudence and Legal Theory* is a core Level 3 module (ranked forthieth); University of Bristol – *Jurisprudence* is a core module in Level 2 (ranked seventy-fourth).

Why is it that most students are averse to 'theory' (i.e. reading Plato or Marx for instance – and I speak here from my own experience of having taught in higher education for the best part of ten years)? Why do the vast majority resist anything that is not visibly identifiable as 'black-letter' law? One reason is certainly the continued reproduction of hierarchy in legal education.[32] Students enter a competitive environment where they face subordination and rivalry from their peers and also from the system, which marks, ranks and labels them (as successful or not); there is a race to qualify, for places on vacation schemes, for training contracts, and so forth. Another reason is that education in today's version of liberal society is a commodity: students buy an education and they expect to get what they pay for – guaranteed entry into the next stage of their law careers, legal *practice*. The relevance of legal theory to practice is so far beyond them that they simply are not interested in investing in something (i.e. doing the reading, attending class) for modules that they think will not strategically benefit them.

And yet law schools continually produce successful students that go on to be successful lawyers. Students produce themselves as effective consumers of the law school education model – they engage in a self-fashioning process (by attending lectures, sitting exams, following careers advice, for example) – which means they become effective legal personae.[33] Teaching through conservative syllabi, fostering a competitive atmosphere – in which law fairs featuring prominent firms are the most readily available options for the future and limiting options available in other disciplines – all work as the minor and mundane functionings of power which produce the governmentable subject that is the graduate law student. And this is not to say that law is not *taught* in innovative ways. I have worked with colleagues, for instance, who put huge amounts of energy into developing new pedagogical techniques – such as 'problem-based learning' (where the traditional lecture mode is abandoned in favour of engaging the whole lecture room in a problem scenario – which may be as simple as the 'traffic light example' – which they have already read up on or been provided with video lectures on;[34]

Available at: http://www.timeshighereducation.co.uk/world-university-rankings/2014-15/world-ranking/region/europe (accessed 10 January 2015).

32 Duncan Kennedy, *Legal Education and the Reproduction of Hierarchy. A Polemic Against the System* (NYU Press 2004).

33 Matthew Ball, 'Becoming a "Bastion Against Tyranny": Australian Legal Education and the Government of the Self' [2012] 23(2) *Law and Critique* 103.

34 See for example, Mohsen al Attar, 'An Introduction to Legal Theory'. Available at: http://mohsenalattar.org/2013/08/30/an-introduction-to-legal-theory/

encouraging and assessing student participation through mooting (using a moot court scenario to facilitate learning of a particular topic);[35] and using a Twitter competition to help collective student learning and allow sharing of ideas.[36] However, the issue here is not about teaching *methods* but the teaching *of methodologies*. It is an issue about the conservative content of law school modules. Why is the conservative content of law modules then a problem? I am not saying that it is a problem *per se* – certainly not that it is bad (we are still producing successful graduates). But it is not 'good' either – because it is dangerous; we are involved, through our role on the operation of pastoral power and the governmentality of legal education, in producing a docile body. Pastoral power refers here to a 'power of care',[37] which literally resembles, in terms of the educator-student relation, the relation of a shepherd towards his flock. It is a relation that involves responsibility and beneficence on the part of the shepherd/educator. By the 'governmentality of legal education', I refer to the processes that regulate the behaviour of students, their 'conduct of conduct' to produce a body that is governmentable, and

---

(accessed 10 January 2015). The 'traffic light example' refers simply to the scenario: would you drive through a red traffic light in a situation where there were no other pedestrians or traffic to witness you do so and no possibility that you might injure someone.

35 This was an activity used by a colleague, Dug Cubie, module convenor on the postgraduate course *Human Rights: Concepts and Institutions* (LAW8100), Queen's University Belfast in the week covering the human rights implications of climate change and was based on two recent New Zealand refugee cases: *AF (Kiribati)* [2013] NZIPT 800413 and *AD (Tuvalu)* [2014] NZIPT 501370-371. The mooting activity was one of a series of activities carried over the semester (others included presentations and debates) that counted for 10 per cent of the overall module mark.

36 @QUBContract and #qconlaw. Another colleague at Queen's University Belfast, Marek Martynisyn, used this on a large undergraduate course, Contract Law (LAW2040). According to Dr Martynisyn's guidelines:

> Tweets are to provide short pieces of information on key points or cases raised in lectures or reading materials, not tutorials. It is hoped these tweets would reflect subject matter that you found useful or helpful in understanding an issue or case. These tweets will hopefully aid your memory of key issues and assist other students in learning.

Prizes were offered as incentive for participation: 'To be counted for the weekly prize students should submit at least three tweets for a week. The overall prize requires students to contribute three tweets for at least five weeks (not necessarily continuous).'

37 Michel Foucault, *Security, Territory, Population: Lectures at the Collège de France, 1977–1978* (M Senellart (ed) (Palgrave Macmillan 2007) 127).

docile (these processes include, for example, the law school curriculum which favours internal interrogation and core topics devoid of theoretical content, the delivery of material in lecture theatres – in which the layout, behaviour of students such as notetaking and performance by the educator is relevant – and, assessment procedures such as exams). The governmentable, docile body is 'dangerous' – or let us say problematic as this sounds less sensational – because it is a body that is not adequately trained since it does not have the skills of interrogation and the application of various modes of thinking to different legal problems.

Different modes of thinking produce different outcomes. Is it important, for example, to shed say a feminist perspective on judicial reasoning and question: what is it important to consider here? What should be magnified under the legal lens? Should it be reasonableness, common sense? Should it be to challenge assumptions, stereotypes and myths about the law's claim to (gender) neutrality? The Feminist Judgments Project, which is a 'unique, imaginative collaboration in which a group of feminist legal scholars set out to write alternative feminist judgments in significant legal cases',[38] represents an original and clever illustration of the importance of a different methodological lens. As Baronness Hale (who remains the first and only female judge of the UK's Supreme Court) suggests:[39]

> It is no longer possible to assert that [...] the law should assign an inferior status to women or deny them the same rights as men; or that the only reality is the reality of men's experience [. ...] But of course it is possible to assert that the substance and practice of the law do not (yet) measure up to either of them.

Moreover, and important from a methodological standpoint:[40]

> *it makes such a difference how the story is told.* Feminist judges will take different facts from the mass of detail to *tell the story in a different way*, to bring out the features which others discard, and to explain the features which others find difficult to understand.

A different lens, be it feminist or postcolonial or poststructural, allows for a different kind of interrogation, a different curiosity about the same things, or facts. Does it not matter that telling the story differently might

---

[38] Rosemary Hunter, Clare McGlynn and Erika Rackley (eds), *Feminist Judgments: From Theory to Practice* (Hart 2009) 3.

[39] Ibid, Foreword by Baroness Hale.

[40] Ibid. (My emphasis.)

lead to a different outcome – to a different judgment or sentence entirely? The range of judgments covered in the project book (23 in total) is broad, from the role of trespass in civil law, to the role of consent in actual bodily harm in criminal law, to cases involving the Human Rights Act 1998. The project is a perfect illustration of the skills of interrogation and application – reading and understanding and *telling* the same facts differently.[41]

The Skills: Interrogation + Application

'Reading law books is like eating sawdust. Few of us have escaped the dry taste in the mouth occasioned by the study of jurisprudence',[42] write Douzinas and Gearey. It is a sentiment that students of course identify with. Jurisprudence can refer to case law – reading endless judgments handed down by, in most cases, old white men does not surprisingly leave a dry taste in the mouth! Yet jurisprudence also has a much more nuanced and challenging aspect which is less passive (reading) and more active (asking the student to think) – it is the 'prudence' of the law (*jus*); that is, 'law's consciousness and conscience', or 'the truth about the law'.[43] To discover this element of 'conscience' or 'truth', necessitates scrutiny – it calls for 'scientific and philosophical investigations of the social phenomenon of the law and justice generally'.[44] I am building up to the point that the study of jurisprudence is about investigation – or what I will presently describe as the skill of *interrogation*. Devlin, tackling the question of 'what is legal theory and why does it matter' answers that it is:[45] 'a multi-dimensional *interrogative process* in pursuit of a *better understanding of the nature and functions of law* … . The interrogative dimension is particularly important.' From this he identifies seven big questions: (1) What is the nature of law? (2) Why, or when, is a law valid? (3) What role do legal institutions, rules or procedures fulfil in society? (4) How does law fulfil those functions? (5) How important is law in society? (6) What perspectives, overtly or covertly, inform legal

---

[41] It is interesting to note that of the six essay questions set for the final assessment on *Legal Theory*, over half of the students chose to answer the question on FJP, showing a strong interest in this 'alternative truths' approach.

[42] Douzinas & Gearey (2005), *op cit* 1.

[43] Ibid.

[44] Suri Ratnapala, *Jurisprudence* (1st edn, CUP 2009) 3.

[45] R Devlin, 'Jurisprudence for Judges: Why Legal Theory Matters for Social Context Education' [2001] 27 *Queen's Law Journal* 161.

institutions, rules and procedures? (7) What is the relationship between law and social change?

Jurisprudence, as legal theory, is fundamentally about *questioning* the claim of the law to neutrality, autonomy and an apolitical character. These questions form a methodological disposition. Devlin's questions are significant from a positivist standpoint. Why does he need to articulate this disposition? Because it informs the types of questions that he will be interested in asking.[46] It is also important to articulate your position and be aware that *there is more than one way to interrogate.* Different methodological positions offer different ways of interrogating – they offer, in other words, different *tools* with which to interrogate the law. Viewed in this way, a methodology is not (just) a theory but a *tool* of interrogation. This is how we market legal theory to our students – as tools of interrogation that are teaching them the skills of interrogation and application. Let me illustrate with the example of an interactive session we conducted on the *Pistorius Trial.*

We chose the trial since students could not help but be familiar with the events given its prominence in the media since the early part of the year (2014). Students were provided with a 'brief' and asked to read the judgment prior to the session.[47] They were asked to consider what I called 'judicial conscience' – the judicial approach according to the conscience of the law. In sentencing Oscar Pistorius to five years in prison for culpable homicide for causing the death of Reeva Steenkamp, Judge Thokozile Masipa said she considered her sentence: '*fair* and *just*, both to society and to the accused … . A non-custodial sentence would send the wrong message to the community. On the other hand, a long sentence would not be appropriate either, as it would lack the element of *mercy*.' Students were then asked to examine the elements of fairness, justice and mercy and their relevance to judicial conscience and reasoning *from a positivist and natural law perspective.* They were asked to think about judicial conscience in light of the themes of these two traditional legal perspectives – that is, the nature of law and why we obey it. So, questions that were of interest were held to be: *What is* law? Why

[46] See Sokhi-Bulley (2013) *op cit,* for an explanation of the relationship between research questions, methodology and the hypothesis of a research project.

[47] The State and Oscar Leonard Carl Pistorius CC13/2013, Vol. 42, pp 3280–3351. Available: https://juror13lw.files.wordpress.com/2014/09/pistorius-trial-judgement.pdf (accessed 10 January 2015).

do we *obey* the law? What is a '*hard case*'?[48] What is the role of the *rule of law?* And they were asked to consider judicial *discretion* and the relationship between law and morality. The actual question for discussion (and which formed the basis of a subsequent formative assessment) was the following: 'Throughout the centuries, there has been an on-going debate between natural lawyers and positivists as to the connection between law and morality. Do you think that Judge Masipa's use of 'fairness', 'justice' and 'mercy' shows that the law is not separate from morality? Discuss all three concepts in your answer.'

The objective of the exercise is to encourage students to *interrogate* and *apply*. That is, to question the role of fairness, justice and mercy in judicial decision-making and in the law itself. Using the tools of positivism and natural law theory, they were encouraged to consider whether Pistorius was a hard case, whether Judge Masipa has fulfilled her 'Herculean' function,[49] and to question the integrity of criminal law and criminal justice. The type of questioning is important as it influences the narrative comment made on the judgment (and what this in turn tells us about the role of fairness, justice and mercy in judicial conscience and in the conscience of the law) – in this instance, looking at the judgment and sentencing from a positivist and natural law perspective incites, for instance, a problematization of the 'reasonableness' standard (that is, the basic criminal law principle of innocent until proven guilty beyond *reasonable* doubt[50] – how is this qualified, according to what standards of fairness, justice and mercy?). It problematizes also 'intention' and 'negligence' (Pistorius was determined to have had the 'intention' to shoot but not to have had the intention to *kill* the person behind the bathroom door and his behaviour was held to be 'negligent',[51] and this resulted in a determination of culpable homicide, rather than murder). Effectively, interrogating the what and why of the law in this way questions the sentence itself – would true 'justice' have been a more

---

[48] See for example, SJ Shapiro, 'The "Hart-Dworkin" Debate: A Short Guide for the Perplexed' [2007] Working Paper No. 77, *Public Law and Legal Theory Working Paper Series*, University of Michigan Law School. Available at: http://papers.ssrn.com/sol3/papers.cfm?abstract_id=968657 (accessed 10 August 2015).

[49] Ronald Dworkin, *Law's Empire* (Hart 1998) 1–86.

[50] See the 'test of the reasonable man' at p. 3329 of the judgment.

[51] The following statements by the judge support this view: 'The accused had intention to shoot at the person in the toilet but states that he never intended to kill that person' (at p. 3325 of the judgment) – and 'I am of the view that the accused acted too hastily and used excessive force. In the circumstances it is clear that his conduct was negligent' (at p. 3334 of the judgment).

severe sentence than five years' imprisonment? To whom does 'fairness' apply – to the victim (Reeva), to the defendant (Pistorius) or to the public? And what does 'mercy' mean – should Pistorius' disability have been taken into account to a greater extent, or was it taken into account too much?[52]

Parallels were drawn here with Lon Fuller's hypothetical case study of *The Speluncean Explorers*, where the five judges in the case differ in their reasoning thereby showing the ambiguous relationship between law and morality (or fairness, justice and mercy).[53] Whether the four surviving explorers of a landslide that left them caved in, are guilty of murder of the fifth explorer (who they killed and ate; following intermittent radio contact which informed them that they were likely to starve before being rescued) is the issue in court, where the judges faced immense public pressure to not convict the survivors despite the wording of the relevant statute being clear in this regard ('Whoever shall wilfully take the life of another shall be punished by death' – NCSA Statute para. 12-A). Chief Justice Trupenny and Justice Keen adopted positivist perspectives – where, observing the letter of the law, they upheld the convictions (with Trupenny putting in a plea for clemency from the Executive). Justice Foster, taking a natural law, purposive approach and advocating an 'inner morality' of law, overturned the conviction. The explorers were, he claimed subject to the 'laws of nature' and acted in self-defence, their actions were thus morally justified. As did Justice Handy, whose argument was based in a pragmatic, common sense approach where he observed that 90 per cent of the public favoured innocence – this is the opinion he sided with. Justice Tatting, able to see both sides of the argument (and indeed the law *versus* morality debate) did not reach a decision and withdrew. Why is it interesting to observe the judicial conscience in this case? What does it matter which perspective or lens the judge uses? It matters because the perspective influences the sentence, the narrative, and the truth. Different verdicts were reached by the

---

52 Note Judge Masipa's comment at p. 3317:

> It is also understandable, that a person with a disability such as that of the accused would certainly feel vulnerable, when faced with danger. I hasten to add however that the accused is not unique in this respect. Women, children, the elderly and all those with limited mobility would fall under the same category, but would it be reasonable if without further ado, they armed themselves with a firearm when threatened with danger. I do not think so, as every case would depend on its own merits.

53 Lon Fuller, 'The Case of the Speluncean Explorers' (1949) 62 *Harvard Law Review* 616.

judges because they came from differing perspectives – those favouring the positivist perspective (who upheld the statute and therefore the rule of law) favoured conviction; those coming from a natural law perspective considered the (inner) morality and purpose of the law and favoured innocence. Theoretical perspectives, or methodological lenses, are thus hugely significant tools for the analysis of legal problems as they determine not only how the case is judged, according to what themes, principles and values, but also determine outcomes. They enable the judge to tell a story – their own version of the *truth*.

We then take this exercise on *interrogation* + *application* further by asking students to consider what the reasoning and sentence might look like from a range of other, alternative perspectives: for instance, feminism, postcolonial theory and a Foucauldian perspective. Table 7.1 below highlights what themes are relevant in terms of the fairness, justice and mercy considerations (underlined and in bold) and, crucially, what different types of questions looking at the same set of facts in *Pistorius* are able to be asked – so, for instance, from a feminist perspective, the theme (or, as I like to call it, 'magic word') of 'gender' (as a power relation) becomes relevant and we ask questions about the victim (Reeva) rather than about Pistorius' sporting career.

Students had the opportunity to answer a question on the use of different lenses to tell alternative truths about the Pistorius Trial in their summative assessments, where the question set was: 'Write a commentary on the judgment and sentencing in the Pistorius Trial from *one* of the following perspectives: natural law, feminist, postcolonial, or Foucauldian. Do you think that this perspective tells an 'alternative truth about the event?' The objective, therefore, of the Pistorius exercise is to show that theory can be a tool for creating alternative truths – alternative narratives about the same event, which change depending on the lens that you look through.

From ILAC to ITAC

Applying theory is then a *skill*. But *how* do you actually 'apply' theory (or a set of methodological tools) to a factual scenario? A useful formula is *ITAC* – Issue, *Theory*, Apply, Conclusion. It is a variation on a formula that students will already be accustomed to when learning problem question-solving; here the technique is ILAC – Issue, *Law*, Apply, Conclusion. When given a problem question (i.e. a factual scenario where they are to 'solve' the problem by giving legal advice), students are taught to write their answer by presenting an Introduction (which should contain the facts and highlight the Issue); they should then identify the

Table 7.1 Perspectives for exercise for interrogation and application

Feminist lens	**Postcolonial lens**	**Poststructural lens: Foucault**
Justice/fairness/mercy – what was being talked about after the sentencing? Was **gender** a relevant consideration? **Question:** Does *violence against women* go ignored in the courtroom? Is sport more important than 'justice'? (See comment in *The Guardian*[1] on what was being talked about: Pistorius' sporting career NOT Reeva Steenkamp's killing).	*Justice/fairness/mercy* – was **race** a factor in the courtroom? **Question:** Were some of the criticisms levelled at Judge Masipa perpetuating the idea of *black* women as less able to be competent judges? **OR** did the trial perpetuate the idea of *the black man as criminal* in South African society (*hypothetical black man in bathroom*)	*Justice/fairness/mercy* – what **power relations** exist in the courtroom, what is being produced? **Question:** Does the courtroom reproduce attitudes of sympathy (or mercy) towards *disabled* subjects? **OR** Was Pistorius given a more lenient sentence due to his status as a vulnerable victim (as a *disabled* person)?

Note: 1. Suzanne Moore, 'Reeva Steenkamp was a victim of male violence. That is the real story', *The Guardian*, 24 October 2014; <http://www.theguardian.com/commentisfree/2014/oct/22/discussion-of-reeva-steenkamp-killing-has-sidelined-male-violence?CMP=EMCNEWEML6619I2> accessed 10 January 2015.

relevant Law and then Apply that law to the facts and issue(s) of the problem scenario. They should end with a Conclusion that summarizes their advice and offers an opinion on the legal advice given or on the law. The ITAC formula thus follows the same basic problem-solving principle that students are already accustomed to, taught in their 'black-letter' modules anyway; the change is simply that rather than thinking *Law* and apply, think *Theory* and apply. In other words, you are teaching students the skill of using the methodological tools or lenses that they have been exposed to (e.g. power, gender, race) to solve the problem. So, for instance, if in the Pistorius question they were to use the 'theory' (or methodological tool) of power or governmentality and look at the problem through the Foucauldian lens, they would be able to make a comment on disability and the treatment of disabled subjects in the courtroom, for example, and as per the table above. It was interesting to observe that the students engaged with the exercise with enthusiasm during the interactive session. The quality of the work produced was of a high standard and the style in which the essays were written was also noteworthy – it seems that students can express their own attitude and curiosity in a more personal and confident way when asked to look through a lens that they identify with. Of course, they were also judged on and made use of the legal skills of how to read and cite a case, how to evaluate judicial reasoning and discretion, and on written presentational skills.

If teaching were to adopt this simple technique of teaching interrogation and application, students would perhaps see the relevance of theory as a methodological tool. The use of case studies, such as the *Pistorius Trial*, illustrates a neat, understandable and contemporary way to 'teach' the usefulness of theory and methodology. By way of another illustration, I convene another module on human rights, which I named quite simply *Understanding Human Rights*. One of its key objectives is to give students a *better* understanding of rights – by asking them to *interrogate* rights through *applying* different methodological tools in different rights situations, or case studies. This means we understand rights using different critical perspectives – namely Marxist, feminist, poststructural, postcolonial and CLS perspectives – and under different thematic headings, namely rights and capitalism (Marxism), rights and power (poststructuralism), rights and bodies (feminist and queer perspectives on rights), rights and imperialism (postcolonial perspectives) and rights and international humanitarianism (CLS critique of rights). Each of these thematic areas is then explored over two weeks. The course intends to highlight how an understanding of critique furthers our understanding of rights – hence it focuses on the *application* of critical perspectives (i.e. why is it useful to understand – and interrogate – rights using, for instance, a feminist perspective? Interrogation here refers to challenging the assumptions that we make about rights – for instance, that they are *only* emancipatory, that they are apolitical and indicators of good state practice), using contemporary examples to be discussed in seminars – such as the Occupy Wall Street movement, rape as a war crime, the war on terror, rioting as resistance, and the role of human rights NGOs in rights protection and promotion, such as Human Rights Watch. Students have a very active role in the sessions (which are run as seminars – with a focus on facilitation of learning, rather than teaching – instead of as lectures) and a component of assessment is student presentations, which happen on each of the case study weeks. I have found that students engage well with the case studies, which are based in contemporary events that they have already some exposure to and so generally have opinions on – so, for example, I 'teach' poststructuralism and Foucault through riots, looking at whether there is a right to resist and a right way to resist and the notion of counter-conduct as the other side of governmentality and do so using the recent example of the London Riots[54] of 2011 and also the Ferguson Riots of 2014.[55] Writing a comment on riots from a positivist perspective may focus on the rule of law, on the need for and level of criminalization and judicial response. However, the Foucauldian lens enables you to tell a different narrative – it highlights the construction of the rioter as 'thug' or '*only* criminal' and thereby highlights the way in which there is a right way to resist in liberal democracy and there is no right to resistance in law. Why is this important? Because it promotes curiosity – about rights, about our society, about its values. It also promotes awareness of different ways of thinking and this is surely a skill that all students should have; law students, who despite doing a vocational course which requires a core knowledge of 'black-letter' law, are no exception since problem-solving is a vital legal skill and can be done using Law (ILAC) but also using theory, or methodological tools (ITAC).

6 CONCLUSION

It seems appropriate, by way of conclusion, to go back to the typical student question of 'Why do I have to study *theory* when I am doing a law degree?' *Theory* does not need to refer to 'high theory' or a set of unapproachable and out-dated philosophical ideas – it is, rather, theoretical frameworks that we should be interested in teaching our law students; theoretical methodologies, perspectives, approaches and lenses.[56] Its practical use, to the student studying a vocational degree such as law, is to provide a skill – namely the skill/s of *interrogation and application*, so as to enable and encourage a *curiosity* … about the law's claim to neutrality, to an apolitical character and to different ways of discarding hierarchy and looking at the same things in a different way. An awareness of methodology provides a way of looking at the world 'out there'; theories 'do not simply explain or predict, they tell us what possibilities exist for human action and intervention; they define not merely our explanatory possibilities, but also our ethical and practical

---

54 Bal Sokhi-Bulley, 'Re-reading the Riots: Counter-conduct in London 2011' (2016) 30(2) *Global Society* 320–339.

55 Bal Sokhi-Bulley (2015), *op cit.*

56 See the range of similar terms used by Burchill (2009), *op cit* 11: 'paradigms', 'perspectives', 'discourses', 'schools of thought', 'images and traditions', 11.

horizons.'[57] There is also, importantly, no 'correct theory' or 'one way' to think; methodology is a personal, critical *attitude* that in the law student needs to be nurtured and encouraged. This is where the responsibility of the educator lies. So that we might advocate a better understanding of the law, where 'better' refers to making law 'more intelligible – to make better sense of actors, structures, institutions, processes and particular episodes mainly, but not only, in the contemporary world',[58] which is largely defined by law. However, not only this; in addition to the responsibility to promote knowledge, we surely have an ethical obligation to educate 'better', meaning to incite curiosity and not to indoctrinate, to instruct in an enlightened way so that our students might also have the 'sharpened sense of reality' Foucault talked about.

57 Ibid 4.
58 Ibid 16.

8. Empirical methodologies knowledge and expertise: a 'necessary' skill for lawyers?[1]

Terry Hutchinson

1 INTRODUCTION

Legal training focuses on the study of the nature of legal rules using 'legal reasoning'. This emphasis on rules has the potential to obscure the importance of facts in the determination of the law. Judges use general facts about the world in developing and interpreting the law in addition to the facts they use that are specific to the dispute between the parties. Practicing lawyers present versions of the facts as truth in arguing their client's case in court. Facts about society also provide an evidence base for lawmakers to formulate policy and draft new laws and rules.

'Evidence-based' practice is used widely in the fields of medicine and business. This chapter describes evidence-based practice. It argues that facts about society gleaned from social research form a legitimate evidence base that is important for legislative reform. An evidence-based approach seems an obvious step in formulating effective laws and providing legal solutions to social problems.[2] Common sense suggests that the existing social evidence base should be used to assist legislators in developing and ensuring well-founded public policies leading to sound legislation. However, in law reform, the evidence base is often overshadowed by populist perceptions and political ideology. A recent

---

[1] Melody Martin, Aaron Walker and Josh Caeiro (QUT Faculty of Law) were the research assistants on this chapter. I also wish to acknowledge the assistance of Professor Charles Sampford.

[2] Brian Head, 'Evidence-based Policy: principles and requirements' in Productivity Commission, *Strengthening Evidence-based Policy in the Australian Federation, Vol. 1: Proceedings, Roundtable Proceedings* (Productivity Commission 2010). Available at: http://www.pc.gov.au/research/conference-proceedings/strengthening-evidence (accessed 2 May 2016).

legislative amendment to youth justice sentencing options provides a pertinent case study where the evidence base was largely disregarded.[3] This chapter argues that there would be more likelihood that 'good' law, that is law that is just and that brings about an intended outcome, would be achieved if the law is based on researched and widely accepted 'facts' about society and the way the law operates within society. Secondly, it argues that empirical research and research about 'facts' in society are important factors in assisting judges in the development of authoritative jurisprudence. The chapter examines examples of the use of the evidence base by judges in the High Court of Australia. In addition, it focuses on one case study from the area of family law where there are debates in the literature questioning the degree of use of empirical research data and the implications for the development of the law.

This chapter argues that there is a need for those lawyers who play a part in law reform (legislators policy officers, academic researchers and those involved in the law reform process) and for those who play a part in formulating common law rules (judges and practitioners) to know more about how facts are established in the social sciences. For this reason, law students need enhanced training and an appreciation of interdisciplinary, and empirical methods in order to effectively use and critique the ever-growing body of evidence from social research. Law students need exposure to basic empirical methodologies skills and a more sophisticated awareness, and knowledge of the ambit of social science methods to fully prepare for legal practice and for the many influential roles law graduates have as advocates, judges, practitioners, legislators, academic researchers and policymakers.

2 THE CONCEPT OF EVIDENCE-BASED PRACTICE AND LAW

The modern concept of evidence-based practice originated within the health services sector. The British physician Archie Cochrane published his *Effectiveness and Efficiency: Random Reflections on Health Services* in 1972.[4] The paradigm of evidence-based practice stipulates that decisions should be based on research-based knowledge collected in a

---

3 *Youth Justice (Boot Camp Orders) and Other Legislation Amendment Act 2012* (Qld).

4 Birger Hjorland, 'Evidence-based Practice: An Analysis Based on the Philosophy of Science' [2011] 62(7) *J Am Soc Inf Sci Technol* 1301.

systematic way using recognized scientific standards with research overviews synthesizing knowledge from multiple primary studies.[5] What effect has the evidence-based practice movement had on the law?

Within the legal academy, the empirical or experiential aspect of law as a central research theme dates as far back as Oliver Wendell Holmes Jr. in the nineteenth century and the American Legal Realist movement in the early decades of the twentieth century.[6] However, particularly in the United States and Canada, the last three decades have witnessed an increasing trend towards the use of the results of empirical research and the use of empirical methods by lawyers.[7] In the US, the Society for Empirical Legal Studies based at Cornell University aims to encourage and hone empirical methodological expertise amongst legal academics.[8] The Society holds successful conferences each year to highlight recent empirical data collected on the legal profession, courts and legal practice. In 2004, the Society launched the *Journal of Empirical Legal Studies* to promote and disseminate its research. Despite this, over the last ten years it seems that only 50 per cent of the articles in the journal are authored by lawyers. The other 50 per cent of authors publishing in the journal comprise those studying the law from external perspectives – economists, criminologists, statisticians, political scientists, psychologists and the like. This may well suggest that only a limited number of lawyers possess the necessary knowledge, interest and expertise to research the law using non-doctrinal methods to the standard necessary for publication in a refereed journal.

The situation within legal academia in Australia also reflects a more positive attitude towards the use of empirical data and the use of empirical methodologies to collect more knowledge about the law. This is spurred on to some extent by the cuts to government funding for universities and the corresponding need for success in external grants, which has resulted in interdisciplinary research teams being developed to apply for extensive grants. Examination of law PhD students' work demonstrates a gradual shift to the use of non-doctrinal methods in

---

[5] Ibid 1302.

[6] Oliver Wendell Holmes, *The Common Law* (Harvard University Press 2009).

[7] Robert Ellickson, 'Trends in Legal Scholarship: A Statistical Study' [2000] 29 *JLS* 517, 528–9; Theresa Shanahan, 'Legal Scholarship in Ontario's English-Speaking Common Law Schools' [2006] 21(2) *Can J L & Soc'y* 25, 32.

[8] Available at: http://www.lawschool.cornell.edu/sels/ (accessed 2 May 2016).

association with the traditional doctrinal outputs.[9] Alongside these forces encouraging changing research patterns there is the ongoing work of interdisciplinary associations – the 'Law and Society' movements.[10] These groups tend to favour more theoretical and philosophical approaches to legal norms but in doing so also force an extension of the methodological boundaries.

In the United Kingdom, the 2006 Nuffield Report signalled a movement towards gathering improved data and ensuring training in empirical methods within the academy.[11] Ten years earlier, the Legal Services Research Centre (LSRC) an independent research division of the Legal Services Commission (LSC) was established to inform legal aid policy and the implementation of reform. The LSRC conducted quantitative and qualitative empirical research on publicly-funded legal services. Unfortunately, changed government priorities resulted in the Centre's closure in 2013.

Are lawyers embracing the new evidence-based paradigm? Rachlinski argues that it is a more difficult or complex process for lawyers to use the existing social evidence base because law lacks the 'uniformity of purpose' seen in other disciplines:[12]

> It is often politics by other means that sorts winners and losers, rather than right and wrong, thereby clouding the normative environment. What is accepted fact in medicine and business is contestable in law. Law's political nature does not render empirical testing of widely held myths a hopeless misadventure but complicates the hope (and the value) of creating an evidence-based law.

Unlike medicine where there is a clear goal of providing 'a positive outcome for the patient's health', or business, where success is judged by the 'bottom line', Rachlinski argues that law lacks 'a unifying, organizing

---

9 Terry Hutchinson and Nigel Duncan, 'Defining the Doctrinal' (2012) 17(1) *Deakin LR* 1.

10 The Law and Society Association of Australia and New Zealand. Available at: http://www.lsaanz.org/ (accessed 15 May 2015); Australian and New Zealand Society of Criminology. Available at: http://www.anzsoc.org/ (accessed 2 May 2016); and their equivalents in the US, UK and Europe.

11 Hazel Genn, Martin Partington and Sally Wheeler, *Law in the Real World: Improving our Understanding of How Law Works* (Report: Nuffield Foundation 2006). Available at: http://www.nuffieldfoundation.org/nuffield-inquiry-empirical-legal-research-law-real-world (accessed 2 May 2016).

12 Jeffrey Rachlinski, 'Evidence-based Law' [2010–2011] 96 *Cornell LR* 901.

principle'.[13] However, in an argument reminiscent of Peter Ziegler's assertion of the 'non-existent legal paradigm',[14] he asserts that efforts to define law's purpose 'lead only to greater complexity' and 'conflicting purpose'.[15] Rachlinski refers to the 'conflicting themes' in the various areas of law, so that tort and contract law, for example, aim for efficiency, but to some degree they also seek to provide fairness for the parties involved, and criminal law needs to balance the rights of the accused 'with society's broader need to control crime'.[16] However, surely, as Rachlinski suggests, the point for Law must be to use the evidence base so as 'to create better law – law informed by reality'.[17] This can be viewed as a separate enterprise to the individual advocacy contests in the courts. Surely the general social rules promulgated in legislation should be progressed based on the best available social evidence base?

3 CONTESTED ROLE OF THE SOCIAL EVIDENCE BASE IN DEVELOPING LEGISLATION

Both in Australia and overseas, recognition has been given to the need to bridge the policy/research divide so as to establish 'mechanisms for identifying and plugging key gaps in research knowledge'.[18] Peter Bridgman and Glyn Davis, for example, have written an influential text on policy research in Australia.[19] In outlining the policy change cycle, they highlight the need for extensive research and consultation.

Accordingly, recent Australian history has numerous examples of governments providing meaningful opportunities for the broader community of interest and non-government policy experts to engage in policy

---

[13] Ibid 918.

[14] Peter Ziegler, 'A General Theory of Law as a Paradigm for Legal Research' [1988] 51 *MLR* 569.

[15] Rachlinski, *op cit.*

[16] Ibid.

[17] Ibid 910.

[18] Sandra Nutley, 'Bridging the Policy-Research Divide: Reflections and Lessons from the United Kingdom' [2003] 10 *Canb Bull Pub Admin* 19–20; Sandra Nutley, Alison Powell and Huw Davies, *Provocation Paper for the Alliance for Useful Evidence* (Research Unit for Research Utilisation (RURU), School of Management, University of St Andrews, 2013).

[19] Catherine Althaus, Peter Bridgman and Glyn Davis, *The Australian Policy Handbook* (5th edn, Allen & Unwin 2012).

analysis and the formulation of options for reform. In 2008, the Australian left wing Labour government announced a positive stance on evidence-led policy:[20]

> The Government will not adopt overseas models uncritically. We're interested in facts, not fads. But whether it's aged care, vocational education or disability services, Australian policy development should be informed by the best of overseas experience and analysis. In fostering a culture of policy innovation, we should trial new approaches and policy options through small-scale pilot studies. Policy innovation and evidence-based policy making is at the heart of being a reformist government.

However, it seems that often as not in Australian politics, the evidence base produced, for example, by specially established government enquiries and academic research submitted in response to departmental discussion papers, is not used within policy development. There is often a lack of any government requirement to disclose or respond publicly to recommendations and submissions. This has led some commentators to question government tactics and query whether governments are only using the inquiries and evidence-gathering processes 'as strategies – to avoid criticism, to be seen to be doing something, to delay action or to divert attention',[21] leading to a growing bank of information which has been labelled by John Lea as 'museums of official discourse'.[22] It would still seem 'that many policy decisions are made in isolation from any real research, and that directions for change, based on anecdotal evidence, are imposed from the top. The community may only be involved at a very late stage through consultation processes designed to justify and legitimise'.[23]

Why is this evidence base being ignored? One very influential tool working against evidence-based practice in the formulation of legislation is 'anecdote'. Politicians use highly publicized stories involving violent criminals to espouse simplistic 'tough on crime' policies that appeal to

---

[20] Kevin Rudd, 'Address by Australian PM to Members Government Senior Executive Service' (speech delivered at the Department of Prime Minister and Cabinet, 1 May 2008).

[21] Elaine Fishwick and Jane Bolitho, 'Politics-led Policy and Policy-led Evidence: The Noetic Review of Juvenile Justice in New South Wales' [2010] 22 (1) *CICJ* 176.

[22] John Lea, 'From Brixton to Bradford: Official Discourse on Race and Urban Violence in the UK' in George Gilligan and John Pratt (eds) *Crime, Truth and Justice* (Willan Publishing 2004) 184.

[23] Terry Hutchinson, *Researching and Writing in Law* (3rd edn, Thomson 2010) 72–73.

broad cross-sections of the community. A single 'bad' decision by a Parole Board can affect the rehabilitation hopes of hundreds. As an example, one widely publicized murder by a parolee in Victoria prompted an overall review of the procedures and parole system in that state which will inevitably result in tighter parole requirements.[24] Just as in the courts, difficult or unusual, or exceptional cases can cause the clarity of the law to be 'obscured by exceptions and strained interpretations', so too unusual and heinous criminal acts can incite public opinion to the point where politicians pass unnecessarily harsh or superfluous laws. Media-inspired outrage can result in 'special' laws, so that for example offences covering looting during disasters are added to the statute books despite the fact that basic stealing offences already cover all pertinent situations.[25]

Modern governments have a tendency to rely on populism and public perceptions of what the voters believe and want from responses to reports in the media. These perceptions and policies are often unsupported by scientific research. If unrestrained by internal government checks and balances, these forces can result in cheap short-term options and simplistic solutions. Therefore, many factors other than research evidence, shape the policy process. These factors include: 'prevailing public opinion'; political policy events such as elections; changes of ministers and governments; fiscal constraints and budgets; institutional constraints; policy actors; political power; policy discourse; organizational cultures; agenda-setting; one-off events; political economy; and 'new managerialism' as well as 'penal populism'; the 'politics of law and order' and 'the performance indicators of the State Plan'.[26]

In a democracy, law emanates from the political will of the people and one recent study has demonstrated that people ignore facts that are contrary to their political beliefs. Confirmation bias comes into play so that empirical findings are taken up selectively and usually only when the findings confirm their point of view. Therefore, when placed in a political

---

[24] Ian Callinan, *Review of the Parole System in Victoria* (Department of Justice – Corrections Victoria, July 2013). Available at: http://pandora.nla.gov.au/pan/144048/20140109-1552/www.corrections.vic.gov.au/utility/publications%252Bmanuals%252Band%252Bstatistics/review%252Bof%252Bthe%252Bparole%252Bsystem%252Bin%252Bvictoria.html (2 May 2016).

[25] See, for example, the Criminal Code (Looting in Declared Areas) Amendment Bill 2013 (Qld) following a few incidents that occurred during the Queensland floods.

[26] Fishwick and Bolitho, *op cit* (notes omitted).

context which is contrary to their political beliefs, people will deny basic numerical facts.[27]

Accordingly, legislative amendments frequently are at odds with the findings from social research. In Queensland, the *Youth Justice (Boot Camp Orders) and Other Legislation Amendment Act 2012* commenced in January 2013. Whilst boot camps may seem a simplistic option to instil discipline and lead young people towards a more appropriate future path, the research demonstrates that the problems being experienced by these youths are not amenable to such simplistic solutions and that positive results are not the actual outcomes experienced by many participants. The weight of social research evidence demonstrates that in the past, boot camps for young offenders have not been effective in reducing reoffending. A meta-analysis of 32 robust research studies of militaristic boot-camps concluded that 'this common and defining feature of a boot-camp is not effective in reducing post boot-camp offending'.[28] Similarly, a meta-review of crime reduction programs conducted in Washington State found that boot camps did not reduce recidivism among participants.[29] At the same time other more expensive diversionary programs[30] with positive evaluations, such as court ordered youth justice conferencing, have been discontinued in order to achieve short-term budgetary gains.[31] Further amendments to the *Youth Justice Act* in 2014 prompted 25 submissions to the Queensland Parliament's Legal and Constitutional Affairs Committee presenting cogent research demonstrating the negative effects of the

---

27 Jeff Nesbit, 'Do Facts Matter Anymore in Public Policy?' *Livescience* (13 September 2013); see also Dan Kahan and others, 'Motivated Numeracy and Enlightened Self-Government', [2013] *Yale Law School, Public Law Working Paper No. 307*. Available at: <http://ssrn.com/abstract=2319992 (accessed 2 May 2016).

28 David Wilson, Doris MacKenzie and Fawn Mitchell, *Effects of Correctional Boot Camps on Offending* (Report, The Campbell Collaboration, 2008) 3.

29 Elizabeth Drake, Steve Aos and Marna Miller, 'Evidence-based Public Policy Options to Reduce Crime and Criminal Justice Costs: Implications in Washington State' [2009] 4 *Victims & Offenders* 170.

30 $11.2 million over the next two full financial years in comparison to $2 million for the new program. Andrew Webber, 'Youth Justice Conferences versus Children's Court: A Comparison of Cost-effectiveness' [2012] 164 *Contemp. Issues Crim & Just* 1; Queensland Government Department of Justice and Attorney-General, *State Budget 2012–13 Service Delivery Statement* (2012).

31 There were 1,691 court-ordered youth conferencing referrals last year (as well as 1,246 police-referred conferences). Court-referred conferencing is reported as having a 98 per cent satisfaction rate. Queensland Courts, *Childrens Court of Queensland Annual Report 2011–12* (2012) 7.

proposed changes on the rehabilitation of young offenders.[32] The arguments in these submissions were not successful in preventing the legislation being enacted. There are long-term risks involved in ignoring the evidence base in important social areas such as youth justice. These risks include increased youth detention rates, higher costs of detention, net widening, and inequitable impacts on indigenous youth.

In addition, many truly serious social problems such as Indigenous disadvantage are not amenable to simple solutions. They require complex multi-faceted long-term adjustments to policy. The evidence base simply does not have the answers to all society's difficult problems. In addition, the research findings are often contradictory or tainted because of bias or questionable research methods. It is not always a simple matter to relate the empirical evidence to the reforms being proposed. However, clear evidence where it exists should not be ignored given the risks (and costs) involved.

4 THE IMPORTANCE OF FACTS IN THE JUDICIAL PROCESS

The heart of the lawyers' craft lies in normative reasoning – the formulation, interpretation and application of legal rules. In the common law world, appellate judges are at the pinnacle of that craft in terms of authority and skill. Those judges have the ultimate responsibility for authoritatively determining the interpretation, meaning and effect of statutory and common law texts.

However, facts are also important in legal disputes. It is clearly recognized that the particular facts alleged and challenged in the matters that come to court constitute the source of, and the reason for more general rules which are determined through the judges' use of inductive and deductive reasoning. These 'adjudicative facts' are the special or particular facts that need to be established in a particular case and to which legal rules are applied. Social scientific studies pertinent to a case are introduced to the court process through expert evidence. Doctrinal scholars have voiced concerns relating to the rules and practice covering the use of social science and expert evidence by the courts. Researchers have examined the

---

[32] Queensland Parliament, 'Legal Affairs and Community Safety Committee: Youth Justice and Other Legislation Amendment Bill 2014' (*Queensland Parliament*). Available: https://www.parliament.qld.gov.au/work-of-committees/committees/LACSC/inquiries/past-inquiries/YouthJustice2014 (2 May 2016).

judges' views on the use of such expert evidence.[33] However, there has been a long tradition of using survey research for specific adjudications in areas such as consumer and trade practices law.[34]

In common law systems, the facts are contested. Factual accuracy has been described as the 'paramount',[35] 'foremost',[36] 'fundamental',[37] 'principal',[38] 'overriding' and 'necessary',[39] and 'central'[40] goal of the trial. Advocates present two versions of the facts rather than an objective truth. As a general rule, 'parties to a court proceeding must prove all facts pertinent to their case',[41] and there are highly developed rules for determining these adjudicative facts centring on the laws of evidence, procedure and discovery.[42] The courts have even been said to exercise a gatekeeping role in keeping out 'junk science'.[43]

---

33 I Freckleton, P Reddy and H Selby, *Australian Judicial Perspectives on Expert Evidence: An Empirical Study* (Australian Institute of Judicial Administration 1999) and I Freckleton, P Reddy and H Selby, *Australian Magistrates' Perspectives on Expert Evidence: A Comparative Study* (Australian Institute of Judicial Administration Incorporated 2001) used surveys to examine the issue of expert evidence in the courts; see also G Edmond, 'Judging Surveys: Experts, Empirical Evidence and Law Reform' [2005] 33(1) *FL Rev* 95.

34 P Shafron, 'Admissibility of surveys in Evidence: Hearsay and Gone Tomorrow? *Shoshana Pty Ltd and Sue Smith v 10th Cantanae Pty Ltd*' [1989] 12 (1) Syd LR 218.

35 Marvin Frankel, 'The Search for Truth: An Umpireal View' [1975] 123 *U Pa L Rev* 1031.

36 Adrian Zuckerman, *Principles of Criminal Evidence* (Clarendon Press 1989).

37 Vern Walker, 'Preponderance, Probability and Warranted Fact-finding' [1996] 62 *Brook L Rev* 1075, 1081.

38 Jonathan Koehler and Daniel Shaviro, 'Veridical Verdicts' [1990] 75 *Cornell L Rev* 247.

39 William Twining, *Theories of Evidence: Bentham and Wigmore* (Weidenfeld and Nicolson 1985); William Twining, 'Rationality and Scepticism in Judicial Proof: Some Signposts' [1989] II *IJSL* 69; David Miers and William Twining, *How to do Things with Rules* (5th edn, CUP 2010).

40 Jack Weinstein, 'Some Difficulties in Devising Rules for Determining Truth in Judicial Trials' [1966] 66 *Colum L Rev* 223.

41 Australian Law Reform Commission, *Uniform Evidence Law* (Report No. 102, 2005) para 17.1.

42 Andrew Ligertwood, *Australian Evidence* (4th edn LexisNexis/Butterworths 2004); Adrian Zuckerman and Paul Roberts, *Criminal Evidence* (OUP 2004); Australian Law Reform Commission, Uniform Evidence Law (Report No. 102, 2005); Dyson Heydon and Rupert Cross, *Cross on Evidence* (9th edn, LexisNexis/Butterworths 2013).

43 Steven Odgers and James Richardson, 'Keeping Bad Science out of the Courtroom' [1995] 18(1) *UNSWLJ* 108; Stuart Washington, 'Tainted evidence:

In addition to adjudicative facts, there are 'empirical facts' (sometimes called 'legislative facts' or 'social facts'). These consist of 'assertions of facts about society, the world and human behaviour', which, in principle, can be tested by 'social science or empirical methodologies'.[44] These facts are neither pure statements of legal principle nor are they adjudicative facts – 'they are assertions used as part of the judicial reasoning process'.[45] Judges can formally take 'judicial notice' of 'notorious facts' and so 'relieve the parties of the burden of proving them'.[46] Judicial notice covers matters of such common knowledge that they are rarely contentious, for example, indisputable scientific, medical, cultural, and historical facts, including: the laws of physical nature; well-known social habits and usages; and notorious historical events, such as World War II; as well as matters the court may be assumed to know already by virtue of its stature and expertise, such as the validity of legislation put before it.[47]

These facts affect the interpretations of norms that judges find most persuasive. Indeed, views about the world may be as important to the choice of the empirical facts used, as a judge's general philosophy and approach to judicial reasoning is relevant to the way they decide cases.[48] There have only been a very small number of studies on the use of empirical facts by Australian courts.[49] There has been a limited discussion in relation to their use in the United States.[50] Research of current Australian, United States and United Kingdom case law demonstrates

---

Science in the dock', *Sydney Morning Herald* (Sydney, 17 December 2011) 1; 'Appeals spark concern over use of scientific evidence', *Sydney Morning Herald* (Sydney, 17 December 2011) 5.

[44] Kylie Burns and Terry Hutchinson, 'Impact of 'Empirical Facts' on Legal Scholarship & Training' [2009] 43(2) *Law Teach* 153.

[45] Ibid; Kylie Burns, 'The Way the World is: Social Facts in High Court Negligence Cases' [2004] 12(3) *TLJ* 215; Kylie Burns, 'The Australian High Court and Social Facts: A Content Analysis Study' [2012] 40 *FL Rev* 317.

[46] Heydon and Cross, *op cit*. See *Evidence Act 1995* (Cth) ss 143–145.

[47] Ibid ch 2.

[48] For example, a judge who protects consumers' ability to challenge standard form contracts might be seen as upholding the principle of consumers' rights or giving recognition to inequality of bargaining power.

[49] Graham Mullane, 'Evidence of Social Science Research: Law, Practice, and Options in the Family Court of Australia' [1998] 72(6) *ALJ* 434; Bradley Selway, 'The Use of History and Other Facts in the Reasoning of the High Court' [2001] 20 *U Tas LR* 129.

[50] Kenneth Davis, 'An Approach to the Problems of Evidence in the Administrative Process' [1942] 55(3) *Harv L Rev* 364; Kenneth Davis, 'Judicial Notice' [1955] 55(7) *Colum L Rev* 945; Peggy Davis, "There is a Book out …". An Analysis of Judicial Absorption of Legislative Facts' [1987] 100(7) *Harv L*

that judges make statements of empirical facts, with or without the support of social science research as part of their judicial reasoning.[51] Empirical facts may be used in a wide variety of ways by judges in their reasoning. They may be used to set background context, in a rhetorical way to support arguments of legal principle, to assist in the determination or interpretation of adjudicative facts, or as arguments of policy or consequence used in the development of law.[52] Sometimes statements of empirical fact are subsumed into statements of legal or social values, 'for example statements that refer to enduring community values such as the value of human life'.[53]

There has been an explosion in social science research on law, the justice system, the context in which law operates, the effects law has, and the social and institutional phenomena that statute law and common law seeks to regulate.[54] Many of the 'home truths' that might have once been considered 'notorious facts' are now subject to sophisticated social science analysis.

In the Family Court jurisdiction empirical facts have been introduced into the courts in a formal manner and thereafter been treated as judicial principle.[55] Extensive research has taken place in areas pertinent to family law disputes. Therefore as Zoe Rathus has pointed out, there is 'a long history of judicial officers referring to social science research in their judgments, the practice having commenced in the first year of operation of the court. The community now expects judges to undertake education about issues central to family law cases, such as gender, race, family violence and mental health'.[56] Much of the information and

---

Rev 1539; John Monahan and Laurens Walker, 'Social Frameworks: A New Use of Social Science in Law' [1987] 73(3) *Va L Rev* 559.

51 See for example *Cattanach v Melchior* [2003] 199 *ALR* 131 (wrongful birth), *Woods v Multi-Sport Holdings* [2002] 208 *CLR* 460 (extra record social scientific material), *St Helens Borough Council v Derbyshire and others* [2007] 3 *All ER* 81 (working lives of women) and *Stack v Dowden* [2007] 2 *All ER* 929 (Cohabitation); Burns and Hutchinson, *op cit*; see also the discussion in Mullane, *op cit*; Kylie Burns, 'It's Just Not Cricket: The High Court, sport and legislative facts' [2002] 10(3) *TLJ* 234; *The Queen v Tang* (2008) 237 *CLR* 1; [2008] 249 *ALR* 200; [2008] *HCA* 39 (slavery).

52 Kylie Burns (2004), *op cit.*

53 Burns and Hutchinson, *op cit*, 156; ibid 219–221.

54 See the examples in Peter Cane and Herbert Kritzer, *The Oxford Handbook of Empirical Legal Research* (OUP 2010).

55 Mullane, *op cit.*

56 Zoe Rathus, 'A Call for Clarity in the use of Social Science Research in Family Law Decision-making' [2012] 26 *AJFL* 81–82.

knowledge absorbed through such judicial education is drawn from the results of social science research. However, within the Australian family law jurisdiction there is growing disquiet towards social science evidence infusing both legal policy and legislation and legal principle.[57] One example of this is the spate of articles critiquing the presumption that 'equal shared parental responsibility is in the best interests of the child' in all parenting decisions in the family court.[58]

This social research is widely publicized in the media and accessible in the community to judges and clients alike. The use of empirical research data by the courts is a contested area. Doctrinal researchers are querying the general acceptance of the results by the courts. Within this environment therefore, it is essential that law schools ensure that the knowledge and skill of critiquing empirical research is not overlooked in legal training. Lawyers do not need to be social scientists or have extensive skills in social science methods. However, lawyers must be able to read, understand and critique the outcomes of this research so that the law develops and functions well in modern societies.

5 THE NEED FOR ENHANCED TRAINING FOR LAWYERS IN UNDERTAKING EMPIRICAL RESEARCH AND IN CRITIQUING THE EVIDENCE BASE

The arguments surrounding the need for lawyers training to be broadened from purely doctrinal research methodologies so as to engage with social research more meaningfully,[59] have been canvassed in the literature

---

[57] Zoe Rathus 'Shifting Language and Meanings between Social Science and the Law: Defining Family Violence' [2013] 16(2) *UNSWLJ* 359; Zoe Rathus, 'The Role of the Social Sciences in Australian Family Law: Collaborator, Usurper or Infiltrator?' [2014] 53(1) *Fam Court Rev* 69.

[58] Zoe Rathus, 'Social Science or Lego-science? Presumptions, Politics, Parenting and the New Family Law' [2010] 10(2) *QUTLJ* 164; J Cashmere and P Parkinson, 'The Use and Abuse of Social Science Research Evidence in Children's Cases' [2014] 20(3) *Psychology Pub Pol'y & L* 239; L. Nielsen 'Woozles: Their Role in Custody Law Reform, Parenting Plans and Family Court' [2014] 20(2) *Psychology Pub Pol'y & L* 164.

[59] Ian Curry-Sumner and Marieke van der Schaaf 'The Theory and Practice of Teaching and Guiding Legal Research Skills' [2011] (1)1 *Law & Method* 64.

previously.[60] The 2006 UK Nuffield Inquiry noted the crucial importance of empirical research to lawyers and recommended that:[61]

> xii. … all law departments should consider enhancing the undergraduate curriculum by offering an option on law in society, or offering options with a significant empirical content … . This would better equip students to deal with a world in which there is an increasing demand for assembling and analysing social data and where, indeed, legal practice requires a wide range of research skills in addition to those of the doctrinal lawyer. Such students should also acquire the technical skills needed to analyse data.

All law graduates would benefit from this training. In the current *milieu*, legal academics are frequently required to take part in interdisciplinary research teams. Interdisciplinary and multi-faceted methodologies are valued by external granting authorities such as the Australian Research Council. Higher degree research students require exposure to the array of methodologies in order to choose the most appropriate way of progressing their research questions and arguments. Even those researchers using strictly doctrinal methods need to have a facility in assessing the legal statistics and social context.

Law students need this training for legal practice. Training in empirical methods will ensure that practicing lawyers have an enhanced ability to locate, read and critically assess the published results of existing interdisciplinary research. Lawyers need to be sufficiently skilled to identify obvious error. The process of evaluation involves reading and assessing reports of empirical research across the spectrum of quantitative and qualitative methodologies, and disciplines. This includes not only the use of statistics, surveys, observations of habitual behaviour and interviews with key players, but also the work of anthropologists, psychologists and sociologists. Reflective critique is necessary to fully assess the abilities of those conducting the research being presented. Lawyers need basic non-doctrinal methodologies knowledge in order to best understand and query expert evidence and research presented by those skilled researchers from other disciplines.

---

60 Terry Hutchinson, 'Developing Legal Research Skills: Context, Framework and Practice' [2008] 32(3) *MULR* 105, 1083–1087; Anthony Bradney, 'The Place of Empirical Legal Research in the Law School Curriculum' in Peter Cane and Herbert Kritzer, *The Oxford Handbook of Empirical Legal Research* (OUP 2010).

61 Hazel Genn, Martin Partington and Sally Wheeler, *Law in the Real World: Improving Our Understanding of How Law Works Report Summary* (Report: Nuffield Foundation 2006) 7.

Many law graduates never practice but instead enter government and politics. Training in empirical research methods will enable this group to become more skilled in formulating evidence-based policy. In Australia, for example, prior to the 2013 federal election, 29 per cent (n=66) federal parliamentarians held law degrees.[62] This continuing trend for law graduates to move into the political arena provides even more reason for the law curriculum to include adequate exposure to social research methodologies.

Fulfilling a requirement for law students to graduate having achieved an enhanced knowledge of social research methods and an ability to validly critique the existing evidence base, is problematic. There are an extensive number of quantitative and qualitative social research methods. Any treatment of the vast array of methods within a law degree would of necessity be superficial. It would be impossible to cover all the methodological possibilities in sufficient depth even within one focused undergraduate unit included in a law degree. Therefore, it may be necessary to limit the skills developed at undergraduate level to learning about the goals and advantages or disadvantages of various research methods. Ideally, the curriculum should also include skills in designing one very basic quantitative method such as a simple online survey, or filling out an ethics application, or critiquing a research study.

Even at the postgraduate level, the coverage of methodologies is of necessity limited. Introductory research training units attempt to open non-doctrinal doors to enable students to gain a basic familiarity with the research methods options for their large projects. When embarking on a higher degree thesis, a research student, for example, may then determine on one or two data collection methods (usually in tandem with doctrinal research), which appear best-suited to their research question and resources. Certainly the chosen methods would need to be mastered to a high standard.

Who will teach the methods courses within the law degree? Few Australian legal academics have dual social science and legal qualifications. In June 2012, the Higher Education Academy's *Social Sciences Teaching and Learning Summit: Teaching Research Methods* continued the discussion within the social science faculty about the best means of

---

62 This contrasts to a small 0.452 per cent of the general public who are lawyers. Evan Whitton, 'The Parliament of Australia (lawyers)' (*Independent Australia*, 23 August 2013). Available at: http://www.independentaustralia.net/2013/politics/the-parliament-of-australian-lawyers/ (accessed 2 May 2016).

teaching these methods effectively.[63] The task is not straightforward. Will law students welcome having such material being included in the curriculum? Australian law students (and legal academics) tend to come from a humanities background and favour text-based studies. Many have not completed advanced mathematics in their final years at school. Therefore, empirical methods will almost certainly need to be taught by academics from other disciplines. There are resourcing (and cost) issues involved in such service teaching arrangements within the universities.

Where should these skills be included in the law degree? In most jurisdictions the law curriculum is already crowded with core units. Is this an effective use of time within the law degree? In Australia, the core units are known colloquially as 'the Priestley Eleven', being named after the chair of the Law Admissions Consultative Committee. This committee completed a review of the requirements for admission to legal practice in Australia in 1992 and this basic list of subject requirements is still being used throughout Australia, although the list of units was reviewed in 2015.[64] Empirical research method is not part of the required list.

However, in the Australian law curriculum, the difficulties in including this material are not insurmountable, and have been canvassed elsewhere.[65] Including empirical research skills within an established incremental skills training program is one option.[66] Inclusion of such knowledge and skills beginning with a first-year tutorial reading and critique module would be sufficient to cover basic skills in reading

---

63 Martyn Hammersley, 'Is it possible to teach social research methods well today?' (paper presented at Social Sciences teaching and learning summit: teaching research methods, University of Warwick, 21–22 June 2012); John MacInnes 'Quantitative Methods teaching in UK Higher Education: the state of the field and how it might be improved' (paper presented at Social Sciences teaching and learning summit: Teaching research methods, University of Warwick, 21–22 June 2012); Mark Garner 'There's madness in our methods: the pedagogical culture of research methods' (paper presented at Social Sciences teaching and learning summit: Teaching research methods, University of Warwick, 21–22 June 2012).

64 Law Admissions Consultative Committee, *Review of Academic Requirements for Admission to the Legal Profession* (Law Council of Australia 2014). Available at: http://www.lawcouncil.asn.au/LACC/index.php/review-of-academic-requirements (accessed 2 May 2016).

65 Terry Hutchinson and Kylie Burns, *op cit,* 74; Hutchinson (2008), *op cit* 1085.

66 Sharon Christensen and Sally Kift, 'Graduate Attributes and Legal Skills: Integration or Disintegration?' [2001] 11(2) *Legal Educ Rev* 207.

empirical research papers. Throughout the academic year levels, there are opportunities to examine examples of empirical research evidence when academics are establishing legal context prior to analysing the substantive law. Statistics on prison populations and recidivism are a logical context for a discussion of the rules in relation to sentencing offenders. Statistics on the incidence of divorce are relevant in a family law unit. The incidence of consumer complaints is good background to a discussion of trade practices and fair trading laws. There are case examples, which highlight where the courts have accepted and used empirical research results.[67]

Final year research units provide an additional venue to introduce non-doctrinal research methodologies. Gradually through individually supervised research project units and Masters or higher degree research, students have opportunities to be introduced to the art of writing surveys and the importance of university ethics clearance regulations. The incorporation of discussion of this material is not onerous and involves organizational emphasis and intention rather than the displacement of other substantive material.

There are other avenues. The universities already promote combined degree or dual degree courses such as Law and Justice or Law and Economics. These are available for those who have an interest in pursuing an interdisciplinary perspective.

The offering of postgraduate Juris Doctor (JD) degrees is a recent trend in Australia. These degrees are 'targeted at graduates (of non-law disciplines) seeking to obtain legal qualifications'.[68] Students completing a degree in another discipline would be more likely to have a basis of research skills from those disciplines. This structure certainly fulfils the requirements of pre-law training covering units such as logic and reasoning, ethics, sociology, economics and communication, which some educators have been expounding for decades.[69]

---

[67] In *Coon and Cox* [1993] 17 *Fam LR* 692; (1994) *FLC* 92–464 an Australian family law decision, the Chief Justice of the Family Court compared the scale of the costs of maintaining children, the 'Lee Scale', to the scale more commonly used, the 'Lovering Scale'. See general discussion and examples in Brenda Hale, *Connections between Practical and Academic Work* (City University London 2013).

[68] Australian Government Productivity Commission, *Access to Justice Arrangements Productivity Commission Inquiry* (Report No. 72, Commonwealth of Australia 2014) 241. Available at: http://www.pc.gov.au/inquiries/completed/access-justice/report (accessed 2 May 2016).

[69] John Pyke 'Why do we Take so Much Upon Ourselves? – The Case for a Prescriptive Pre-law Year', (1997) 3(2) *ALTA Newsletter* 1.

Not all law graduates in Australia enter practice. Survey data from Graduate Careers Australia suggest that law graduates enter employment in a range of roles, from practising lawyers, in roles directly involving law in firms and government, to roles where knowledge of law is useful but not core to the job.[70] These graduates are still influencing the development of the law and it could be argued they also need an ability to critique social evidence and policy.

It is imperative that shifts occur within the law degree curriculum so that there is more recognition of current research realities. The methodologies used in research emanating from the law faculties are expanding beyond purely doctrinal work. The number of higher degree students in law is increasing. There is a corresponding increase in the number of interdisciplinary methods being employed by both academics and students at that level.[71] The time is ripe for change.

6 CONCLUSION AND FURTHER WORK REQUIRED

This chapter has argued that facts gleaned from social research form a legitimate evidence base that should be used to assist legislators in developing, and ensuring well-founded public policies and to assist judges in the development of authoritative jurisprudence. This argument is in some respects simplistic because it ignores the complexities involved in the development of a valid evidence base pertinent to any specific jurisdictional legal problem, or specific legal dispute, and it also ignores the complexities involved in contested legislative reform underlaid by political reality in democratic government structures. This chapter maintains that law graduates need enhanced facility in dealing with non-doctrinal methods so as to fully prepare for legal practice and the many influential roles lawyers have as advocates, judges, practitioners, legislators, researchers and policymakers in modern democracies.

---

70 Australian Government Productivity Commission, *op cit*, 245–246; Graduate Careers Australia, '2012 Graduate Destinations Tables and Figures (2012 Table 19)' (2013) cited in Australian Government Productivity Commission, *Access to Justice Arrangements Productivity Commission Inquiry* (Report No. 72, Commonwealth of Australia 2014).

71 Hutchinson and Duncan, *op cit* 13–14.

9. Visuals for a critical legal profession[1]

Wibo van Rossum

1 INTRODUCTION AND OUTLINE

Not only the law itself is 'dead material' that needs to be brought to life, the same goes for texts that describe, explain or critique the law. I do not mean to downplay the creative-writing capabilities of many legal scholars, but I think more than text is necessary to infuse students with a critical outlook on legal phenomena. In today's visual culture, law is often seen in Hollywood movies and series such as *CSI*. Law students – just like many others – are permanently 'online', using Facebook, Instagram, YouTube and other visual social media to connect, exchange information and make public their current social status. When they enter the classroom however, they often have to go back to the 'old days' (of the teacher) of reading large amounts of text and a few lecture slides (also with text) to support that process. Including visuals (e.g. photos, documentaries, etc.) brings teaching more inline with the ordinary way students process and produce information. However, a second and more important argument is that 'bringing the visual in' in teaching law, will help students develop a more imaginative critical perspective on law. Photos and film confront students with real-life situations, which together with a case or social issue, and the story behind it enables them to put themselves in the shoes of the people concerned. There is a third reason for why using visuals are good. That argument relates specifically to the courses I teach, and holds that photos and documentaries show empirical data from society. They socially contextualize a legal case or legal issue.[2]

---

[1] This chapter is an extended and adapted version of an article that will be published in Marie-Claire Foblets, Gordon Woodman and Anthony Bradney (eds), *The Trials and Triumphs of Teaching Legal Anthropology* (Ashgate forthcoming).

[2] The arguments are partly connected to the 'law and film' movement (and the 'law and literature' movement). The 'law and film' movement analyses on the

Currently I teach three different socio-legal courses: *Anthropology of Law*, *Comparative Legal Cultures*, and *Sociology of Law* (the last one is taught in Dutch). I teach all three courses in law schools. *Sociology of Law* (± 150 students) and *Comparative Legal Cultures* (± 90 students) are courses at the third year bachelor level at Utrecht University, whilst *Anthropology of Law* (± 10–15 students) is a course for both bachelor and master students at Erasmus University Rotterdam. Bringing the socio-legal perspective to law students is a challenge. They have to leave the idea behind that there is a right and a wrong answer to questions, that law is always a good thing, that a normative focus on law is the only relevant focus and the hardest thing, that there is only one type of law. These preconceptions about what law is and should do, settle themselves in the minds of law students because of the specific function of academic legal training in the Netherlands. I will explain this in section 2. In section 3 I will describe the differences between the courses I teach by using the images I start off with in the first meeting with students. In section 4 I will argue why the use of (parts of) documentaries and films in class help accomplish the goal of a critical reflection for our future legal professionals. I conclude in section 5.

2 THE FUNCTION OF ACADEMIC LEGAL TRAINING IN THE NETHERLANDS

Legal education in Dutch universities is restricted by what is commonly called the 'requirements for the professions of the gown', officially called

one hand how law is reflected in popular movies and documentaries ('law in film') and on the other how film can contribute to the development of law and legal arguments ('film in law'). A recent example of the first is Steve Greenfield, Guy Osborn and Peter Robson (eds), *Film and the Law. The Cinema of Justice* (Hart 2010). This chapter is more inline with the second approach in that it argues that including visuals in teaching law creates better legal professionals. An example of an interesting documentary that is able to do this is 'Hot Coffee' available at: <http://www.hotcoffeethemovie.com> on the lawsuit against McDonald's because of serving coffee too hot and the burns it caused in a woman's lap. A related, but different discussion is on what the increasing use of visuals in courtrooms mean for doing justice. See Neal Feigenson, 'The Visual in Law: Some Problems for Legal Theory' [2014] 10 *Law, Culture and the Humanities* 13–23.

'civil effect'.[3] It means that professional organizations of lawyers and judges have a large say in the curriculum of law schools. Universities educate their students in order to become judges, lawyers, or (most of them) legal professionals working at ministries, municipalities, or other policy-making institutions. Courses in legal theory, philosophy of law, jurisprudence, and sociology of law are not compulsory for the 'civil effect'. The study of the core of black letter law in the field of civil law, constitutional and administrative law, and criminal law is the main focus, while law faculties are free to decide on the inclusion of courses that offer a reflection on law from other disciplines.[4] These courses tend to be scheduled in the curriculum after the first and most of the time second year bachelor. This means that when students in their third or fourth year of study choose for, or need to do one of those courses at the fringes of the law, they are already trained (some say brain-washed) in looking in a legal way at the world. This 'legal view' means that students take the law as a given, know some of its systematic whole and hierarchy, know where to find relevant legal rules in order to solve legal cases, and know how to apply and legally argue a case in the light of previously decided cases by higher courts. This leads to the main focus of 'legal problem solver'. They are trained to find answers to questions as either right or wrong, to address each problem or social issue with that normative dichotomy in mind. Acceptance of the current legal system as a given means alternatives to law or even alternative laws only very rarely enter the discussion. I do not mean to argue that this dominant legal training is not useful. Most law students end up in jobs in which 'questioning the law' is seen as a waste of time. Also, many indeed have jobs in which they need to take well argued and legally sound decisions. The discussion on the legal curriculum, therefore, is always on the right balance between black letter law *versus* other courses, and on how much 'context' is needed in black letter law courses themselves.

In this chapter I do not address that discussion. I merely state that courses that consist of a mixture of law and another discipline usually have a hard time to land in the minds of students. Being trained in 'either-or questions' of the sort of there being a civil contract or not,

---

3 The higher educational system in law in the Netherlands is divided between universities and 'hogescholen' (higher professional education). Hogescholen have taught law at the more practical level since around 2000. Students generally become law clerks at courts, assistants to lawyers, legal bureaucrats, etc. They cannot become a lawyer or a judge.

4 See Margreet Ahsmann, 'Civiel effect, keurslijf of keurmerk?' [2015] *Nederlands Juristenblad* 1355.

someone being liable for damage or not, having a procedural right or not, etcetera, makes it hard to suddenly consider rather 'vague' (we say 'nuanced') answers to whether social rules in a community 'coerce' people to behave in a certain way, whether a value like 'tolerance for uncertainty' influences precautionary policy and practice on the terrain of environmental law, or to think of a theory that considers rules to be 'more' or 'less' legal.[5] In other words, law students in the Netherlands are usually taught 'how to think like a lawyer', and only for a few courses have to temporarily forget that way of thinking.[6]

3 IMAGES OF GRANDFATHERS AND BIKES

In this section I describe my three courses – *Anthropology of Law*, *Comparative Legal Cultures*, and *Sociology of Law*. I highlight their differences by explaining how I use some photos at the start of each course. In the next section I will argue why the use of (parts of) documentaries and films in class should help accomplish the goal of a critical reflection.

Anthropology of Law

The most 'extreme' course I teach is *Anthropology of Law*. Compared to *Sociology of Law* and *Comparative Legal Cultures*, it makes one more theoretical step. The extra step is to discuss empirically the concept of law itself.[7] In my opinion, the discussion of the concept of law is what distinguishes anthropology of law from other studies in law and society. In the sociology of law, for example (but also in almost all modern legal philosophy) state law is taken for granted and as the start-and-end point of the analysis. Modern concepts of law are almost always tied to the State. In the anthropology of law, State law is 'just another folk system of law', alongside many others in modern societies (such as Jewish law, the

---

[5] See Wibren van der Burg, *The Dynamics of Law and Morality: A Pluralist Account of Legal Interactionism* (Ashgate 2014).

[6] Recent debate about the function and curriculum of the law school is by Carel Stolker, *Rethinking the Law School; Education, Research, Outreach and Governance* (CUP 2015).

[7] I say 'empirically' because legal theory and legal philosophy also discuss concepts of law. These discussions are mostly conceptual and normative. In the anthropology of law it is necessary to analyse the workings of law based on empirical findings, and to think 'outside' of the State.

law of Inuit groups in Canada, etc.).[8] That is why I started this year's course with an image of Uluru/Ayers Rock.

Figure 9.1 Photograph of Uluru, Ayers Rock

Uluru was formed through the fight of Aboriginal ancestors and lies in the middle of the Australian desert. It is a Dreaming place of 'the human beings'. For the Aboriginals it is a place of law. Aboriginals walk the paths, renew the paintings, sing and dance the songs connected to the place, because that is the law. If that law is not respected, it disappears. Aboriginals make law appear.[9] In one article an Aboriginal woman is cited:[10]

> The law transcends all things, guiding us in the tradition of living a good life, that is, a life that is sustainable and one which enables our grand-children yet to be born to also experience a good life on earth. The law is who we are, we are also the law. We carry it in our lives. The law is everywhere, we breathe it, we eat it, we sing it, we live it. And it is, as explained by George Tinamin: *Ngangatja apu wiya, ngayuku tjamu.* This is not a rock, it is my grandfather. This is a place where the dreaming comes up, right up from inside the ground.

---

[8] Wibo van Rossum and Anita Böcker, 'Death and Resurrection of Anthropology of Law', in Anita Böcker, Wibo van Rossum and Heleen Weyers (eds), *Legal Anthropology from the Low Countries* (Reed/Elsevier 2009) 9–21.

[9] See among many other relevant research Stephen Muecke, Paddy Roe and Krim Benterrak, *Reading the Country; Introduction to Nomadology* (Fremantle Arts Centre Press 1996); Bruce Chatwin, *The Songlines* (Random House 1987); Ronald M Berndt, Catherine H Berndt, *The Speaking Land: Myth and Story in Aboriginal Australia* (Penguin 1989).

[10] Irene Watson, 'Indigenous Peoples' Law-Ways: Survival against the Colonial State' [1997] 8 *Australian Feminist Law Journal* 39.

Law students are at a loss with citations like this, because it turns their world upside down as to the question 'what is law?' If law is connected to the dreaming, and the dreaming is connected to the songs and the stories, and the stories are connected to the rocks and the waters and the trees, and the rocks and the waters and the trees are connected to the ancestors and the ancestors to the dreaming – then law is everywhere.

Disbelief is what usually remains after the first class: 'This cannot be true'. Fortunately in the following classes we delve deeper into not only the social and legal situation of Aboriginal people in Australia, but also what the anthropology of law entails, what its history as a scientific discipline is and how it struggles not only with the concept of law, especially 'Other law', but also with the idea of 'the Other' in general. My greatest inspiration in these classes is a short chapter by Jean Baudrillard, 'The Melodrama of Difference'. It inspires me to invite students to think in 'exclusions' instead of the usual 'inclusions', in other words to 'discriminate' instead of to think in terms of universals. I want them to take self-designation seriously. Above I wrote that 'Uluru is a dreaming place of the human beings', since 'Anangu' (the name of the group of Aboriginals who are the caretakers of Uluru) means 'human being'. Like 'Inuit' means human being; like 'Roma' means human being. In Baudrillard's theory, this means that creatures that are not part of the 'in group', are not human beings. In fact, they are not interesting. They could just as well not exist. As Foucault says, '[it] is a source of profound relief to think that man is only a recent invention';[11] the idea of human being as a universal concept only exists in the West since about 1800. This also means that students need to learn to think of law in these terms: law is the law of the group, and there is no universalizing tendency. No proselytizing of law and of universal human rights.

The first part of the course is an introduction to the discipline of the anthropology of law, with Australian Aboriginal law as empirical ground and illustration at the same time.[12] We touch on the first empirical legal

---

[11] Michel Foucault, *The Order of Things: Archaeology of the Human Sciences* (Tavistock 1970) xxiii.

[12] In the first eight classes we, inter alia, read Collier, *Analyzing Witchcraft Beliefs*, an interview of Peter Weir on his making of *The Last Wave*, Toohey, *Understanding Aboriginal Law*, several chapters of the Law Reform Commission of Western Australia final report of 2006, Marchetti, *Delivering Justice in Indigenous Sentencing Courts*, Moore, *The Early Classics of Legal Ethnography*, part 1 of Malinowski, *Crime and Custom in Savage Society*, Baudrillard, *The Melodrama of Difference*, Schreiner, *Observing the differences*, and Weiner, *Culture in a Sealed Envelope*. As a 'general introduction', we also read and

anthropological studies, how the research methods developed, and how the concept of legal pluralism entered the socio-legal sciences. We close the first part with an exam. In the second part we discuss, inter alia, based on required readings, the struggle of anthropologists with the idea of universality and human rights, the complexities of fighting FGM/C in Africa, the concept of 'Dharma' in relation to Hindu law, multiculturalism in Europe, and the existence and forms of Roma law. Students need to do a presentation on one of the topics, and they need to do a final paper based on a topic of their choice.

In short, students in this course learn about fundamentally different concepts of law, connected to different, often incommensurable views on what it means to be 'human' and part of a community. Compared to my other two courses, *Anthropology of Law* is radically different. The course not only questions common sense, theoretical notions of law, and how law functions in society, but it also presents alternatives for the concept of law that is dominant in our ordinary discourse. It does that empirically, which should be distinguished from philosophical or overly theoretical accounts of law.

Comparative Legal Cultures

My course in *Comparative Legal Cultures* starts with several images of randomly parked bikes at the train station in my hometown Haarlem.

I ask students 'what they see'. They first have to discover the official sign that forbids to park bikes outside the designated areas and racks, and that many bikes are parked outside the racks. We discuss that this is quite normal, that these legal rules are hardly ever enforced, so there is a 'gap' between black letter law and their working in society. We continue by discussing whether a certain tolerance toward following legal rules, tolerance toward disregarding rules even, may be related to Dutch cultural values. Would the situation be different in France, or in China?

The images thus serve to illustrate at least two basic goals in this particular course. First, that the relationship between legal rules, their interpretation and actual working in society, is culturally specific. Second, that comparing black letter law is not enough when you want to understand law comparatively. Comparing 'parking rules' across countries would give a completely distorted picture of the meaning of law in different countries. You would also need to know, as in the photos,

criticize Fernanda Pirie, *The Anthropology of Law* (OUP 2013). Visit my website www.wibovanrossum.nl for the latest descriptions.

Figure 9.2 Randomly parked bicycles at the train station in Haarlem

whether people actually comply with the law, whether non-compliance is seen as a problem, if rules are enforced and if so, in what manner. In other words, the study of law comparatively can only meaningfully be done when studying legal cultures comparatively.[13]

By then, the course has actually only started. We read about how 'culture' can be understood, whether cultures should be considered bounded wholes and internally consistent, and to what extent legal transplants are possible, taking into account that legal systems and practices sometimes (but not always) actually resist and transform transplanted rules. Alongside these discussions we treat the question 'why' we should compare, and also 'what' we should compare. Should we compare in order to improve other legal systems or our legal system?

---

[13] In my opinion, traditional comparative law focused too much on black letter law to make comparison meaningful. Most comparative law scholars today would agree. See for example the many works of David Nelken, specifically D Nelken, *Legal Cultures*, in: DS Clark (ed), *Comparative Law and Society* (Edward Elgar 2012), G Samuel, *An Introduction to Comparative Law Theory and Method* (Hart 2014), and J Husa, *A New Introduction to Comparative Law* (Hart 2015).

Or should we compare in order to better understand our own legal culture? Considering the 'what to compare' question, should we start with comparing similar legal rules and then find out what happens in society, or should we compare similar social situations and then find out how the law deals with these? By the way, how are we able to say anything is 'similar' if we do not even speak the same language so we have to translate? On top of these complex questions with no definite answers, students also need to know about the difference between qualitative and quantitative sociological research, and about the difference between explanation and understanding. We read, for example, Nelken on the concept of legal culture, the Legrand/Watson debate on legal transplants and the 'closed-ness' of cultures, Teubner because of his ideas on tight- and loose-coupling, and Flood, Friedman and Rosen on ethnographic and historical research. Alongside this, we read *Cultures and Organizations* written by Hofstede, Hofstede and Minkov.[14] This book is meant to give students some empirical ground to compare different cultural values that may lie 'behind' legal rules and that possibly influence their interpretation, application and popular acceptance. In three weeks students are supposed to have the knowledge and flexibility to work with these tools in order to do explorative comparative

[14] This is the literature for the first three weeks of the course: John Flood 'Socio-Legal Ethnography' in: Reza Banakar & Max Travers (2005) *Theory and Method in Socio-Legal Research* (Hart 2005); Lawrence Friedman, 'A Few Thoughts on Ethnography, History, and Law' in June Starr & Mark Goodale (eds), *Practicing Ethnography in Law* (Palgrave Macmillan 2002); Ido de Haan, 'Politics between Accommodation and Commotion' in Emmeline Besamusca & Jaap Verheul (eds), *Discovering the Dutch* (Amsterdam University Press 2010); Geert Hofstede, Gert Jan Hofstede and Michael Minkov, *Cultures and Organizations, Software of the Mind* (3rd edn, McGraw-Hill 2010); Pierre Legrand, 'The Impossibility of "Legal Transplants"' [1997] 4 *Maastricht Journal of European & Comparative Law* 111; Wijnand Mijnhardt, 'A Tradition of Tolerance' in: Emmeline Besamusca & Jaap Verheul, *Discovering the Dutch* (Amsterdam University Press 2010); David Nelken, 'Legal Cultures' in David S Clark (ed), *Comparative Law and Society* (Edward Elgar 2012); Lawrence Rosen, *Law as Culture; An Invitation* (Preface) (Princeton University Press 2008); Wibo van Rossum, 'Legal Culture' in Emmeline Besamusca & Jaap Verheul (eds), *Discovering the Dutch* (Amsterdam University Press 2014); Gunther Teubner, 'Legal Irritants: Good Faith in British Law or How Unifying Law Ends Up in New Divergences' [1998] 61 *The Modern Law Review* 1, 1–14; Alan Watson – Legal Transplants and European Private Law, Ius Commune Lectures on European Private Law, see: http://www.ejcl.org/44/art44-2.html (accessed 21 August 2015).

research.[15] In the second part of the course, students do presentations in pairs on a specific legal topic and based on their own research. For example, they choose a specific problem in tort law, for example, the liability of medical doctors for mistakes on patients, and compare France and the Netherlands. Or they study the legal regulation of religion in the UK as compared to Spain, and discover that concepts such as 'secular' and 'separation of church and state' actually do not make us understand much.

At the end of the course students write a research paper in which they compare a legal phenomenon in two countries. In line with the purpose of the course their conclusions on the connection between a specific legal regulation or complex set of rules and the broader values of a country, are rather diverse but nonetheless can be theoretically classified as seen in Table 9.1. They necessarily generate new questions.

Table 9.1 Relation between legal rules, legal practices and cultural values

Situation number	**Legal rules**	**Legal practices**	**Cultural values**
1	similar	similar	similar
2	different	similar	similar
3	similar	different	similar
4	different	different	similar
5	different	different	different
6	different	similar	different
7	similar	different	different
8	similar	similar	different

Situation 1 covers a comparison of countries, in which for a certain issue, for example, whether same sex marriages and registered partnerships are allowed, the legal rules are similar, legal practice is similar (for example, relative numbers of marriages), and the cultural values of the countries are largely similar. As I hope the reader will understand, this situation, as

[15] The course does not pay much attention to the traditional 'legal families' such as modern law, Islamic law, Hindu law, etc. In my opinion, styles of legal regulation cut across these families. Environmental law regulation in China may take a similar form as in Turkey.

with situation 5 (only differences), is the least interesting. All other situations are much more interesting. Consider the treatment of prostitution in Sweden compared to the Netherlands. In Sweden, prostitution is not forbidden, but users should be prosecuted and fined. In the Netherlands, prostitution is regulated, but allowed. In both countries the numbers of prostitutes do not differ much. In Sweden, it appears difficult to prosecute users. Culturally both countries very much look alike. In other words, this is situation 2. The question students need to reflect on after they have researched the above, is why the two countries have such a different legal approach, while legal practice and cultural values do not seem to differ much? Another example is a comparison of the juvenile criminal justice system in Belgium and the Netherlands. Belgium on paper seems to be much more protective towards the prosecution of juveniles than the Netherlands (no criminal liability in Belgium below the age of 18 while Netherlands has the minimum age set at 12-years-old) but how juveniles are actually treated in both systems is rather similar. Culturally, however, both countries show some similarities but also rather large differences. So why do the two countries show such similarities in practice, while the law and underlying cultural values are different (situation 6)?

In short, students in this course learn how to question their – sometimes inconsistent – common sense assumptions, such as that law and culture necessarily are two sides of the same coin, that law and legal practice necessarily coincide, that modern legal cultures are largely alike, and that the harmonization of law in Europe is simply a question of harmonizing the rules.

Sociology of Law

The *Sociology of Law* course this year also started with an image of bikes at the train station in my hometown Haarlem. After asking the first simple questions like ‘what they see’ and a short discussion of their answers, the first lesson we draw is that legal rules ‘on paper’ differ from how they work out ‘in society’. A second image shows the seemingly chaotic placement of bikes, that on second sight is not that disorderly.

A better look shows people have put their bikes in rows. My question ‘whether they are required to do so by law’ of course generates laughter. But the question brings them to think about what does induce people to behave orderly. We discuss psychological (do like others do), economical (easy to find your bike again and stands the least chance of the bike to be wrecked), and social (this way other people can still easily take their bike) considerations people might have. The second lesson is thus that

Figure 9.3 Bike placement detail

even though law is not fully effective (or not effective at all), this does not necessarily mean that there is chaos. 'Law' and 'Order' are not each other's mirror. Then I show a third image, in which the same place shows painted yellow lines on the pavement designating new areas where bikes can legally be placed.

The lesson is that the informal order in society that was against the law now has become formalized and legalized. The question attached to this photo is a blow in the face of law students: Who made that law? They have to admit that although formally it was the lawmaker, empirically it was society itself.

Even though a start like this is funny, interesting, sets students off balance and takes them out of their comfort zone, I also hope that from now on they will look differently at law and their own social surroundings. They should not only remember the pictures of the bikes whenever they visit a train station and look for signs of prohibition, but hopefully also use this perspective when they hop on the bus (contract?) or order two beers by raising two fingers at the bar man.

Sociology of Law has an introduction in which we read texts on the definition of sociology of law, its main focus of what legal rules 'do' in

Figure 9.4 Yellow lines designating new areas where bikes can be legally placed

society (the other being how society influences the development of law), its methods, and some 'classics'.[16] The rest of the course is structured around the three basic questions of law and society studies, and their pioneering scholars, namely Marx and 'law and power/inequality', Durkheim and 'law and social solidarity', and Weber and 'law and legitimacy'. We read parts of original texts from those pioneers, summaries of their work, and how they approached their questions. However, we also read contemporary empirical and theoretical research that relate to those basic questions. In 'law and power' we read about how the rule of law is used to further economic and global power interests, but also research at

[16] Classics in the introductory part of the course are S Macaulay, 'Non-contractual Relations in Business: A Preliminary Study' [1963] 28 *American Sociological Review* 1; V Aubert, 'Enkele sociale functies van wetgeving' in John Griffiths (ed) *De Sociale Werking van Recht* (Ars Aequi Libri 1996) 113; SF Moore, 'Law and Social Change: The Semi-autonomous Social Field as an Appropriate Subject of Study' [1973] 7(4) *Law and Society Review* 719.

the micro-level on unequal parties in court.[17] 'Law and social solidarity' brings us texts on and of Durkheim, and to contemporary research on practices of social exclusion, the requirements for Dutch citizenship, and texts on Dutch cultural identity.[18] The third question we address is on 'law and legitimacy'. It brings us to contemporary Dutch research on trust in the legal system, distrustful citizens, bottom-up lawmaking, and the transparency of institutions.[19]

The course takes eight weeks and is fully packed. There is a general weekly lecture of four hours and a discussion meeting of two hours. The lecture is not only a 'talking head'; I use selections from documentaries to illustrate sociological concepts and show some documentaries in full. In the second part of the course students need to write a short paper. To force them out of their comfort zone, they have to base their paper on interviews with two real people. Another requirement that brings them off balance is that they can write on any topic they find interesting, as long as it is connected to one of the three basic questions (see above) and is approached in a socio-legal way. Law students find this difficult because the usual assignments in their studies are variants of 'solve this legal case' or 'contrast the opinion of X and Y on this matter, and give your own opinion'. They finish the course with an exam on the literature.

The main goals of the course can all be squared under the heading 'see law as being part of society', and especially understand that law is not always that effective and has unintended consequences, that law not only

---

17 Part of the literature on law and power is Marc Galanter, 'Why the "Haves" come out Ahead' [1974–1975] 9 *Law & Society Review* 95; and Ugo Mattei & Laura Nader, *Plunder, When the Rule of Law is Illegal* (Blackwell 2008).

18 All texts are in Dutch; among them are A Böcker & B de Hart, 'Wat zijn de bedoelde en onbedoelde gevolgen van het migratierecht?' [What are intended and unintended consequences of migration law?] in M Hertogh, H Weyers (eds), *Recht van onderop, Antwoorden uit de rechtssociologie* (*Ars Aequi Libri*, 11th edn 2011) 409; Robert Knegt, *Burgerschap en niet-statelijk recht* [*Citizenship and non-state law*] [2012] Recht der Werkelijkheid 41–58, and two chapters from Herman Pleij, *Moet kunnen, op zoek naar een Nederlandse identiteit* [*Why not?! Looking for a Dutch identity*] (Promotheus 2014).

19 Most research on this question is in Dutch, e.g. Marnix Croes, 'Heeft de burger vertrouwen in de rechter?' ['Do people trust judges?'] in Marc Hertogh en Heleen Weyers (eds), *op cit*; Jonathan Jackson et al, *Policing by Consent: Trust in Justice. Topline Results Round 5 from European Social Survey* (ESS 2011), and Nick Huls & Suzan Stoter, 'Welke rol spelen ambtenaren achter de schermen van het wetgevingsproces?' (What is the role of civil servants behind the screen of the official lawmaking process?) in Marc Hertogh en Heleen Weyers (eds), *op cit*.

empowers but is also used by powers, that law not only enhances social solidarity but also excludes people, and finally that we have to admit that we have hardly anything empirically to say as to what enhances the legitimacy of State institutions and actors. In short, students in this course learn to relativize law's role in society.

4 WHY USE VISUALS?

As I said in the introductory section of this chapter, I think ways of teaching should relate and adapt to the ways students in contemporary societies take in and produce information. This probably makes it easier to remember. More important, however, is that visuals in my opinion will help students develop a more imaginative critical perspective on law.[20] Photos and film confront students with real-life situations, which together with a case or social issue and the story behind it enables them to put themselves in the shoes of the people concerned.[21] There is another reason why using visuals is good, specifically in the described courses. Photos and documentaries bring society into the classroom.[22] In the rest of this section I will illustrate these interrelated arguments with a few examples.

I feel law students mostly have forgotten that society is a complex thing and have come to think that law is applied to a set of pre-given facts or an abstract description of a situation ('A contracted B …', etc.). Real life however is different and more complex.[23] The cases and social issues discussed in class are about indigenous groups and minorities, about cultural routines and value-laden habits, and about the actual behaviour of people in relation to legal rules. This is never a question of

---

[20] This argument is also used by Joseph W Dellapenna, 'Peasants, Tanners, and Psychiatrists: Using Films to Teach Comparative Law' [2008] 36 *International Journal of Legal Information* 156. Available at: http://ssrn.com/abstract=1126762 (accessed 10 August 2015).

[21] See for an overview of recent studies the excellent review by Leslie J Moran, 'Visual Justice' [2012] 8 *International Journal of Law in Context* 43.

[22] In anthropology a recent debate was on how using visual material should help in improving the situation of suppressed people. Visuals are then used in an activist programme. See Mac McLagan, 'Introduction: Making Human Rights Claims Public' [2006] 8 *American Anthropologist (Special issue: Technologies of Witnessing: The Visual Culture of Human Rights)* 191.

[23] A valid counterargument here is that photos and documentaries are constructed facts as well. I would then say that one has to start somewhere, and that students will hopefully experience the real life of the law later in their career.

black and white – of dichotomies. Confronting law students with documentaries that show those people, their life circumstances and their routines and values, means confronting them with real-life situations in which the 'legally relevant facts' still need to be carved out. In socio-legal courses we do not primarily discuss legal cases; we discuss behaviour and social structures in relation to the law. For example, in sociology of law one of the discussions is on the influence of corporate actors in the lawmaking process. Democratically and legally speaking, only voters have an influence in lawmaking. In practice, many professional lobby groups work in and around 'The Hague circles' and also internationally in Brussels, or New York for example, in order to make sure that certain corporate interests are taken into account. Moreover, they may have a direct interest in selling their products to State agencies, for example in the area of safety and surveillance. Students may read about and discuss this, but the impact is far greater when they also view the documentary *The Security Complex* (*Het veiligheidscomplex*) about how the perception of too many asylum-seekers entering Europe, and the threat of terrorism is captured by corporate actors in the safety industry, eager to sell their technical solutions, e.g. iris scans for airport control and camera software to analyse street movements. And hearing EU Commission members say that this is a EUR100 billion market (and growing) for the coming years.[24] The security complex is indeed the complex entanglement of governmental security demands, the safety wishes of civilians, and the corporations whose primary purpose is to make the largest profit possible by selling their new technologies on a market they themselves help create. However, it is too easy to dismiss this entanglement as illegal, out of line, or unwanted. Somehow, the EU and European States need the corporations if they want to secure their borders. Civilians do want to live a safe and secure life. Seeing (part of) society and the lawmaking process in this documentary and discussing it with the help of literature, gives a better insight in the rather vague and messy actual process of lawmaking than if they had merely read it from paper.

As for the argument that visuals add to students' imagination, I believe that a message of a 'Rom Baro' (literally 'big man') saying directly in the camera 'of course we have our own jurisdiction and it is none of your business', tends to stick much more compared to when I would say such a thing as a teacher. Because the rest of the documentary on groups of

---

[24] Available at: http://tegenlicht.vpro.nl/afleveringen/2013-2014/veiligheids complex.html (accessed 10 August 2015).

Roma and Sinti in the Netherlands makes very clear why they have their own laws different from Dutch State law.[25] Their particular legal culture or what is left of it needs partly be maintained by not speaking about it, by the refusal to reflect on it. Reflection in their eyes means one starts to question the laws that were made 'by the forefathers'. And once you start to question traditions, they are usually on the verge of being broken down or at least adapted to current circumstances. That is why the Rom Baro does not want to discuss their jurisdiction and how it works, with the filmmaker. The documentary can be connected to scientific studies of Roma worldwide. Students read about romaniye (Roma law) and its seemingly irrational rules e.g. taboos on talking about sex and death, rules on gender divisions, norms to throw away stuff that has become 'impure', etc. These rules are accompanied by the strong norm, upheld by social control, to not talk about romaniye at all in order to keep it safe from non-gypsies.[26] It is one thing to read about these laws, but another to see that actual human beings live up to these rules and consider their law to be an integral part of their social life. To make clear what 'secrecy' and 'outsiders' mean for these people I also show parts of a documentary in which an older Roma couple discusses whether they should agree to be interviewed by the filmmaker. The older Roma woman out of habit evades questions and makes up stories during the interview, and the man then tells her: 'She [the filmmaker] is not a bad *gaji*. Tell her the truth.'[27] At the same time these documentaries show the ordinary life and living conditions of several families, which also makes clear that norms do change and that traditions do slowly adapt to new circumstances. Bringing these families and their issues 'into the class room' induces students to connect to their lives. I do not mean to say that reading scientific texts is boring and that students will quickly forget about it. But a message *plus* image and sound, just stands a higher chance of being remembered, because it induces students to put themselves in the shoes of others. The impact of visuals hopefully produces better professionals that more often say: 'Wait a minute, this can be seen differently/is probably more complex than we think!'

---

[25] The quote is from the documentary *Volk zonder eigen land* by Bob Entrop, Sol film producties, 2007. Available at: http://www.npo.nl/sinti-roma-in-beeld-volk-zonder-eigen-land/31-05-2008/RVU_103452 (accessed 10 August 2010).

[26] See for example Walter Weyrauch and Anne Bell, 'Autonomous Law-making: The Case of the "Gypsies"' [1993–1994] 103 *Yale Law Journal* 323.

[27] A *gaje* is a non-Roma, an outsider, literally a 'non-human'. Citation is from *American Gypsy, A Stranger in Everybody's Land*, a documentary on legal pluralism in a lawsuit in the USA, by Jasmine Dellal, 1999.

Text combined with visuals enhances the urgency of seeing law as part of social relations. Reading about why and how people consider female genital-cutting already has a large impact ('how can people support this awful practice?!') – seeing women in a family setting actually discussing the practice, some supporting and some denouncing it, makes clear that these women are and want to be part of a group in which some practices are consciously upheld, whilst others are strongly contested. Law is part of a group process, is always part and parcel of social relations.[28] Law students should realize that law, because it depends on social relations, is a phenomenon embedded in the broader culture of a country. Teachers can only show this by making use of materials outside of the domain of the legal system, namely by using philosophy to shed light on the principles underlying the law, by looking at the law as it historically developed due to changes in society, and by embedding law in social relations and circumstances. In all disciplines visuals will enhance the learning process, but especially in courses related to the domain of the social (including social history) documentaries and photo's can enhance the critical potential of law students.

5 CONCLUSION: VISUALS FOR A CRITICAL LEGAL PROFESSION

Important goals in the three courses are to make clear that law is part and parcel of social relationships; that modern legal cultures are difficult to compare; and that laws can be based on foundational principles and practices that are incommensurable to the ones we find valuable. These goals, is my guess, will probably *not* stick in the minds of students. These courses only form a small part of their professional education, so I would already be happy if they would remember two or three insights when they need it, and my conviction is that visuals help do that. These insights hopefully function as triggers in their later career to 'take a step back and think'. Suppose they work at a ministry or policy bureau and need to write on a regulation empowering citizens to address pollution of their living environment by local companies. I should hope this professional would remember that the 'individual rights strategy' (individuals need to take action to secure their rights) might not be very effective when the people to complain about are part of the complainants' daily

---

[28] I refer to Kim Longinotto's 2002 documentary *The day I will never forget* about FGM/C in Africa. Available at: http://www.imdb.com/title/tt0342265/ (accessed 10 August 2015).

social circles. 'Wait a minute!', our future policy maker should say, 'Do we expect citizens to take action even when it's not a personal problem and file a written complaint in an office they have to travel two kilometres for, about a company their neighbour is working for?'

Suppose another professional works in Brussels for the EU on a directive requiring Member States to work towards better protection of young people at work.[29] The directive prohibits the employment of people under 18-years-old, but under certain conditions national legislation may allow exceptions to that rule. This professional should immediately realize, when s/he did a course on comparative law and culture, that the 'exceptions to the rule' will probably be interpreted very differently from one country to another ('wait a minute!' again). What is considered to be 'light work' for example, or 'work which exceeds the mental or physical capacities', depends partly on cultural values, such as how tough and assertive people are expected to be, or on value-laden assessments of what people at certain ages are capable of. Our professional should discuss assumptions underlying the directive in order to decide more properly on whether to grant Member States a certain leeway in this, or to describe more strictly what is expected.

And suppose yet another professional who has done a course in legal anthropology works at an agency to help build-up the rule of law in developing countries. Confronted maybe with resistance from the local population, despite democratic support, she should wonder about customary legal practices on, for example, the power of traditional chiefs, or the consultation of forebears ('wait a minute!' again). I believe that some of them will remember what they have *seen* in class.

Disregarding the specific professions, such as judge, lawyer, civil servant, etc., a good professional in my view is someone who is willing to go against the current when necessary – but not too often, because going along with the routine is important too. A good professional is able to present an issue in a broader perspective, for example, concerning social and legal problems between a specific minority group and the State, and s/he is able to draw historical parallels and compare with other minorities. Also, good professionals dare to question common sense assumptions: Why should education be *that* important? Why should law only be attached to the State? Why should we expect any compliance with this regulation?

---

[29] For example, on what is now Council Directive 94/33/EC of 22 June 1994 on the protection of young people at work.

In other words, I would like the future legal professional to think for herself/himself, to ask critical questions, and to be able to see the broader social context of law. Visuals can support this.

10. For a new and more diverse comparative legal education[1]

Sabrina Germain

1 INTRODUCTION

Comparative law became a part of American law schools and European law faculties' curriculums shortly after the Second World War.[2] Its expansion and its rise as a standalone course were due in part to the success of the 1937 Round Table of Comparative Law of the Association of American law schools where the province of the subject-matter and the methods of teaching had been abundantly discussed.[3] In the aftermath of the war, many scholars felt compelled to write on the merits of comparative law, its importance as a research topic, and its role in the education of young legal minds and future practitioners.[4]

Unfortunately, the usual absence of a defined legal corpus and the reference in a vague sense to 'any juristic activity which pays attention to one or more law [sic] or system of laws'[5] as comparative law has led American and European law students to perceive courses in comparative

---

[1] This contribution builds on an article published in the *Journal of Criminal Justice Education*, see: Sabrina Germain, 'Prison-based Education and Its New Pedagogical Perspective' (2014) (ahead-of-print) *Journal of Criminal Justice Education* 1. This article is dedicated to Professor Patrick Glenn, outstanding scholar, fantastic mentor and wonderful human being, may you rest in peace.

[2] George Winterton, 'Comparative Law Teaching' [1975] 23(1) *The American Journal of Comparative Law* 69.

[3] Mathias Reimann, 'The End of Comparative Law as an Autonomous Subject' [1996] 11 *Tul Eur & Civ LF* 49.

[4] See generally, John N Hazard, 'Comparative Law in Legal Education' (1951) 18(2) *The University of Chicago Law Review* 264; Angelo Piero Sereni, 'On Teaching Comparative Law' [1951] 64(5) *Harv Law Rev* 770.

[5] Edward D Re, 'Comparative Law Courses in the Law School Curriculum' [1952] 1 *Am J Comp L* 233.

law as superfluous rather than indispensable.[6] Indeed, comparative law does not constitute a branch of law in itself. There are no rules of comparative law nor does it constitute a body of law compromising normative prescriptions. This may explain why a variety of courses and programs labeled as 'comparative law' in American law schools and European faculties widely differ in their content and delivery. For the purpose of this contribution I chose to focus on comparative law as a topic 'going beyond mere knowledge of foreign rules, [broadening] the understanding of how legal rules work in context'.[7] I also limit the analysis to the teaching of comparative courses that flesh out multiple legal traditions, and set aside the academic research of comparative law.

Comparative legal education seems to be simultaneously undergoing a crisis and a revolution. The decline in enrollment and loss of interests in these classes signal outdated teaching methods, while North-American law schools calling for the death of comparative law as a self-contained area of study are now exploring trans-systemic law teaching.[8] Perhaps this paradoxical phenomenon can be explained by a need for more diverse and better-adapted teaching methods to train a new generation of lawyers that will inevitably be confronted to issues of transnational, international and comparative law in its practice.[9] For this, it is imperative that we start perfecting the training of future lecturers by taking them to alternative teaching venues.

For my part, having had the chance to attend trans-systemic courses at the McGill Faculty of Law, and having received my legal education in an American law school and a French '*École de Droit*', my training as a common and civil law lawyer inevitably led me to choose comparative law as one of my main research interests. In the spring of 2011, entering my second semester as a doctoral candidate I had the desire to invest myself in a meaningful project and confront a different academic reality. I decided to take part in the Cornell Prison Education Program (CPEP) as a law instructor. Since the 1990s, the CPEP has brought together faculty and graduate students to teach courses in liberal arts to groups of inmate-students at a maximum security correctional facility (Auburn),[10] with the goal of contributing to the successful re-entry into society of

---

6 Michael P Waxman, 'Teaching Comparative Law in the 21st Century: Beyond the Civil/Common Law Dichotomy' [2001] 51 *J Legal Educ* 305.

7 Mathias Siems, *Comparative Law* (CUP 2014).

8 Mathias Reimann [1996], op cit, 49.

9 Ibid.

10 'Cornell Prison Education Program': <http://cpep.cornell.edu/_Home> (accessed on 8 September 2013).

incarcerated persons by supporting their academic ambitions,[11] and providing scholars with an invaluable teaching experience.

This experience triggered in me a reflection on legal education outside the classroom, and more particularly on the importance of a comparative legal education to reveal diverse voices in traditional and untraditional teaching environments. I understood that the solutions and alternative methods acquired in unconventional teaching environments can and should be applied to all traditional topics offered in European faculties and North American law schools. It also seemed to me that comparative law required a superior level of introspection on the part of the student and the instructor making it a more fertile ground for learning through alternative approaches.

Indeed in order to acquire a clear understanding of another legal system it is imperative for students to be taught with a more global and diverse view on the law. I believe that this can only be achieved by having instructors turn to alternative venues to broaden their own understanding of legal teaching. Future and young lecturers must adopt a different perspective on the law to revive the teaching of comparative law in traditional venues. For this, the more diverse student-body present in unconventional environments can inspire and provide them with alternative teaching tools. Thus, in this chapter, I wish to share how the teaching of comparative law in prison led me to develop better-adapted teaching techniques to shape a more critical attitude towards law and legal reasoning in traditional law school students. Through the narrative of my own experience I hope to offer a critique of the traditional comparative law-teaching paradigm and provide constructive solutions to improve comparative legal education.

2 TEACHING LEGAL TRADITIONS IN AN UNTRADITIONAL ENVIRONMENT

Prison is commonly thought of as a place that houses the abandoned, angry, and the marginalized. The talent and creativity of inmates enrolled in education programs is hardly ever highlighted. Most certainly it is because of the controversial nature of these initiatives that the impact and benefits of prison education programs has often been questioned. Nonetheless, the abundant scholarship supporting prison-based education programs as a way of reducing rates of recidivism had a significant

---

11 Ibid.

influence on my approach as a law instructor. Developing my lesson-plan and planning my course objective I tried to fit, as closely as possible, the aims of this body of literature expanding on education as a reinsertion process. While this contribution does not have the goal of establishing a direct correlation between education and successful reinsertion, the conclusions I draw nevertheless support the findings of other empiricists on the topic.[12]

Comparative law being one of my main research interests, I offered to teach a weekly seminar on *Comparative Legal Traditions* at Auburn. This course was designed to give students a basic understanding of some key legal traditions: Talmudic law, Civil law, Islamic law, Common law, and Asian legal traditions. Similarities and differences between the traditions were put forward through the examination of their historical backgrounds, constitutional systems, and interpretation through the reading of Patrick Glenn's book on *Legal Traditions of the World*,[13] and various practical exercises.

My 22 male students, with a rough age range of 21 to 55, coming from diverse social, cultural, economic, religious and educational backgrounds offered me a new perspective on legal education. By the end of our class my students had convinced me that traditional legal education could benefit from a new perspective on its approach of comparative law teaching. Through their understanding of my contextualized methods I noted that comparison had become part of their thought process as they referenced to their own 'prison legal tradition' when addressing the seminars' topics. Adapting to their unique outlook led me to adjust my teaching style and to understand that comparison lies beyond the study of foreign systems of laws. It should be applied to different legal concepts in varying degrees.

The Importance of Comparison

I have wondered what had made my experience so deep and beneficial. The increased security of the facility certainly created an unusual work environment, however I believe that it is the exceptional student-body

---

[12] John Dewey, *Democracy and Education* (Courier Dover Publications 2004); James S Vacca, 'Educated Prisoners are Less Likely to Return to Prison' [2004] 55(4) *Journal of Correctional Education* 297; Bruce Western, Jeffrey R Kling and David F Weiman, 'The Labor Market Consequences of Incarceration' [2001] 47(3) *Crime & Delinquency* 410.

[13] Patrick H Glenn, *Legal Traditions of the World: Sustainable Diversity in Law* (OUP 2007).

with its ability to approach comparative legal topics in a completely novel manner that made the experience extra-ordinary. Their atypical interpretation of religious legal traditions and their refreshing presentation of principles of civil law and common law, time and again surprised me and challenged me as an instructor.

Many psychologists and sociologists have been interested in the prison environment, mostly in its culture, its codes and its lifestyle. As I started teaching my seminar, I myself became fascinated with this universe, and naturally the following passage of Professor Patrick Glenn's book on *Legal Traditions of the World*, came to mind:

> There are other traditions, however, which do not seek to play a major role for an entire community, and do not seek its good or well-being. They are parasitic traditions, living off a larger one and profiting from its adherents in a way antithetical to their welfare and well-being. These are traditions of crime- either generally or in more particular form, such as those of the mafia or the narcos, and there may be others of more recent generation.[14]

I had thought of my students as founder and perpetrators of traditions of corruption. However with students coming from such different ethnic, social, and economic backgrounds, it was incorrect to assume that a prisoner archetype really existed. Also, I could not believe that they had dedicated their lives to parasitizing larger traditions. In fact they had not, but they were members of a unique legal tradition, one that arose in prison.

The 'prison legal tradition' is strong and continuous within the walls. It rewards great learning skills, membership and loyalty to a group, and shuns betrayal and arrogance. Although at times questionable, it is a tradition with its own axes of morality and decency, one of humility and great knowledge with customs and rites of passage. It stands on its own and nourishes itself from religion and a conflicted sense of rationality. It is in no way the corruption of an already existing tradition. The prison legal tradition does not parasite, it crafts and perfects its own rules.

For example, after a few weeks I noticed that the students had established that witty interventions or good answers were to be rewarded with a piece of candy, and that older and more experience inmates were in charge of communicating this rule. This instant gratification was just one of many examples of how the tradition had developed its own rituals, means of transmission, and vision of justice and fairness. Introducing the

---

14 Patrick H Glenn (2007), op cit.

biblical story of Solomon's Judgment the students unpacked their definition of equity. Some of them saw Solomon's ruling as wrong and unjust. In their opinion it was only right that the baby be physically separated in half between the two women claiming to be his mother. In my students' eyes there was nothing wrong in the dismemberment of an infant if it were to give out an equal 'lot'. This explanation made me uneasy, and I found myself wondering how I would enter into a dialogue with a group that had an extremely different outlook on ethics, law and morals. The comparative experience had to take another dimension. I had to teach them about justice but also about fairness, to show them that the law adapts to social life and values, and that our sense of decency also shapes the legal corpus.

Thanks to our in-class discussions, their presentations and essays, I was able to adjust to this untraditional environment. Within my first week of teaching, I had undergone something close to what the literature describes as an Inside-Out experience. Professor Lori Pompa, founder of the celebrated Inside-Out Program, explains that the goal of her project was to provide a transformative experience, focusing on an embodied method of teaching.[15]

The Inside-Out Program promotes teaching law to 'inside' and 'outside' students within the prison environment. Law school and inmate-students develop a relationship around their understanding of legal topics and get to experience each other's point of view and realities. Law school students are provided with a shock therapy to spur questions about prison life, inspire them to improve the prison system and become better legal practitioners. The program provides a great stepping-stone to these students, but it also offers inmates an exceptional learning opportunity. Traditional law school students contribute to the mutual learning process by helping their inmate comrades nuance their sometimes sharp and counter-intuitive assumptions about the law. The 'Inside-Out' method is not a single-sided learning tool, just like many other prison-education programs it has a multi-directional dimension.

Law professor Giovanna Shay used the Inside-Out method to structure her class at the Western Massachusetts Correctional Alcohol Center. She later transposed the methodology to her lectures at Western New England University School of Law. She writes that the program made her adopt a more creative teaching style. She went back to the drawing board and

---

[15] Lori Pompa, 'Breaking Down the Walls: Inside-Out Learning and the Pedagogy of Transformation' in Stephen John Hartnett, Jennifer K Wood and Bryan J McCann (eds), *Turning Silence into Speech and Action: Prison Activism and the Pedagogy of Empowered Citizenship* (Taylor & Francis 2011).

simplified her approach. She rethought her class preparation and teaching techniques to adapt to a more diverse audience. For my part, drifting away from the traditional methods towards a more fluid and organic lecturing style, I also experimented with alternative teaching techniques. Initially approaching my student with a classic approach focused on black letter law, I quickly shifted to constructivist and methods better-adapted to my unconventional audience. I focused my teaching on the students' needs and became more creative in my presentation of classic legal topics.[16]

I had an outstanding group of students, who were interested in sharing their work through original presentations, but also eager to give their opinions on a variety of legal issues ranging from the role of equity in common law to the importance of Sharia investments in 21st century finance. At times the debate had to be refocused as the desire to drive the discussion towards philosophical and quasi-metaphysical questions rather than adopting legal inductive or deductive reasoning was strong.

My students remained fundamentally positivist in their analysis of the law. The image they painted of the judicial power was one of an arbitrary government of the judges. They believed a just and good system should not be subject to interpretation, and that the letter of the law should be laid down in order to avoid any misinterpretations. To me this was paradoxical given their attachment to divine legal traditions, where more often than not the law is the heritage of a messiah's interpreted transcriptions of God's revealed message.

I was surprised to see how religious legal traditions resonated with my students, and impressed by their quasi-scientific knowledge of Islam. In upstate New York facilities, one in three inmates converts to Islam upon incarceration. This may be explained by the rhythm this religion gives to one's life. Daily rituals can be accomplished in prison, since no temple, or church buildings are required for prayer, making it an easier religion to practice in confinement.

I spent a lot of time theorizing as to why my students had more trust in the divine judgment than any of the occidental dispute resolution systems. Perhaps it is because they have received harsh judgments from their peers and trust that, when the time comes, God will be more lenient in his judgment. I believe that the possible redemption offered by religious law validated their faith and gave them the confidence that they were not hopeless.

[16] Giovanna Shay, 'Inside-Out as Law School Pedagogy' [2012] 62 *Journal of Legal Education* 207.

The comparative process that I had triggered between the prison legal tradition and the legal traditions studied during the course of the seminar had fostered a novel learning process. It was the meshing of omnipresent spirituality and the unconventional environment that allowed for more diversity to be voiced, and the comparative teaching of different legal principles that had the students reflect deeply on different questions beyond the mere absorption of jurisprudence or codified law.

A Constructivist Approach to Comparative Law Teaching

The diverse background of my students and their varied acquaintance with legal studies required a constructivist teaching approach. The constructivist method helps students learn pro-actively by building on pre-existing knowledge and skills to ignite a reflection on the law. Instead of the students being fed the information or confined to a passive role, knowledge becomes part of a construct they assemble under the guidance of their teacher.

Course materials are used as more than supports, they provide the stimulus that sparks the learning process. With this approach prior knowledge is the tool that helps discover new concepts and build new ideas.[17] The professor helps students select and transform the information, formulate hypotheses and make decisions relying on their cognitive structure. An active dialogue is naturally installed, not with the purpose to 'socratically' forge a legal mind, but rather to have students spontaneously discover 'legal things'.[18]

Thus, my teaching had to be comprehensible and accessible to optimize my students' learning experience. For this, I had them use prior knowledge, legal or other. I did not want to lecture them and they did not want me impose my knowledge on them. I understood that a harsh Socratic method would also be unsuccessful, I had to develop contextualized teaching methods to help them acquire knowledge by filling the gaps. Given their particular personal experience with the American legal system I assumed some prior knowledge of the law even though my goal was not to have them gain factual knowledge of the legal traditions, but rather to guide their already existing 'legal minds' to make logical reasoning rather than simply memorizing legal concepts.

---

[17] Jaakko Husa, 'Turning the Curriculum Upside Down: Comparative Law as an Educational Tool for Constructing the Pluralistic Legal Mind' [2009] 10 *German LJ* 913.

[18] Ibid.

Early on my students showed me that their understanding of comparative law was dependent on their ability to relay the course material to their own experiences, daily lives, and personal beliefs. For most the study of comparative law was a novelty. All came in with expectations and preconceived judgments about the topic. I already knew that legal studies could trigger a fair share of issues, but after the first student presentation it was obvious that comparative law constituted a greater challenge with its own particular set of difficulties. In fact, the group struggled to transpose itself into different legal universes to proceed with proper comparative work.

I strongly believed that the complexity of comparative law with its methodology and the unique nature of the themes analyzed had to be demystified with concrete illustrations. Right from the start, I gave the students a basic understanding of what the topic entailed and initiated a relationship on a different level in order to discover the context in which they were going to transpose my teachings.

I decided to share trivial details about myself: my passion for cleaning and an early start to the day. This personal information made my students uneasy and left them wondering why I wanted to provide them with this unusual insight on my life. I made them do the same. I had them share their favorite food, color, animal, and hobby. This created even more confusion, but ultimately made them bond with each other and me. I had made a simple, basic but crucial connection with my group. Using simple examples, I created an opportunity to turn the 'de-personalized' setting of the prison classroom into a more intimate learning environment. I had provided them with a human connection rarely present in prison and an unexpected comparative perspective.

I had to explain that legal rules are meant to frame human behavior and create a harmonious social life irrespective of individual likes and dislikes. Therefore, if I were to create disturbance with my habits I would have to be penalized with a fine because I was disrupting social harmony. This example showed them that all our choices and preferences, even at the most personal level, can impact society, and that law has the potential to regulate the most intimate aspects of our day-to-day life. I stressed that our study of comparative law and legal traditions through principles and vivid examples would require respect and that we cultivate our differences in order to better understand our diverse outlooks.

After the success of this experience, I explained almost any other concept by starting with a concrete relatable example to move on to a greater level of abstraction. This anecdotic exercise can and should certainly be transposed in traditional classrooms because our comparative legal teaching currently lacks meaningful dialogue, leaving students confused and unable to contextualize the foreign and domestic cases they are presented with.

Throughout the class I was able to give basic examples to illustrate intricate legal paradigms and had my students understand that although they perceived the fundamental principles of law as arbitrary, legal traditions came to life in the concrete application of a set of rules, and that for most part these rules were the expression of a democratic majority, or a divine revelation used to provide guidance to followers.

At a later stage it became more important to have the students own the class materials. I did not want them to memorize or be persuaded by the readings. I wanted them to internalize the information to reason in an inductive or deductive manner, and to apply the theoretical concepts to concrete sets of facts. Role-playing was crucial. The students argued different positions to understand rules and exceptional cases. Among many exercises, I had them defend a woman in a divorce proceeding under two different legal traditions and compare the outcomes. Not only did this exercise demand that they interpreted the legal corpus of an unfamiliar legal tradition, they also had to step in the shoes of a woman to appreciate her situation and provide a critical analysis of the proceedings. Having perfected their analytical skills, students started to coin their own hypotheticals and explain complex legal issues and concepts to their fellow classmates. Critical legal thinking was coming from within without probing. Adding their perspective to my explanations, they were finding their voices individually and as a group.

I quickly understood that the use of legal paradigms and citations of authorities did not resonate with my students. I had to prove assumptions and accept that the most fundamental statements of law would always be challenged. Teaching legal traditions in prison was not about laying down the law; it was about opening my eyes and their horizon to a new language using a constructive and alternative form of dialogue.

Irrevocably, I am convinced that all this tedious comparative learning strongly influences my students' re-insertion process. I was not able to measure how much they were taking away from my class, but without a doubt they were able to foster the culture of understanding, compromise and open-mindedness I tried to instigate over the course of our seminar. The diversity in topics covered and the traditions we chose to study led us to reach an interesting middle ground. My students understood that all legal traditions had to be subject to interpretation and had to develop some adaptive qualities in order to be sustainable. For my part, I saw stability and a great sense of justice in religious law, understanding that divinity was not a synonym of arbitrariness.

I like to believe that I was successful in constructing a more pluralist legal mind for my students and myself thanks to an unconventional teaching environment that seemed more favorable to the development of different perspectives on the law. My students proved to me that their ability to 'learn the law' or to 'learn how to think the law' was much greater when constructing their own legal understanding of concepts derived from multiple sources. In order to replicate this method we must, as lecturers, find a place for the constructivist approach in our traditional law schools and apply it across the curriculum to better teach comparative law.

Indeed, varied teaching approaches are more likely to reach a greater number of students. Legal educators trained through untraditional environments will prepare future lawyers to complex work environments and raise their awareness to a set of skills they need to develop as future counsels. It is now time for legal academia to change its point of view on the teaching of law and relay the valuable contribution of untraditional teaching approaches. For this prisons are ideal microcosms that challenge young academics. Diversity in the student body as well as the unusual setting of the facility can expose a new comparative dimension to the teaching of many legal topics.

3 TRADITIONAL COMPARATIVE LAW TEACHING

A case can certainly be made for comparative law in any law teaching institution. The sense of open-mindedness inherent to this subject liberates students from the narrow confines of their national legal systems. It is also right to believe that '[t]he work of comparing laws and institutions is very necessary, for the only way to perceive any object clearly is to compare it with something else'.[19] Thus, taking a closer look at the initial goals set forth by European faculties and American law schools for comparative law teaching in the 1990s can help understand where and how these curriculums have failed in their enterprise. Most importantly, reflecting on the issues affecting these courses and their approach to the comparative subject-matter is crucial in order to turn to more adapted methods for comparative law teaching. This analysis may lead us to conclude that the teaching of comparative law should be no more divorced from the teaching of any other core topic or taught as a

[19] Walter Joseph Kamba, 'Comparative Law: A theoretical Framework' [1974] 23(03) *International and Comparative Law Quarterly* 485.

standalone upper-level course, but should be presented through the use of a more diverse and progressive pedagogy and integrated into other law courses.

The Initial Objectives

European law faculties and American law schools differ in some respect in their approach to comparative law teaching. This may be because for most part a tradition of self-reflection has endured in American legal education with scholars dedicating entire publications to topics in legal education, whereas in Europe, law professors tend to give little to no attention to these issues. Historically, European legal scholars have defined themselves exclusively through their production of doctrinal work rather than their teaching, thus a reflection on the pedagogy was never initiated as part of the scholarship. The potential critical outlook on teaching methods was also stumped down because of the slim impact of the realist current in Europe in comparison to the support it received in the United States.[20]

Thus, while the body of law created by the Institutions of the European Union, such as European Commission, Parliament and the Court of Justice, has become omnipresent in the legal discourse, legal education is somehow resisting Europeanization and almost exclusively focused on training lawyers within the confines of their jurisdictions. In Europe, comparative law teaching has never completely shifted away from the positivist and quasi-scientific teaching of law. Programs have been created to expose students to the national law of different member states, but do not engage in a thorough jurisdiction to jurisdiction comparison. Students are also encouraged to participate in *Erasmus* exchange programs or joint programs where they are able to learn through many disciplines the culture and law of other European countries; however even in the most ambitious of these programs students only acquire a partial understanding and knowledge of two jurisdictions to be awarded a dual degree.[21]

This phenomenon in some respect is also present in the United States where what is encompassed in the realm of the legal education tends to be more focused on domestic law. Indeed, despite the globalization of legal services, comparative law is still not playing a prominent role in

---

[20] Helge Dedek and Armand De Mestral, 'Born to be Wild: The Trans-Systemic Programme at McGill and the De-Nationalization of Legal Education' (2009) 10 *German LJ* 889.

[21] Ibid.

law schools' curriculums. Perhaps it is the diversity of the American legal system with its two levels of jurisdiction (state and federal) that already make the study of national law a complex and somewhat comparative enterprise that discourages students to enroll in courses dedicated to the study of a foreign system of law.[22]

Mathias Reimann and many other scholars have also blamed 'the parochial attitude and the lack of international sophistication of American lawyers for the marginal role of comparative law'.[23] However, it may be more the case that the objectives American scholars have set for themselves with regard to the teaching of this topic are too broad and confusing. Courses in comparative law in the United States aim at tackling too many topics. The following are only the 10 reasons most often cited by Professors to justify engaging in the comparative study of law:[24]

1. Provide foreign models for the improvement of domestic law.
2. Promote the international unification (or at least harmonization) of law.
3. Reveal the common core of all law.
4. Teach basic skills for international legal practice.
5. Provide an overview of law on a world-wide scale by introducing the major legal families.
6. Acquire some knowledge about certain foreign legal systems.
7. Become familiar with foreign rules, concepts, and approaches in order to facilitate communication with foreign lawyers.
8. Compare the national system of law with foreign alternatives in order to provide critical perspectives on the domestic legal system.
9. Help students understand law as a general phenomenon, in particular its contingency on history, society, politics, and economics.
10. Provide critical perspectives and functionally explain alternative approaches, in order to foster tolerance towards other legal cultures and thus overcomes parochial attitudes.

This agenda is unrealistic for a single comparative law class but also lacks clarity. These various goals call for different teaching styles and differences in substance that can trigger serious pedagogical challenges. While wanting to engage with all of these aspects of comparative law teaching, American legal education is primarily focused on practical

[22] Mathias Reimann [1996] op cit.
[23] Helge Dedek and Armand De Mestral [2009] op cit.
[24] Mathias Reimann [1996] op cit.

training. The confusion and impossibility to meet expectations in comparative law courses frustrate students and faculty, leaving the discipline ill-defined and unattractive. Comparative law is left on the margin of the mainstream course offering.[25]

Nonetheless, much can also be said in defense of the traditional objectives of comparative law teaching. Not only does the study of other legal systems or foreign law provide students with a different perspective on their own legal system, it also engrains a sense of modesty and promotes the transplantation of cutting-edge legal concepts. The study of comparative law even in the most traditional setting cultivates the student's curiosity and imagination and prompt critical thinking *vis-à-vis* existing norms and legal solutions.

Ultimately, what needs to be further emphasized to provide students with a more progressive and diverse comparative legal education is the interdependence of the law and other social phenomenon not to confine comparative study to a descriptive task. Notable efforts have been made in this direction in a few law-teaching institutions over the past decade. Modern comparative law teaching now impels on increasing the student's understanding of the law and on broadening perspectives with the help of other core topics or disciplines outside the legal realm. Interdisciplinarity has started to be seen as key in the teaching of comparative law.[26] However, this novel approach is not yet the norm. Thus, prison and other alternative teaching venues could further demonstrate that the law should not be taught as a static science but as a social phenomenon that reflects societies' desire to structure human behavior.

The Inadequacy of Traditional Comparative Law Teaching Methods

Comparative law may not be any worse off than other upper level subjects such as legal history or jurisprudence that seem to present no real appeal to future practitioners. However, the increasing internationalization of legal transactions should prompt students' interest in comparative legal matters. It is now time, more than ever before, that future practitioners become aware, at the earliest stages of their legal education, of the diversity of legal systems and rules that compose the current legal world.[27] Undeniably, the European and American approach to comparative legal education fails to provide students with an integrated

---

[25] Mathias Reimann [1996] op cit.

[26] David Nelken and Johannes Felst, *Adapting Legal Cultures* (Hart Publishing 2001).

[27] Mathias Reimann [1996] op cit.

framework from which they can develop some comparative, trans-systemic or global learning skills.[28] Students get to learn national law but their knowledge of another legal system is limited.

Unfortunately, the laudable European comparative law and exchange programs described above only provide an alternative perspective to a small percentage of students. For most part European students are still taught as though only one legal system exists. Professors most oftentimes trained in a single jurisdiction provide their students with a reductionist vision of the law.[29] However, the mastery of multiple bodies of laws or at least of the comparative methodology and its reasoning should no longer be taken as a specialty area confined to masters/upper level courses or to classes touching upon topic of European law. It needs to be integrated in core classes. Curriculums must be revised and the teaching methodology needs to account for the growing needs of jurisdictions seeking comparative and European law specialists. Among others, the pioneer work of Professors R Cotterell and J Husa should be taken as example of what can be accomplished through interdisciplinary legal teaching and an innovative curriculum.[30]

In the United States teaching methods are also maladapted to the practice of law. Students are required to gain solid knowledge of their national system before exploring any type of foreign law. In a purely descriptive exercise they are encouraged to pinpoint some of the similarities and differences present between their legal system and the few elements of foreign law they have gathered during the span of a seminar. In a final identification phase, they are expected to juxtapose their superficial analysis of both systems to present some pertinent conclusions.[31]

This teaching approach fails to bring more open-mindedness to students or to provide them with essential practical tools for the practice of law. These courses simply do not offer relevant knowledge of comparative law. Even though the descriptive exercise is an essential first step in the comparative pedagogy, comparative law teaching needs to go beyond a superficial account of legal systems to build strong comparative analytical skills.[32] Limiting the teaching of comparative law to this

---

28 Helge Dedek and Armand De Mestral [2009] op cit.

29 Ibid.

30 Roger Cotterrell, *Law, Culture and Society Legal Ideas in the Mirror of Social Theory* (Ashgate 2007); Jaako Husa, *A New Introduction to Comparative Law* (Hart Publishing 2015).

31 Walter Joseph Kamba [1974] op cit.

32 Mathias Reimann [1996] op cit.

traditional methodology will only breed legal technicians and not excellent lawyers.[33]

It may be more adequate to have students reflect on socio-economic problems and legal solutions related to the application of these rules in different jurisdictional contexts to appreciate the importance of comparative studies for their career as transnational counsels. Vocational training can be achieved using comparative methods, and the teaching of comparative law can be simplified to make the topic more attractive to students. The key is to have students reflect on the role of law and the meaning of legal norms as means of social control rather than self-sufficient instruments. In this respect, integrated comparisons are crucial in developing this perspective. Also essential to vocational training is an increased awareness to different mode of legal reasoning and problem solving.[34] Legal practitioners need to be adaptable thinkers, thus law students must be taught to be flexible in their approach to domestic and foreign law and to adjust their reasoning to different legal environments and social settings.

Another detrimental consequence of traditional comparative legal education is the tendency to treat non-western legal traditions as less perfected systems of law, and thus as incomparable to Western legal traditions. Based on this assumption many comparative legal scholars posit that only systems that have attained the same stage of legal development can be compared.[35] In order to remedy this biased and ethnocentric perspective more progressive methods of teaching must be employed.

For this, the 'kitchen sink' approach must disappear and instructors must set clear course objectives without completely disregarding traditional methods. Lecturers must define and simplify their teaching goals. They should also make use of alternative methods to reach these targets. Only then will students start to understand the law in a global context. It may be best to decentralize the teaching of comparative law. Comparative legal teaching should not be an isolated province but should incorporate comparative elements in the core courses already part of the traditional law school curriculum.[36] Altogether this will not only clarify the essence of comparative law but also ignite a renewed interest for comparative legal studies.[37]

---

33 Walter Joseph Kamba [1974] op cit.
34 Mathias Reimann [1996] op cit.
35 Walter Joseph Kamba [1974] op cit.
36 Mathias Reimann [1996] op cit.
37 Ibid.

4 CONCLUSION

Some law schools like the Faculty of Law at McGill University, Quebec have paved the way for progressive comparative teaching methods. For the past 17 years McGill's law professors have taught in a trans-systemic manner. Overtime the law faculty has developed a three-year curriculum that teaches even first year introductory courses, such as contracts and torts, simultaneously from a civil and common law perspective. The ultimate goal of the program has been to transcend the fixation of the study of law as 'the study of legal systems'. Certainly, Quebec's mixed jurisdiction system inspired and called for the implementation of this program, but the model could be transposed to European faculties and American law schools.[38]

The trans-systemic project is one of many options that should be explored by lecturers in redesigning their comparative teaching methods. It should not be confined to mixed jurisdictions.[39] Constructivist teaching techniques building on the student's existing knowledge, as well as contextualized teaching methods adapted to diverse groups of students can supplement traditional comparative teaching techniques. A more diverse comparative legal education will reach a larger group of students and will ultimately redefine the contours of the discipline to make it more attractive to future practitioners.

For academics much can be learned from those who have experienced the law differently – not as 'law-abiding' citizens, but as 'law-contravening' ones. The legal perspectives of those who have been most violently affected by the law should also be heard in the conventional law school environment to inspire a new type of 'trans-systemia' for the teaching of traditional legal topics. Young lecturers need to be trained differently to experiment with different perspectives on the law. The training of comparative law instructors in unconventional environments, such as the prison system, must become part of the apprenticeship of young legal scholars to spontaneously instill more progressive comparative teaching skills. Ultimately these methods will not only benefit unconventional students and young lecturers. The transposition in conventional teaching venues will also provide a broader more accurate perspective on the law to law students in European faculties and Law Schools making them aware that the multifaceted functions of the law in

---

38 Helge Dedek and Armand De Mestral [2009] op cit.

39 Ibid.

our societies. We can now only hope that unconventional teaching environments will inspire different training tools to foster some more critical teaching of comparative law in traditional settings.

PART III

Didactic innovations and learning experiments

11. Orchestrating encounters: teaching law at a liberal arts and sciences college in the Netherlands

Barbara Oomen

1 INTRODUCTION

It was an October meeting in my 'Transitional Justice' class of 30 sessions, with the rain pouring outside of our Gothic town hall, and the 25 students playing out an exercise on Truth Commissions inside. I'd asked them to focus on one single testimony in the Truth Commission Reports of South Africa, Sierra Leone, Guatemala and Argentina. 'Choose the life story of one person who is closest to you – possibly a student like yourself – and be prepared to describe what happened to you during the war. After that, we can discuss the tensions between truth and reconciliation from the perspective of your persona'. As the students gave their testimony one by one there was a focused atmosphere. One told the story of a young warrior from South Africa. The other was a girl from Guatemala, who saw her brother being killed. Tears welled from her eyes as she told how his head was smashed against a rock. The subsequent discussion on whether knowing the truth leads to healing, and whether reconciliation can replace accountability was of remarkable depth and seriousness.

The exercise above is one of many attempts to achieve the objectives of a liberal arts undergraduate program within my law classes over the past years. On the basis of my experience, having moved from teaching law within classical mono-disciplinary Dutch legal programmes to doing so within one of the newly-founded Liberal Arts and Sciences honours' colleges in the Netherlands, I have come to see the role of the instructor in such a context as one of orchestrating encounters: between perspectives, between people, and between positions. Such encounters, I will argue, are the best way to achieve classical Liberal Arts and Sciences objectives such as stimulating critical thinking, honing research skills, benefiting from interdisciplinarity, fostering the narrative imagination and educating for (global) citizenship. The narrative imagination, here, can be understood as the ability to truly envisage someone else's story, in relation to his or her context and past, however different that person's situation may be from that of the student, and to empathize with the other on that basis. Global citizenship education equips students with those values, knowledge and skills that are based on and instil respect for human rights, social justice, diversity, gender equality and environmental sustainability, and that empower learners to be responsible global citizens.[1]

The argument will be illustrated with examples coming from my own experience in teaching courses such as 'Law, Society and Justice', 'Origins and Implementation of Human Rights', 'Law and Cultural Diversity', 'Transitional Justice' and various research seminars at University College Roosevelt. This undergraduate college is one of the seven Dutch University Colleges that have been founded since 1999, as a way of implementing the Bologna Declaration for Higher Education in the Netherlands.[2] Situated within the large Dutch research universities, these undergraduate programmes are characterized by their selection of students, residential character, emphasis on the academic community, intensive, interactive and small-scale teaching, undergraduate research, an international student body and – above all – a broad liberal arts and sciences program. Amongst the Dutch University Colleges, the University College Roosevelt distinguishes itself by its stand-alone character.[3]

---

[1] This is the definition used by UNESCO: Unesco, *Global Citizenship Education: Preparing learners for the challenges of the 21st century* (2015). More critical understandings of global citizenship can, for instance, be found in: Vanessa Andreotti, 'Soft versus Critical Global Citizenship Education' [2006] 3 *Policy & Practice: A Development Education Review* 40.

[2] See Bob Reinalda and Ewa Kuleszka, *The Bologna Process: Harmonizing Europe's Higher Education – Including Essential Original Texts* (Barbara Budrich Publishers 2005) and Marijk van der Wende, 'The Bologna Declaration: Enhancing the Transparency and Competitiveness of European Higher Education' [2000] 25 *Higher Education in Europe* 305. One of the main features of the Bologna Process was the introduction, in the whole of Europe, of two cycles: a broad bachelor degree followed by a more discipline-specific master degree. For an overview of the Dutch University Colleges and their mission see: www.universitycolleges.info (accessed 20 August 2015).

[3] Whereas UCR is part of Utrecht University, it is based in the relatively sparsely populated Province of Zeeland, which leads to tight town-gown relationships, a focus on undergraduate research and on global citizenship; the latter is

This contribution will be structured as follows. It will first offer a general introduction into the tradition of liberal arts and sciences education, both in Europe and in the United States, and the key educational objectives of such an education. Subsequently, I will discuss the place of the study of law within these programmes, the relationship with disciplinary legal masters and the core educational objectives of law courses within a liberal arts context. The next section then discusses my own experiences in translating these objectives into the contents and pedagogics of a variety of liberal arts law courses. In conclusion, I will argue how the common thread in all these experiences is that of orchestrating meaningful encounters.

2 THE LIBERAL ARTS TRADITION

Modern liberal arts and sciences education was defined by Bard College's vice president Jonathan Becker as:[4]

> A system of higher education designed to foster in students the desire and capacity to learn, think critically and to communicate proficiently, and to prepare them to function as engaged citizens. It is distinguished by a flexible curriculum that demands breadth as well as depth of study, encourages inter-disciplinarity, and enables student choice. It is realized through a student-centered pedagogy that is interactive and requires students to engage directly with texts in- and outside of the classroom.

Whereas the tradition of 'Liberal Arts & Sciences' has come to be associated with the American residential colleges such as William's College, Swarthmore and the Harvard, Stanford, Yale, MIT and Princeton undergraduate colleges, such colleges build on a much longer tradition that goes back to Ancient Greece. Seneca emphasized the importance of such a 'liberal' education, one that would free the mind and of 'cultivating humanity'.[5] Before him, many Greek philosophers pointed out how

---

also as evidence of the historical connection between Theodore, Franklin and Eleanor Roosevelt and the Province of Zeeland.

[4] Jonathan Becker, 'What a Liberal Arts and Sciences Education Is … and is Not' (2014) 4. Available at: http://iile.bard.edu/liberalarts/index.php?action=getfile&id=8123006 (accessed 20 August 2015).

[5] Seneca, Letter 88, in Lucius Annaeus Seneca and Charles Desmond Nuttall Costa, *17 Letters* (Aris & Phillips 1988). See also Cicero, PG Walsh (trs) *On Obligations: De Officiis* (Oxford World's Classics 2000) 13; Angelo Bottone, 'The Influence of Cicero on Newman's Idea of Liberal Education' [2009] *Yearbook Irish Philosophical Society* 1, 6.

'an examined life' is the best preparation for citizenship.[6] Plato, for one, stressed the importance of responsible citizenship, setting out how within each society there should be philosophers, or lovers of wisdom to study the ends of existence in order to bring justice to society. Aristotle, in turn, emphasized the value of education in the liberal arts and sciences in order to cultivate liberally-educated – that is open-minded in its most literal sense – rational individuals who can use reason to make decisions in society.[7] Building on the Greek tradition, Marcus Cappelus, in the fifth century AD, presented the seven liberal arts – grammar, rhetoric, logic, music, arithmetic, geometry and astrology – as bridesmaids to the marriage of Mercury and Philology, thus consolidating the type of knowledge deemed essential for an educated man.[8] Enlightenment itself, of course, was a celebration of the *homo universalis* and was consolidated in the nineteenth-century ideals of scholars such as Von Humboldt, who emphasized the importance of *Bildung*, a broad education and the close connection between teaching and research that resounds in today's liberal arts and sciences programmes.[9]

Nevertheless, it was in the United States that the ideal of liberal arts was developed and institutionalized further with the founding of the first residential liberal arts colleges of Harvard in 1636, and of William and Mary in 1693.[10] By now, there are about 125 independent and residential bachelor programmes that fall under the Carnegie liberal arts classification, based on the idea of a broad bachelor and discussion-led classes, taught by scholar-teachers.[11] With the tradition of such institutions comes the tradition of defending their intellectual premises. Thomas Jefferson was as proud of having founded the University of Virginia as he was of his Presidency. In a famous defence of liberal arts in 1854, Cardinal Newman defined a liberal education as a 'broad exposure to the outlines

---

6 'An Unexamined Life is a Life Not Worth Living', Socrates as quoted in Plato's *Apology*. Available at: http://classics.mit.edu/Plato/apology.html (accessed 20 August 2015).

7 Aristotle, *Politics*. See also Allan Ornstein, Daniel Levine and Gerry Gutek, *Foundations of Education* (Wadsworth 2014).

8 William Harris Stahl, *Martianus Capella and the Seven Liberal Arts* (Columbia University Press 1992).

9 Wilhelm Von Humboldt, *Zur Theorie der Bildung des Menschen* (First published 1793, GRIN 2005).

10 Steven Koblik, 'Foreword' in Steven Koblik & Stephen R Graubard (eds), *Distinctively American: The Residential Liberal Arts Colleges* (Transaction Publishers 2000).

11 Eugene M Lang, 'Distinctively American: The Liberal Arts College' in ibid 133–134.

of knowledge for its own sake', scorning critics who – according to him – kept asking 'To what then does it lead? Where does it end? Who does it profit?'[12] John Dewey provided further intellectual foundation in stating that liberal education should engage students in the surrounding community, should be focused on problems to be resolved rather than academic discipline, and should collaboratively involve students and faculty.[13] A liberal education, in his mind, was an education, which leads to 'hospitality of mind, generous imagination, trained capacity of discrimination, freedom from class, sectarian or partisan prejudice and passion, faith without fanaticism'.[14]

Even if the dedication to pursuit of knowledge *per se* in liberal arts and sciences has been criticized from the seventeenth century onwards, the past decade, in America, has been characterized by evermore scholars, parents and students asking for a stronger emphasis on vocational training.[15] They, in turn, were met by a number of vociferous defenders of the liberal arts tradition.[16] Michael Roth, for instance, argues that replacing:[17]

> life-long learning with targeted vocational undergraduate instruction is a critical mistake, one that neglects a deep American tradition of humanistic education that has been integral to our success as a nation and that has enriched the lives of generations of students by enhancing their capacities for shaping themselves and reinventing the world they will inhabit.

Proponents like Martha Nussbaum have emphasized the inherent value of a liberal education, including the element of educating for democratic

---

[12] John Henry Cardinal Newman, *The Idea of a University: Defined and Illustrated* (First published 1854, Regnery Publishing 1999) 94.

[13] John Dewey, *Democracy and Education* (First published 1916, CreateSpace Independent Publishing Platform 2009).

[14] John Dewey, On Education, *The Middle Works of John Dewey, 1899–1924* (Southern Illinois University 1983) 201.

[15] Victor Ferall, *Liberal Arts at the Brink* (Harvard University Press 2011).

[16] Stefan Collini, *What are Universities for?* (Penguin 2012); Martha Nussbaum, *Not for Profit: Why Democracy Needs the Humanities* (Princeton University Press 2010); Helen Small, *The Value of the Humanities* (OUP 2013); William Deresiewicz, *Excellent Sheep: The Miseducation of the American Elite and the Way to a Meaningful Life* (Free Press 2014); Mark Roche, *Why Choose the Liberal Arts?* (University of Notre Dame Press 2010).

[17] Michael J Roth, *Beyond the University: Why Liberal Education Matters* (Yale University Press 2014).

citizenship.[18] Others have taken a more instrumental standpoint in defending the liberal arts, pointing out how well liberal arts graduates do on the labour market, but also how broadly educated academics are prepared for every kind of job, including the ones that do not exist yet.[19] At college, as Menand put it, you 'acquire the knowledge and skills important for life as an informed citizen, or as a reflective and culturally literate human being. College exposes future citizens to material that enlightens and empowers them, whatever careers they end up choosing'.[20]

Over the past years, liberal arts thus underwent some of the most vociferous attacks in history in the United States – with some observers even speaking of 'disappearing liberal arts colleges'.[21] Out of concerns pertaining to the labour market (many of them unjustified) more students opt for a vocational degree, and many liberal arts colleges find themselves forced to introduce vocational forces to stay afloat.[22] It is interesting to note how, in the same years, liberal arts has undergone a steady rise in Europe, a continent classically known for its mono-disciplinary education.[23] In the Netherlands, liberal arts and sciences programmes have undergone a particularly rapid expansion. Since the founding of the first 'University College' at Utrecht University, seven of such residential, international, small-scale programmes have been founded in the Netherlands, and a variety of other liberal arts and

---

[18] Martha C Nussbaum, *Cultivating Humanity: A Classical Defense of Reform in Liberal Education* (Harvard University Press 1997).

[19] Debra Humphreys and Patrick Kelly, *How Liberal Arts and Science Majors Fare in Employment: A report on eEarnings and Long-term Career Paths* (2014). Available at: https://www.aacu.org/sites/default/files/files/LEAP/2013_EmployerSurvey.pdf (accessed 20 August 2015).

[20] Louis Menand, 'Live and Learn: Why we have College', *The New Yorker* (6 June 2011). Available at: http://www.newyorker.com/magazine/2011/06/06/live-and-learn-louis-menand (accessed 20 August 2015).

[21] Scott Jaschik, 'Disappearing Liberal Arts Colleges', *Inside Higher Education* (11 October 2012). Available at: https://www.insidehighered.com/news/2012/10/11/study-finds-liberal-arts-colleges-are-disappearing> (accessed 20 August).

[22] Ferall, *op cit.*

[23] On the mono-disciplinarity, see Nussbaum (2002), *op cit.* Examples of novel liberal arts programmes can be found all over the Continent, such as the Bratislava International School of Liberal Arts, Kings College London, University College London, Bard College Berlin, University College Freiburg and St Mary's University College in Belfast.

sciences bachelor programmes have been introduced.[24] Driving forces behind the Dutch development included concerns about the low results of university programmes, the degree to which equal access had led to overfull lecture halls, the emphasis on mono-disciplinary programmes and the academic preoccupation with research over teaching.[25] One ambition of the founders of the Dutch University Colleges was to overcome the 'two cultures', the divide between the Sciences and the Humanities as described by Snow.[26] Another one was to cross the divide between research and teaching at university.

For all the differences between liberal arts and sciences programmes worldwide, there are also similarities, both in institutional and programmatic terms and in specific learning outcomes.[27] Institutionally, all the colleges discussed are small-scale and residential institutions, that seek to create and foster an academic community. Learning takes place in the context of small, interactive seminars, with great emphasis on academic skills in general, and on writing and argumentation in particular. As a result, the faculty is stimulated to put teaching first, and there is a great deal of attention for pedagogics and didactics, and for fostering teaching excellence. As Yale president Giamatti put it: 'A liberal education is at the heart of a civil society, and at the heart of a liberal education is the act of teaching'.[28] Programmatically, there is a great deal of emphasis on academic skills but also on reading the classics. The rationale for reading the classics is to forge an intimate connection with the intellectual tradition at hand, which often has roots going back to Ancient times, and to equip students to work with original sources.[29]

The essential endeavour is to set the foundation for a lifetime of learning, and to transmit 'the sheer joy associated with exploring the life of the mind and asking the great questions that give meaning to life'.[30] Students are stimulated to foster curiosity and learning for its own sake,

---

24 Marijk van der Wende, 'The Emergence of Liberal Arts and Sciences Education in Europe: A Comparative Perspective' [2011] 24 *Higher Education Policy* 233.

25 Ibid; Netherlands Scientific Council for Government Policy, *Higher Education in Stages* (1995) Wende Herman Tak and Barbara Oomen, *De disciplines voorbij: De colleges van Hans Adriaansens* (De Drukkerij 2012).

26 CP Snow, *The Two Cultures* (CUP 2012).

27 Becker, *op cit.*

28 As quoted on the memorial for the former Yale president in the Old College Hall.

29 Anthony Kronman, *Education's End: Why Our Colleges and Universities Have Given Up on the Meaning of Life* (Yale University Press 2007).

30 Roche, *op cit* 10.

as opposed to working towards a specific objective (a grade, a job) and to acquire those habits of the mind that come with this – discipline, close reading and critical thinking. In the formulation of the Association of American Colleges and Universities 'Liberal Education is an approach to learning that empowers individuals and prepares them to deal with complexity, diversity, and change. It provides students with broad knowledge of the wider world (e.g. science, culture, and society) as well as an in-depth study in a specific area of interest. A liberal education helps students develop a sense of social responsibility, as well as strong and transferable intellectual and practical skills such as communication, analytical and problem-solving skills, and a demonstrated ability to apply knowledge and skills in real-world settings'.[31]

All this is translated into a number of learning outcomes, which will be organized as follows in this contribution: critical thinking, conducting research, multi- and inter-disciplinarity, fostering the narrative imagination and global citizenship.[32] The centrality of stimulating *critical thinking* in a liberal arts program was set out most forcefully by Martha Nussbaum in *Cultivating Humanity,* in which she speaks of 'an education that is "liberal" in that it liberates the mind from the bondage of habit and custom, producing people who can function with sensitivity and alertness as citizens of the whole world.'[33] Critically examining oneself and one's traditions, and those of others, is crucial to make sense of today's interrelated and complex world. As Giamatti would tell the Yale freshers: 'a liberal education is defined by the attitude of the mind toward the knowledge that the mind explores and creates'.[34]

The ability to think critically is closely related to the ability of conducting informed, methodologically sound research. Research here can be understood as – the thoroughly thrilling but laborious – activity of generating new knowledge on the basis of a well-formulated research question, grounded in theory, on the basis of suitable research methods.

---

[31] Available at: http://www.aacu.org/leap/what-is-a-liberal-education (accessed 20 August).

[32] Of course, these learning objectives differ per college. See, for an overview of those learning outcomes most commonly shared amongst American liberal arts colleges: http://www.aacu.org/leap/essential-learning-outcomes (accessed 20 August 2015); for a general statement on the objectives of all Dutch University Colleges, see: www.universitycolleges.info (accessed 20 August 2015).

[33] Nussbaum, *op cit* 8.

[34] A Bartlett Giamatti, 'The Earthly Use of a Liberal Education' in Pearson (ed), *College: We Make the Road by Walking* (2007), 58. See also Bart van Klink in this volume.

Roth speaks of 'an emphasis on inquiry and critical thinking – learning to develop as an autonomous person by shedding illusions and acquiring knowledge through research'.[35] Collini reminds us how schoolchildren are taught, and students at university study, and:[36]

> undergraduates are being introduced to the modes of enquiry appropriate to various disciplines; what they develop, ideally, is not simple mastery of a body of information, but the capacity to challenge or extend the received understanding on a particular topic.

It is not without reason that undergraduate research is such an important part of liberal education all over the world.[37] The added value of a liberal arts and sciences context is that of *multi-* and even *interdisciplinarity*, the perusal of a wide range of disciplinary perspectives that can add depth and context to the academic enquiry on any given topic.

An often-stated objective of a liberal education is fostering the *narrative imagination*. Human beings, as Michael Sandel put it, are storytellers:

> There is a growing danger that, individually and collectively, we will find ourselves slipping into a fragmented, storyless condition. The capacity for a narrative would amount to the ultimate disempowering of the human subject, for without narrative there is no continuity between present and past, and therefore no responsibility, and therefore no possibility of acting together to govern ourselves.[38]

A true understanding of people's stories, whether as individuals or collectives, as these stories come about via literature, poetry, interviews and archival research strengthens empathy, and the ability to overcome one's own prejudices. A student who can truly see, feel, hear what another individual's life, in a different context, with a different position, past, present and future is like, will also be able to empathize with such an individual more easily, and act upon these feelings of empathy.

Such action is related to a final key objective of many liberal arts programmes, and of liberal education as it has been understood since Ancient times: strengthening the capacity for democratic citizenship,

---

35 Roth, *op cit.*

36 Collini, *op cit.*

37 See, for instance, the Council for Undergraduate Research. Available at: www.cur.org (accessed 20 August 2015). The first Dutch undergraduate research conference was an initiative of University College Roosevelt.

38 Michael Sandel, *Democracy's Discontent: America in Search of a Public Philosophy* (Harvard University Press 1996) 351.

whether this is understood as one's relation to the national or to the global community. Democracy is, after all, all about deliberation, and about understanding a variety of positions and coming to decision-making in a process that takes all these positions into account, just as citizenship can be as much about responsibility as it is about rights. In America the emphasis has long been on a 'well-rounded man' and 'social service'.[39] The philosophy of liberal arts is:[40]

> the philosophy of a democratic society in which citizenship, social responsibility and community are inseparable. An education citizenry is the essential instrument for promoting responsible action and community well-being'.

It is precisely the value of this aspect of the liberal education that has been emphasized over the past decades, for instance by Benjamin Barber who argued that undergraduate education should foster in students:[41]

> the willingness to engage in public issues (which grows out of self-esteem); empathy and respect for differences; commitment to non-violence and conflict resolution; and the ability to analyse information, evidence and argument'.

This has didactical consequences. Social responsibility is, as Berman set out, 'a personal investment in the well-being of others and of the planet-doesn't just happen. It takes intention, attention, and time'.[42]

How, now, does law fit into such an educational enterprise?

3 TEACHING LAW IN THE LIBERAL ARTS

For Aristotle, but also for Thomas Jefferson, the pursuit of justice and a just society constitute the main reason for propagating a liberal education.[43] The legendary first British law professor Blackstone considered

---

[39] Hugh Hawkins, 'The making of the Liberal Arts College Identity' in Koblik, *op cit* 5.

[40] Lang, *op cit* 140. See also Sandel, *op cit.*

[41] As quoted in Lang, *op cit* 144.

[42] Sheldon Berman, 'Educating for Social Responsibility' [1990] 48 *Educational Leadership* 75.

[43] Thomas Jefferson, for instance, in founding the University of Virginia, wrote how its purpose was to 'Preach a crusade against ignorance; establish and improve the law for educating the common people', T Jefferson, Letter to George Wythe Paris, 13 August 1786. Available at: http://www.nps.gov/nr/twhp/wwwlps/lessons/92uva/92facts1.htm (accessed 20 August 2015).

the study of law 'an almost essential part of liberal education'.[44] Nevertheless, the place of the study of law in the liberal arts curricula in the United States has never been self-evident, and has had a 'checkered history'.[45] In 1954, for instance, a Conference on Teaching Law in the Liberal Arts Curriculum held at Harvard University sought to strengthen the study of law within the liberal arts, if only to avoid undergraduates entering law school full of 'misconceptions about law [...] planted there by their teachers in the social sciences'.[46] Ever since, both legal scholars and other academics have argued for the study of law in the liberal arts, for a variety of reasons, and with different degrees of success.[47]

Those opposing a key role for legal studies in the liberal arts curriculum point out how the study of law, in the United States as in many other countries, is essentially vocational, seeking to equip students with that knowledge, that vocabulary and those techniques that enables them to apply the law, for instance, to decide on cases as judges, or to serve their clients' interests as lawyers. Goodman and Silbey, for instance, consider professional education in law to be mere training; 'the acquisition of techniques for which norms and standards have been commonly agreed upon, as in the trades and professions'.[48] Rosenberg, even more viciously, labelled law schools as 'essentially anti-intellectual institutions incapable of meeting the standards of any genuine academic discipline'.[49] Liberal arts, in contrast, seeks to provide an education, in which 'norms and standards are explored, critically examined, discussed

---

44 As quoted in Harold J Berman, 'Teaching Law Courses in The Liberal Arts College: A Challenge to the Law Schools' [1961] 13 *Journal of Legal Education*, 47.

45 Elizabeth Gee and Barbara S Webber, 'Historical Development of Law in Liberal Education' [1986] 10 *Legal Studies Forum* 7, 7.

46 Berman, *op cit* 50.

47 J Samaha, 'Law and Liberal Arts at the University of Minnesota' [1976] 28 *Journal of Legal Education* 80; P Lader, 'Experiments in Undergraduate Legal Education: The Teaching in the Liberal Arts Curriculum of American Colleges and Universities' [1973] 25 *Journal of Legal Education* 125; FE Barkman, 'Law in the Liberal Arts: An Appraisal and a Proposal for Experimentation' [1966] 19 *Journal of Legal Education* 1; A Sarat, 'Situating Legal Scholarship in the Liberal Arts: An Introduction' in A Sarat (ed), *Law in the Liberal Arts* (Cornell University Press 2004).

48 Douglas J Goodman and Susan S Silbey, 'Defending Liberal Education from the Law' in ibid 17.

49 As quoted in Keith J Bybee, 'The Liberal Arts, Legal Scholarship and the Democratic Critique of Judicial Power' in ibid 46.

and submitted to continuous challenge'.[50] The essence of a liberal arts education is anti-vocational, as it prizes generalized instruction over training for a single profession. 'When law is considered as a liberal art, the prospect of becoming a lawyer is subordinate to the task of cultivating the mind and instilling a sense of what it means to be human'.[51] If law is to be taught within a liberal arts and sciences college, in short, this has to be in other ways than providing mere training for the legal profession.

The division between a liberal arts program and good legal education need not be as stark as it is depicted here. Many scholars have pointed out how the study of law can enrich a liberal arts curriculum and vice versa. For one, the difficult dilemma's that come with legal deliberations hone the critical thinking that is expected from liberal arts and science students, and add depth to them.[52] The need, in addressing such dilemmas, to take actual decisions, and the threat of violence behind the enforcement of such decisions, equips this particular study with a weight and sense of responsibility not found in, say, the study of many social sciences or rhetoric.[53] The degree to which actual dilemmas come together in particular cases feed the narrative imagination in a way that adds to literary scholarship. 'Stories and storytellers', as Cook expresses it, 'pervade the legal culture; Law professors tell war stories to their students; clients tell their stories to lawyers; lawyers, in turn, provide judges and juries with stories on behalf of clients. The courts ultimately relate stories through judicial opinions'.[54] Whereas law itself is not one of the classic *artes liberales*, the disciplines that are key to being a good lawyer, such as rhetoric and logic, are.

Another reason to include law in a liberal arts curriculum is related to the objective of stimulating global citizenship. A certain degree of legal literacy is needed to meet the demands of 'intelligent citizenship', whether of a nation or of the world.[55] Taking this as a point of departure, many have argued for the inclusion of law not as an elective, but as part of the core of any liberal arts curriculum.[56] Departing from the old adage

---

50 Goodman and Silbey, *op cit.*

51 Bybee, *op cit* 42.

52 Ibid.

53 Sarat (2004), *op cit* 5.

54 Nancy L Cook, 'Outside the Tradition: Literature as Legal Scholarship' [1995] 63 *University of Cincinnati Law Review* 95, 95.

55 Goodman and Silbey *op cit* 17.

56 John D Appel, 'Law as a Social Science in the Undergraduate Curriculum' [1958] 10 *Journal of Legal Education* 485.

that 'law is too important to be left to lawyers alone', Woodrow Wilson argued in 1894 that 'we need laymen who understand the necessity of law and the right uses of it too well to be unduly impatient with its restraints'.[57] Such a course, in his opinion, should teach *all* students 'what law is, how it came to existence, what relations its form bears to its substance, and how it gives to society its fibre and strength'.[58] As Giamatti put it:[59]

> The medium of cohesion and conflict, ligature and litigation, that is the law, must be part of the educated person's perspective in order to appreciate one of the grandest, systematic ways of thinking human beings have developed for their survival.

Looking at what the liberal arts offer to the study of law, many teachers and scholars have pointed how much an interdisciplinary approach can add to classical legal studies. Applying insights from psychology, statistics, political science and economics to the study of any subject in the field of private, criminal or public law can enhance insight into the topic and provide the necessary context.[60] An interdisciplinary study of law helps us to 'see the complex connections of law, culture and society in all their variety' and to connect legal theory to insights from the humanities and social sciences.[61] Sociologists of law and legal philosophers, often marginalized in law schools, often marvel at the possibilities provided by a liberal arts context, where they find the intellectual habitus missing in law schools. As Sarat puts it: 'if law schools did anything like what I am describing, then it might be less necessary to study law in the liberal arts'.[62] The 'law and justice' or 'law and society' programmes offered at liberal arts colleges throughout the United States are, in this perspective, considered to be an illustration of what law schools *should* be doing.[63]

These insights have not lead to a wholesale adoption of legal programmes in liberal arts and sciences curricula: a 2004 study found that

---

57 Quoted by Bybee, *op cit* 54.

58 Ibid.

59 Austin Sarat, 'From Disciplinary Perspectives to an Integrated Conception of Legal Scholarship', in Sarat (2004), *op cit* 103.

60 Derek Bok, 'A Flawed System of Law Practice and Training' [1983] 33 *Journal of Legal Education* 570.

61 Sarat (2004), *op cit* 3.

62 Ibid.

63 Donna E Arzt, 'Too Important to Leave to the Lawyers: Undergraduate Legal Studies and its Challenge to Professional Legal Education' [1989] 13 *Nova Law Review* 125.

only 60 colleges in the United States enabled their students to focus on legal studies or law and society, with only a handful offering majors in law. They are typically taught in departments of political science, sociology or history.[64] If we look at a number of high-ranked liberal arts colleges, Wellesley, for instance, offers courses such as 'courts, law and politics', 'constitutional law', 'inequality and the law', 'gender and the law', 'international law', 'law and economics', 'philosophy of law' and 'roman law'.[65] Pomona College offers six law courses: 'critical race theory, representation and rule of law', 'law and economics', 'philosophy of law', 'law and politics', 'topics in law and society', and 'love, labour and law across borders'.[66] Williams College, finally, offers a concentration on justice and law studies that consist of an 'introduction to justice and law', 'images of law' and 'race and American law'.[67] A consortium of undergraduate law and justice programmes that sought to exchange expertise stopped its activities in 2012.[68]

In Europe, law is studied at both the undergraduate and the graduate level. Nevertheless, its main characteristics, and critiques, do not differ much from the American situation.[69] The study of law is largely vocational and mono-disciplinary, geared towards preparing students for positions as a lawyer or a judge, even if most law students do not enter the legal profession in the end. In the Netherlands, as in many other European countries, the emphasis lies on the systematic study of the various fields distinguished within the civil law tradition and their judicial interpretation. In spite of the way in which the Bologna process sought to introduce broad bachelor programmes in combination with more vocational masters, a practicing lawyer in the Netherlands still needs to have obtained both an LLB and an LLM degree.[70] This means

---

64 Sarat (2004), *op cit* 3.

65 Wellesley, course catalogue 2013–2014.

66 Pomona College, course catalogue 2013–2014.

67 Williams College, course catalogue 2013–2014.

68 Available at: http://culjp.sharepointsite.net/ (accessed 20 August 2015).

69 Margreet Ahsmann, 'Het civiel effect biedt niet wat het pretendeert: over de aansluiting de universitaire studie op de togaberoepen' [2011] 2 *Nederlands Juristen Blad* 66; Freek Bruinsma, 'De ondraaglijke lichtheid van de rechtenstudie' [2000] 28 *NJB* 1371; Martijn Snoep et al, 'Opleiding jurist moet breder' *NRC Handelsblad* (17 March 2014). Available at: http://www.nrc.nl/handelsblad/van/2014/maart/17/opleiding-jurist-moet-breder-1358770 (accessed 20 August 2015).

70 Art. 1 Besluit Beroepsvereisten Advocatuur. There is a tension here with the Bologna Process and the European emphasis on separate bachelor, master and doctorate educational cycles: Julian Lonbay, 'The Changing Regulatory

that the Dutch Liberal Arts and Sciences Colleges, in seeking to enable their graduates to also pursue a legal career, need to somehow cover the basic material discussed in legal bachelor programmes. Often, after such programmes, students need to do a number of extra Dutch law courses elsewhere to be admitted to the bachelor degree.[71]

The difference between studying law within a regular legal bachelor program, and within a liberal arts and sciences program are sizeable, in terms of objectives, material covered and pedagogics. Whereas the objective of a regular legal bachelor program is preparing students for a career as a lawyer, liberal arts programmes seek to stimulate critical reflection upon the law and its role in society. The intensity of the courses within a liberal arts context enables instructors to cover much more material: a course typically taught to hundreds of students in a lecture hall in ten sessions at a regular university, will be taught to a maximum of 25 students over 30 sessions in a liberal arts context. This enables more Socratic discussions and variety in student work and forms of assessment. The challenge for a law instructor in a Dutch University College is thus not only to train students in the tricks of the legal trade, but to also equip them for the open-ended inquiry, multi-facetted approach, critical reasoning, reflections on justice and their own contribution towards achieving it in the world around them that have been the hallmarks of liberal education since the Ancient Greeks. During the introduction to 'Law, Society and Justice', I typically draw a box on the whiteboard, explaining to students that I will show them not only how to work inside of the box, but also how to look at the box from the outside and – hopefully – to wonder whether the box should be there at all, or whether it should have a wholly different shape altogether.

How, now, are the classical liberal arts and sciences objectives met in one particular Dutch Liberal Arts and Sciences college, the one in which I teach? Here, the Law Track consists of seven courses: 'Law, Society

---

Environment Affecting the Education and Training of Europe's Lawyers' [2012] 61 *Journal of Legal Education* 479.

[71] Out of the Dutch University Colleges, Leiden University College and University College Utrecht have met this challenge by offering a four-year double degree program, in which the three-year Liberal Arts and Sciences bachelor degree is supplemented with a year of largely vocational legal studies, in Dutch, that leads up to a LLB. Others, such as University College Roosevelt, seek to provide both adequate preparations for further legal studies within a law track in their three-year program, whilst also meeting the wider liberal arts and sciences objectives. This system is, however, under discussion at the time of writing.

and Justice', 'International and European Law', 'Law, Medicine and Healthcare', 'Principles of Private Law', 'General Theories of Law', 'International Human Rights', and 'Crime and Law Enforcement'. In addition to this, students can do an Honour's Thesis or an Independent Research Project in the field of law. Each course consists of 30, 2-hour sessions, and has at least 5 different forms of assessment, ranging from presentations to papers, case briefs and exams. The law track has three key objectives: First, introducing students to the general theory of law and the crucial concepts, main legal texts and case law in particular fields of law, and familiarizing them with the most important legal institutions but also with key skills as legal research, drafting and argumentation. Next, firmly placing the understanding of law within a wider social science curriculum, leading to an understanding of 'law in action' and its interrelationship with disciplines such as political science, philosophy, economics, psychology, sociology, anthropology, argumentation and rhetoric. Finally, in contrast to American counterparts, preparing students for admission to prestigious legal masters programmes, whether in the Netherlands or elsewhere. The following section will discuss the way in which the general liberal arts and sciences objectives are addressed within a number of courses in this curriculum.

4 LIBERAL LEGAL EDUCATION AT UNIVERSITY COLLEGE ROOSEVELT

How, as a law instructor at a Dutch Liberal Arts and Sciences College, to straddle the dual objectives of introducing students to the legal discipline, but also stimulating them to approach that discipline with an open mind, a critical attitude and those skills that promote the liberal education objectives set out above? Before offering a few examples from my own classroom practice, it is important to emphasize once more the pedagogical and didactical approaches in a liberal arts education, that are all about creating meaningful learning experiences.[72] Instead of engaging in one-way monologues, liberal arts teachers seek to create true encounters in the classroom, stimulating Socratic discussions and applying a variety of teaching methods, that do not only lead to deeper knowledge, but also to changes in mindset, nudging students, conversation-by-conversation, exercise-by-exercise, towards academic rigor, an open mind and an

72 Ken Bain, *What the Best College Teachers Do* (Harvard University Press 2004); James Lang, *On Course: A Week-by-Week Guide to your First Semester of College Teaching* (Harvard University Press 2008).

examined life. This contribution can only offer a few snapshots of the type of exercises and approaches that seek to structure, and give rise to such conversations.

As an instructor, I like to think of my main role as that of 'orchestrating encounters'. These encounters take place among individual students on the one side, and with other students, great books, compelling ideas, and the world outside on the other. Education rather becomes like a social event, in which the teacher, who knows the student well, introduces him or her to a fellow student with a different background, a relevant work or field of study, a new perspective or a real world event, to then stimulate a true encounter between the two. As this point, the instructor should not withdraw from the 'conversation', but listen in, steer where necessary, and crosscheck whether there is true understanding.

Let me provide some examples. In order to stimulate the first, and arguably foremost, liberal objective of *critical thinking* I like to ask the freshers taking the 'Introduction to Law, Society and Justice' course to write a 1000-word essay on the question 'Should one disobey unjust laws?' in their second week of college.[73] This forces students to formulate their own thoughts on one of the classical questions in legal philosophy, but also provides a great introduction to discussions on natural law and legal positivism, and the classical texts by Aristotle and Thoreau on the topic. This exercise is also premised on the intimate connection between writing and critical thinking, as is an in-class exercise in the very first week in which I ask students to write up their very own definition of 'law', after which we classify the definitions together. Another way in which I seek to stimulate both legal doctrinal analysis and critical thinking, is via a constitutional essay. Students discuss a constitutional issue – like the legalization of same-sex marriages, the prohibition of ritual slaughter – from the perspective of one given national constitution, and the relevant case law. In class, however,

---

[73] The course itself has 30, 2-hour sessions, and forms of assessment that include a take home exam on searching for and quoting legal literature, and observing a court case, a classical exam on the textbooks, a constitutional essay, an interview with a lawyer, a research paper and participation in various classroom activities, e.g. a moot court.

The literature used in 2014 was: Kitty Calavita, *Invitation to Law and Society: An Introduction to the Study of Real Law* (Chicago University Press 2010); Tony Honore, *About Law: An Introduction* (OUP 1996); Anthony Walsh and Craig Hemmens, *Law, Justice and Society: A Sociolegal Introduction* (OUP 2013). Whereas, I recount a number of personal experiences below, many of the exercises were developed together with the other law faculty.

they are stimulated to debate that issue in more normative terms, often having to argue the opposite of what they put down in writing. An important classroom activity is to not only discuss a legal institution – such as inheritance law – but to also debate its effects, for instance, on the basis of De Tocqueville's analysis of the relationship between America's inheritance law and its democracy.[74]

A key skill in enabling critical-thinking is the ability to conduct independent, academic *research* on questions anchored in theory, answered in using the most suitable research methods and presented, both orally and in writing, in a convincing manner. Here, the challenge is to make perfectly clear to students what doctrinal legal research entails, and to have them practice this via case briefs, case analysis and legal papers, but to also stimulate them to include empirical and philosophical insights on the topic at stake. The paper that students produce at the end of the 'Introduction to Law, Society and Justice' should thus include a legal, a socio-legal and a normative discussion, for instance of a particular tax law. The liberal arts tradition of *undergraduate research* goes further than simply stimulating students to recite existing research; it is also about students uncovering new knowledge shoulder-to-shoulder with established scholars, on a topic of social relevance whenever possible.

In one first-year class, for instance, students studied how a local chemical plant involved in environmental pollution violated environmental law, thus diving deep into national and international administrative law. Apart from issuing a research report, they published an op-ed on this in the local newspaper and organized a seminar on the topic, visited by policymakers, lawyers and concerned citizens.[75] Another research group looked into the degree to which judicial reorganization affected access to justice in the local province. The fact that these were real issues, and the combination of legal analysis with interviews of stakeholders, stimulated students to delve much deeper into the topic than they arguably would have done otherwise.

Taking an *interdisciplinary* approach is central to a liberal education, and each student in a class takes a different combination of disciplinary insights to a given topic. Over the three years that the undergraduate program lasts, conducting independent research and including a variety of perspectives becomes more and more important. In a course on 'Law

---

74 Alexis De Tocqueville, *Democracy in America* (First published 1835, Pinguin 2004).

75 Laurie van Dalm, 'Zaak Thermphos werpt juridische vragen op' *Provinciale Zeeuwse Courant* (17 December 2010).

and Cultural Diversity', for instance, students wrote their own textbook, thus learning how an authoritative text is constructed on the basis of a variety of sources. My course 'Origins and implementation of human rights' always includes an extensive research project. One year, students conducted archival research on the history of the Universal Declaration of Human Rights, and turned this into an edited volume. Two years later, students focused on Human Rights Cities, those cities that base their local policies on international human rights, and turned their empirical research, based on interviews in cities all over Europe, into an edited volume as well.[76] Whereas these projects involved entire classes, I have fond memories of conducting research with smaller groups of students as well: for instance, on the social effects of court cases on discrimination by the orthodox protestant SGP party in the Netherlands.[77] The students' backgrounds in religious studies, research methodology, and other disciplinary fields contributed significantly to the publications that came out of the research, just as participating in the research enhanced their interest in academics.[78]

Whereas these assignments stimulate critical-thinking and research skills, the essential attitude that a liberal education seeks to develop is that of *empathy*, and the ability for a *narrative imagination.* In the Introduction to Law, Society and Justice, students visit both a local courtroom session and one in an international court, and interview a legal professional to write a report about this. Last semester, I started a class on justice by asking them to write a poem on the topic. Students play out a moot court, like the case of *Donoghue v Stevenson* that formed the basis of the common law case law on negligence, learning first-hand about both the doctrinal issue at stake ('who, in law, is thy neighbour')

---

76 Jordy Van Aarsen et al, *Human Rights Cities: Motivations, Mechanisms, Implications. A case study of European Human Rights Cities* (Report of an undergraduate research project), University College Roosevelt, Middelburg, 2013.

77 Barbara Oomen et al, *Recht op verschil? Percepties en effecten van de implementatie van gelijkebehandelingswetgeving onder orthodox-protestanten in Nederland* (University College Roosevelt, Middelburg 2010); Barbara Oomen et al, 'Van Walswetten en de Wil van God: orthodox protestantse perspectieven op de gelijkebehandelingszaken' [2010] *NJB* 165.

78 Barbara Oomen & Niels Rijke, 'The Right to be Different: Homosexuality, Orthodoxy and the Politics of Global Legal Pluralism in Orthodox-Protestant Schools in the Netherlands' [2012] XXVIII *Journal of Law and Religion* 361; Barbara Oomen, Joost Guijt and Matthias Ploeg, 'CEDAW, the Bible and the State of the Netherlands: the struggle over orthodox women's political participation and their responses' [2010] 6 *Utrecht Law Review* 158.

but also playing out the part of the young woman who found a decomposed snail in her ginger beer, or the factory owner who faced liability for this.[79] In the third year course on 'Origins and Implementation of Human Rights' I was inspired by *A people's history of the European Court of Human Rights* in asking students to not only write a paper about the doctrinal importance of a ECtHR case of their choice, but also about the actors involved in the case, the trajectory followed in taking the case to Strasbourg, and its legislative and social impact.[80] This particular class' understanding of the story behind a given case was also fuelled by an excursion to Strasbourg, where we watched the hearing of *Jaloud v the Netherlands*, to subsequently interview and hear presentations by the Dutch judge, the representatives of the Dutch State, and the lawyers representing the Iraqi plaintiffs.[81]

Such an approach does not only stimulate empathy, but also shows students the degree to which the abstract ideal of justice is man-made, and thus what their personal contribution towards issues of social justice can be. This final objective of a classic liberal education, stimulating *critical democratic citizenship*, is the furthest removed from what is classically expected of a Dutch law teacher, and has thus removed me furthest out of my comfort zone.[82] I vividly remember sitting in a park in the middle of our quaint college town, in early Spring, watching students intently interviewing a group of Iraqi undocumented migrants, who told tales of being thrown in and out of alien detention, sleeping in the park, not being able to reach their lawyer, and not daring to go to the doctor. This encounter stimulated students to organize a policy seminar, taking these stories to local politicians and policymakers, and calling on them to take action. Similarly, I have proudly witnessed how first-year students organized the local Four Freedoms Awards, a corollary to the wider event, with a popular contest in the local newspaper to elect who – at the local level – contributed to the freedom from want and from fear, and of

---

79 Available at: http://www.scottishlawreports.org.uk/resources/dvs/minitrial/index.html (accessed 20 August 2014).

80 Michael D Goldhaber, *A People's History of The European Court of Human Rights* (Rutgers University Press 2009). The book on the Dutch Supreme Court F Bruinsma, *De Hoge Raad van Onderen* (Kluwer 1999) provides similar inspiration. Students also translated their case into a moot court.

81 *Jaloud v The Netherlands* (2014) app no. 47708/08 (ECHR, 20 November 2014).

82 See also B Oomen, 'De brede bachelor: ruimte voor bildung, bezieling en een bepaald soort burgerschap' in Herman Tak and Barbara Oomen (eds), *De disciplines voorbij: De colleges van Hans Adriaansens* (De Drukkerij 2012).

expression and religion.[83] Students have worked on cases with the local refugee council, anti-discrimination bureau, organization that works with the disabled and immigration lawyers, have received credit for it but – more importantly – developed a sense of their own potential and responsibility as citizens and contributed to social justice. The program 'Going Glocal', in which students seek to straddle global and local action is another example of such an endeavour.[84]

5 CONCLUSION

The very essence of liberal education is opening the mind, and stimulating an interest in obtaining knowledge and understanding as goals in themselves. Such a pursuit does not always combine logically with the specific, vocational approach of classical legal education. At the same time law – as has long been recognized in America – has an important contribution to make to a liberal education: it adds a particular type of reasoning, and many moral dilemmas and stories to go with it, introduces students to one of the most important institutions devised by man to overcome irrationality and arbitrariness, and equips them with the understanding and the tools needed to effectively function as a democratic citizen. Simultaneously, the liberal arts approach adds much to classical doctrinal education, by introducing interdisciplinarity, a focus on narratives and adding purpose to such education.

Having taught various law courses in a Dutch liberal arts context over the past eight years, I have come to consider my own role as that of orchestrating encounters. Such encounters can be between various perspectives on the law and the positions of various actors in the legal process. They can take place within the confines of the classroom, but just as often outside of it: by sending students out to do research, observe court cases and to conduct interviews. Out of such encounters, with classical texts, between law and reality, arises an insight in not only the law taught at law school, but also in what law does, and how this does – or does not – contribute to justice. This is quite an open-ended process that calls for a specific attitude in the teacher. On the one hand, there is the need to have a keen interest in the students' backgrounds and ideals, and to have the time to develop this. On the other hand, this calls for a sound legal education, but also a knowledge of related disciplines and real-world issues and people. It is also important not to shy away from

83 See: www.fourfreedoms.nl (accessed 20 August 2015).
84 See: www.goingglocal.nl (accessed 20 August 2015).

open-ended inquiry, much like research, and of undertaking a journey of intellectual discovery together with students, instead of the more classic unidirectional model of teaching. As such, classes that are about orchestrating encounters also become great learning experiences for teachers themselves. The final advantage of this type of teaching concerns its contribution to society. After all, properly orchestrating such encounters, and the reflection upon them, does not only make for better lawyers, or for better scholars, but also for a better world.

12. Students' perception and legal education

Gülriz Uygur

1 INTRODUCTION

The relationship between ethical awareness and legal education can be discussed in different contexts. Here, I discuss it in the context of seeing injustice.

Seeing injustice is important to lawyers for different reasons. In this chapter, my primary aim is to argue for a close relationship between seeing injustice and virtue. After elucidating the nature of this relationship, I will explain why legal education should include education in the ethical virtues and how this improves students' ethical awareness. The focus lies in particular on the virtue of attention. I do this with an example of experiential learning, taken from my classroom practice.

The question of how virtue can play a role in legal decision-making may be answered in different ways. Generally, the subject of virtue is discussed in the context of legal ethics. As Amalia Amaya argues, the role of virtue in legal ethics is accepted by most legal theorists. Hence, it is plausible to think that there is indeed a relationship between a good legal decision and the possession of virtue. Amaya states that:[1]

> Good legal-decision making, particularly in hard cases, requires the possession of capacities that go beyond the ability to properly assess relevant consequences and the mere compliance with a number of duties. The possession of some character traits, such as prudence, courage, wisdom, or justice, is arguably conducive to good (justified) decisions as well as constitutive of the conception of a good judge, good lawyer, or a good prosecutor.

[1] Amalia Amaya, 'The Role of Virtue in Legal Justification' in Amalia Amaya & Hock Lai Ho (eds), *Law, Virtue, and Justice* (Hart Publishing 2013) 52.

There is then, a connection between legal decision and virtue, in that virtue has a constitutive role in the legal decision-making. Virtue's connection to epistemic injustice is that it can block such an injustice.

To elucidate this point, it is important to take virtue epistemology into account. Amaya argues: 'The central commitment of virtue epistemology is that intellectual agents and communities, instead of beliefs, are the primary focus of epistemic evaluation'.[2] According to Ernest Sosa who coined the term virtue epistemology, it is possible to make significant progress on epistemological problems by adopting virtue theory.[3] So virtue epistemology and virtue ethics can be seen as related. In this chapter, within the context of seeing injustice, I will take up and explore this relationship.

I do so, as my main question is: how is it possible for the law students to see injustice? I claim that to see injustice has much to do with the possession of certain virtues, in particular the virtue of attention.[4] But to properly *attend* requires the ethical awareness that is at the core of my main question, how is it possible for law students to gain ethical awareness so as to be attentive to incidents of injustice?

To explain this, in the first part of the chapter, I will concentrate on seeing injustice and explain its critical importance for ethical awareness. Then, I will try to explain one of the main obstacles that block the seeing of injustice, that is to say, systematically-produced prejudices. However, to be aware of prejudices requires intellectual effort. Therefore, I will claim that it is paramount to teach law students virtues. In the second part of the chapter, I will claim that since experience is required to see injustice, experiential learning is a valuable methodology in teaching virtues. Finally, in the third and last part of the chapter, I will use Michel Foucault's example of 'the mirror', together with the discussion of the prison experience and claim that the viability of the ethical awareness on the part of students is closely connected with their ability to think in intersubjective terms, i.e. thinking of the self together with others.

---

[2] Amalia Amaya and Hock Lai Ho, 'Of Law, Virtue, and Just Introduction' in Amalia Amaya and Hock Lai Ho (eds), *Law, Virtue, and Justice* (Hart Publishing 2013) 2.

[3] John Greco, 'Virtue Epistemology' in Jonathan Dancy, Ernest Sosa and Matthias Steup (eds), *A Companion to Epistemology* (Blackwell Publishing 2010) 75.

[4] Attention as a virtue see: Gregory Reichberg, *Studiositas, the Virtue of Attention*. Available at: http://maritain.nd.edu/ama/McInerny/McInerny11.pdf (accessed 14 March 2015).

2 SEEING INJUSTICE AND VIRTUES

In the Preface of his book *The Idea of Justice*, Amartya Sen writes:

> "In the little world in which children have their existence", says Pip in Charles Dickens's *Great Expectations*, "there is nothing so finely perceived and finely felt, as injustice". I expect Pip is right: he vividly recollects, after his humiliating encounter with Estella, the "capricious and violent coercion" he suffered as a child at the hands of his own sister. But the strong perception of manifest injustice applies to adult human beings as well. What moves us, reasonably enough, is not the realization that the world falls short of being completely just – which few of us would expect – but there are clearly remediable injustices around us which we want to eliminate.[5]

In some respects this idea might be true. I agree with Sen that what moves us is the will to eliminate injustice. But for this to be realized we must, first of all, be able to see injustice which, as I have said, is quite hard and not at all straightforward. There are various impediments that are not easy to be aware of or to overcome, such as strong prejudices and biases preventing one from noticing injustice. In this chapter, I am mainly concerned with the possibility of the kind of legal education that would make the students aware of these prejudices and biases. To answer the question as to how students can see injustice in a particular case then, we should ask how they can be made aware of their own prejudices and biases.

To see injustice is an ethical question requires the possession of virtue.[6] Although there are various ways to define virtue, I want to look at Claudio Michelon's definition of virtue which provides a particular understanding of virtue to be discussed in relation to the seeing of injustice. Michelon says:[7]

> [V]irtue is a settled disposition or *habitus* that allows you to do, perceive or think certain things effortlessly and intelligently (McCabe 2008:56). As such, they are (a) subjective traits that include (b) a motivational element, since they are inclinations to react to certain stimuli (c) a perceptive element, that is to say, a capacity to see something as something, or as Wittgenstein would put it, a capacity for aspect-seeing.

---

5 Amartya Sen, *The Idea of Justice* (Penguin 2010) vii.

6 Gülriz Uygur, 'Seeing Injustice' in Guttorm Fløistad (ed), *Philosophy of Justice* (Springer 2014).

7 Claudio Michelon, 'Practical Wisdom in Legal-Decision Making', [2010] 6. Available at: http://ssrn.com/ abstract=1585929 (accessed 10 September 2014).

Moving on from this definition, if 'the 'act' that I am motivated to perform by the perception is to investigate beyond appearances',[8] we should focus on the meaning of the concept of seeing, particularly as presented by Simone Weil and Iris Murdoch.[9]

Murdoch says that it is a duty to see the world as it is.[10] For this, it is necessary to pay attention to the particularities of the situation as it is being presented. Weil regards paying attention as a means for understanding things. She says that it is a method for the exercise of intelligence and it requires looking into things, until they can be seen clearly.[11]

However, seeing is not synonymous with being attentive. Ethically speaking, the concept of the seeing means to see injustice. Following Weil and Murdoch, since seeing injustice is not easy, I claim that it requires the possession of certain virtues, of which attention has a special place. The attention that allows for the clarity of vision, is closely connected to seeing injustice or to recognizing the cry of pain.

There are some cries that can be recognized more easily than others. Weil distinguishes between two types of cries.[12] One of them is explained in terms of the language of rights. It is possible to claim that this cry may be easily recognized by law students without ethical awareness, since their minds might be formed to solve problems according to rules. However, it is harder to recognize the other cry, since it is not possible to account for this cry in the abstract language of rights. In that case, seeing injustice requires looking beyond the positive law and recognizing the cry of pain. In other words, it requires us to see hurt.[13] For this purpose, to see something clearly requires paying attention, and paying proper attention requires being able to see the particularities of the situation.[14]

Seeing injustice, then, is connected with seeing the particularities of the situation. It is possible to connect the seeing of injustice with legal decision-making. If the decision-maker cannot see injustice or cannot recognize the reasons for injustice in a particular situation, her or his

---

8 Ibid 7.

9 Iris Murdoch, *The Sovereignty of Good* (Routledge 1970) 91; Simone Weil, *Simone Weil: An Anthology*, in Sian Miles (ed) (Virago Press 1986) 21.

10 Murdoch (1970) *op cit* 91.

11 Weil (1986) *op cit* 215.

12 Simone Weil, 'On Human Personality' reproduced in: McLellan D. *Utopian Pessimist: The Life and Thought of Simone Weil* (Poseidon Press 1990).

13 In this part of the chapter, I am indebted to Zenon Bankowski for valuable suggestions on the content.

14 In the relationship between seeing and attention, I was inspired by Zenon Bankowski. See especially: Zenon Bankowski, *Living Lawfully Love in Law and Law in Love* (Kluwer 2001).

decisions will mostly be wrong. As Michelon stated in connection with the failure of the decision-making processes, it is possible to claim that there are two general categories of mistakes:[15]

> Namely, weakness of will (which is often conceived as a gap between a reasoned conclusion and the motivation to act on that conclusion) and ignorance (which is often characterized as a failure to grasp all the reasons applicable to the case and their relative weight).

Seeing injustice then provides a means to overcome prejudices and prevent these mistakes.

Since prejudices and biases can come into play in legal decision-making, they affect the acquisition of knowledge about the particularities of the situation. To explain this point, I will refer to Miranda Fricker and her arguments concerning epistemic injustice. Fricker explains that epistemic injustice is connected with ignorance in relation to someone's capacity as a knowing subject. According to Fricker, there are two kinds of epistemic injustice, testimonial injustice and hermeneutical injustice:[16]

> Testimonial injustice occurs when prejudice causes a hearer to give a deflated level of credibility to a speaker's word; hermeneutical injustice occurs at a prior stage, when a gap in collective interpretive resources puts someone at an unfair disadvantage when it comes to making sense of their social experiences. An example of the first might be that the police do not believe you because you are black; an example of the second might be that you suffer sexual harassment in a culture that still lacks that critical concept. We might say that testimonial injustice is caused by prejudice in the economy of credibility; and that hermeneutical injustice is caused by structural prejudice in the economy of collective hermeneutical resources.

Following Fricker, it is possible to say that epistemic injustice affects the process whereby the knowledge of the particular case is acquired. For example, in Turkey, some legal officers are insensitive to domestic violence and conceive it as a familial and private matter. Thus they are reluctant to interfere when there is a complaint. They turn a blind eye when a woman who is being abused by her husband or her father appeals for help. The woman is crying for help and says that she is suffering, but

---

[15] Michelon, C, 'Practical Reasoning and Character Traits', in: Z Bankoswki & J Maclean, *The Universal and the Particular in Legal Reasoning* (Ashgate 2006) 126.

[16] Miranda Fricker, *Epistemic Injustice: Power & the Ethics of Knowing* (OUP 2007) 2.

they do not hear her voice. In other words, they do not see the hurt. The *Opuz* case is a clear example of the hurt going unseen.[17]

Nahide Opuz and her mother were abused by Nahide's former husband. The Turkish State authorities failed to protect them. Despite the fact that the authorities had been repeatedly alerted to the former husbands incessant threatening and violent behaviour, they did not do anything. The result was the death of Nahide's mother caused by her former husband.

In this example, it is possible to see both testimonial injustice and hermeneutical injustice. I claim that the police or judges did not believe Nahide because she is a woman – she suffers domestic violence because the culture still lacks the critical concept of a private sphere. This is an example in which a person suffers because of epistemic injustice. Fricker states that this epistemic climate 'must be regarded a seriously defective both epistemically and ethically'.[18] To combat this injustice, we need to apply virtues. At this point, as Sosa stated, progress on epistemological problems is only viable by looking at virtue.

For the purposes of this chapter, I focus especially on how we can combat epistemic injustice.[19] In order to pay attention properly, we should be aware of our prejudices. Prejudices come in many forms and I do not claim that it is possible to act completely free from them. Starting with the fact that we have prejudices, I claim that not all but only some prejudices cause epistemic injustice. Fricker states the general conception of prejudice as follows:[20] 'Prejudices are judgements, which may have a positive or a negative valence, and which display some (typically,

---

17 Since Turkish authorities did not do anything, Nahide Opuz applied to the European Human Rights Court. The Court decided that the State did not act with due diligence to protect women against domestic violence. See *Opuz v Turkey* (2009) App no. 33401/02, of the European Court of Human Rights. Available at: http://hudoc.echr.coe.int/eng?i=001-92945#{'itemid':['001-92945']} (accessed 10 August 2015).

18 Miranda Fricker, '*Epistemic Injustice and a Role for Virtue in the Politics of Knowing*' (Blackwell Publishing 2003) 172. Available at: http://ruconnected.ru.ac.za/pluginfile.php/225921/mod_resource/content/2/EJ%20%20Role%20for%20Virtue.pdf (accessed 20 December 2014).

19 This does not mean there is no relationship between testimonial injustice and hermeneutical injustice. There is relationship between them and in some cases we cannot easily make a separation between them. I also think that legal education is very important regarding hermeneutical injustice for creating a culture.

20 Fricker (2007), *op cit* 35.

epistemically culpable) resistance to counter-evidence owing to some affective investment on the part of the subject'.

Following Fricker, it is possible to say that negative prejudices are the reasons why individuals are reluctant to reach out to the worlds of the others. I am particularly interested in negative prejudices in connection with injustice, especially systematic injustice which distorts ethical imagination. It is in this sense that we need to distinguish negative prejudices from positive prejudices. What I claim is that in negative prejudice, there is a clear relationship between prejudice and systematic injustice. For instance, in the *Opuz* case, due to the negative prejudices of the authorities against women, Nahide's voice was not heard.

Systematic injustice may be explained on the basis of Iris Marion Young's views. Young takes up the subject of injustice in connection with oppressed groups, such as women, gays, lesbians, etc. In this context, to talk about oppression means to describe the conditions under which injustice occurs. Being oppressed, the members of these disenfranchised groups are hindered from realizing their capacities and meeting their needs. Young states that forms of oppression, such as marginalization, violence and cultural imperialism are produced in the normal process of everyday practices.[21] For example, some groups suffer as a consequence of unconscious assumptions and reactions of well-meaning people in ordinary interactions, media and cultural stereotypes, structural features of bureaucratic hierarchies and market mechanisms.[22] In those cases, there is a relationship between oppression and prejudices which is produced by different dimensions of social activity (e.g., religious, sexual, educational and others).

At this point, it is important to be aware of the kind of prejudices which block the seeing of injustice or hurt. In this regard, the perceptive element of the virtue, namely a capacity to see something as something, is necessary for the awareness of prejudices. Although that element is present in all moral virtues, I focus on attention. Because, following Weil and Murdoch, my main claim is that to see something as something we need to *attend to* it properly. We need therefore, to explain attention.

As I have stated before, we need attention to see injustice or to hear the cry of pain of the particular who suffers injustice. Since attention requires care for the particular, we should be open to the other and so we should think of attention together with the virtue of openness. I claim that

---

[21] Iris M Young, *Justice and the Politics of Difference* (Princeton University Press 2013) 40.

[22] Ibid 41.

the particular element of openness is ethical awareness. This element is a bridge between attention and openness.

Since prejudices may hinder us from seeing something as something, from *attending* properly to it, we need ethical awareness. Martha Nussbaum argues that 'humanity does not automatically reveal itself to strangers'.[23] Ethical awareness is intimately connected with seeing the particular in its relation to the conditions that give rise to injustice. In other words, we can be said to be ethically aware only when we are ever vigilant about our own prejudices and are able to see harm.

The virtue of openness, then, can help us in seeing injustice. Openness is closely connected with the virtue of attention, with being attentive to the particular. Openness means to be open to the particularities of the situation and to others' worlds. To attend properly requires being open. Though interdependent, these virtues nevertheless are to be distinguished from one another.

Ethical awareness is a particular element of the openness we talk of here. To be open to the particular means to take notice of the complexities in which it is situated. Therefore, if we are not aware of our prejudices, we also cannot be open to the particular. To understand this point, it is necessary to explain our experience in such a way as to make us aware of our prejudices. Ethical awareness in subjects should start with the awareness of their prejudices. As we become more and more aware of our prejudices, we simultaneously develop our capacity to be open to the particular. Hence, we start a journey that brings us face-to-face with our own prejudices.

3 HOW CAN LAW STUDENTS LEARN THE VIRTUES OF OPENNESS AND ATTENTION?

How can we initiate this journey of ethical experience in legal education? Our goal is to see injustice and the virtues of attentiveness and openness are important means. Then, we should start from teaching these virtues.

There are many approaches to teaching virtues. Some people claim that it is not possible to teach virtues. If we insist that legal education should improve ethical awareness, we run into arguments ranging from 'cynicism that the teaching of ethics can make any difference, or that ethics is simply a matter of personal opinion, or that the study of ethics must start

---

23 Martha Nussbaum, *From Disgust to Humanity* (OUP 2010) xvii.

with the study of ethical theory rather than practical experience',[24] and even to various myths. One of these myths is connected with a particular belief about human nature that is clearly expressed in the following claim of one of my students: 'a person's character is determined at an early age and you cannot change it'.

To counter these claims, I want to stress that to teach virtues is different from creating ethical persons. In other words, teaching virtues does not mean that once a person acquires the knowledge of virtues, by this same act, she or he becomes an ethical person. No one can compel the other to be ethical. Regarding this point, Aristotle sets outs the Hesiod state:[25]

> The best person of all is someone who understands everything for himself; a good person, too, is the fellow who accepts on trust the well-spoken word of another; but the person who neither grasps something for himself, nor arrives at heartfelt conviction through listening to others – he's a waste of a human life.

In other words, although there are some people who can see the hurt, not everyone is capable of it. This is why I insist on the necessity of the teaching of ethical virtues. We need to inculcate this ability in our students. My ongoing aim is to provide the students with the experience of ethical awareness. But obviously there are prejudices which make injustice go unseen. Here, as I said before, I insist on negative prejudices which may be explained as connected with power in the context of structural oppression. These prejudices are the reason why some groups suffer epistemic injustice. This is connected with hermeneutical injustice and Fricker claims that this injustice results from situated hermeneutical inequality and is a kind of structural discrimination.[26] This yields to some groups being hermeneutically marginalized. Fricker comments on this:[27]

> When there is unequal hermeneutical participation with respect to some significant area(s) of social experience, members of the disadvantaged group

---

[24] Bryan Howieson, 'Can We Teach Auditors and Accountants to be More Ethically Competent and Publicly Accountable?' in: Tom Campbell & Keith A Houghton (eds), *Ethics and Auditing* (ANU Press 2005) 265.

[25] Michael Pacaluk, *Aristotle's Nicomachean Ethics: An Introduction* (CUP 2005) 36.

[26] Miranda Fricker, *Powerlessness and Social Interpretation* (Episteme 2006) 103.

[27] Ibid 9.

> are hermeneutically marginalized. The notion of marginalization is a moral-political one indicating subordination and exclusion from some practice that would have value for the participant. In that case, hermeneutical marginalization manifests itself as a form of powerlessness.

Here we can ask how we can expect students to think beyond taking these kinds of prejudices and become ethically aware. It is not easy and so I argue that they need special experientially-based teaching that is connected with ethical practice. I believe a methodology can be developed based upon Foucault's ideas in his later works. My aim is not to discuss Foucault's ethics or to take-up real political and ethical dilemmas on the basis of his view. Rather, I want to argue that particular questions of attention and ethical awareness are meaningful only when we take power and political awareness into account. With the insights Foucault provides us, we can move from political awareness to ethical awareness. In this journey, we can start by guiding the students until they are faced with their own prejudices and help them transform themselves as they transgress these prejudicies. As Allen puts it, 'This invitation enables individuals ... to see themselves as the main source of transformation, rather than waiting for a more substantial structural or material change'.[28]

In what follows, I will try to specify a mode of experiential learning based on Foucault's 'mirrors'. Here, students will establish a relation with themselves in a practice that will enable them to change. As teachers, we can play different roles in that experience. Here, Plato's allegory of the Cave can help teachers by letting the students establish a relation with themselves in order to become ethically aware. There are many interpretations of this allegory, but for the purposes of this chapter, I will focus on the subject of gaining awareness. In Book VII of *The Republic*, Socrates and Georgias discuss the effects of the education of the rulers. In this discussion, it is possible to see that the knowledge of justice is not sufficient for the just state. The rulers must also act in a just fashion.[29] Similarly, I claim that to see injustice, the mere recognition of injustice is not sufficient. Students should also act in a just fashion. It is for this that I claim ethical awareness to be necessary. As Plato writes in *The Republic*:[30]

---

[28] Julie Allan, *Rethinking Inclusive Education: The Philosophers of Difference in Practice* (Springer 2008) 92.

[29] Michael Cormack, *Plato's Stepping Stones: Degrees of Moral Virtue* (A&C Black 2006) 92.

[30] Plato, *Republic* in GRF Ferrari (ed) (T Griffith (tr) CUP 2000), § 514b, 220.

> If we're thinking about the effect of the education – or the lack of it – on our nature, there's another comparison we can make. Picture human beings living in some sort of underground cave dwelling, with an entrance which is long, as wide as the cave, and open to the light. Here, they live from earliest childhood, with their legs and necks in chains, so that they have to stay where they are, looking only ahead of them, prevented by the chains from turning their heads. They have light from a distant fire, which is burning behind them and above them. Between the fire and the prisoners, at a higher level than them, is a path along which you must picture a low wall that has been built, like the screen which hides people when they are giving a puppet show, and above which they make the puppets appear.

Being restrained, the prisoners in the cave can only see the shadows of the objects. But with the guidance of a mentor, it is possible for them to see injustice. Education is 'like putting sight into eyes which were blind'.[31] But to see injustice is not easy. It requires proceeding step-by-step: 'When one of them was untied, and compelled suddenly to stand up, turn his head, start walking, and look towards to the light, he'd find all these things painful'.[32]

This allegory explains that being acquainted only with reflections, both with those of people and of other things, for so long, it is hard to see things clearly as they are. 'He'd find it easier to look at the light of the stars and the moon by night than look at the sun, and the light of the sun, by day'.[33]

With this allegory in mind, I will now describe my experiential class. In this, I tackle a hard topic of which people have strong prejudices and make them reconsider it, and, by doing so, they gain a new experience.

4 AN EXAMPLE FROM THE MIRROR-PRISON

Prison Clinic Course

My experiential class is part of a prison clinic course with 20 students taking it. Before attending the clinic, students must have already taken and completed courses on legal ethics, philosophy of law, sociology of law, law and literature, and women and law. In addition to these courses, the students *should also have fufilled the requirement to* attend a number of group sessions specifically designed to instill some preliminary

---

31 Ibid. § 518c, 224.
32 Ibid. § 515d, 221.
33 Ibid. § 516b, 222.

insights into the students. This is to ascertain that these students, before they attend my course, have theoretical knowledge of virtues, and theoretically and practically they know that there are biases and prejudices which hinder the seeing of injustice. For example, all of them have examined court decisions which are based on prejudices. Thus they know that there are prejudices and biases which cause injustice and they also know that they themselves might have prejudices. But though they might know this in the abstract, they are not experienced at recognizing in the particular situation that they themselves have certain biases, including the prejudices systematically produced by their environments, against prisoners. At this stage, students do not yet have sufficient ethical awareness. Hence, as Foucault puts it, 'it is hard to distinguish the form and effects of the relation to the self as particular elements in the constitution of this experience'. There was always 'the risk of reproducing'[34] prejudices regarding prisoners.

To see the light in the darkness of the prejudices, we should go beyond the texts in legal education. For this purpose, I make use of Bankowski's 'Beyond Text in Legal Education' project which aimed at creating 'a space where the ethical imagination can be inculcated and the movement beyond can be experienced in non-textual ways'.[35] Regarding this project, it is possible to use non-textual research for legal education. For example, one can use different mediums, like art, to explore legal problems or 'different ways of designing and interacting with spaces for exploring legal issues'.[36] Using non-textual resources is also important for the development of the students' imagination. In this regard, I am interested in the ways in which we can develop ethical or moral imagination by using non-textual resources.[37] For this part of my course, I use Foucault's mirrors.

---

[34] Michel Foucault, *The Foucault Reader* in Paul Rabinow (ed), (Pantheon Books 1984) 339.

[35] Maksymillan Del Mar & Zenon Bankowski, 'Introduction' in Maksymillan Del Mar & Zenon Bankowski (eds), *The Moral Imagination and the Legal Life: Beyond Text in Legal Education* (Ashgate 2013) 3.

[36] Ibid 1.

[37] However, as Del Mar & Bankowski argue, this claim does not mean that legal education should only include non-textual resources. We need to go beyond the text for ethical training. See: Del Mar-Bankowski, *op cit* 4.

Foucault's Mirrors

The mirror is a space in which one loses and finds oneself, realized through the other person. Ethical awareness starts from the idea of seeing the other, and is connecting with our ethical personality. Since we situate this awareness within the context of paying attention, it also includes ethical imagination and openness to others. In other words, when this awareness occurs, we also open up to others. In that space, we pay attention to others and we realize ourselves as ethical persons unhindered by the boundary of prejudices.

It is not easy to determine the space in which we belong. As social beings, we are affected by different spaces. As Foucault said, it is possible to say that our lives are governed by opposites, like public-private space or workplace-familyplace.[38] The place in which we are located is neither homogenous nor simple. According to Foucault, there are two main types of these sites which are not only linked to other sites, but also contradict all other sites. One is called 'utopias' and the other is called 'heterotopias'.

Foucault says that utopias do not have real places yet they are connected with society's real places. These kinds of real places are connected with the culture. These are heterotopias in which their places 'are outside of all places, even though it may be possible to indicate their location in reality'.[39] One sort of heterotopia is a prison. According to Foucault, heterotopias isolate themselves from other places. You cannot enter prisons without permission.[40] Prisons are created for the other, namely prisoners. They serve specific functions and they are the 'smallest parcel of the world'.[41]

The 'real' place I focus on in my experiential learning project is the prison. In this space, how can we ethically deal with the other? For this, we need specific experience about heterotopias: 'We need to experience a genuine heterotopia to potentially come up with an idiosyncratic strategy to deal ethically with otherness'.[42] According to Foucault, to ethically

---

38 Michel Foucault, 'Of Other Spaces' [1986] *Diacritics*, 23.

39 Ibid 24.

40 Ibid 25.

41 Peter Meyer, 'Dimension Space' in Trygve Whyller & Hans Günter Heimbrock (eds), *Perceiving the Other: Case Studies and Theories of Respectful Action*, (Vandenhoeck & Ruprecht 2010) 172.

42 Ibid 172.

deal with otherness requires self-training, one that can be acquired by the specific experience.[43]

For the training of the self by the self, another space is needed besides the prison. Foucault says that between utopia and heterotopia 'there might be a sort of mixed, joint experience, which would be the mirror'.[44] Foucault states that the mirror functions as a utopia, since it is a placeless place. The mirror also functions as a heterotopia, since it reflects the real.

It makes this place that I occupy at the moment when I look at myself in the glass at once absolutely real, connected with all the space that surrounds it, and absolutely unreal, since in order to be perceived it has to pass through this virtual point which is over there.[45]

As one's own visibility to her/himself requires the awareness of one's own invisibility to her/himself, in the experiential learning project, I start by using the mirror as a medium to distinguish the visible and the invisible. According to Foucault, one establishes a relationship between self-sovereignty and self-possession to oneself, and prepares oneself to face the world.[46] Ethics means a kind of relationship each individual ought to have with oneself. It 'determines how the individual is supposed to constitute himself as a moral subject of his own actions'.[47] Our being-with-others 'is what establishes the relation with oneself and with others, and constitutes the human being as ethical subject'.[48]

Foucault's second mirror, the mirror in Velasquez's *Las Meninas* helps us in this particular step of the project where we concentrate on the requisite awareness of our-being-with-others as a condition for ethical relation. Connected with this picture, we can determine the space in which we and others are situated. Foucault regards the mirror in this picture in the context of representation. He starts by drawing the attention to the fact that the mirror in the picture does not reflect any figures within the picture. Rather than reflecting visible objects, the mirror reflects what is outside of the spectator's view.[49] In this way, any spectator can see things which are represented in the picture. Second,

---

43 Allan, *op cit* 291.

44 Foucault (1986), *op cit* 24.

45 Ibid 24.

46 Cressida J Heyes, *Self Transformations: Foucault, Ethics, and the Normalized Bodies*, (OUP 2007) 115.

47 Foucault (1984), *op cit* 352.

48 Ibid 334.

49 Michel Foucault, *The Order of Things: An Archaeology of Human Sciences* (Routledge 2005) 8.

Foucault says that the mirror in the picture is ignored by all. This mirror reflects both figures which the painter is looking at and figures which are looking at the painter.[50] Foucault:[51] 'The mirror provides a metathesis of visibility that affects both the space represented in the picture and its nature as representation; it allows us to see in the centre of the canvas, what in the painting is of necessity doubly invisible'.

To explain the significance of the first mirror – where spectators can only see their own reflections in the mirror – for the project of experiential learning in the particular case of the prison to be examined below, it is possible to think of the prisoners as the people in the picture, and of the students as the spectators. Although they see the prisoners who are represented in the picture, they are neither aware of their own invisibility, nor of the invisibility of the prisoners. In this invisibility, how should the spectators act to reverse it? For this, Foucault uses another mirror in Manet's *A Bar at the Folies Bergères*. In this painting, spectators act freely and can see different perspectives. Connected with Manet's painting and *Las Meninas*, it is possible to say that the mirror reflects how our minds relate to imaginary worlds.[52] 'The mirror re-doubles the incompatibility of vision and representation, allowing the spectator to comprehend the imaginary experience of the gaze via its imaginary displacement'.[53]

At this point, the self may also find a way for reconstituting herself/himself. In this stage, when we turn first to the mirror which is stated above, the self discovers the space between the image in the mirror and herself/himself. This space also includes the answer to the question of how we can deal with other worlds.

Mirrors-Prison in the Class: 'losing-finding self'[54]

Connected with the space in which our ethical awareness occurs, my main claim is that one cannot see prisoners or others without getting into

---

50 Ibid.

51 Ibid 9.

52 M Christine Boyer, 'The Many Mirrors of Foucault and Their Architectural Reflections' in Michiel Dehaene and Lieven De Cauter (eds), *Heterotopia and the City: Public Space in a Postcivil Society* (Routledge 2008) 62.

53 Ibid 62.

54 I took this term from David Blacker; see: David Blacker, 'Intellectuals at Work and in Power: Toward a Foucauldian Research Ethic' in Thomas S Popkewitz & Marie Brennan (eds) Foucault's Challenge: Discourse, Knowledge, and Power in Education (Teachers College Press 1998) 393.

contact with them. In other words, to see something as something requires that one be involved in that particular thing. These practices permit openness which means that one does not only open to oneself, but also opens to the particular.

In the clinical course, my aim is to make students meet the groups against whom they have strong prejudices. One of these groups is prisoners. Before going to a prison, I try to give them some experience connected with themselves. For this purpose I start the students with the mirror experience to consider what is visible and invisible. In this way, they can compare their virtual images in the mirror and their image of themselves – they try to recognize themselves in the mirror.

In the first stage of this, each of the students takes a mirror and I ask them, 'What do you see and not see in the mirror in terms of yourself?' Most of them reply that they see themselves physically, but do not see their feelings or thoughts.

As a second question, I ask them, 'Can we separate these fully, in other words, is one's physical appearance entirely independent of one's thoughts?' The following interaction among the students concerning this question is relevant in seeing how this experience affects them. In response to this question, one of the students said, 'I saw that I should change my hair colour'. Another student replied, 'Don't do it, you look amazing'. Then the first student looked in the mirror again and said, 'OK, I'll think about it'. This and similar interactions clearly show that students are aware of the relationship between their physical appearances and their thoughts. They are also aware of their need to be recognized by the others. In that case, awareness is linked to recognition of other people.

The third question is connected with character: When asked whether they see anything about their character in the mirror, students generally reply in the negative. Following the individual answers, I pick a student and ask other students, 'Can you see anything about her/his face connected with her/his character?' They always say something, for example, that she or he looks like an honest, lovely or innocent person. Then, I ask the student about whom we are talking, 'Why can't you see yourself as a lovely person in the mirror?' The student's usual reply to this question is something like, 'OK, sometimes I do not want to look at the mirror'.

My fourth question is: 'When is it that you do not want to look at a mirror? Or 'When is it that you do not want to see your face in the mirror?' Most of them say: 'If I made a mistake or, if I am embarrassed or if I did a wrongful action, I would not want to see my face'.

Thus, in this first stage of the mirror experiment, students come to connect with their personality. They become aware that they have a relationship with themselves.

In this relationship, they recognize their prejudices through the mirror and from within their own position. For this, it is not sufficient to see themselves in the mirror. They also need the mediation of another eye. It is like an exercise of the self upon the self.[55] For this we need to move to the second stage of the mirror.

In the second stage of the mirror experiment, I ask students about the prisoners. In this stage, some students say that prisoners should not have good living conditions and that some criminals such as rapists deserve to be treated very badly. This stage of mirror reflects that there is no place for prisoners in the place of their mirrors. Like the *Las Meninas* painting, the mirror in the picture does not reflect any figures within the picture itself.

In that stage, it is not hard to notice that a number of students respond on the basis of their own prejudices, some of which we will mention shortly. To address this particular issue, first, I select a case which is connected with the murdering of a child. In Turkey, the examination of certain court cases reveals that, under the pressure of harmful customs, some women kill their own children. These cases are hard cases and to see harm in these cases requires having one's eyes wide open. When I tell the story of a woman who was accused of killing her step-child by burning the child in the stove, most of students respond, 'Oh no, there is no reason to behave ethically toward this person'. Some of them turn their eye against her. At this stage, they have the theoretical knowledge, but they cannot see the particular. Prejudices are taken as a given, as the norm. Like the *Las Meninas* painting, spectators take the image as reality. But this image has some problems. They cannot see the mirror in the picture and they are not aware of their own prison.

After that, I explain the details of the case to students and they read the reports connected with the case. Subsequently, they do not find enough evidence to blame the woman. In this stage, students start to see the prisoner in the mirror, but not yet clearly.

It is not until the third stage of the mirror experiment that the students start to be aware of the particular's space. For this purpose, I invite people who work with prisoners, such as judges, prosecutors, and lawyers. They inform the students about the prisons, their conditions and the problems that prisoners face. They tell stories about the prisoners

---

55 Foucault (1984), *op cit* 365.

and their behaviours. After this stage, I show Las Meninas once more to my students. At this point, they all see the mirror which they did not see before in the picture. In this stage, students are also aware that they may move actively. They can see the possibilities that Manet opened up.

During the fourth stage, students meet the particular and the particular's place. In this stage, together with the students, I go to the women's prison. Each student listens to two or three prisoners who need legal advice. These prisoners are poor and uneducated women. They generally do not have a lawyer. We also meet the woman whose case we examined. Upon meeting this woman and getting to know the particulars of her situation, the students were able to reach the awareness that she is also a human being and not a 'monster'.

When students meet the prisoners, like the *Las Meninas* painting, they look at each other, but they do not know who is seen or seeing. As spectators students look at the picture and see only the visible.[56]

> As soon as they place the spectator in the field of their gaze, the painter's eyes seize hold of him, force him to enter the picture, assign him a place at once privileged and inescapable, levy their luminous and visible tribute from him, and project it upon the inaccessible surface of the canvas within the picture. He sees his invisibility made visible to the painter and transposed into an image forever invisible to himself.

Similarly, when students start to talk to the prisoners, the prisoners force them to enter their world and to see their pain. Namely, the invisible comes visible in that stage.

This stage is very critical because it is only in this stage that the students encounter the particular as they come into real contact with the prisoner and the prisoner's place. Hence, this stage fulfils three functions. One of the students said that, 'Firstly, I could not know how I would behave toward a prisoner who killed two people'. This is the space in which the student feels herself or himself lost. After that meeting, for example, one of the students said, 'I listened to this woman patiently, I learned of her story and her conditions'. In this space, the student let go of her feeling of being lost and sees herself through the other. It is very common that in this stage a question comes to the minds of the students: 'What should I do for this person?' Indeed, it is this space that, as a teacher, I want to bring the students into. In this space, students not only see the particular and the particular's place, but also themselves. In this stage, when the students look at the mirror, they can clearly see the

---

[56] Foucault (2005), *op cit* 5–6.

particular and come to realize that to have contact with the particular depends on them. They become aware that what the mirror reveals is also themselves connected with their visibility and invisibility.

I suppose it comes down to the idea that students learn to see others (such as prisoners) as individuals like themselves and on that basis are able to ethically evaluate their own acts. I believe that, as a virtue, paying attention is also to understand.

After this stage, I show Manet's *A Bar at the Folies Bergères* to my students most of whom have not seen this picture before. When I ask them the meaning of the mirror in this picture, they say that it represents the possibility of different perspectives. They also say that the spectators move very actively. Manet opened them up, since they reach the awareness that they can move actively.

At the end of the course, I give my students a form and ask them to write their opinions about changes they observe in themselves. This year, like other years, they generally said that they became aware of their own prejudices and that they have changed their minds about the prisoners. The effect of this experience on the students is exemplified in the first-person testimony of a student:

> Before going to the prison, I thought that prisoners were not normal persons. After the prison, I saw that there is no difference between us and I felt that I could find myself together with this person. I will never forget a prisoner's word. She said that "we were not criminals all our lives". She was right. I at once became aware that she is a human being. Another student realized that 'we can cause suffering to people when we call them criminals'. And a third confessed: 'before this course, I did not see it to be my job to understand the conditions of the criminal. Now, I do'.

They have also expressed that they felt dilemmas. Most of them said that when they meet a case which seems unfair at first, they reduce their pace and listen to people patiently. Some of them also said that they have in general started to listen to people who had different opinions. One of them, upon talking with a gay prisoner, said, 'I never before met a gay person and I did not know what he would look like'.

Regarding the mirror experience, they generally said that it is not enough to regard a case according to the painter's gaze and it is necessary to look very carefully at the mirror until seeing the particular's place. Most of them agreed that the meaning of the mirror is no longer the same for them. A few students even said that they now look for a mirror in every painting.

As to the question whether they think this particular method of teaching helped them learn, they in general agreed that it did. They were very appreciative of being able to see the real problems of the prisoners and understand the meaning of the prison in a dynamic intersubjective atmosphere. They said they saw that each case is too complicated to be handled with theoretical knowledge only. Finally, they came to realize that law is not a practice of approaching cases merely in terms of rules but needs to ethically take the particulars of the case into view.

5 CONCLUSION

Foucault reminds us of the following:[57]

> I also reminded myself that it would probably not be worth the trouble of making books if they failed to teach the author something he hadn't known before, if they didn't led to unforeseen places, and if they didn't disperse one toward a strange and new relation with himself. The pain and pleasure of the book is to be an experience.

The pain and pleasure of education is an experience. I try to construct this experience in a special way. For this, I claim that to see injustice, students should have ethical awareness. Connected with seeing injustice, attention and openness are the important moral virtue in this respect.

I tried to explain openness in connection to ethical awareness. As I said before, to see injustice requires paying attention. A person who is attentive toward something needs ethical awareness, to overcome the obstacle of prejudice. I then tried to explain the meaning of being open in the context of ethical awareness as an anti-prejudicial virtue.

Ethical awareness occurs in the space where we meet and get into contact with the particular. This space is one that reflects our ethical personality. And it is in that space that attention to the particular begins. However, for ethical awareness, students need experience. I discussed a particular sort of experience in which students begin by losing themselves to find themselves. This entails an awareness of how one's actions get absorbed by prejudices. In this experience, starting from the chains of prejudices, we try to move to the particular's place. Like the journey in Plato's allegory of the Cave, this journey is paved with difficulties.

To see injustice then, it is necessary to be aware of our prejudices. In this chapter I argued – in connection with epistemic injustice – that it is negative prejudices that get in the way and therefore hinder us from understanding the particularity of the case.

---

57 Foucault (1984), *op cit* 339.

If this is so, legal education should include training in virtues like attention and openness – the ethical training which I believe to be the only one with the power to improve the ethical awareness of the students.

Another aim is to work on and develop the experiential learning project that I have devised for my students. I think it merits attention as a interdisciplinary method using real cases, art and literature to get into contact with real spaces (such as the prison). Real spaces are at the core of this project because this is where students meet the particular. To reiterate, my argument, is that it is only in our contact with the particular that we can see the other. The experiential learning project that I have carried out with my students can be said to confirm the truth of that claim. The practice of the interactive learning method of 'losing-finding oneself in one's own prejudices' which was the topic of this chapter is a major step in my project. While acknowledging that no method of teaching can completely eradicate all traces of prejudice from the minds of the students, I think this method to be quite successful in relation to the prejudices giving rise to structural injustices.

13. Learning how to read a case: resources from the visual and dramatic arts

Maksymilian Del Mar[1]

'The aesthetic "attitude" is restless, searching, testing – is less attitude than action: creation and re-creation.'[2]

1 INTRODUCTION: TOWARDS LEARNING BY PLAYING

It is not often that a legal academic has the opportunity to work closely, and over the period of an entire year, with a visual artist and an actor. I was put in this very fortunate position thanks to a generous grant from an internal funding scheme (the Westfield Fund for Enhancing Student Experience) at Queen Mary University of London, awarded for the year 2012–13. The aim of the project was to design and deliver a number of pilot workshops (primarily with students, but at least one with staff) exploring the potential for drawing on resources from the visual and dramatic arts for teaching law and legal reasoning. In this chapter, I report on two of the pilot workshops for students, both of which focused on 'How to Read a Case', or more broadly, precedential reasoning. The other workshop for students focused on 'How to Read Statutes' or statutory interpretation, and the workshop for staff looked primarily at

---

[1] Many thanks to Bart van Klink and Bald de Vries for the invitation to participate in this collection, and for their helpful comments on an earlier draft. Great thanks are due to Alicja Rogalska and Jacqueline Defferary, my collaborators on this project. Thank you also to the students and staff at Queen Mary University of London who participated, and then filled out detailed post-workshop questionnaires.

[2] Nelson Goodman, *Languages of Art* (Hackett 1976) 242.

the teaching of substantive areas of the law (e.g. the various principles and rules of contract law).

Epistemological justifications for engaging in art-based research and art-based pedagogy are slowly making their way into the legal academy – this collection is itself a sign of that.[3] Nevertheless, there remains very little philosophically-rigorous explanation of the epistemological benefits of drawing on art and artistic processes to, for instance, model legal knowledge and train legal reasoning.[4] I will say a little more about the epistemological justifications for the workshops developed in this project below, but this is but a snapshot of the more holistic account we need. My principal aim in this chapter is to set out the 'how' of the project – the 'why' will need to be left for a later discussion.

A few words about the way in which the three of us – the visual artist (Alicja Rogalska), the actor (Jacqueline Defferary) and I – collaborated will be in order. It is pertinent to note that neither the visual artist nor the actor were legally trained – and equally pertinent to note my own anti-talents in art and drama. From the beginning, then, it was obvious to us that much time and energy will need to be invested by: (1) discussing the processes and techniques drawn on by visual artists and actors in their work; and (2) discussing the basic principles and materials of the legal examples we were exploring. This was necessary in order to make sure that the exercise was genuinely collaborative: that it was not a mere matter of me identifying learning outcomes and the artist and actress proposing matching resources and activities from art and drama. In fact, one of the most surprising and beneficial results of the collaboration was that I changed the way I thought of, and explained, not only the specific principles and materials we were looking at, but legal reasoning in general, while the artist and actress changed and further developed their pool of resources and activities that they can draw on in their own artistic and dramatic work. In more practical terms, the final program of the

---

3 For two recent collections outside of the legal context that give a flavour as to what is possible in art-based research and pedagogy, see Shaun McNiff (ed), *Art as Research: Opportunities and Challenges* (Intellect 2013) and Maggi Savin-Baden & Katherine Wimpenny, *A Practical Guide to Arts-Related Research* (Sense 2014). For the legal context, see also Zenon Bankowski, Maksymilian Del Mar and Paul Maharg (eds), *The Arts and the Legal Academy* (Ashgate 2012) and Zenon Bankowski and Maksymilian Del Mar (eds), *The Moral Imagination and the Legal Life* (Ashgate 2012).

4 I am endeavouring to contribute, with a monograph currently in progress: *Imagination in Legal Cognition*, under contract with Bloomsbury/Hart Publishing.

workshops, which, as will be clear in a moment, contained learning outcomes matched with resources and activities, had been formulated and reformulated by all three of us over the course of many meetings and further correspondence online.

It is also significant to stress that our approach to art and drama was not about the products of art (e.g. paintings) or drama (theatrical or cinematic performances). Instead, we were clear from the start that the focus would be on resources and activities used by artists and actors in their processes of making an artwork and preparing for a performance, e.g. techniques for visually exploring a particular image or theme, or techniques for exploring a script. We wanted workshop participants to be as active as possible, and also not concerned about their own level of artistic or dramatic ability. This was, then, an approach to art and drama as cognitively-rich processes, which involve skills that were potentially transferrable to other domains. Thus, for example, we took the cognitive skills of seeing complex patterns, of discerning relationships between shapes or other forms, or of holding in suspense potential storylines (e.g. in the course of an improvization) and considered how similar they were to the cognitive skills exercised in lawyering.[5] Put another way, we approached art and drama here as laboratories or spaces for cognitive work, for epistemological experimentation, for the training of the imagination – in short, for learning by playing.

The structure of the chapter is as follows: in the first section, I briefly present the background hypothesis for the more specific learning outcomes that were the subject of the two workshops; in the second section, I turn to the first workshop and present its teaching and learning program, zooming-in on a number of activities that were particularly challenging and/or particularly successful; and in the third section, I do the same for the second workshop. The two workshops were complementary (as they focused on two different, but closely-related, aspects of precedential reasoning), and had the same participants (12 students from all years in the undergraduate program).[6] Each workshop was also supported by group discussions after each activity, as well as numerous opportunities for reflection throughout (including audio recorders, personal notebooks and a post-it corner). Finally, each workshop lasted

---

[5] One source of inspiration for this approach is the cognitive turn in literary theory, see e.g. Joshua Landy, *How to Do Things with Fictions* (OUP 2012).

[6] The mixture of years was deliberate – and indeed part of the pedagogical success of these workshops (as measured by student feedback).

approximately three hours, followed by lunch (the workshops were held on successive days in drama studios at Queen Mary).[7]

2 THE BACKGROUND HYPOTHESIS

Reading Actively and Imaginatively

The hypothesis in the background to all the more specific learning outcomes, and their matching resources and activities developed in the two workshops, is that legal reading is an active and imaginative form of reading. More specifically, this is a kind of reading that involves constructing and considering alternatives and possibilities, e.g. alternate descriptions of the legal significance of a past case or a string of past cases, or alternative versions of the material facts of the present case. The specific resources and activities developed below were all geared towards enabling the student to be active and imaginative in this way, offering a myriad of opportunities for re-imagining the significance of the case, and also occasions for discussing the importance and benefits of doing so.

This hypothesis as to the active and imaginative form of legal reading was developed in part by reference to the theoretical literature on precedent. Consider, briefly, the debate over the determination of the *ratio decidendi* (RD). For argument's sake, let us conceive of this as the reason for the decision together with the material facts that support it. The orthodox view, articulated, for instance, by Arthur Goodhart,[8] was that there is a RD to be found or discovered in any past case, i.e. the case wears its RD on its sleeve, as revealed by the reason for the decision together with its material facts. When it comes to a judge resolving the present case, the judge takes the RD at face value, and his or her judgement is restricted to ascertaining whether the facts of the present case are sufficiently similar to the material facts of the past case so as to render that past case a precedent to follow in the present one. There is, certainly, some scope for judgement as to the applicability of the past case, as in any situation where one needs to decide whether a likeness obtains. However, at no point in that process is the judge revisiting and

---

7 It helped the budget that these rooms did not cost us anything to hire – our costs were mainly spent on the time of the project leaders and on materials for the workshops (photocopying, props, etc.).

8 See Arthur Goodhart, 'Determining the Ratio Decidendi of a Case' [1930] 40 *Yale Law Journal* 161–83; and Arthur Goodhart, 'The Ratio Decidendi of a Case' [1959] 22 *Modern Law Review* 117–24.

revising the RD of the past case itself. On this view, then, there is no scope for actively re-imagining the legal significance of the past case.

This orthodox view was famously challenged by Julius Stone,[9] though one can also see a similar view in Karl Llewellyn's notoriously rich list of techniques for avoiding precedent.[10] Stone argued that there was no single RD to a past case, and certainly not one that was somehow 'there', awaiting our 'discovery' of it.[11] Instead, he said, the judge in the present case revises and re-constructs the legal significance of the past case. The judge can do that more or less actively and imaginatively, e.g. she can do it relatively passively by not applying the case and saying little about why it is sufficiently dissimilar not to apply it (this changes the legal significance of the past case, but does not actively re-construct it) or she can actively and imaginatively reconstruct the legal significance of the past case.

Stone had a rather ingenious account of how that more active and imaginative reconstructing of the RD (as it was previously understood) could be, and was sometimes, done. His suggestion was that the material facts of the past case could be re-described at different levels of generalization, which would change the understanding of its RD and, therefore, also its legal significance (at least until such time as it would be changed again). He illustrated this in the context of the well-worn case of *Donoghue v Stevenson*.[12] Stone took the material facts of the case, and showed the different possibilities (the different levels of generalization) for articulating them. For example, consider the first two:

> *Fact as to Agent of Harm*: 'Dead snails', or 'any snails', or 'any noxious physical foreign body', or 'any noxious foreign element, physical or not', or 'any noxious element'.
>
> *Fact as to Vehicle of Harm*: 'An opaque bottle of ginger beer', or 'an opaque bottle of beverage', or 'any bottle of beverage', or 'any container of

---

[9] See Julius Stone, 'The Ratio of the Ratio Decidendi' (1959) 22 *Modern Law Review* 597.

[10] See Karl Llewellyn, *The Common Law Tradition: Deciding Appeals* (Little, Brown & Co. 1960).

[11] This echoes Simpson's observation that the common law 'lacks an authoritative authentic text'; AWB Simpson, 'The Common Law and Legal Theory' in AWB Simpson (ed), *Oxford Essays in Jurisprudence, Second Series* (OUP 1973) 77–99, 88. It follows that each subsequent court has to re-describe, re-construe, re-construct the past case and/or strings of past cases.

[12] *Donoghue v Stevenson* [1932] AC 562.

commodities for human consumption', or 'any containers of any chattels for human use', or 'any chattel whatsoever', or 'any thing (including land or buildings)'.

Even just isolating these two material facts, one can immediately see the difference between a RD that is narrowed to 'dead snails' and 'opaque bottles of ginger beer' on the one hand, and, on the other hand, expanded to include 'any noxious element' in 'any thing'. These are, of course, the extremes, but one can imagine more subtle options in between, and then also a great many different combinations of the various degrees of generalization of all the material facts.

The point, then, that Stone was making was that a judge in a present case is not necessarily a passive recipient of how the RD has been characterized in the past (including in subsequent cases that have returned to that case). Certainly, the judge may adopt some prior characterization of the case, but the point is that it is open to the judge to revise it – e.g. by changing the level of generalization of one, or more of the material facts, and thereby altering the scope of the RD. What this approach makes room for, then, is an active and imaginative reading (or, better, re-reading) of the past case, or strings of past cases.

To Stone's idea of changing the level of generalization of one or more material facts, one may add a few other techniques, such as creating new material facts (i.e. elevating to legal significance a fact in the case that was not thought to be material); being strategic in how one refers to and describes the persons in the case (some commentators in *Donoghue* referred to Mrs Donoghue as a 'beautiful widow'!); and being strategic in one's spatio-temporal lens on the facts,[13] i.e. focusing the judgement on just one transaction, or zooming-out and examining the broader context and history of the transaction. Techniques such as these are indicative of the role for the active imagination of the reader of legal cases. They are techniques that are employed by judges in their search for a way to decide the case, and, therefore, they are also techniques that need to be employed by lawyers in their dual quest to pursue their clients' interests and assist the court. They are, then, also techniques that students ought to learn in law school.

This all-too brief venture into the thickets of precedential reasoning reveals, it is hoped, the need for more work on the centrality of the imagination in legal reasoning. In a moment, it will become clear how the specific learning outcomes, and resources and activities developed in

---

13 Geoffrey Samuel, *Epistemology and Method in Law* (Ashgate 2003) 210–212.

the workshops were built on this background hypothesis as to the active and imaginative kind of reading required in the legal context.

The Chosen Case(s) for the Workshops

Before proceeding to the workshop programs, I need to briefly outline the case(s) that the workshops focused on. I decided to focus on a case that would have been well-known to the students who had done our contract law course, and one from relatively early on in the curriculum (so that the first year students participating would be familiar with it). The case I chose came from the area of consideration, which I have always found a challenge to teach. I needed a case I could look at on its own terms, but one to which I could add a prior case and a later case, so as to put it in some precedential context. The case I chose was *Williams v Roffey Bros*,[14] with the prior case being *Stilk v Myrick*,[15] and the later case *Re Selectmove*.[16] Students are often asked to read these together, with tutorial questions typically asking them to reconcile the first two.

For readers unfamiliar with these cases, let me very briefly introduce them.[17] As noted above, all three cases fall under the general requirement (under English law) of 'consideration'. Consideration is one of the requirements for a valid contract (others being that there be an offer which is accepted and an intention to create legal relations). Consideration has been described – needless to say, controversially – as 'the price one pays for a promise'. The point in general terms is that the law will not enforce gratuitous promises. If you (as the promisor) promise something off-hand, and you receive nothing in return (from the promisee) then the law will not hold you to your promise. The rationale is that the law is only concerned with serious promises, i.e. those that you can be reasonably taken to have intended to be binding on you, and for that to be so, the law assumes you must get something in return. In other words, there must be an exchange of sorts, some kind of bargain – some sort of reciprocity.

The line of cases beginning with *Stilk v Myrick* revolves around promises (mostly for extra payment) by a promisor to a promisee to

---

14 *Williams v Roffey Bros* [1991] 1 QB 1.

15 *Stilk v Myrick* [1809] EWHC KB J58.

16 *Re Selectmove* [1995] 2 All ER 531.

17 I have written about the relations between these cases at length elsewhere, from a narratological angle: see Maksymilian Del Mar, 'Exemplarity and Narrativity in the Common Law Tradition' [2013] 25(3) *Law & Literature* 390–427.

perform (arguably) the same work they had already promised to do. The issue in these cases is whether there is any consideration for such a promise, given that the promisor is (again, arguably) not getting anything (extra) in return.

Very briefly – though again controversially, given what has been said above about there being no neutral, objective way to describe cases – the first case (*Stilk v Myrick*) involved sailors being paid more to do arguably the same job, i.e. sailing the boat back home (the captain promised the sailors who stayed on, after some deserted, that he would pay them more if they returned the ship home). The second case – *Williams v Roffey Bros* – involved a subcontractor being promised more money by the builder of some flats to finish (as he was already contracted to do) his work on those flats, it having emerged that the subcontractor might not finish on time. Finally, the third case (*Re Selectmove*) involved the enforceability of an agreement to accept less in tax arrears by the Revenue office, after it emerged that the company might not be able to pay those arrears (because it was in financial difficulties). The issue in all three cases is: is there consideration for the promise?

For the purposes of the workshops, the students were asked to read *Williams v Roffey Bros* as preparation. The case has the benefit of having multiple judgments (though with one leading judgment by Glidewell LJ), which was useful for it allowed us to develop activities that drew on the comparisons and contracts of the various judgments (including differences in descriptions of the facts). As noted above, the workshops were divided into two: one dealing with techniques for the active and imaginative re-reading of the facts, and the other for the active and imaginative re-reading of the reason for the decision.

3 WORKSHOP 1: EXPLORING THE FACTS

Learning Outcomes and Associated Activities

I will describe the program of the workshop in two stages – first, by giving a quick overview of the learning outcomes and how they were matched by particular activities; and second, by zooming-in to say a little more about how the activities were conducted, including the comments and questions that we had prepared to ask the students during or after each activity.

The following Table 13.1 summarizes, on the one hand, the learning outcomes for exploring the facts of the past case so as to read it actively and imaginatively, and, on the other hand, the matching 'learning activities'.

Table 13.1 Learning outcomes matched with activities for Workshop 1

Learning outcomes	Activities
• Paying attention to what facts are described.	• 'Walk-n-Read': Walking around the room, reading out loud, and changing direction with each punctuation mark.
• Paying attention to how the facts are described.	• 'The Echo Game': echoing words out loud that resonate for whatever reason (e.g. emotionally).
• Paying attention to, and exploring, what facts are not described.	• 'Sketch the Facts': Sketching the facts, with one's eyes closed, when another person reads excerpts of the judgment out loud. • 'Extra Materials': Considering extra resources, including non-textual ones, such as props, images and imaginary facts.
• Paying attention to, and exploring, the differences between different judgments in the one case as to: (1) what facts are described; (2) how they are described; and (3) what facts are not described.	• 'Whiting Out': Whiting out those parts of the descriptions of the facts in other judgments that are familiar. • 'The Cast List': Writing down the cast list of characters of all three judgments, including how they describe them. • 'Who is Hooper?': Imagining in more detail the physical characteristics, status and profession of certain persons in the case.

In preparing for the workshop, the three of us rehearsed the instructions we would give to the students (so as to make sure they were clear) and we also prepared a rough transcript of the kinds of questions we wanted to ask and comments we wanted to give. This has to be planned carefully, as we scheduled the activities in a logical sequence, moving from the simplest learning outcomes to more complex ones. Here is a selection of questions and comments related to each of the activities:

Table 13.2 Questions/comments linked to activities for Workshop 1

Activities	Questions/comments
• 'Walk-n-Read'	• How was reading the case out loud different to the way in which you normally read a case? • Did any terms/phrases jump out at you that you did not pick up on when reading this case as preparation? • Why did those particular terms/phrases jump out at you?

Activities	Questions/comments
• 'The Echo Game'	• What terms/phrases did you echo? • Why do think you echoed them – why did they 'strike' you, or 'jump out' at you? • Consider the differences between what is echoed.
• 'Sketch the Facts'	• What appeared in your mind's eye? What images did you see when you were listening and sketching? • Did you find yourself imagining any particular fact in detail? Did you get stuck on any particular fact?
• 'Extra Materials'	• How did the image affect your description of the facts? Did it influence you to one side with a particular party? • How did you relate the object to the facts? Did you imagine any of the facts in a different way, as a result of having to relate them to the object?
• 'Whiting Out'	• By now you are very familiar with the facts as described by Glidewell LJ – but you've now just read an excerpt from Russell LJ. How did that feel? Did it feel strange – was there something unfamiliar or indeed familiar about this description? What did you not white-out? What was unfamiliar? Did we agree on what is familiar and what is not? What significance do you think these differences might have?
• 'The Cast List'	• What characters did you write down? What differences were there amongst the judges in that respect? Did anyone notice the difference in the spelling of the surnames?
• 'Who is Hooper?'	• We've picked out Hooper here, as he is differently described in Purchas LJ than in Glidewell LJ and Russell LJ. How did you imagine Hooper? Do you think in any particular way of imagining him and how his role might be legally relevant?

The judges in the case spelled the surname of one of the persons who appear in the facts differently – this was a rather unusual way to highlight to the students the differences between the ways facts are described in the judgments. Nothing was said to turn on the differences in spelling.

Again, here there were some interesting differences in how this person was described by the judges, e.g. as 'Mr Hooper', as 'Hooper', or simply as 'a man'.

One of the most challenging activities in this workshop was that of 'Extra Materials'. This activity was designed with a view to encouraging students to read a case with one eye on what facts are not being described, but could be, and thus what further detail could be introduced into the description of the material facts of the case (thereby potentially also changing its legal significance). The participants were put into two groups, and each group was given a different set of extra materials – one set that was pro-plaintiff and one that was pro-defendant. These extra materials all shed more detail on certain facts where the judgments were silent. The pro-plaintiff (i.e. pro-contractors, Williams) group had the following extra materials:

> An image of the flats as dilapidated/in a very bad state, requiring lots of further work.
>
> Some bandages.
>
> The following sentence: 'It is known in the building industry that Roffey Bros are a nightmare to work for – they always underpay you – and as a result have incurred many previous complaints by workers' unions.'

The pro-defendant (i.e. pro-building company, Roffey Bros) in turn, had the following:

> An image of the flats as in good working order, with little repair work left to do.
>
> Some empty beer bottles.
>
> The following sentence: 'It is known in the building industry that Roffey Bros are a reputable company, with no previous complaints against them by the workers' unions'.

Here is a picture of one of the groups with the extra materials:

Figure 13.1 Extra materials

We had prepared each of the extra materials with a particular insight in mind. For example, in the case of the pictures of the apartment blocks, where they were in a very bad state, the idea was that this could change the way we viewed the facts, for now it is more understandable why the contractors took such a long time in repairing the flats. One could thus potentially turn the state of the flats being repaired into a material fact in the case (which might enable one to either make an analogy easier or more difficult in relation to some present facts). The insights were similar for the other two sets of extra materials: (1) the bandages might encourage one to consider the danger of the work to be performed, and the beer bottles raised the possibility of the lack of discipline by the lead contractor; and (2) the two different sentences raised the potential relevance of the industry history/reputation of the contractors or the building company. As it turned out, the students developed their own interpretations of these extra materials. The exact interpretation did not matter, of course, what was important was that the students began to see that it was possible to change the legal significance of a case by introducing a certain material fact (for instance, by imagining something already mentioned in the facts in more detail, or imagining further reasons for why certain things in the case happened).

In terms of student feedback on these activities, a detailed table with feedback matched to each activity is included as Appendix 1.

4 WORKSHOP 2: EXPLORING THE REASON(S) FOR THE DECISION

Learning Outcomes and Associated Activities

Here is the table of learning outcomes for the active and imaginative re-reading of the reasons for the decisions in past cases, including matching activities:

Table 13.3 Learning outcomes matched with activities for Workshop 2

Learning outcomes	**Activities**
• Comparing differences in the formulation of the reason for the decision between different judgments in the one case.	• 'Cutting out the Ratio': Cutting out candidate statements of the reason for the decision in each judgment and sticking them onto a large poster. • 'Poster Session': A poster session follows the above, in which similarities and differences in the substance and the form of the candidate statements are identified.
• Inserting facts (including both facts mentioned, but not included, by the judges themselves, as well as those not mentioned by them) into the *ratio* (and thus elevating them to legal significance).	• 'Playing the Clerk': Each participant is a clerk, and the clerk's judge comes in with a draft *ratio*, and one or more facts that she or he wants incorporated into the *ratio*. The clerk is asked to redraft the *ratio* by including (appropriately reformulated) the fact(s) into the draft.
• Generalizing or particularizing the *ratio* as articulated by the judge(s).	• 'Particularizing/Generalizing': Participants are asked to either maximally particularize or maximally generalize the reason for the decision of a judge. The two formulations are then compared, and elements of each can be swapped to produce a mixture of particular and general formulations.
• Categorizing the case under a different legal category.	• 'Choose your Island': Three islands are prepared on the floor. Each island contains a large sheet containing an alternative categorization/framing of the case. Participants are given time to read and (silently) choose which is the most persuasive to them. Participants on each island are then given a chance to discuss their reasons amongst themselves. The debate is then opened up between the islands, with participants being free to vote with their feet during the debate.

It is a little more difficult in the context of this second workshop to select questions and comments, as we were building ever more detail and complexity into those questions and comments. But here is a brief selection to provide a taste:

Table 13.4 Questions/comments linked to activities for Workshop 2

Activities	**Questions/comments**
• 'Cutting out the *Ratio*'	• What did you notice when you compared the three groups of statements side-by-side? What kinds of differences were there? Whose 'test' is broader/narrower? Do you think it is possible to find commonality amongst them? • How can you spot a candidate reason for a decision? There being a list of criteria can be a sign; and various turns of phrase can also be signs, e.g. the judge saying 'the present state of law on this subject can be expressed in the following proposition' can be a sign, or saying 'the approach to take on this issue is …', etc. Also putting things in the form, 'If so and so … then … so and so …' suggests a test/a rule/ principle.
• 'Poster Session'	• N/A (Discussion focused on differences between the groups' posters).
• 'Playing the Clerk'	• How did you articulate the first fact? How did you articulate the second fact? How did the new test strike you when you did so? In both cases, what was the effect on the test – did it make it narrower (i.e. applicable, in future, to fewer cases)? Do you think you could successfully persuade a court that the legal significance of the case should include such an extra criterion (the new fact elevated)?
• 'Particularizing/Generalizing'	• What was your experience of articulating the individual criteria at different levels of generality? It is not easy to do in some cases – and in others it is easier? • Even at the lowest level of generality, there is still some generality isn't there? We are talking about degrees of generality/particularity, rather than something being completely general, or completely particular. • We took things here to an extreme, in that we tried to re-articulate the level of generality of each part of the criteria, but already articulating just one criterion can change the significance of a case drastically, so, e.g. changing the first criterion to 'any contract', and not just a contract for the supply of goods or services, might then mean you can extend the case to promises to accept less in contracts where money is owed – recall, this was precisely the issue in *Re Selectmove.*

Table 13.4 (continued)

Activities	Questions/comments
• 'Choose Your Island'	• Why did you find one more persuasive than other? What facts did each make you think of? • More substantively: the three frames are different ways of describing the legal significance of the case. What is interesting is how the story changes – the relevance of facts change – depending on how you frame it. Sometimes, the frame can change bottom-up – as with yesterday, when we explored the facts. This exercise shows you can also do it top-down. • The second way of describing the case is based on a part of the judgment of one of the judges in *Williams v Roffey Bros*: Russell LJ said (at para 19B–C): *there was further a need to replace what had hitherto been a haphazard method of payment by a more formalised scheme involving the payment of a specified sum on the completion of each flat … the plaintiff did not undertake to do any work addition to that which he had originally undertaken to do but the terms upon which he was to carry out the work were varied … ?* • The other judges did not give this much significance, but if they did, could this not have formed an alternative RD that would have rescued the 'strict approach to consideration' in *Stilk v Myrick*? • The third framing of the case was in fact suggested by an academic. What do you think would be the effect if we were to see *Williams v Roffey Bros* in this way? It would mean it was not very controversial, wouldn't it? It would retain the orthodox (traditional) approach to consideration, and would not need to put more pressure on the doctrine of duress.

The two most successful activities in this workshop – and indeed probably over the span of both workshops – were 'Playing the Clerk' and 'Choose Your Island', with the latter being the most successful overall. Again, by this stage, the atmosphere in the group was warm and friendly, and these activities also lent themselves to laughter (e.g. as a result of the acting of the actor playing the Lady Justice).

In terms of 'Playing the Clerk', the students were given the general test articulated by Glidewell LJ (which they were already very familiar with from previous activities). Here are the two extra 'fact cards' brought in by LJ Glidewell, which they were asked to incorporate (by rephrasing at their chosen level of generalization) into the test (the reason for the decision given by Glidewell LJ):

> 'Mr Cottrell, the surveyor employed by Mr. Roffey, told Mr. Roffey that the original price was too low, and that the price should have been £23,783'.
>
> 'The completion of the flats (on time) was 'the critical path of the defendant's global operations'.

Students responded well to the dramatic aspects of this activity – the student representative from each group had to knock on an imaginary door, and read out the newly revised general test to the judge. What was perhaps most insightful about this activity was hearing the different ways in which the two groups incorporated the extra facts into the test.

In terms of the 'Choose Your Island' activity, the three different alternative framings of the case were:

> 'This case is best understood as being about the presence or absence of duress. Consideration based on identifying 'practical benefit' is just a camouflage or empty vessel (for it can easily be satisfied – anything can be a practical benefit), and the case really turns on the absence of duress'.
>
> 'This case is best conceived as a consideration case – in the traditional, rigid sense of *Stilk v Myrick* – because there was actually a legal (not merely practical) benefit that both parties acquired, namely a more structured method of payment for the carpentry work. The case, then, is best understood as a consideration case, but does not at all introduce a modern, more flexible approach to consideration'.
>
> 'This case is best conceived as a 'collateral contracts' case, i.e. there was not one contract and then a variation to it regarding the completion of all the flats on time, but rather the original contract, and then 18 new separate unilateral contracts of the promise to pay £575 upon the completion of each flat. The issues of consideration and/or duress need not even have been considered.'

Here are two pictures from this activity – the first with the students walking around silently, reading and initially choosing their 'island':

Figure 13.2 'Choose your island' 1

And the second with a group of students in discussion on their chosen 'island':

Figure 13.3 'Choose your island' 2

What made this activity successful was that a real debate ensued about the alternative overall categorization/framing of the case. Although no student actually changed their 'island' in the debate (law students hold their ground!) they also realized (perhaps more clearly than before) that they actually disagreed as to their understandings of the case, or the best way to frame it. On reflection, it may be that such an exercise could also be introduced earlier, so as to enable this kind of discussion at an earlier stage of the workshop – whilst still leaving a final discussion at the end.

What is noteworthy, in general, about these two successful activities is that they were both ways of dramatizing disagreement, and bringing it to the surface in a playful way.

In terms of student feedback, students generally preferred the second day – which was perhaps unsurprising, as exploring the reasons for the decision was more familiar to them and therefore appeared more immediately relevant. It is also possible that the second day was more successful because there was already a better atmosphere, as the initial ice had been broken, between the students as well as between the students and the instructors; and there were fewer activities in the second workshop, and more time was spent on each. A detailed table matching activities on this second day with specific feedback on them is included as Appendix 2.

5 CONCLUSION: WHAT WE LEARNED

Both the design and the delivery of the workshops conveyed clearly two strong messages: first, legal reasoning was even more active and imaginative than I had assumed before this project; and second, students were keen to learn to be active and imaginative in these ways.

As described briefly above, my initial hypothesis as to the active and imaginative character of legal reasoning was formed in the context over the debate over determining the *ratio decidendi*. As a result, the primary technique I had in mind that illustrated that active and imaginative dimension was Stone's different levels of generalizations at which material facts could be articulated. What this project showed me was just how much more there is to the active and imaginative aspect of legal reasoning – that it is pervasive and integral to the practice of law. Judges and lawyers have to be incredibly nimble and subtle in their constructions of facts – adopting a variety of different perspectives or frames, and elevating certain facts (framed in a certain way) to legal significance and dropping others – and not only in the context of the present case, but also keeping in mind the effects on both the past and the future shape of the law. Judges and lawyers constantly imagine possible ways of constructing the facts of past, present and even future hypothetical cases. They discuss these possible constructions amongst each other, using them to experiment with and to test possible legal rules and principles – thereby refining them to balance all the various interests they need to balance.

Given the pervasiveness of this activity and imagination in the practice of law, it really is astonishing just how few opportunities we provide to law students to really play with facts – to practice this nimbleness with constructions of the facts of past, present and future hypothetical cases. If these workshops taught us anything, it was that there is great pedagogical richness in staying close to the facts – even so far as bringing in the physical materials, and experiencing them in an embodied, interactive way – and then creating a learning space in which students feel free to experiment, to engage in fantasy, to ask 'what if' and 'so what', and to do all this together in a group that is not afraid of disagreement and debate.

As noted above, the workshops also showed that the students were very keen to learn by playing in these ways. They also emphasized the benefits of doing so together in an environment that mixed the year levels of students, and that allowed them to interact with their teachers in a more relaxed, less hierarchical atmosphere. They spoke about how liberating it was to do all this in very different physical conditions: there were no chairs or tables in the studio, so we sat on the floor or walked around the room, and some of the reflective learning was done in the context of a communal lunch at the end of each workshop.

A lot of the time in legal education we, as educators, feel obliged to cover a huge amount of substance, squeezing in as many rules, principles and cases as we can in each lecture and tutorial. Despite the efforts of many, educators in the legal academy still find themselves caught up in the model of the active teacher and the passive student. There is clearly a need – most pressing in the legal academy – for greater variety in the spaces in which we teach and learn (and interact, in general) and more room for experimenting together, for testing, probing and exploring the limits of what we know. What law schools need, in short, is more spaces, more time, for students to play.

APPENDIX 1

Table 13A.5 Feedback from activities for Workshop 1

Activities	Feedback
• 'Walk-n-Read'	• 'I loved this, I found this incredibly useful and stimulating.' 'I enjoyed reading the case out loud. I think doing this just once, you probably remain too focused on getting used to the new situation rather than concentrating fully on the text .... Just doing it once did still allow you to appreciate the way the text was written (long/short sentences, use of story-like narrative/ expressions, tone etc.).
• 'The Echo Game'	• 'I think this encouraged you to view a case not as an intimidating bit of text but essentially a collection of words that the author has simply chosen where they might well have chosen others ...'. • 'I also really enjoyed this exercise. I found it interesting to see who was sensitive to which words'.
• 'Sketch the Facts'	• 'This was a fun activity. I could see it as a warm [...] or an icebreaker in the future'. • 'This activity was really enjoyable. You appreciated where you struggled to envisage the facts of the case, which shed light on why a bit of a case might appear difficult. It also allowed you to engage with the text in a new way, which did not focus on the exact facts over the course of the chronology, but rather patterns in the text for example.' • 'I had fun with this. I can't really say I explored further facts in this exercise, but it made out the dealings between the parties really clear.'
• 'Extra Materials'	• 'I liked this for looking at the different factual backgrounds of the cases, interesting to create a story in your head.' • 'Wasn't too good with coming up with ideas personally, but listening to others' thoughts was helpful. Many possible explorations to be done with the facts. Some could even be used to manipulate the direction of the case.' 'This was good fun, and a useful activity. What are our biases when reading a case? If we do not have (perceived) biases, what are the facts that we have not considered that are nevertheless shadowing the judges' perceptions of a case, or form the reasons that the parties feel aggrieved? I think this gave us an important lesson in thinking broadly and resisting jumping to conclusions, which is essential for answering problem questions. When distinguishing cases (for example, in the course of answering a problem question) it is vital to keep an open mind as to subtle differences in cases, and this activity encouraged us to take the facts (including omitted facts) seriously.' • 'This activity did help us see how different people think. I would keep it for the future.'

Table 13A.5 (continued)

Activities	Feedback
• 'Whiting Out'	• 'This was a good activity to help you see the differences. I strongly recommend to keep this activity.' • 'Saw how different judges approached the case.' I really liked the use of large chunks of text which one could highlight, cut out, manipulate etc. It made engaging with the text much more manageable. It is so important to understand where the judgments differ in determining the *ratio*. This includes an appreciation of the different facts they are basing the decision on. I think this process should be encouraged, and doing it like this in groups was fun and meant there was fruitful discussion. • 'This was useful to see some judges present cases clearer than others, usually I only read leading judgment.'
• 'The Cast List'	I think the main benefit of this activity was that it encouraged us to consider how the facts (not just relating to the 'cast list') of a case can differ across judgments, and the significance of this. There is no such thing as an objective judgment, and the fact that we see all the judgment in our justice system (including those that dissent or differ widely in their reasoning) means that we have excellent opportunities to discuss the reasons judges come to conclusion; we should make the most of this, which we did creatively in this activity.
• 'Who is Hooper?'	• 'This was really cool – coming up with different characteristics made the considerations to be made in the case livelier, and showed me how the characteristic of one person can be interpreted in so many different ways as to result in so many different attitudes in deciding the case.' • 'Again, this helped coax out our biases and also drew attention to the potential biases of the judges based on their descriptions of persons. This was a very fun activity, and perhaps the best one in terms of getting to know our contemporaries.'

APPENDIX 2

Table 13A.6 *Feedback from activities for Workshop 2*

Activities	Feedback
• 'Cutting out the *Ratio*'	• 'Great activity, keep it, it really helped to see *ratios* better.' • 'I liked this. I thought it was useful and enjoyable particularly for people that like the physical touching aspect'. • 'This was one of the most useful activities. I think students get the impression that there is 'a *ratio*' in a case, that this is the law, and that it is only a matter of finding it. In fact, there are many subtleties surrounding the *ratio*, and this activity teased out the various aspects of the *ratio* that exist; demonstrated that it is not in one place but may be spread across the judgment; and that it may not be a definitive statement of the law, but could in fact be in more humble terms and make references to particular facts of the case etc. This is vital for the student to understand. I think that even for tutorials, if a case is up for discussion, students should come prepared with their own ratio, ready to defend it.'
• 'Poster Session'	N/A
• 'Playing the Clerk'	• 'This activity is a must keep. It is the kind of thing you would expect from this type of workshop. Helps you understand the different tests written by judges, their thinking. So you really have an advantage when studying or analysing law.' • 'Personally, I think this wasn't too hard, but having too many people on the team can potentially lead to too many ideas! But I guess that also shows how the exact same facts, when translated into legal *ratio*, can end up with different expressions that may be subtly somewhat more substantially different.' • 'This was enjoyable. This was probably one of my favourite activities. You had to think on your feet and really assess what were the facts/*ratio* of the judge.' This was fun! Jacky was an excellent judge .... It goes without saying that the performance opportunity for the students was great for building confidence and the ability to articulate oneself clearly. Also very good from the perspective of teamwork, as we effectively all had a go at writing a line and then negotiated which one was more suitable for inclusion. I think this activity was perhaps the strongest from the perspective of teamwork therefore, as it is a really important balance to develop: that of putting your own case forward, while also being open to the merits of other cases and being to articulate your thoughts persuasively and tactfully either way.'

Table 13A.6 (continued)

Activities	Feedback
• 'Particularizing/ Generalizing'	Very useful and well designed. Encouraged you to engage with the facts and the law, and consider what the relevant bits were of each (which also entailed a memory test!). In problem questions you effectively need to demonstrate how the facts fit the law you are citing; and, perhaps in an essay question or in distinguishing a case, you need to demonstrate how the law made in a case is contingent on certain facts. This is no easy task! And indeed, this activity was challenging; its difficulty and relevance made it incredibly useful.
• 'Choose Your Island'	• 'This was a great activity. It should remain. It sparked debates between the groups. Helped us see how different approaches work.' This was one of the best activities. Assessing the wider significance of cases is not only valuable for essay questions, but encourages us to look at cases critically which is essential for problem cases. Cases clearly do not fall objectively into one category or another, but can be used in different ways depending on how we interpret them, which must be supported by the facts. It also had the added bonus of encouraging public speaking and articulating our arguments. I think it more fun and more useful to do this standing up in an environment such as this rather than sedentary in a tutorial.' • 'This was interesting for debate. I liked the fact that there were three options and we could really explore what the underlying motives are when judges make their verdicts/ when barristers make their submissions.' • 'I think this exercise if done more regularly will help anyone reading a case, not just with the case but also generally. It's not difficult to stand one's ground and defend, it really makes one think deeper about why (I) am thinking this way and what the effects of choosing such a position [are].'

14. Law & lounge: an experiment on student self-organization and critique as skeptical reflexivity

Ubaldus de Vries[1]

1 INTRODUCTION

This contribution reports upon an ongoing experiment that aims at contributing to the academic development of law students at Utrecht University. It does so from the perspective of legal and social theory. The experiment contains a type of learning in which students reflect critically upon ready legal knowledge, based on the study and discussion of fundamental and primary texts that provide a theoretical framework for this knowledge. This type of learning is characterized by self-organization in the sense that students are responsible themselves as to how the class meetings are conducted and the insights gained.

In section 2, I report upon the experiment and describe how the experiment has been developed in three phases. I first explain the assumptions that led to developing the experiment and describe the set-up of the experiment in its initial appearance. I then summarize the

[1] I thank Minke de Haan who helped reporting the student evaluations, Bart van Klink and Jetta Spaanenburg for their helpful and insightful comments. A previous version of the experimental report featured in a co-authored article from 2013; see Bart van Klink & Bald de Vries, 'Skeptical Legal Education. How to Develop a Critical Attitude', [2013] 3(2) *Law and Method* 37.

I thank the students from ULC Tilia and the student-mentors who, like me, supervised the student sessions: Minke de Haan, Roy Heesakkers, Paul Tanja, Jo-Anne Nijland, Jip Mennema, Frans-Jan Hulsbergen, Tessa de Zeeuw, Tessa Groen, Jasmin Buijs, Wieke Vink, Hugo Boon, Tom Walter, Danielle Snaathorst, Laura van den Berg and Rutger Fransen. I also thank the faculty for their grant to conduct the experiment, in particular Jetta Spaanenburg. The experiment was part of my honours teaching course at the Centre of Excellence for University Teaching, Utrecht University.

conclusions drawn from my own observations. Subsequently, I report upon the follow-up of the experiment in its second and third guises, and summarize the findings that came out of the student evaluations. In section 3, the experiment is placed against the background of the meaning of academic development. In essence, I understand legal academic learning as learning to know the law, having the skills to work with the law and, fundamentally here, the ability to reflect critically upon the law and its use (why is the law the way it is and could or should it be different?). In developing the notion of critique, I build upon the concept of skeptical legal education (SLE) as worked out in the contribution of Van Klink in this book, and I introduce the notion of intellectual uncertainty and the idea of reflexivity, derived from the work of Beck, Giddens & Lasch.[2] The latter, applied to the study of law, can be understood as a constant self-confrontation of our assumptions about law and its social context, both for academic self-development and the development of law. The contribution concludes with a number of observations about what legal and social theory offers law students and about its place in a law curriculum.

The contribution, as said, reports upon an educational experiment conducted by the author in his role as a teacher. I strive to do more than suggesting how legal education could be improved or strengthened in showing how this can take shape, what the pitfalls might be and which criteria should be met when introducing new methods of teaching and learning. The contribution does not pretend to have the scholarly quality of an author who is an expert in the field of educational studies and education theory.[3] In essence, it is an anecdotal testimony of how I seek to be innovative in ways of teaching and how these innovative endeavours reflect upon and contribute to academic legal learning, as I understand it and builds upon previous publications and conference presentations.[4]

---

[2] U Beck, A Giddens & S Lash, *Reflexive Modernisation. Politics, Tradition and Aesthetics in the Modern Social Order* (Polity 1994).

[3] I have benefitted from expertise of COLUU (Centre for Education and Learning, Utrecht University) in particular from Hanne ten Berge. I also benefitted from the academic work of K Scager, SF Akkerman, A Pilot & Th Wubbels, 'Challenging High-Ability Students' [2012] 39 *Studies in Higher Education* 1; and K Scager, *Hitting the High Notes. Challenge in Teaching Honors Students* (Scager Utrecht 2013).

[4] For example, Bart van Klink & Bald de Vries (2013), *op cit*; Lyana Francot & Bald de Vries '"Adieu Von Humboldt?" Over Domme Organisaties en Slimme mensen', in LJ Dorsman & PJ Knegtmans (eds), *Het Universitaire*

2 LAW & LOUNGE: THE EXPERIMENT

The Introductory Course

As explained in Van Klink's contribution in this book, SLE requires active students and detached teachers. A skeptical attitude entails that knowledge claims and value judgments are questioned from a detached point of view in which judgment is suspended and the art of conversation is enhanced. The experiment sought to bring this into practice.

The experiment, colloquially called 'Law & Lounge', was embedded in the introductory course 'Foundations of Law' and was mandatory for those students who were selected to take part in the honours degree programme. These students are deemed high-ability students and greatly motivated to study within a distinctive academic community, named the Utrecht Law College.[5] They are selected on the basis of past (school) results, the enthusiasm to learn, academic curiosity and societal interests. As the groups stay together from day one, they quickly get to know each other, creating with the teachers a distinct 'academic community'. Indeed, research shows that honours students score high in terms of intelligence, creative-thinking, openness to experience, desire to learn, and a drive to excel: provided the 'right' environment is created.[6]

The introductory course itself provides students with the philosophical and theoretical foundations of Dutch contemporary law, addressing themes such as *Rechtsstaat* and legality, law and morality, justice, liberalism, equality and solidarity, adjudication and legal interpretation. These themes are explained in textbooks. The students study these books

---

Bedrijf: Over Professionalisering van Onderzoek, Bestuur en Beheer (Verloren 2010) 73–86; Bald de Vries & Lyana Francot 'The Legal Method Reconsidered: Contextual Legal Research from an Interdisciplinary Perspective – Towards Developing a New Paradigm' in M Karanika-Murray and R Wieseme (eds) *Exploring Avenues to Interdisciplinary Research* (Nottingham University Press 2009) 167–178; Lyana Francot & Bald de Vries 'Legal Education Re-Enchanted', [2006] 3 *European Journal of Legal Education* 3 (actually published in April 2007).

[5] This honours degree programme consists of two *colleges* (Utrecht Law College Sirius and Utrecht Law College Tilia) of about 75 students each and is open for first year students who pass the selection criteria. (The regular law programme consists each year of about 650 non-selected enrolled students.) The experiment was carried out with students of Utrecht Law College Tilia.

[6] See K Scager, SF Akkerman, F Keesen, MT Mainhard, A Pilot and Th Wubbels, 'Do Honors Students Have More Potential for Excellence in Their Professional Lives?' [2012] 64 *Higher Education* 19.

at home in preparation for the lectures as well as the smaller classroom sessions in which the themes are reviewed on the basis of questions and assignments. The course takes 12 weeks and consists of a multiple-choice exam after 3 weeks (testing ready legal knowledge), a written assignment (paper) and a final open-essay-questions exam.

The approach taken in the introductory course tends to discourage students to access primary sources (fundamental texts in legal and social theory) and to critically assess the conceptual, moral, political and sociological ideas these texts address. The teacher focuses on knowledge transfer through the use of textbooks in which these primary sources are summarized and explained. The teacher may teach students 'the rules of the language' but he or she does not show 'how students can make their own contribution to the on-going conversation'.[7] This approach is defended with the idea, or so the argument goes, that first year students are not yet able to read and assess primary sources, because these sources are deemed to be too difficult or complex.

Two Assumptions

The Law & Lounge experiment intends to encourage students to make their own contribution to the conversation, building upon two basic assumptions. The first relates to difficulty. It is important, in my view, that we as teachers confront students from the very start of their academic career with fundamental texts that underscore a broader understanding of law and legal concepts. It may well be that first year students find these texts difficult and understand only part of the theory presented in the texts at hand. We as teachers should not expect students to understand the texts in the way we do – it took us time and effort too to grasp them (and we often still doubt). Furthermore, students will read many such texts and become familiar with the themes these texts address (such as power, legality, equality, etc.) repeatedly in different courses during their academic career and over time their understanding of these texts will improve; so why not start early? The aim of the experiment does not lie in teaching students how to study such texts, as if it were a course in exegesis. Rather, the aim is to awaken in students a critical potential, and assess the worth of the theories presented in the selected texts as such, and in the social context of today's world and the legal system they study.

---

[7] Van Klink & De Vries (2013), *op cit* 39. See also Van Klink's contribution in this book, pp. 15–34.

Research shows that challenging high-ability students appropriately improves their capacity to learn.[8] The trick, so to speak, is to trigger their intrinsic motivation by providing the appropriate balance between challenge and ability, in the literature on learning described as a flow-model. Indeed, Scager *et al.* defines flow as 'a state of intrinsic motivation in which people are fully engaged in a task for the sake of the activity itself' of which an important condition is 'the compatibility of the perceived levels of skills and challenge'.[9]

The other assumption relates more directly to the first two conditions that were described above: the attitude of students and the position of the teacher. These are communicating vessels: when a teacher puts him or herself at the centre of the learning process, telling students what they must know, giving them the 'right' answers, the teacher creates a passive audience of students, who are merely encouraged to process information and apply – unreflectively – the trick of legal analysis as exemplified by the case study method. James Boyd White already pointed out, in a somewhat caricatured fashion, to the numbing experience of students of the case study method: 'a wonderfully exciting educational experience degenerates into a mechanical and empty ritual that robs it of almost every value, a transformation in which both sides are complicitous'.[10] Is it possible that students 'take over' and are put in full control of the classroom sessions? Pedagogically, this was one of the central aims of the experiment.

Phase 1 – Initial Set-up (September–December 2012)

The experiment consisted of ten sessions that ran in addition to the 'normal' classroom sessions of the introductory course, and were offered to three groups of first year college students; the groups consisting of about 17–22 students each. The sessions were part of the honours programme and they were mandatory. Students did not receive a grade, nor was there a final exam or a paper to write in respect of the Law &

---

8 See K Scager, SF Akkerman, A Pilot & Th Wubbels (2012), *op cit* 3, referring to Csikszentmihalyi's flow theory. (The theme of challenging high-ability students is more fully addressed in K Scager, *Hitting the High Notes. Challenge in Teaching Honors Students* (Scager Utrecht 2013)).

9 Ibid 2.

10 JB White, 'Doctrine in a Vacuum: Reflections on What a Law School Ought (and Ought Not) to Be', [1986] 36 *Journal of Legal Education* 155–156.

Lounge sessions. Each session lasted an hour. The selected texts (preselected literature and one documentary) were linked, directly or indirectly to the themes of the introductory course. See below Table 14.1:

Table 14.1 The texts in the initial experiment

Course themes	**Law & Lounge: Selected texts**
1 Legitimacy of Power	Locke, *Second Treatise* (excerpts)
2 Sovereignty	Hobbes, *The Leviathan* (excerpts)
3 Research Methodology	Siems, 'Legal Originality' [2008] 28 *Oxford Journal of Legal Studies,* 147
4 Fair Trial/Authority	Documentary: 'The Milgram Experiment'
5 Judicial Autonomy	Wiarda, *Drie typen van rechtsvinding* [excerpts], (Kluwer 4th edn, 1999) (*Three types of finding law)*
6 Law & Sociology	Schwartz, 'Social Factors in the Development of Legal Control' [1953] 63 *Yale L J* 471
7 Justice	Wissenburg, 'Aristoteles over rechtvaardigheid' [*Aristotle on justice*]
8 Liberty	Mill, *On Liberty* [excerpts]
9 Equality & Solidarity	Oscar Wilde, *The Soul of Men under Socialism*
10 Legal Education	James Boyd White, 'Doctrine in a Vacuum' [1986] 36 *Journal of Legal Education*, 155

All students were expected to read the texts in preparation for the class discussion. In addition, in each session a small group of about three students was responsible for organizing the session as they saw appropriate, and to then lead the discussion. Two graduate students and myself supervised the sessions. Our role was limited to that of an observer and 'coach'. We would, if asked, discuss prior to a session with the students who were responsible for that session, their view on how to shape the format of the session. Afterwards we would give feedback on the chosen format.

We did not interfere with the content of the discussions about the texts. No 'right' answers were given, nor did we explain to students the essence of the texts. It was up to the students themselves to figure that out together during the group discussion. In general, the sessions had the following pattern: a brief introduction of the author of the text; a short presentation of the essence of the text; and a discussion based on one or two theses formulated by the group responsible. Usually, these theses sought to link the text to contemporary societal problems.

As the experiment itself was innovative and exciting, so was my decision to involve older-year (graduate) students in supervising or 'coaching' the groups. These students I had taught myself, or were part of my reading club and I felt comfortable to give them this teaching responsibility. This would have been different if they had to be involved in any formal assessment, which the experiment did not provide for. For them, it was a learning experiment also. They were not paid or enlisted as student-assistants by the department. They did this voluntarily. As will be described below, the group of student-instructors increased in each new phase of the experiment and in the end consisted, for the most part, of older year students of the honours programme who had been subject to the experiment in their first year. This aspect is outside the scope of this contribution, but I have found that involving students in teaching is feasible and provides them with a unique experience that strengthens their academic development also.

First Evaluation – Some Preliminary Findings

After having completed the first version of the experiment in December 2012, I could make a number of (preliminary) observations and draw some conclusions. These formed the basis to alter the experiment and to make the experiment, in its second phase, subject to empirical evaluation. The observations related to the central pedagogical aim of students 'taking over', the format chosen by the students, and the role and position of the teacher in the sessions (including my role in terms of the selection of the texts, my scholarly assumptions and perspectives). In the last two observations I develop a preliminary link between the experiment and the concept of SLE. The conclusions provided valuable input to alter the experiment into its second phase.

The use of self-organization (as a pedagogical tool) without 'supervision' is feasible if certain conditions are met. As said before, the students were honours students, selected to take part in the honours degree program referred to as *Utrecht Law College*. It was obvious for them that we expected them to come prepared to class and to have an active attitude during class sessions. The students took the experiment seriously and took responsibility for their learning process. (This is not to say that all students equally 'liked' reading the texts and discussing them and were always equally well prepared.) However, the task of choosing a format for the individual sessions, proved to be a cause for concern. The format students chose to organize the sessions in, caused students to study and discuss the texts on a level that appeared too superficial. They felt like being thrown in at the deep end without the tools for reading such fundamental texts and discussing them. After each session, they felt uncertain about their efforts in understanding the text and its essence. However, as the initial experiment progressed and students found connections between the texts, and between the texts and the normal sessions of the introductory course, students slowly started to understand (and accept) the value and function of what I term 'intellectual uncertainty', which will be addressed below. Although the texts were connected to the themes of the introductory course, students felt these connections were not explicit enough.

By and large, the experiment in its first guise suggests that the 'flow',[11] the balance between challenge and ability, was not always properly made, leading to anxiety and hence, a decline in (intrinsic) motivation. This balance was also distorted by the fact that students didn't gain anything materially in return – no exam or assessment was prescribed, and no mark or grade was given. Attendance and preparation were merely mandatory for their status as *college* student. There was no carrot so to speak, only a stick and students complained about this. The experiment in its second guise sought to make improvements to address the side-effects. It was also clear that the students did not fully understand what our role as teacher or instructor was. As we did not interfere but at the same time were present during the discussions, the students were at a loss and felt 'observed'. This inhibited them to show their uncertainty about the text.

Phase 2 – Experiment in its Second Guise (September–December 2013)

In its second guise, I sought to be clearer in my expectations, aims and set-up of the reading and discussion sessions of Law & Lounge. I also addressed in more detail what students could expect from us as instructors. Again, graduate students assisted me, this time three of them as we had four groups. Each of us was committed to one group of about 20 students. We drafted a more extensive instruction manual to set out the aims of Law & Lounge and the set-up of the sessions.

The instruction manual explained the three aims of Law & Lounge (with the main aim to awaken a critical potential):

---

[11] See K Scager, SF Akkerman, A Pilot & Th Wubbels (2012), *op cit.*

(1) To allow a deeper analysis of the themes of the course by studying fundamental texts.
(2) To get familiar and experienced in studying such fundamental texts.
(3) To discuss these texts on the basis of self-organization.

In essence, it would allow students to get acquainted with fundamental texts on law in a free and informal setting with aim to learn to critically reflect upon these texts.

Each week, students met for an hour to discuss and share their ideas, and insights about the texts they had read at home, without a formal assessment. Law & Lounge, we explained, was not about finding the 'right answers' but rather about the importance to pose the 'right questions'. We explained that group discussion helps understanding the texts better, and allows students to learn from each other's insights, so as to better determine one's own understanding and perspective, awakening their critical potential. Exchanging and expressing ideas out loud is a valuable contribution to academic learning. Subsequently, we explained the set-up of the sessions.[12] Again, we were prescriptive about the set-up whilst it remained the responsibility of the students to organize them. We provided suggestions as to how to give shape to the discussion (after a brief introduction of the authors and summary of the text). These suggestions included round table discussion, group discussion, different debating styles or formats, and Socratic conversations, etc.

I selected a somewhat different set of texts to ensure a better connection with the themes of the introductory course. These texts are set out in Table 14.2 (nb. within the left column is the theme of the introductory course). An innovation was to include chronological study questions to most of the texts. These questions were not meant to be discussed in class, but were intended rather to guide students through the texts – as the answers to them were easily found in the texts.

Another innovation was the integration of the paper (which students had to write as part of the assessment and grading of the introductory course). It allowed me to connect the paper to the Law & Lounge texts. I asked the students to write a paper, in couples, on a particular social problem and 'translate' this problem into a legal philosophical question relating it to the tension between freedom, equality and solidarity, using one or more of the relevant Law & Lounge texts. As an example of such a problem I referred to the shortage of donor organs and the extent to which this could be addressed by, for example, changing the law from

---

12 See also Del Mar's contribution in this book.

Table 14.2 The texts in the experiment in its second guise

Course themes	Law & Lounge: Selected texts
1 Introduction	Explaining the set-up, group formation
2 Legitimacy of Power	Locke, *Second Treatise* [excerpts]
3 Sovereignty	Hobbes, *Leviathan* [excerpts]
4 Paper Instruction	Hage, 'Hoe moet recht worden onderwezen' [2012] *Law and Method* 25 [*How to Teach Law?*]
5 Fair trial	Veraart, 'Ik lijd, dus ik heb rechten', [2013] *Ars Aequi* 582 [*'I suffer, therefore I have rights'*]
6 Judicial Autonomy	Vranken, 'De kunst om met een casus om te gaan', *Algemeen Deel – Een Vervolg*, (Kluwer 2006) ['The Art of Handling Cases', *Exploring the Jurist's Frame of Mind*]
7 Law & Sociology	Schwartz, 'Social Factors in the Development of Legal Control' [1953] 63 *Yale L J* 471
8 Justice or Truth	Van den Berge, *'Oresteia and Molora'*, [2013] 42 *NJLP* 125
9 Justice	Wissenburg, 'Aristoteles over rechtvaardigheid' [*Aristotle on Justice*]
10 Liberty	Mill, *On Liberty* [excerpts]
11 Equality & Solidarity	De Vries & Francot, 'Recht en Armoede' [*Law and Poverty*]

voluntary registration towards a system of automatic registration and deregistration. How would such a shift affect the notion of freedom, equality and solidarity? One Law & Lounge session was reserved to discuss the set-up of the assignment.[13]

[13] It is outside the scope of this chapter to address the paper assignment more fully. To note: the student-instructors had no role in assessing the paper. This was done only by me.

The experiment in its second guise was subject to a more extensive evaluation, to which I shall turn now.

Second Evaluation – Methodology, Empirical Findings and Conclusions

After the conclusion of the sessions, students were asked to fill in a questionnaire.[14] The aim of the questions was to determine the extent to which the student responses corresponded with the aims of Law & Lounge. Out of about 80 students, 39 students filled in the questionnaire.[15] The questionnaire was followed-up by a panel discussion with about ten students. This questionnaire consisted of 17 open-ended questions.[16] These questions related to:

(1) The aims of Law & Lounge, including questions about the development of academic skills, the level of difficulty of the texts, the extent to which the sessions contributed to a better understanding of the texts, cooperation among the students, creativity in presenting the texts, teacher guidance and the awakening of a critical potential.
(2) The set-up of the sessions, including questions about the set-up of the individual sessions by the students and their preparation, the ability to gain insight from fellow students, preparation and the value of the study questions.
(3) How the students experienced the Law & Lounge sessions, what the students thought the experiment had meant for them. These questions sought to uncover what students felt about the aim of Law & Lounge, its weak and strong points and any suggestions for change, etc.

---

[14] The questionnaire was drafted with the aid of Hanne ten Berge of COLUU (Centre for Teaching and Learning, University Utrecht). The complete report is on file.

[15] The evaluation and the subsequent reporting of the findings were drafted, in Dutch, by Minke de Haan, under my responsibility. A copy of the evaluation report is available upon request. This paragraph summarizes the conclusions of the questionnaire.

[16] There were also questions related to the virtual learning environment (VLE), a web-based platform for the digital aspects of the introductory course and Law & Lounge. The VLE provided students with access to the learning materials – textbooks, assignments and study questions, the Law & Lounge texts, etc. It allowed for interaction between teacher and students and amongst students themselves. These questions are not further addressed in this contribution.

The evaluation provided valuable feedback to assess whether to continue the experiment, making further improvements, or to conclude that the experiment in its set-up and main aim had failed. On the whole the group of students appreciate the free and relaxed environment Law & Lounge created. They valued the opportunity to discuss issues of law and theory, to critically reflect upon it and to gain together new insights as a result. Students stated that reading and discussing the texts started their 'thought process' and made them understand that 'different perspectives' could exist.

They also agreed that the experiment stimulated the development of a critical attitude. I found evidence of this in many of the papers the students had to write (as part of the introductory course): I detected a critical attitude in how the students came to select their paper topic, how they formulated the research question and how they connected the topic to the texts they had studied and discussed in the sessions. It is worth noting that students came up with interesting topics, such as new developments in euthanasia case law, the debate about 'Zwarte Piet' (Black Peter), legal aid, etc. The papers showed that to a large extent students had gained a better grasp of the texts they had used for the paper.

The students indicated that the sessions contributed greatly to their understanding of the texts. They obtained a lot of information from the presentations and learned from each other's insights from the discussions. They also noted the value of preparing a presentation in the sense that it helped them understanding the texts better. Half of the respondents felt positively challenged to make a creative presentation (using YouTube films, for example, or other supporting tools).

Furthermore, perhaps Law & Lounge has a so-called 'delayed learning effect', in the sense that students later in their studies realize the value of Law & Lounge, and how it contributed to their academic learning and the development of a critical attitude.[17] To this end, further evaluation of the groups, toward the end of their undergraduate career might provide some evidence of this and I seek to conduct some further investigations in this

[17] In the academic literature on memory and cognition, scholars speak of a delayed-JOL (judgment of learning) effect. Dunlosky & Nelson, in a 1992 study, describe the effect as 'the finding in which judgments of learning (JOL) are more accurate at predicting eventual recall when they are made a short time after study rather than immediately after study'; see J Dunlosky & Th O Nelson, 'Importance of the Kind of Cue for Judgments of Learning (JOL) and the Delayed-JOL Effect' [1992] 20(4) *Memory & Cognition* 374.

regard. One student who participated in the first guise of the experiment stated in her portfolio two years later:[18]

> During Law & Lounge in the first year we had to study difficult texts. Often I understood only half of it and I was not able to get to the essence of the text. As we listened to a presentation of the text later, I started it to understand it better. Also in later courses we had to read difficult texts. You realise that the more often you do this the better you understand such texts. Now I am able to read a complex text and to understand what the text is about.

It is possible, I believe now for sure, to confront students with difficult texts, debunking the assumptions that these would be 'too difficult and complex' for first year students. Other evidence of this comes out of conversations I had with the students of the experiment in the first guise who took upon the role of Law & Lounge instructors in the third guise of the experiment to which I now turn.

Phase 3 – Experiment in the Third Guise (September–December 2014)

The experiment in the third guise allowed me to strengthen the set-up of Law & Lounge, based upon the findings of the evaluation. The evaluation showed that there was room for improvement in respect of preparation and the role of the instructors. About the first aspect, students complained in two different ways. First, they complained about the lack of preparation by their fellow students, which caused a negative impact on the sessions and their learning experience. Second, they complained that they found it difficult to prioritize preparation for Law & Lounge as preparation for other courses interfered and were deemed more important ('mandatory') as these would be assessed through an exam. As to the second aspect, students were uncertain about the role of the teachers and their guidance. Although students appreciated the minimal role of the teachers, they did feel that better guidance in understanding the texts would contribute to their learning process in a positive way.

Thus, my task was two-fold: to create an environment in which the students would come to the session better prepared, and to reconsider the role of the teachers to improve the guidance for those who needed it. I revised the format of the Law & Lounge sessions in three ways: I made the groups smaller, I had each group coached by two older (graduate)

---

[18] The portfolio is on file with the author. (Each student must prepare a portfolio for graduation in which they reflect on amongst other things their programme of study and their academic and legal skills.)

students and I integrated more fully the paper assignment into the sessions. The individual Law & Lounge groups now consisted of about ten to twelve students. Each individual group was coached by two graduate or older-year students. (It is a privilege to teach within such a strong community Utrecht Law College represents and to have the opportunity to involve older-year students in teaching.) It allowed the students-instructors to divide the group up in an even smaller group of five to six students, either for the whole or part of each session. I made the decision to *not* take part in the sessions, leaving all to students and instructor-students. I felt that my position in the previous guises of the experiment was problematic in two-related ways: I was deemed to be an authority too much, which inhibited students to be fully free in their discussions and this had an impact as well on my student-instructors for whom I became a point of reference for the students. I also made adjustments to the texts and their order, which is visible in Table 14.3.

The student-instructors took their role seriously and created a close bond with the students. The latter accepted them as instructors, also because, contrary to my position as an academic lecturer, they were still students themselves. It allowed them to take a more active role without them immediately being recognized as an authority. They were considered to be first among equals as they had two or more years student experience. I noted this on a few occasions when I observed a number of sessions, and when I reviewed the sessions with the student-instructors each week.

From these observations and review sessions I arrived at additional conclusions. To have the groups smaller and more intensely supervised proved to be a success. This may be obvious, but the point I want to stress here is that I was actually able to organize this, making use of the community of Utrecht Law College students without this putting pressure on time and budget. In addition, the sessions became more 'intimate' and as a consequence, students felt a stronger commitment to come to the sessions fully prepared. The discussions were on a higher level, due to the fact that the student-instructors took a more active part in the discussions and the understanding of the texts. (Indeed, one group continued meeting for the remainder of the academic year after the conclusion of the course!) Furthermore, the extended time dedicated to the paper proved to be successful too. Law & Lounge became somewhat of a 'home' for the paper. In the dedicated sessions, students could discuss and review each other's theses, paper structure and problems they would encounter when writing the paper. Again, when reading and assessing the papers, I was impressed by the scope of topics, the originality of the research questions and the ways in which the students analysed the problem in the context of the texts they had studied.

Table 14.3 The texts in the experiment in its third guise

Course themes	Law & Lounge: Selected texts
1 Introduction	Explaining the set-up, group formation
2 The Need for Law?	Schwartz, 'Social Factors in the Development of Legal Control' [1953] 63 *Yale L J* 471
3 A Just War	Piret, 'Amerikaans unilateralisme en de actualisering van de bellum iustumtheorie' [2007] R&R 345
4 Paper Instruction	Students brainstorm and discuss about a paper topic
5 Paper Pitches	Students present their research question through an elevator pitch
6 Paper: Peer Feedback	Students provide peer feedback upon each other's draft versions.
7 The Nature of Law	Hart, *The Concept of Law* [excerpts] (OUP, 2nd edn 1994)
8 Justice or Truth	Van den Berge, *'Oresteia and Molora', 2013*] 42 *NJLP* 125
9 Justice	Veraart, 'Ik lijd, dus ik heb rechten', [2013] *Ars Aequi* 582 [*'I suffer, therefore I have rights'*]
10 Liberty	Mill, *On Liberty* [excerpts]
11 Equality & Solidarity	De Vries & Francot, 'Recht en Armoede' [*Law and Poverty*]

Based on the data of the student evaluations, panel discussions, feedback from my student-instructors and my own observations, I can conclude that the perspective taken in the experiment has contributed to awakening and enhancing the critical potential in law students, and strengthened their academic development in various ways.

3 ACADEMIC EDUCATION – ACADEMIC DEVELOPMENT

I would like to make some observations about this potential and elaborate on the idea of intellectual uncertainty (as a legal scholarly 'translation' of the idea of flow that I introduced at the beginning of this contribution) and the notion of reflexivity as part of the concept of SLE.

Law as an Academic Discipline

As already set out in the introductory chapter of this book, there has been an ongoing discussion in the Netherlands whether the study of law is an academic activity. The discussion focussed for a large part about the absence of a clear methodology in legal research, contrary to other disciplines like, in particular, the social sciences (with whom scholars have to compete for research money). It was Carel Stolker, former Dean of the School of Law of Leiden University (the Netherlands) who prompted the discussions.[19]

In my view, the study of law is academic. In terms of the scope of law curricula in the Netherlands and the extent of legal knowledge (both at the bachelor and master level) sufficient reasons exist to infer that the study of law is an academic endeavour. Although methodology is perhaps too implicit, it is but one part of academic endeavours and we seem to 'suffer', so to speak, of the huge emphasis placed upon the natural and social sciences when talking about the university. Reasons to accept that law is academic exist in terms of scholarship, in-depth knowledge and insight, reflection and critique. They exist in the ability to lay bare social consequences and side-effects of scientific discoveries that impact upon human relations and how law can be formulated, adapted and used to address these side-effects. They exist in exposing the consequences and side-effects of legal rules, and judicial decisions in order to detect instances of injustices that law may generate. They exist in keeping track of law's development in an increasingly complex world that confronts law with new problems like the consequences of globalization, climate change, immigration, etc. They exist in new moral and ethical dilemmas,

[19] CJJM Stolker 'Ja geleerd zijn jullie wel. Over de status van de rechtswetenschap' [2003] *NJB* 1409.

for example, in the field of beginning and end-of-life decisions, demanding a new or different normativity.[20]

Our scholarship is academic. What could be improved is the extent in which students learn the law and are enabled to think about the law. The study of law is more than vocational training (at least in the continental tradition). Stolker's conclusion that 'our students are studying law not philosophy',[21] sells both law and philosophy short. To think about the law (what it is, why it is as it is and whether it could be different; how it relates to social developments, etc.) is, essentially, a philosophical activity. Fundamental texts, such as in the field of jurisprudence, legal and social theory as well as other disciplines provide a frame of reference for this activity. Indeed, as Stolker points out, law remains a normative activity in which a single right answer, based on the case study method is not sufficient to grasp law as a normative activity – it demands different, additional perspectives.

Skeptical Legal Education and Intellectual Uncertainty

This intellectual activity is by definition 'uncertain'. There is nothing wrong with students feeling uncertain about what they have to study, and whether they understand it, and to point out that clear answers do not exist but that questions demand *creative* solutions. The idea of intellectual uncertainty is considered to be a positive effect in shaping a critical attitude insofar this uncertainty triggers curiosity – the desire to find out and discover. As the Law & Lounge experiment progressed and students found connections between the texts, and between the texts and the 'normal' course sessions, the majority slowly started to understand (and accept) the value and function of this uncertainty. And in a later stage of their studies they were reminded of this, when the 'delayed learning effect' kicked in, particularly for those that had acted as student-instructors.

The idea of intellectual uncertainty provides a connection between the observations about the format of the experiment and the observations relating to SLE and the role and position of the teacher. Skeptical legal education, as explained by Van Klink, stresses the importance of conversation, discussion and suspended judgment and in doing so, it promotes

---

[20] See for example, Lyana MA Francot and Ubaldus RMT de Vries, 'Normativity in the Second Modernity' [2008] 39(4) *Rechtstheorie* 477. (Actually published in 2009.)

[21] Carel Stolker, *Rethinking the Law School. Education, Research, Outreach and Governance* (CUP 2014) 152.

the students' critical potential. A skeptical attitude starts with the intellectual awareness that knowledge claims cannot be taken for granted but must continuously be questioned in order to properly understand and use them in a critical way, and to do so from a detached point of view rather than on the basis of a particular political ideology. After they are graduated, lawyers can use their skeptical attitude to contribute in a critical way to the development of law. After all, legal education is to a large extent oriented towards legal practice and those who we teach law will shape legal practice, albeit indirectly.

The experiment allowed students to engage with each other by discussing ideas, theories and concepts, found in the authoritative texts that underpin the understanding of (positive) law. In doing so, students are put in a position to develop their own view about law and its foundations, formulating answers to the fundamental questions such as: What is law? How does it operate in society? How to recognize law as valid or just? It allows for developing a critical potential. This view and these answers may be naïve at first but as students are progressing in their studies, I observe (as most of us do as teachers) that their view on law does become more sophisticated and academically sound. As far as the position of the teacher is concerned, the experiment takes 'detachment' quite literally, in the sense that the teacher gives over 'control' of the learning process. Teaching, in this sense, following Biesta, is not about an 'experience that can be produced by the teacher' – the power to teach is 'a weak and existential power' and relies on professional judgment as to how to give shape to teaching.[22]

I do not promote, to be sure, this (giving up control) to be a pedagogical *Leitmotiv* in the entire curriculum but it is worthwhile to give students in some courses (in the shadow of the current approach in which the teacher is in control) the opportunity to take over, as it does seem to inspire them. It makes them realize the responsibility they have, as students, for their own learning process and how they can 'be taught by'.[23] The experiment presupposes a skeptical attitude: the awareness that theories about, for example, power, equality, freedom, punishment and so on are diverse, and can be questioned. Questioning is instructive – a means of learning and academic self-development.

---

22 See Gert JJ Biesta, *The Beautiful Risk of Education* (Paradigm 2013) 53.
23 Ibid 44.

Reflexivity[24]

I seek to go one step further and to make the skeptical attitude instrumental in the sense that students will eventually make a judgment about law and its functioning in contemporary modern society. I do this by introducing the idea of reflexivity. Reflexivity – as a social theoretical concept – may provide a yardstick or reference point with which law can be taught and thought about in a critical way. Reflexivity not only refers to one's own learning process but also to the social context of modernity in which legal learning takes place, as described by scholars such as Beck, who holds that '"reflexive modernisation" means the possibility of a creative (self)destruction for an entire epoch: that of industrial society' and it entails 'first the disembedding and second the re-embedding of industrial social forms by another modernity'.[25]

Beck suggests that reflexive modernization is a task (as well as a process); a task to modernize modernity; a task to deal with the radicalization of the processes of modernity that is visualized in all kinds of side effects. To properly fulfil this task the ramifications of this radicalization must be known and problematized in order to realign the direction of progress. Reflexivity is to Beck a means of self-confrontation – reflection (thinking) *and* corresponding action – to lay bare and deal with the uncertainties produced by the successes of modernity through a reconfiguration of its foundations.

I refer to this notion of reflexivity, to make the point what is at stake: how to deal with contemporary, modern, and uncertainty. Hence, I take reflexivity to mean a task to understand structural social processes, and attendant incidents in order to find out what they mean for the structure of society and its foundations, particularly in politics and law. Reflexivity, then, is at first a means to process information into knowledge. Knowledge, here, is not merely academic or theoretical knowledge, but also knowledge about social expectations and interests. It enables reflection upon what these expectations and interests mean, and what their impact is, both positive and negative. Second, the purpose of it is to lay bare, as far as is possible, the 'blind spots' or loopholes of modern thought. Blind spots refer to existing circumstances or self-evident assumptions that direct observation, preventing alternative ways of

---

[24] This section expands upon the concluding paragraph of Bart van Klink & Bald de Vries (2013), op cit 37.

[25] U Beck, A Giddens & S Lash, *Reflexive Modernisation. Politics, Tradition and Aesthetics in the Modern Social Order* (Polity 1994) 2.

observing. It helps, thirdly, in re-evaluating modern self-evident foundations in law and politics with a view to establish a new normative field for choices and decisions, and corresponding action. Uncertainty is threatening but also creates possibilities insofar one has the courage to embrace uncertainty. Communication (conversation) is a means by which uncertainty can be embraced.

4 CONCLUSION

This contribution dealt with an experiment in which students took responsibility for their own learning process, supervised (in the last guise) by their fellow but older-year students. Students met once a week to study and discuss fundamental texts in the field of legal and social theory with an aim to learn how to read and discuss such texts, and to develop their critical potential. It reported upon the experiment over a period of three years, with an aim to provide some insight about the weak and strong points of such an innovation, and the conditions necessary to make it successful.

After that, I placed the experiment in a theoretical framework concerning academic development and legal education. Law & Lounge can be seen as a way to give shape to SLE, as introduced by Van Klink in his contribution of this book, building upon the concept of liberal legal education, as espoused by Oakeshott. Whereas Oakeshott stresses the importance of the 'interval' – a non-instrumental moment of learning and suspended judgment through the art of conversation – Van Klink put moral and intellectual integrity in the centre of legal education. It refers to the requirement that students feel responsible to use their own faculty of judgment when encouraged to do so while studying and discussing legal texts. Skeptical legal education stresses the importance of conversation, discussion and suspended judgment, and in doing so it promotes the students' critical potential. It poses a challenge to legal education, its teachers and students as well as the organization of law faculties. The Law & Lounge experiment is an illustration as to how one could give shape to SLE. What the experiment showed is that learning and teaching must be a collective activity where learners and teachers each have their responsibilities, which law faculties must be able to provide and facilitate, for example, the involvement of older year students as student-instructors.

Skeptical legal education can be *reflexive* in the sense that it aims at questioning current assumptions about what law is, how it functions in society and what or whose purposes it serves. To this end, I emphasize the 'social end of legal education' – education with a mission rather than for its own sake.[26] Reflexivity means that modern law calls for an understanding of modern society and the processes of modernization that shape society. Applied to legal education, it means an attitude towards the law and its foundations, such as the rule of law, causality, responsibility and so on, in order to find out whether these foundations have to be reconsidered or are changing in nature in the context of contemporary society.[27] A reflexive approach aims at exposing the seemingly self-evident assumptions of (any) authoritative interpretation of law and presupposes an intellectual position towards the study of law rather than a particular political position as advocated by, for example, critical legal studies (CLS). Skeptical legal education serves no immediate political purposes nor is it part of an existentialist quest for the meaning of life. Reflexivity exists in a constant questioning of current assumptions about law, for the benefit of our knowledge of the law and its operations as well as for the intellectual development of the student.

It may be that at first sight this mode of education fits well within the so-called meta-juridical courses, such as jurisprudence, legal theory, the sociology of law, comparative law, but it is not necessarily restricted to these kind of courses. At each level and in each course skepticism as a way of teaching and learning enables students to understand, and question the law as it is and *why* it is as it is. It provides an intellectual or theoretical context for existing positive law. It enables students to reflect upon law and its theoretical context in order to be able to draw their own conclusions about the law and its meanings, and operations when they leave the university (in the awareness that these conclusions are temporary and uncertain). It also allows them to raise questions about their role as a lawyer: What type of lawyer do I want to be? How do I shape my career as a lawyer? Questions that equally apply to us teachers: What are our moral and political values? How do I want the law to be and why? What kind of law teacher do I want to be for my students? How do I want them to prepare for the practice of law? How do I want to teach?

---

[26] This distinction is worked out in the introductory chapter.

[27] Cf. U de Vries, 'Kuhn and Legal Research, A Reflexive Paradigmatic View on Legal Research' (2013) 3 *Law & Method* 7.

15. Epilogue: an overview, reflections and a student's perspective

Tim Bleeker[1]

1 INTRODUCTION

In the introductory chapter of this book, the many challenges that legal education faces today are discussed. Teachers and students call for a critical re-evaluation of the purpose, curriculum and teaching methods of academic legal education. This edited volume adds various, sometimes conflicting, positions to the already complex and multifaceted debate on academic learning. It would seem desirable to briefly reflect on the positions discussed in this book. Therefore, in section 2 of this afterword, I submit an overview of this book, providing concise summaries of the contributions, reflecting on the general themes and discussing the relation between the positions taken. The overview need not to be read integrally from beginning to end. It can be used to get a short introduction to particular texts or themes and their relation. The concluding remarks in section 2 contain a syntheses of all contributions and can be consulted for an answer as to how the academic nature of law can be reinforced building upon the contributions in this book.

In the debate on academic learning in legal education, the student and his or her development have returned as important topics. However, the student is often the object of study rather than a participant in this debate. This is odd, because critics in this debate tend to agree that students should become critical peers in society and take responsibility for their own intellectual development. This apparent contradiction was the reason that De Vries and Van Klink gave me, a (graduate) law student, the opportunity to give my point of view on the challenges that legal education faces today. In short, in my view, teachers should transmit the open and undetermined character of law to students, in order to stimulate

[1] I would like to thank Bald de Vries, Bart van Klink, Thijmen Nuninga and Willem Both for their helpful comments on earlier versions of this chapter.

students' eagerness to learn and be taught, and to achieve a solid understanding of law. I briefly set out this view in section 3 of this afterword.

2 OVERVIEW

Structure and Purpose

The contributions are divided in three parts: theoretical perspectives on legal education (Part I); experimental courses (Part II); and didactic innovations and learning experiments (Part III). However, this division is not to be regarded as too rigid. In the editing process, we choose these three focal points as general themes and the contributions were categorized after submission. Of course, the contributions may discuss topics that are connected to other themes of the book as well, and to some extent all the themes are connected and overlap.

The overview in this section follows the structure of the book. I elaborate on the general theme of each part. Subsequently, each contribution is discussed. Of each contribution, first, I give a concise summary of the contribution (first paragraph), followed by a reflection on some implications of the contribution at hand for the ongoing debate on legal education, and its relation with other texts and themes of the book (second paragraph). In the concluding part of section 2, I summarize the positions and consensus contained in this book.

PART I – THEORETICAL PERSPECTIVES ON LEGAL EDUCATION

In Part I, five authors set out their theoretical positions on the nature of legal education. These theoretical perspectives are related to contemporary questions concerning the purpose and function of legal education. For example, how can we conceive of academic learning and how can we stimulate students to reflect critically on the theory and the practice of law? On what notions of learning are these conceptions based and how do they promote academic learning? Which (external) trends interfere with the purposes of academic learning?

The answers to these questions have implications for the design of the curriculum and the teaching methods used. What is more, the positions taken by the authors bear implications for different actors in the academic learning debate. This is because the theories discussed by these authors also produce certain responsibilities for teachers, students, administrators, etc. In the context of this book, Part I functions as a theoretical framework and argumentative basis for the texts in Part II and III. It is, so to say, the meta-discussion on the topics dealt with in the rest of the book. It is important to first take position on the purpose of legal education, because this can provide direction in the debate on content and process.

Van Klink: Knowledge and Aphasia

Van Klink aims to discuss what it means to be critical, and why it is important. In this regard, Van Klink presents the notion of skeptical legal education (SLE) inspired by Oakeshott's idea of liberal learning. Oakeshott characterizes learning as a strictly non-instrumental activity. He describes education as an interval free from contingent wants, in which a transaction between generations can take place where newcomers are introduced to an 'intellectual, imaginative, moral and emotional inheritance'.[2] Following Oakeshott, Van Klink argues that the teacher has the responsibility to teach students how to develop their own voice in the ongoing academic conversation.[3] For this purpose, students should be encouraged to critically reflect on their assessment of information, and learn to build critically and hermeneutically on the values and knowledge that is already accepted in a community.[4] Skeptical legal education involves a detached mode of teaching in which the teacher provides a neutral account of the information. Also, in order to suspend judgment, the teacher should expose contradictions to the students by engaging in a Socratic dialogue. For SLE, it is furthermore required that students actively participate in education. With regard to the institutional context, SLE requires that the university management makes sure that the teachers have different social and intellectual backgrounds, and that the curriculum allows for different perspectives. Skeptical legal education is useful on different levels.[5] On the individual level, it can be liberating to discover that there is no ultimate truth, but many different perspectives on reality. On the scientific level, as Gadamer argues, raising questions will stimulate the quest for knowledge and finding new answers, building on ideas of earlier scholars. On the social level, finally, a skeptical attitude

2 Van Klink, 18.
3 Ibid 20.
4 Ibid 21.
5 Ibid 33–34.

may help to think society anew by raising critical and uneasy questions about the current state of affairs.[6]

Van Klink conceives of legal education's purpose as 'the ability to assess knowledge claims critically drawing from the reservoir of accepted ideas'.[7] As I see it, there is a tension between SLE and the current demand for practical knowledge in the curriculum. After all, by questioning basic assumptions, students will likely as not adopt a very practical view on the law, which is often regarded as useful for legal practitioners. Although Van Klink holds that this critical attitude is connected to the intrinsic purpose of education, he also provides instrumental reasons for creating critical students, such as the requirements that lawyers find alternative avenues and are able to take a normative position in order to improve the law as it is. As Van Klink elaborates a theoretical perspective on liberal and critical learning, he furthermore provides a normative basis for the critical teaching methods that are advocated by various authors in Parts II and III.[8] An illustration of how SLE could be applied can be found in De Vries' chapter on the Law & Lounge experiment.

Francot & Corrias: Re-*Bildung*

Francot & Corrias criticize the tendency of instrumentalization and economization of legal education. They use Von Humboldt's conception of 'Bildung' in their argument for reviving intrinsic education, free from market-forces and societal demands into the notion of *Re*-Bildung. According to the authors, the purpose of academic education is to teach an 'investigative attitude', or 'reflective stance'.[9] In *Re*-Bildung Francot & Corrias rethink Humboldt's connection between the inward and outward dimension of Bildung. Echoing Gadamer, the inward dimension of Bildung – which regards the unfolding of the potential and qualities of a student – requires that the student should question the knowledge and prejudices that make up his or her horizon.[10] The outward dimension then – which involves social interaction and exchanging ideas – is derived from Arendt's idea of education as a transitional space, in which the teacher has the responsibility for preparing the student to be a responsible

---

6 Ibid 34.

7 Ibid 31.

8 Francot & Corrias; Schwöbel-Patel; Sokhi-Bulley; De Vries ('Law & Lounge'); Del Mar; Oomen; Van Rossum.

9 Francot & Corrias, 45.

10 Ibid 46.

inhabitant of the world.[11] *Re*-Bildung as an ideal can guide legal education to arm itself against the economic rationality that erodes the underlying interests of academic legal education.[12]

An important function of *Re*-Bildung, is that it can provide a normative basis for various institutional changes. These changes include the questioning of the proliferation of economic rationality in universities and a reconsideration of the focus on audit, assessment, accreditation and accountability. These are trends broadly recognized in the course of this book, in particular problematized by Bradney. In addition, *Re*-Bildung requires the state to step back as a mediator between Academia and economical and societal demands,[13] in order to create space for the university to focus on what is valuable in the long run. Also, it explains why students and teachers should embrace contemporary uncertainty, rather than to stack up readymade knowledge. In other contributions, elaborations can be found of how this state of uncertainty can be achieved. For example, Van Klink engages in a Socratic Dialogue to postpone judgment, Del Mar uses exercises from the visual and dramatic arts to construe alternative descriptions of the legal significance of a past case, and Sokhi-Bulley provides an account of how methodology allows the student to find alternative truths. De Vries places such exercises in a theoretical context, as he examines how 'intellectual uncertainty' in connection with reflexivity can contribute to challenging the foundations of society.

Anja Böning: Academic Education and Socialization

Böning reports on an explorative study regarding the social dynamics and disciplining effects that traditional forms of examination in German law schools have on students. By examining interviews with law students, she connects factors in the learning environment with subjective learning experiences. She uses Bourdieu's methods of educational-sociological research and Foucault's power-analytical studies as a frame of reference for the interpretation of the interviews. This perspective reveals underlying structures of meaning and effects that are hidden behind the neutral regulations of legal education.[14] One of the reported effects is a massive psychological pressure on the students, which could negatively influence the students' motivation and self-efficacy, and can hinder academic

---

11 Ibid 48.
12 Ibid 44–45.
13 Ibid 44.
14 Böning, 63.

maturation. She also examines the effect of the anonymized examination apparatus, which means that students are essentially reduced to their grade and student number. As a result, the grade becomes the students' first priority and overtakes intrinsic reasons to study. Böning elaborates on various other mechanisms that would result in selective destruction of 'successful socialization', which she links to total institutions such as the military and prisons.[15] She concludes that legal education has the important task to teach students to be reflexive and how to become responsible and critical citizens.[16] She reminds the readers of the importance of looking at learning the law from the students' point of view.

Böning notes that 'pioneer status'[17] could be awarded to her research, as law's education praxis and the experiences of law students is still a 'white spot in the research map'.[18] This author, too, seems to recognize that students are still too often object rather than subject in the debate on academic legal education.[19] Although Böning acknowledges that further study is required, several detrimental underlying mechanisms can already be deduced from the examination of the students' subjective learning experience. This illustrates that using different perspectives can expose the blind spots that still exist in this debate. Böning's sociological approach provides an empirically grounded account of why trends and mechanisms such as massification, and a focus on grades are harmful for the university's academic core and marginalizes students. Bradney also argues that these trends are undesirable, but puts the teacher central in his argumentation. Furthermore, emphasizing the importance for successful socialization, Böning provides a sociological argument for conceiving of legal education as a transitional space, which has also been argued by various other authors from a philosophical and pedagogical perspective.[20]

Anthony Bradney: The Necessary Loneliness of Teaching

Bradney argues that academic autonomy is impinged for two reasons: teachers frequently work as members of teams, and institutions and

---

[15] Ibid 76.

[16] Ibid 77–78.

[17] Ibid 60.

[18] Ibid 63.

[19] In section 3, I also argue that perspectives from discussants of all levels of legal education should be included in the debate on the nature and purpose of law school.

[20] Including Van Klink; Francot & Corrias; and Oomen.

external bodies audit the work of academics (managerialism). He furthermore maintains that university teaching in law is a key professional activity, because it is the starting place for 'acculturation into the legal professions'.[21] Therefore, it is particularly important for academics to understand what it means to be a 'professional', which he connects to values such as responsibility and altruism.[22] Professionals are expected 'to place the good of the clients, the public, or the development of a discipline over their own economic interest'.[23] Then, from a historical point of view, Bradney frames 'Lehrfreiheit' as 'the core mission of the university'.[24] He argues that this kind of freedom also creates certain obligations for academics. In this regard, Bradney argues that academics have the uncompromising responsibility for speaking out what they think is true, which is coined by Dworkin as 'ethical individualism'.[25] Autonomy, according to Bradney, is therefore a duty rather than a right, and at the same time is academic freedom the only way to ensure that teachers meet the responsibility to teach professionalism as a virtue. Subsequently, Bradney describes various pervasive trends that threaten academic freedom, such as the massification and managerialism. He also notes that resistance against these trends exists, and that their efficacy can be doubted.[26]

Like many authors in this book,[27] Bradney recognizes trends such as massification, managerialism and economic rationalism as threats for academic learning. However, he takes a different approach than the other contributors. Rather than prescribing a particular theoretical perspective on the nature of academic learning and legal education, he puts the teacher's position central in his argument. Typical in this regard, is that students are the object rather than the subject. It seems that instead of liberal learning, teachers should communicate a predefined attitude (that of professionalism), and the teachers also have the obligation to present

---

[21] Bradney, 81.

[22] NB Bradney does not mean to say that being a 'professional' requires (practical) experience.

[23] Ibid 81–82.

[24] Ibid 83.

[25] Ibid 84.

[26] Ibid 92.

[27] Including Van Klink; Francot & Corrias: Böning; Schwöbel-Patel; Sokhi-Bulley; Germain; Oomen; and Van Rossum.

the information accordingly to their (political) views.[28] It is interesting to note that even though Bradney has a very different approach to support his conclusion, the importance of teachers' autonomy could also be supported by the theoretical positions in other contributions.[29]

PART II – EXPERIMENTAL COURSES

The trends broadly recognized in Part I have had their impact on the curriculum of law schools. Today, there seems to be a specific focus on reading black-letter law and providing the student with primarily ready-to-use information. As a result, meta-juridical courses, aimed at interpreting law in a moral, social or political context, are under pressure.

In Part II, five authors advocate courses and teaching perspectives they believe are paramount for the students' development as critical thinkers and able jurists. In their argument in favour of teaching particular topics, the authors, implicitly or explicitly, also take part in a broader discussion with regard to the function and purpose of the law school. However, the main purpose of Part II is to provide inspiration for the design of the curriculum and teaching perspectives. What is more, the contributions provide means of how to go beyond black-letter law and how students can develop a critical attitude towards legal doctrine.

Schwöbel-Patel: Teaching International Law Critically

Schwöbel-Patel notes that, due to the predominance of neoliberalism, vocational training rather than learning has become the key objective in law schools.[30] The curriculum is skill-focused and instrumentalized to produce apt professionals for market-focused legal practice. In doing so, as Schwöbel-Patel sees it, teachers portray international law as neutral and rational, and omit to explain how it enables inequality and unfairness.[31] As a result, students are left with a very 'thin' and unproblematic understanding of international law. What is more, the students are taught a Eurocentric and neoliberal perspective on international law, in which

---

[28] Cf. Van Klink, Van Klink argues differently that teachers should maintain a detached point of view when teaching; cf. Sokhi-Bulley, Sokhi-Bulley emphasizes that the teacher should expose that there are different ways to look at a subject.

[29] Cf. Schwöbel-Patel and Oomen.

[30] Schwöbel-Patel, 99–101.

[31] Ibid 103–105.

Western traits such as individualism, competition and free market are dominant. The students tend to be passive and mimic the teachers' attitude; they are disciplined to embody tainted perspectives and hierarchies without questioning them. This is how 'cultural hegemonies' are preserved: 'the construction of particular cultural norms, sustaining and endorsing them as natural and inevitable, for the purposes of domination'.[32] Schwöbel-Patel discusses how counter-hegemonic conditions can be created when teaching (international) law. The notion of Bildung could be helpful for sensitizing education to the inequalities that are produced by cultural hegemonies. Furthermore, following Freire and Canaan, she suggests that the teacher should engage in a critical pedagogy, destabilize power relations in the classroom, and should touch upon cultural, historical, socio-economic, religious and political context of international law.

The purpose of legal education is debatable, but few will disagree that it should contribute to a just society. Schwöbel-Patel's argument on how legal education possibly facilitates injustice should induce the law school to take responsibility for creating awareness about the epistemic injustice that could follow from seemingly neutral norms. An interesting parallel exists with Böning's contribution, in which she explains how 'neutral' rules and mechanisms benefit specific traits and cause a 'grade nobility': it could well be argued that the law school's method of examination leads to a reproduction of hierarchies. Furthermore, knowledge of cultural hegemonies should bring about a wariness of the instrumentalization of legal education, the neo-liberalist rationality, the limited academic freedom for lecturers and the power-structures in universities. Also, these hegemonies produce normative implications for the institutional design of universities, the curriculum and the teaching methods. In this regard, Schwöbel-Patel's position is closely connected to Sokhi-Bulley's contribution, in which she argues that it is the teacher's responsibility to provide different 'lenses' for examining legal issues. Also Van Klink's appeal for teachers of diverse backgrounds can be seen as a means to challenge cultural hegemonies.[33]

Sokhi-Bulley: Learning Law Differently

Sokhi-Bulley notes that in law schools there seems to be an aversion to theory and methodology. However, the author understands methodology

---

32 Ibid 100.

33 Van Klink, 33.

as an important tool: a lens that can magnify certain themes, a perspective that can be changed in order to ask different questions about the same subject in order to find alternative truths.[34] However, she notes that there exists nowadays a lack of awareness and a resultant lack of curiosity amongst students and teachers with regard to legal research methods. Illustrative in this regard, is the absence of a canon of legal methodologies, in sharp contrast to other scientific disciplines. The aversion to theory and methodology results from a strong focus on legal practice and doctrinal research methods, and a very competitive atmosphere. However, she argues that teachers have a responsibility to teach students to read, understand and tell the same facts differently, exposing students to a range of legal research methodologies.[35] Jurisprudence, which she explains as the conscience of or truth about law, is fundamentally about investigation:[36] it requires questioning law's claim to neutrality, autonomy and apolitical character. Methodology is the required tool for interrogation to challenge our assumptions about law. This tool could be applied using the ITAC formula – 'Issue, Theory, Apply, Conclusions'.[37] Applying different theories as lenses is important because it promotes curiosity – 'About rights, about our society, about its values' – and it also promotes a critical attitude and awareness of different ways of thinking and looking at the world 'out there'. 'They define not merely our explanatory possibilities, but also our ethical and practical horizons'.[38]

The author notes that methodology and legal theory cope with an image problem, and she suggests to 'market' these topics as 'tools for interrogation'.[39] Sadly, the need for the marketing of courses that fall outside the vocational scope, perhaps tells us something about the expectations that law students have. Sokhi-Bulley links the aversion to particular topics to the grade-driven competitive culture in legal education, as is elaborated upon by Böning, Schwöbel-Patel and various other authors. Nevertheless, this 'framing' may be useful to turn aversion

---

34 In this regard, Sokhi-Bulley coins two skills associated with methodology: that of interrogation (being able to ask different questions about the same topic) and application (the skill to find different outcomes by using different methodologies). Sokhi-Bulley, 122.

35 Ibid 133.

36 Ibid.

37 Ibid 138.

38 Ibid 140–141, citing S Burchill et al, *Theories of International Relations* (Palgrave Macmillan 2009).

39 Ibid 137.

around and to make students aware of the importance and utility of unpopular courses. Sokhi-Bulley observes that legal research does not have a canon of research methodologies; methodology is implied rather than explicit and it hardly deserves attention in the legal curriculum, in opposition to other disciplines, as already observed by Stolker (see the introductory chapter of this book).[40] Finally, the idea of 'alternative truths' is, as I see it, in stark contrast with traditional teaching methods in law schools. This is because they focus on teaching doctrine, and in doing so law schools refute alternative views as 'merely an aberration': a distraction from the actual 'rules'.[41]

Hutchinson: Empirical Methodologies Knowledge and Expertise

Hutchinson argues that empirical methodology should be a core subject in the legal curriculum, because it enables students – in their future influential roles as advocates, judges, practitioners, legislators, academic researchers and policymakers – to create better case law and legislation.[42] With regard to legislation, Hutchinson notes that lawmakers often rely on populist and anecdotal evidence, and sometimes even use evidence-gathering as a strategy to delay or distract from the real issue.[43] Law graduates in the political arena with an understanding of empirical methods can play a role in securing internal government checks and balances, and ensure well-founded policy. Furthermore, Hutchinson sees factual accuracy as paramount in legal trials. Research indicates that judges often make (incorrect) assertions about empirical facts as part of their legal reasoning, without due support of social science research.[44] Hutchinson argues that if law is to develop and function well in modern societies, lawyers and judges must be able to read, understand and critique the outcomes of social science research.[45] Moreover, she argues that training in empirical methodologies in legal education could advance the students' normative reasoning, and that they will need this training to be fully prepared for (legal) practice.[46] The author proposes teaching one

---

40 De Vries (Introduction), citing Carel Stolker, *Rethinking the Law School. Education, Research, Outreach and Governance* (CUP 2014) 88.

41 WJ Witteveen, *Evenwicht van Machten* (Tjeenk Willink Zwolle 1991) 99.

42 Hutchinson, 143.

43 Ibid 147.

44 Ibid 150.

45 Ibid 150–152.

46 Ibid 155.

quantitative method tutorial at undergraduate level, and further elaboration on one or two methods at graduate level. Throughout the curriculum, courses could also incorporate empirical examples.

Hutchinson tries to open up the emphasis on the study of rules in legal education, by elaborating on the importance of empirical methodology. It appears that the argumentation relies primarily on the instrumental value of empirical training. Although it is refreshing – in the context of this book – to hear a plea in favour of particular vocational skills, there seems to be a tension with the call for intrinsic education (learning for the sake of learning) by other authors. On the other hand, perhaps the relation between law and empirical studies requires a reassessment. At the moment, empirical methodology is hardly ever included in the legal curriculum, and if it is, it is the odd man out. But, various other authors in this book reiterate that law cannot be studied in a vacuum, and that due attention is to be paid to the socio-economical context of law.[47] In order to do justice, justice needs to be done to reality, for which empirical methods can be important means. What is more, the importance of interdisciplinarity for the academic maturation of students and a critical attitude is also stressed by various other authors.[48] Hence, both instrumental and intrinsic reasons could be thought of why empirical knowledge and normative reasoning should go hand-in-hand when studying law.

Van Rossum: Visuals for a Critical Legal Profession

In his contribution, Van Rossum first notes that the law school has a vocational character, as students in the Netherlands are usually taught 'how to think like a lawyer'. Only a few courses nuance the 'legal view' that students attain.[49] Van Rossum describes three courses – Anthropology of Law, Comparative Legal Cultures and Sociology of Law – in which he uses visual materials to challenge his students' assumptions about respectively the nature of law; the relation of law, legal practice and culture; and the function and place of law in society. For example, in Comparative Legal Cultures, he displays the gap that might exist between law and legal practice by showing a picture he made in his hometown, in which bikes are parked next to a prohibitory sign, and discussing the connection with law enforcement and Dutch values.[50] Van Rossum

47 See, for example, Germain; Schwöbel-Patel; Van Rossum; and Oomen.
48 Particularly Oomen and Van Rossum.
49 Van Rossum, 162.
50 Ibid 166.

believes that teaching methods should be adapted to the ways in which students take in and produce information.[51] Visuals make it easier for students to remember material, and it provides them with a more imaginative and critical perspective on law. Also, visuals help to connect legal issues to society, it confronts them with 'the real life'.[52] Watching documentaries about lobbyists or Roma, for instance, has a bigger impact on students than only reading about these topics, because it induces the students to 'put themselves in the shoes of others'. In these courses, with the help of visual materials Van Rossum hopes to induce students to ask critical questions and see the broader social context of law.[53]

Van Rossum was categorized under Part II, because his main argument appears to be that an anthropological, sociological and comparative perspective can turn the students' understanding of law upside down, and he explains why this would be an important complement to vocational courses. In this respect, his text corresponds with the positions of Sokhi-Bulley and Schwöbel-Patel. Another important purpose of his chapter is connected with particular teaching methods, this theme is elaborated further in Part III. In this regard, Van Rossum's and Del Mar's teaching methods have in common that they both rely on visual means to establish a more imaginative understanding of the law. Del Mar focuses on constructing alternative interpretations of the *ratio decidendi* and facts of the case, whereas Van Rossum deals with the implications of the social context for the concept and functioning of law. Also interesting to note, is that there are various authors in this book who argue that it is important for students to 'engage with the other'. Three different means are discussed to achieve this learning outcome: Van Rossum through visual materials, Uygur through a Foucauldian mirror in a prison setting, and Oomen through orchestrating encounters.

Germain: For a New and More Diverse Comparative Legal Education

Germain believes that it is paramount for students to be taught with a more global and diverse view on the law, and she argues that this can be achieved if teachers turn to alternative teaching venues to broaden their own understanding of legal concepts, and use better-adapted teaching tools.[54] In this regard, she believes that teaching in an unconventional environment, such as a prison, contributes to the pedagogical qualities of

---

[51] Ibid 174.
[52] Ibid 174–177.
[53] Ibid 179.
[54] Germain, 182.

the teacher. Germain reports on the Cornell Prison Education Program (CPEP) in which she participated as a law instructor. As a teacher, she benefitted in this programme from the exceptional student-body, the extraordinary approach they had to comparative legal topics and being subjected to the unique legal tradition that existed. Germain used a constructivist approach for teaching the inmates-students, in which 'students learn pro-actively by building on pre-existing knowledge and skills to ignite a reflection on the law'.[55] Germain is convinced that the comparative law course strongly influenced the students' re-insertion process, particularly because it helped them to develop adaptive qualities and open-mindedness.[56] Finally, she elaborates on the place and the importance of comparative law in the legal curriculum, and how it should be improved. She argues that comparative law teaching is currently too descriptive and superficial. Students should be made more aware of the socio-economic context, remedy their ethnocentric perspective, and reflect on the role and meaning of legal norms. Furthermore, teachers should experiment with unconventional teaching methods, and comparative law elements should be integrated in other courses as well.

Germain notes that there is a decrease of comparative law courses in the legal curriculum, whilst – now more than ever – comparative courses are unmissable for the students' understanding of law and the development of a critical attitude.[57] Interestingly, she does not frame this as a problem of market pressures and instrumentalization only, but also as a pedagogical problem. Van Rossum takes a similar position, he argues that the teaching methods should be better adapted to the contemporary ways in which students take in and produce information, for which he suggests using visual materials. Hence, the solutions to this problem are not only to be found in an institutional or management context, but it also implies a responsibility for teachers to explore different teaching methods in order to achieve the full potential of a course. In this regard, prisons can be both an environment to confront students with their prejudices, like Uygur elaborates on in her contribution, but also a setting in which a teacher develops pedagogical skills. After all, prison is law school upside down: Germain notes that she 'had no intention on lecturing them and they most certainly had no intention of letting me impose my knowledge'.[58] In other words, normal teaching methods may not work and

---

[55] Ibid 187.
[56] Ibid 189.
[57] Ibid 193.
[58] Ibid 187.

even the most fundamental statements of law are questioned. This forces the teacher to find new teaching avenues.[59]

PART III – INNOVATIVE TEACHING EXPERIMENTS

In Part I, the authors agreed that the study of black-letter law as such is not enough to provide students with a critical attitude and thorough understanding of the law. Altering the curriculum to include contextual and reflexive classes, as has been argued in Part II, may not be sufficient either to achieve the purposes of academic legal education. Indeed, content should be accompanied with the right teaching methods, pedagogical knowledge and didactical tools. In Part III, four authors discuss concrete examples of innovative learning experiences and give their view on how law could be taught. In doing so, they also address other challenges, such as how to enhance student participation and what this means for the role of the teacher.

The teaching methods discussed in this part are often accompanied with a view on the purpose and function of academic legal education, which exemplifies again the interconnectivity between the nature of legal education, the curriculum and the teaching methods. In the context of the book, Part III focuses on creating conditions for achieving the goals discussed in Part I, and provides inspiration and tools for teaching. The methods discussed in Part III are not necessarily tied to a particular course.

Oomen: Orchestrating Encounters

In her contribution, Oomen explains the concept and tradition of liberal arts and sciences (LAS), the place of law within these programmes and her own experiences in teaching law in these programmes. Oomen's starting point is the assumption that law is not only about rules and institutions, but essentially about balancing conflicting interests, both at individual level and society at large. The role of the lecturer in teaching law then, especially in a LAS context, is to orchestrate encounters

---

[59] Of course, the prison environment and inmates-students should never be reduced to tools for legal education. Germain argues that teaching inmates-students is a goal in itself, as well as instrumental for the re-insertion process. Comparative law as a course, in this regard, can be seen as a vehicle for the development of open-mindedness of inmates.

'between perspectives, between people and between positions'.[60] Oomen describes LAS as a system of higher education with a flexible and diverse curriculum. Moreover, it aims to foster the students' desire to learn, trains them to think critically and prepares them to be responsible (global) citizens.[61] Law in the context of LAS is not a vocational training programme, but rather a vehicle to cultivate the mind by critically examining norms and rules and dealing with dilemma's. LAS in turn, is valuable for the study of law as it enables the student to 'see the complex connections of law, culture and society in all their variety'.[62] Oomen discusses five learning objectives of LAS, being: stimulating critical thinking; improving academic research skills; interdisciplinarity; fostering the narrative imagination; and educating for (global) citizenship, and provides various exercises to achieve these learning outcomes.[63]

Law in a LAS context and 'regular' legal education make for an interesting comparison. It would seem that the kind of law education many critics call for, already exists in LAS University Colleges. According to Oomen, it has a great focus on critical pedagogy;[64] it proved more resistant to market-forces imposing economic rationality, instrumentalization and managerialism;[65] it has a diverse curriculum;[66] and in essence LAS is 'anti-vocational'.[67] The purpose of law in LAS context may be somewhat different from traditional legal education, but to what extent does it fulfil the same function? For example, does it produce apt professionals? Could it even be that, ironically, anti-vocational training is the best vocational training? If so, then why is there a trend of an increasing focus on positive law and practical skills? Of course, it can be argued that LAS is successful because it has more resources available and high entry-requirements for the students. Nevertheless, it deserves attention in the debate about academic legal education, as it already embodies several features that critics call for.

---

[60] Oomen, 201.

[61] She refers to Becker's definition, Ibid 203.

[62] Ibid 213.

[63] Ibid 218.

[64] This is argued by Francot & Corrias; Germain; and Sokhi-Bulley.

[65] This is argued by Van Klink; Francot & Corrias; Böning; Bradney; Schwöbel-Patel, Sokhi-Bulley; and Van Rossum.

[66] This is argued by Van Klink; Francot & Corrias; Schwöbel-Patel; Del Mar; Van Rossum; De Vries (Law & Lounge).

[67] Other authors who advocate (partly) non-vocational legal education include: Van Klink; Francot & Corrias; and Böning.

Uygur: Students' Perception and Legal Education

Uygur explains how law students should gain ethical awareness in order to be attentive to incidents of injustice. In the first part of her contribution, Uygur discusses the complex relationship between ethical awareness, moral virtues and seeing injustice in the context of legal education. She frames seeing injustices as an ethical problem, for which moral virtues are required.[68] She notes that prejudices are an obstacle for seeing injustice. The virtue of attention, then, can block the epistemic injustice that may result from prejudices. This requires students to take account of the particularities of the subject – for example, a suspect or convicted person – in order to truly see it.[69] In the second part, she elaborates on her prison-seminar involving the Foucauldian mirror metaphor: 'The mirror is a space in which one loses oneself, realised through the other.'[70] The seminar aims to confront students with their prejudices about inmates, to achieve an open attitude and to be involved with 'the other', allowing them to see the particularities of the case.

Law and retribution are inherently connected. Yet, many prejudices exist with regard to prisoners. Critical thinking involves questioning one's knowledge. This is particularly important if one's view may impact the freedom of others. In this regard, the prison clinic that Uygur reports on serves two purposes. On the one hand, it improves the students' critical attitude by revealing the contrast that may exist between a student's prejudice and a confrontation with reality. On the other hand, it allows to better understand the people who may be future subjects of their responsibilities as lawyers and judges, and to connect with these subjects. Interestingly, we see that the prison environment serves a different purpose than it does in Germain's chapter. Whereas Uygur focuses on the benefits for students, Germain discusses how teaching in a prison-environment enhances pedagogical skills and induces the teacher to look differently at law.

Del Mar: Learning How to Read a Case

Del Mar reports on two workshops that use resources from the visual and dramatic arts in order to help students to read case law actively. The underlying hypothesis is that legal reading is an active and imaginative

---

68 Uygur, 225.
69 Ibid 229.
70 Ibid 233.

form of reading.[71] In this context, Del Mar's workshops focus on exploring respectively the facts of a case and the reasons for the decision. Del Mar, together with a visual artist and an actor, aimed to create workshops that would allow the students to explore legal materials in a playful way, making use of the resources, and activities used by artists and actors in their cognitively-rich process of making art.[72] They came up with various exercises, such as 'playing the Clerk';[73] adding or subtracting details in the *ratio decidendi*; and making a 'cast list' of the parties involved. In his contribution, Del Mar describes the exercises, didactic techniques and evaluation methods, and also shows the feedback that he received from the students. The students considered the workshops as 'a good social event', and they found it liberating to study in a different physical environment in which they could be active in ways that have been all too rare in their law school experience.[74] The author concludes that 'what law schools need, in short, is more spaces, more time, for students to play'.[75]

Referring to the debate on the determination of the *ratio decidendi*, Del Mar argues that reading case law 'involves constructing and considering alternatives and possibilities, e.g. alternate descriptions of the legal significance of a past case'.[76] It assumes that the judge can use interpretation methods and framing techniques to construct the *ratio decidendi* of an earlier case. As I see it, Del Mar infers that there is not 'one right answer' and that learning to read law is not about reproducing doctrine, but rather that it is a creative activity that requires a critical attitude, deploying various perspectives and the courage to form a position. This illustrates that the view we have on the nature of law, and also has implications for the way in which lecturers teach law. Del Mar refers to various other contributions, as he provides playful exercises to 'suspend judgment',[77] tell the same story from different perspectives,[78] understand that facts require interpretation,[79] and to destabilize power-relations.[80] A noticeable 'side-effect', that was also experienced by

71 Del Mar, 247.
72 Ibid 246.
73 Ibid 259.
74 Ibid 263–266.
75 Ibid 262.
76 Ibid 247.
77 Van Klink.
78 Sokhi-Bulley.
79 Hutchinson.
80 De Vries; Oomen; and Schwöbel-Patel.

Germain, is that this teaching experiment changed the way Del Mar looks at legal principles in general.[81] This exemplifies that the teacher can learn from teaching in unconventional settings or by unconventional means.

De Vries: Law & Lounge

De Vries reports upon 'Law & Lounge', an experiment that focuses on the students' self-organization in reading and discussing fundamental texts in the field of legal and social theory, with the purpose to awaken the students' critical potential.[82] In this experiment, the students are free to determine how the class meetings are conducted and how insights are gained, and the teachers do not interfere. De Vries elaborates on the problems and successes he encountered in three editions of Law & Lounge, and how the experiment developed. After reporting on Law & Lounge, De Vries places the experiment in a theoretical context. He argues that law inherently involves normative activity, as well as uncertainty.[83] De Vries embraces this state of uncertainty, which he coins as intellectual uncertainty, and links it to Van Klink's SLE. According to De Vries, a skeptical attitude begins with intellectual awareness that knowledge cannot be taken for granted, and with accepting the value and function of uncertainty.[84] Subsequently, referring to social theorist Beck, he elaborates on the notion of reflexivity. Reflexivity is a task as well as a process, which entails self-confrontation and corresponding action to expose, and deal with the uncertainties produced by modernity, 'through a reconfiguration of its foundations'.[85] De Vries argues that reflexivity induces to challenge the self-evident assumptions we have about law – even if this leads to uncertainty – to lay bare the blind spots of modern thought and to establish a new normative field for choices and decisions.[86]

De Vries' experiment addresses several challenges in legal education. First of all, self-organization can break the pattern of a passive student and an active teacher. Furthermore, students are challenged to formulate their own answers, as there is no authority to dictate the 'right answer'. Even more: the uncertainty connected with legal argumentation is embraced and deployed to increase the students' critical potential. Also, asking the senior students to supervise small groups of first year students

---

81 Del Mar, 245.
82 De Vries, 270.
83 Ibid 283.
84 Ibid 283.
85 Ibid 285.
86 Ibid 286.

is a creative remedy to massification, and it challenges and benefits students from different year levels. Moreover, De Vries developed a strategy for coping with the potential lack of intrinsic motivation, the 'massive psychological stress', and the focus on grades in legal education, as noted by Böning. Some methods include studying the materials in small groups, destabilizing power relations, the absence of a grade and making students responsible for their own intellectual development. Finally, De Vries' notion of reflexivity in legal education could facilitate normative action in a society in which the logic of risk-prevention overtakes the focus on wealth-distribution,[87] and help to embrace the uncertainty that is connected with challenging our foundations.

CONCLUDING REMARKS

'Legal education is and should be academic'.[88] But what does this entail? In the course of this book, three dimensions of this question are addressed: the nature and purpose of legal education and the challenges it faces, the topics legal education should deal with, and the teaching methods to be used.

In the contributions, the authors have different views on the purpose of the law school. What they have in common, is that the contributors agree to some extent that the purpose of the university legal education is connected to the development of the students' critical attitude.[89] Moreover, various authors assert an *intrinsic* purpose of legal education, they see the university as a (transitional) space in which students can unfold their potential by 'learning for the sake of learning' and by engaging in the intellectual heritage.[90] Others say that legal education has an instrumental function (as well), such as creating responsible citizens,[91] preventing (epistemic) injustice,[92] socialization,[93] or improving society in other

[87] This idea is coined by Beck as the 'Risk Society'. See U Beck, *Risk Society, Towards a New Modernity* (Sage 1992).

[88] See Van Klink & De Vries (Introduction), 5.

[89] Van Klink; Francot & Corrias; Schwöbel-Patel; Germain; Hutchinson; Del Mar; Oomen; Van Rossum; Uygur; and De Vries (Law & Lounge).

[90] Oomen; Francot & Corrias; Van Klink; Schwöbel-Patel; and De Vries (Law & Lounge).

[91] Francot & Corrias; Böning; and Oomen. Bradney arguably as well, although he has a more predefined image of the values that these students should attain.

[92] Schwöbel-Patel and Uygur.

[93] Böning.

ways.[94] There is some tension among these goals, as a focus on particular (intrinsic) goals may be at the cost of other (instrumental) goals. This tension is an imperative to continue the debate at this fundamental level, in order to strike a proper balance between the purposes and to determine general direction for improving legal education.

It is remarkable how much the contributors agree on the threats that exist for academic legal education. Market pressures, instrumentalization, massification and managerialism are broadly recognized as negative trends in the contributions. Some authors also mention the law school's lack of attention for pedagogy[95] and methodology,[96] the effects of the method of examination[97] and the teachers' compromised autonomy as threats for the academic nature of law school.[98] Various authors stated that the academia should arm itself against market forces.[99] But how this can be accomplished, and what role teachers have in this regard, are questions that seem to require further elaboration.

Concerning the topics legal education deals with: despite the aversion to the instrumentalization of law schools that many authors have in common, nearly[100] every author agrees that vocational training and courses (solely) on 'positive law' should not be removed altogether from the legal curriculum. However, a general consensus exists that such courses should be complemented with knowledge aimed at challenging the assumptions we have of law, such as law's determinacy and neutrality. In this regard, the authors propose that knowledge of – inter alia – sociology,[101] legal theory,[102] comparative law[103] and (empirical) methodology[104] should be included in the curriculum. These subjects can provide a critical lens for looking beyond black letter law and the effects of a legal system.

---

94 By creating better law, for example (Hutchinson and Van Rossum), or re-configuring its foundations (De Vries (Law & Lounge)).

95 Germain and Francot & Corrias.

96 Sokhi-Bulley and Carel Stolker as referred to in De Vries (Introduction).

97 Böning and Sokhi-Bulley.

98 Bradney; Schwöbel-Patel; and Oomen.

99 Inter alia Francot & Corrias; Bradney; Schwöbel-Patel; and Germain.

100 One notable exception is Oomen's approach of anti-vocational education.

101 Hutchinson and Van Rossum.

102 Van Klink; Francot & Corrias; Sokhi-Bulley; Schwöbel-Patel; and De Vries (Law & Lounge).

103 Germain; Francot & Corrias; Schwöbel-Patel; and Van Rossum.

104 Sokhi-Bulley; Hutchinson; Van Rossum.

What do the various alternative teaching methods – including SLE;[105] Re-Bildung;[106] counter-hegemonic teaching;[107] imaginative learning;[108] law in liberal arts and sciences context;[109] anthropology and sociology of law;[110] methodology,[111] and Law & Lounge[112] – have in common? Each in their own way, they aim to prevent a thin and uncomplicated understanding of the law, and expose that there is not such a thing as 'one right answer'. This learning objective is connected to a purpose of legal education echoed by many authors: teaching students to be critical. Various different teaching methods are examined to achieve this learning objective, ranging from (supposedly 'harsh'[113]) Socratic-dialogues[114] to playful exercises derived from cooperation with visual artists.[115] By doing so, this book provides a myriad of pedagogical perspectives and exercises to strengthen the academic nature of legal education.

Everything considered, there is consensus on various topics in this multi-faceted debate on academic legal education. An important question that follows is *why* various persistent trends exist, such as managerialism, that do exactly the opposite of what many teachers believe is good for academic (legal) education? Should all these trends be reversed? Or are there simply practical, institutional or other factors that are not taken into account in the argument in favour of teacher's autonomy, meta-juridical courses, and abolishing standardized answers? In short, could 'we' be wrong? When the academia requires students to be critical and reflexive, shouldn't it also ask this from itself in this debate? Therefore, it would seem desirable to actively involve discussants at all levels of legal education in this debate, such as students, management and practitioners. After all, different perspectives on a (educational) challenge allow for different stories to be told, and perhaps finding better solutions.

---

105 Van Klink; De Vries (Law & Lounge); Francot & Corrias.
106 Francot & Corrias.
107 Sokhi-Bulley.
108 Del Mar and Van Rossum.
109 Oomen.
110 Van Rossum and Hutchinson.
111 Sokhi-Bulley.
112 De Vries (Law & Lounge).
113 Germain proposes the constructivist method as an alternative for the 'harsh' Socratic method.
114 Van Klink.
115 Del Mar.

3 A STUDENT'S PERSPECTIVE

In addition to the various teachers' perspectives in this book, I conclude this afterword with a short reflection on legal education in the Netherlands from my own student's perspective. It expresses my personal experience, and admittedly, this example neither proves anything nor lends itself for generalization. Nevertheless, it can be illustrative for various themes dealt with in this book. In doing so, I submit my view on how the critical potential of students can be enhanced. I argue that teachers should communicate the open and undetermined character of law to students in order to preserve students' eagerness to learn, to achieve a solid understanding of law, and to provide them with a sense of responsibility for the development and morality of law.

First, I believe that it might be useful for teachers to be aware of the expectations and assumptions about law that exists among first-year students. Before I commenced my undergraduate studies, I envisioned the university as an institution of certainty, and law as the ultimate instrument to find objective and just solutions. What else than a syllogistic system could deliver legal certainty and just solutions? My high expectations of law's determinacy and the scientific qualities of legal education, resulted in a particular focus on internalizing doctrine and finding the 'right answer'.

Perhaps I was naïve at that time, but I believe that various factors in Dutch legal education confirmed the assumption I had about the existence of the 'right answer' in law.[116] These factors are also discussed by the authors in this book. From my experience as a student, I believe that the massification of legal education, the emphasis on the study of doctrinal law and the limited time and resources teachers have for lectures, resulted in limited space for debate, standardized answers, and conservative teaching methods.[117] The learning objective of nearly every course was simple: learn a set of doctrinal rules. A critical attitude, then, did not contribute to this learning objective. The teacher had clear and

---

[116] The contributions in this book already mentioned trends such as instrumentalization, ethnocentricity, and massification, that could partly explain this assumption. For example Sokhi-Bulley; Schwöbel-Patel; and Oomen.

[117] In this regard, I was fortunate enough that I was enrolled at the honours programme called Utrecht Law College, which is a programme with additional resources for extra courses and assistance, and small-scale discussion groups. I can imagine that the effects I noticed are even stronger in the regular legal education in the Netherlands. For more on the Utrecht Law College, see De Vries' contribution in this book on Law & Lounge.

unambiguous formula for all the exercises we dealt with, and the right answer could apparently be captured in a handful of bullet-points. Hence, law appeared to be a coherent and complete system, with an authoritative inner logic.[118]

What is more, law seemed to be neutral. After all, it was a body of democratically legitimate rules, and they applied to everybody equally. An implied division of roles followed from this assumption: 'we' lawyers should internalize law and apply it, the problematization and improvement of law was a task for politicians.[119] Of course, nobody explicitly taught us to think this way. Yet, there was little reason to assume responsibility for the injustice that could be produced by law.[120] The question we were responsible for, as I saw it then, was whether 'it was legal'.

Cramming all the study material a week before the exams proved to be an efficient and successful way for internalizing the information, and it was often rewarded with good grades. It was not a lot of fun though, and the pressure to score well was high.[121] At some point, I found that my curiosity lessened as my focus shifted from understanding to reproducing. Looking back, it would seem that the examination-methods in legal education better reward short-time memory than a critical attitude.[122]

Only later, particularly after participating in classes on legal theory, I developed a better understanding of law's nature, and with that a different attitude to law. My current understanding of law corresponds with various contributions in this book. As I understand it now, law is an argumentative discipline. What is and what ought depends on the perspective used[123] and the social and cultural context at hand.[124] The meaning of rules is determined by the interpretation of countless related concepts, ranging from the meaning of a particular word in a statute to the balancing of underlying (conflicting) principles. With some creativity,

---

118 Schwöbel-Patel elaborates further on how the inner logic of law remains unquestioned in legal education.

119 The depoliticization of law is further problematized by Schwöbel-Patel.

120 I found Scott Veitch's account of how law can facilitate injustice truly eye-opening. S Veitch, *Law and Irresponsibility: On the Legitimation of Human Suffering* (Routledge Cavendish 2007).

121 The competitive culture in Utrecht Law College contributed to some extent to the psychological and social pressure to score high grades. See Böning for the problematization of examination pressure.

122 Ibid.

123 This is also argued by inter alia Sokhi-Bulley; Schwöbel-Patel; and Oomen.

124 Further elaboration by inter alia Van Rossum and Schwöbel-Patel.

the essence of a case can even be interpreted and constructed with opposite outcomes.[125] There are always arguments for another point of view, leaving those who work with law in a permanent state of contemporary uncertainty.[126] As I see it now, it is inherent to determining the meaning of law that choices have to be made. This awareness made me shift my focus from reproducing a particular 'right answer', to understanding the argumentation that leads to it.

I believe that many law teachers would to some extent agree on law's fluid and argumentative nature. But then why does legal education rely on standardized answers? Witteveen argued that it is connected with the human need for structure and clarity, which sometimes even leads to denial.[127] In his inaugural speech, he rightfully describes various contradictions in legal education: 'we expect the law to provide certainty, while at the same time we understand that language is ambiguous; we expect all judges to act consistently, while we also apprehend that they are only humans of flesh and blood'.[128] To meet these paradoxical expectations, Witteveen argues, teachers present simplified examples, didactical formulas and standardized answers as the undebatable truth. In this sense, deviation of paradigm is by default 'against the rules'.[129]

As I see it, doctrine still has an important role in legal education, because it can be considered as a skilled and authoritative attempt of explaining and structuring law.[130] Furthermore, doctrine and simplified examples serve a didactical purpose.[131] Nevertheless, doctrine is a human construction, and it is limited by practical and human shortcomings. Therefore, its truthfulness can never be taken for granted. Consequently, studying law should not be about reproducing doctrine, but should be an intellectual, active and uncertain activity.

Studying law in such a way, as a 'Herculean exercise',[132] is not for everyone. Many students will probably have trouble deciding on hard

---

125 Del Mar.

126 De Vries (Law & Lounge); Van Klink; and Francot & Corrias.

127 Witteveen, *op cit* 95.

128 Ibid 99 (paraphrased and translated by author).

129 Ibid 99.

130 Parallel with Van Klink's idea of intellectual inheritance, that the student should critically and hermeneutically build on. See Van Klink.

131 Witteveen argues that these are primarily didactical tools, that can be used to gradually achieve an understanding of more complex 'stories'. However, he states that this didactical process is often discontinued prematurely, as teachers linger in dogmatic teaching. Witteveen, *op cit* 99.

132 I refer to Dworkin's hypothetical rational hermeneutic Hercules, a judge that can make a coherent and complete construction of the system of law and

cases, because it is not easy to find an answer to a legal question if there are conflicting interpretations and perspectives possible. Would it then be more useful for struggling students to teach them a simplified notion of the law? I think not, the intellectual activity that finding law requires, should not be reduced to reproducing what we already know. Biesta calls this the inherent risk of academic legal education. He explains that the risk inherently exists because the outcome of education cannot be controlled, as students are 'subjects of action and responsibility', not objects 'to be moulded and disciplined'.[133] Hence, education cannot be reduced to input: 'education is not about filling a bucket of water but about lighting a fire'.[134]

In sum, I believe that communicating the fluid nature of law at an early stage serves three important purposes. First, it nourishes the students' critical attitude. As they understand that law inherently involves making choices, they will look for different possibilities and understand that the choice they make requires thorough argumentation. Second, it creates a responsibility for lawyers and for law students to examine whether law is just. After all, injustice cannot be justified by seemingly neutral rules or mechanisms, because an immoral outcome would imply a wrong interpretation of what law requires and the social and cultural context. Third, it will preserve the students' eagerness to study law. Framing law as an active and intellectual activity rather than an exercise of reproduction triggers and maintains the students' curiosity. For these reasons, in order for legal education to be truly academic, I believe that teachers have a responsibility to challenge the unproblematized image of the law that beginning students may have. The contributions in this book provide a myriad of teaching methods and experimental courses to achieve this objective.

---

moral principles, which would lead him to the 'one right answer' to any legal question. Dworkin acknowledges that it requires more time and skill than human judges have at their disposal to take into account all relevant factors and to achieve full rationalization of law and moral principles. Nevertheless, Dworkin argues that the judge needs to presume and pursue a one right answer and engage in the Herculean exercise of finding law – as far as practical and human limits permit. RM Dworkin, *Law's Empire* (Harvard University Press 1986).

133 GJJ Biesta, *The Beautiful Risk of Education* (Paradigm 2013) 1.

134 For this citation, Biesta refers to WB Yeats in ibid.

16. Conclusions: concrete proposals for change: 14 theses

Hopefully, the reader of this book will be inspired by the previous chapters to experiment in his or her teaching with some of the ideas discussed and the theoretical viewpoints presented in the first part. Teachers may be tempted to revise the perspective taken in a course, devise new interactive methods or reflect on their own teaching philosophy. For that purpose, each contributor has drafted a concrete proposal in the form of a thesis that might serve as a stepping-stone for actual change in the educational system in general or learning methods in particular. The theses listed below follow the order of the contributions.

PART I THEORY AND LEGAL EDUCATION

Bart van Klink

Instead of looking for the 'right answer', academic legal education should focus more on raising the right questions.

Scientific inquiry always starts with a question. If it is a good question, it opens up a whole new field of research which may lead to innovative and interesting answers. However, every answer in science has a provisional character, and can and will be challenged by further research. That makes the quest for knowledge endless. In legal education, however, there is a tendency to present knowledge as a fixed and indisputable set of descriptive statements about the law – the legal doctrine – which the student is expected to learn by heart and to reproduce at the exam. Skeptical legal education questions this doctrinal approach. It promotes interactive practices of questioning in the classroom that destabilize certainty and cast doubt on widely-shared beliefs. For that purpose, a variety of educational methods and techniques can be used, for instance the Socratic method of interrogation, De Bono's thinking hat-method and the neo-Skeptic reading practise of deconstruction. During the whole curriculum, students have to be exposed to a plurality of voices and be encouraged to use and develop their own voice in the ongoing academic conversation. Moreover, next to the regular law courses, philosophical, empirical and historical courses have to be provided that promote reflection on the foundation and the functioning of law, now and in the past. In that way, legal education contributes to the training of critical minds which is what the Academia is all about.

Lyana Francot and Luigi Corrias

*The contemporary reign of market rationality and managerialism in universities necessitates the defense of Academia's intrinsic value by means of Re-*Bildung.

Re-*Bildung*, as we understand it, contributes to a much needed second emancipation of the individual from the iron cage of economic rationality. More specifically in the case of legal education, Re-*Bildung* seeks to resist the demands of professional practice and to reinvigorate legal education as *academic* education. We hold that this can only be done by breathing new life into the core of *Bildung*, i.e. the unity of research and education. Practically, this means maintaining and fortifying the academic core of the curriculum by giving due place to such courses as legal philosophy, legal sociology, legal history, methodology, etc. Only through these subjects, Academia will remain a place where not just any lawyer, but the *good* lawyer is educated, the Re-*gebildete* lawyer.

Anja Böning

Structures of legal education and institutional requirements should be reviewed not only to encourage the students' self-control, self-regulation and self-improvement but also to ensure there is space left for reflexivity and critical thinking: rethink the purpose of examination.

When we look at learning in legal education we should not disrespect the students' point of view. Stress and anxiety seem to be part of a hidden curriculum of legal education, with its emphasis on summative assessment. Law teachers should be aware of the fact that it can have fatal socializing effects on students. A learning setting which triggers excessive stress and feelings of anxiety can hinder successful academic maturation. In the face of neoliberal tendencies in Academia advancing the students' empowerment and 'output' orientation, it is important to offer curricular spaces in order to enable the development of critical distance to legal positivism and legal practice. In other words, reflexivity lies at the core of academic thinking and seems to be suitable to counteract risks of the new economy of knowledge which turns students into objects of their individual learning story.

Anthony Bradney

Law is an argument and a debate not a description.

Propositions about law are the subject of almost endless debate and speculation; being a student of law means immersing yourself in those debates. Enhancing learning for students involves both giving them the intellectual tools to take part in the debates, and helping them to develop the emotional resilience that will allow them to ignore glib answers and accept the likelihood of uncertainty whilst always trying to improve their knowledge of law. For academics, who always remain students of law, acknowledging the uncertainty in what we are doing involves accepting nothing will ever enable us to be sure that what we have done is right or even worthwhile; as TS Eliot writes in *Four Quartets*: 'For us, there is only the trying. The rest is not our business.'

PART II EXPERIMENTAL COURSES

Christine Schwöbel-Patel

Legal education should be less focused on skills training and more focused on law in context.

The neoliberal market pressures to focus on skills training of students should be recognized as creating and sustaining hierarchies inside and outside of the classroom and should therefore be resisted. Rather than a focus on skills, there should be a focus on knowledge exchange, what Paolo Freire called 'dialogical teaching'. This means an emphasis on learning *from* the students as well as teaching them. Students should, for example, be encouraged to see their own context (e.g. gender, background, language, education) as relevant to their developing legal consciousness. Dialogical teaching therefore goes some way in addressing the privileged position of the educator as the individual who imparts knowledge. Moreover, a focus on law in context recognizes the importance of theory as something that underpins legal doctrine and law's social relations. The current market orientation of law, legal education and lawyers has seemingly given prominence to doctrine over theory. This often leaves law's complicity in inequality, unfairness and bias uncontested and in turn maintains and strengthens the *status quo*. Alongside dialogical teaching, as a form of addressing hierarchies in the classroom, a prominent place should therefore be given to theory, as a means of addressing hierarchies outside of the classroom.

Bal Sokhi-Bulley

Legal education needs to foster curiosity by making methodology a key 'transferrable skill' that is part of all law courses, and to teach through contemporary case studies where we can identify dominant narratives and magnify alternative truths.

There is an inherent lack of curiosity within legal education, which means that both law academics and the students we teach are disengaged from alternative methodologies. These students go on to become lawyers, experts and even educators who are unaccustomed to asking the *how* question. An understanding of 'methodology' (as a way of *thinking*) ought to be ingrained as a learning objective or 'transferrable skill' in all law courses and teach not 'theory' but the skills of *interrogation* and *application*. A course on human rights, for example, ought to present what human rights (in law) are *and* be curious about the *how* of rights; that is, how are they practiced, measured, narrated? Can we understand rights better if we examine them through the experience and struggle that informs different critical perspectives – such as feminism and post-colonialism? What do these lenses magnify? Teaching through contemporary case studies is a great way to show how the story can change depending on what lens you use to magnify the details. The interactive session on the *Pistorius* trial that I use as an example in my chapter shows how to encourage students to *interrogate* the dominant narrative and *apply* alternative perspectives, or lenses, to the same set of facts and arrive at alternative truths, or counter-narratives, that mean we produce more curious, less docile, less governed, graduates.

Terry Hutchinson

Law graduates need skills in understanding and using the social evidence base.

In the twenty-first century, social research, often used in conjunction with sophisticated algorithms, is providing our law graduates with an increasing and more reliable social evidence base. The law curriculum must reflect this paradigm shift and empower graduates to function effectively within a context marked by a plethora of accessible social data. Law graduates need to have the ability to read, understand and critically analyse the results of social and scientific research. It enables students to make use of the fact base and allows the law to develop and remain relevant to changing social contexts. The modern law school curriculum needs to include incremental interdisciplinary research skills exposure throughout the degree to ensure graduates are competent in dealing with the outputs of social research. In this way, tomorrow's graduates will be best prepared to understand and use the expanding social evidence base.

Wibo van Rossum

The law must also be seen: use visuals like film and photo to enable students to view law as more than black letter law.

Apart from black letter law, law is about arguments. Law is stories. Law is power. Law is lobbying. Law is identity. Law is enforcement and non-enforcement. Law is compromise. Law is living law. Law is action. Law is education. Law is culture. Law is regulation of behaviour. And yes, law is the wisdom of the old and the senses of the young. In order to make this clear, the law must also be seen. In education we need to show the law in images, cartoons, photos, documentaries, and movies. Seeing law makes for better lawyers.

Sabrina Germain

Young lecturers need to be trained differently to experiment with different perspectives on the law and teach more creatively comparative law.

The training of comparative law instructors in unconventional environments, such as the prison system, must become part of the apprenticeship of young legal scholars to spontaneously instill more progressive (comparative) teaching skills. We can only hope that unconventional teaching environment will inspire more adapted methods for a more critical teaching of comparative law in traditional settings. Furthermore, twenty-first century law instructors should be required to use constructivist methods when introducing comparative law in core subject teaching. This will allow students to feel empowered and become more creative in their approach of comparative law and other core legal subjects.

PART III DIDACTIC INNOVATIONS AND LEARNING EXPERIMENTS

Barbara Oomen

Feed students literary imagination when studying law – go beyond the rules and into the story.

The law is all about stories. Stories of individuals encountering injustices. Stories of competing interests, and finding a balance between them. Stories of legislators seeking to structurally curb lawlessness. This is why I feel that it is so important to feed the narrative imagination of students, and to stimulate them to see and to learn about the stories behind the rules, and behind the case law. My emphasis on the importance of an encounter between the law and the liberal arts in this book concerns a general plea for more interdisciplinarity, but puts a particular emphasis on the humanities. The literary imagination can be fed in many ways – through stimulating students to conduct socio-legal research, through reading Kafka, for example, through stimulating them to write a poem about justice. Whatever the form, more attention for the story of, and behind the law would not only serve law students well but, ultimately, also their pursuit of justice.

Gülriz Uygur

If we want students to observe the other's face in particular cases, legal education should include training in virtues like attention and openness, together with experiential learning that puts a focus on the person who suffers injustice.

Since attention requires care for the particular, we should be open to the other and think of attention from the perspective of the virtue of openness. Openness occurs in the space where we meet and get into contact with the particular. This space is one that reflects our ethical personality. And it is in that space that attention to the particular begins. However, for openness, students need experience. I try to specify a particular sort of experience in which students begin by losing themselves to find themselves. This entails an awareness of how one's actions get absorbed by prejudices. To see injustice then, it is necessary to be aware of our prejudices. The experiential learning project merits attention as an interdisciplinary method using real cases, art and literature to get into contact with real spaces (such as the prison). Real spaces are at the core of this project, because there students meet the particular. Acknowledging that no method of teaching can completely eradicate all traces of prejudice from the minds of the students, I think this method is quite successful; in relation to the prejudices giving rise to structural injustices.

Maksymilian Del Mar

As legal educators, we ought to create more spaces in which students can learn by playing – in particular, developing new physical games thanks to which students learn to relate to legal materials actively and imaginatively.

Being able to read a past case (a potential precedent) actively and imaginatively is essential to legal practice. In constructing an argument, an advocate will often have to find a way of narrating the facts of a past case and articulating its legal significance that fit and support the overall ruling being offered to the judge as deciding the present case. To develop that skill, students have to be given opportunities to play with the facts and the ratio of a past case. For instance, on the facts side, this will require students to learn to pay attention to what facts are described and how they are described, to what facts are not described, and to differences between descriptions of facts in cases of multiple judgments. Learning to pay attention in this way is a first step in re-narrating the case actively and imaginatively, e.g. by suggesting that there was a fact that was not described in the case but that played a vital role in guiding the judges to make the ruling they did. That active and imaginative re-reading of the case may then open up the possibility for distinguishing the past case from the present (in situations where the past case is an obstacle to the ruling desired). Acquiring these abilities for attention and active and imaginative re-reading is enhanced by educators creating spaces – literally different physical spaces, an empty space, for example – and by drawing on certain techniques used by artists and actors.

Ubaldus de Vries

If we want students to take responsibility for their learning, give them the opportunity to 'take over' the classroom, allowing them to be creative.

We tend to teach students in a one-dimensional way. When we teach, we emphasize instruction (lecturing them) too much. We tend to believe that as long as we have told students what they need to know (what the law is), we have discharged ourselves of our responsibility. In doing so, we remain in control – learning through teaching. It leads to a passive student attitude. It carries the danger of eroding their curiosity and intrinsic motivation to learn. More importantly, it prevents them to think. The Law & Lounge Project encourages the opposite. As a group of students, they are responsible to organize the class sessions and to discuss the literature. It allows them, as Bart proposes, to formulate the right questions and, I add, seek the answers to the questions together, by themselves and without instruction. It allows them to think first before being instructed and lectured. They learn (first) without teaching. It prepares them for post-academic life in which they must be creative in order to formulate answers to yet unknown questions.

Tim Bleeker

Reproducing standard answers does not produce critical minds: teachers should render law as an intellectual and argumentative activity.

It is my impression that law students focus on internalizing doctrine. In doing so, they often assume that teachers transmit the 'right answers'. Teachers subliminally reinforce the idea of 'right answers' because they use simplified examples with standardized answers and translate complex issues into a couple of bullet points. Also, the methods of examination used by teachers are often attuned to testing the students' ability to reproduce. If teachers want to nourish a critical attitude and foster the students' eagerness to learn, they should prevent a thin and uncomplicated understanding of the law. To achieve this, the teacher should use different perspectives and interpretation methods on complex examples to illustrate that law inherently involves making choices. Also, the examination methods should reward argumentation over reproduction. Finally, teaching should be an interactional process in which the student is regarded as a 'subject of action and responsibility' (Biesta) rather than merely a receiver of information.

Index

ability
  cognitive skills 246
  high-ability students in Law and Lounge experiment 269, 271
  knowledge assessment 19, 31, 45, 46–7, 54, 188, 190, 231, 291
  narrative imagination 202, 209, 212, 219–20
  performance-related self-image 74–5
  training for lawyers, need for enhanced 154–9
academic debate, ongoing 3–7, 282–3
academic education
  anonymized examination apparatus 66–9
  Bildung ideal 43–6
  Bologna Process and educational program 77
  collegiate social controlling network 73–4
  competition for good grades, effects of 73–4, 76
  educational climbers, rise in 70
  eliticization and social climate 70–71, 77–8
  examination 68
  grade nobility 72–3
  'interpretative and discovering' approach 59–60
  interview scripts and research methods 63
  law students, lack of research into 60–61
  newcomers' status 70–71
  organized uncertainty 74–5
  performance-related self-image 74–5
  proposals for change 314–21
  self-discipline efforts 74–5
  self-estrangement tactics 65, 73, 76–7
  socialization 58–78, 292–3
academic freedom, legal academics 82–5, 91–2
academic obligations, legal academics 83–4, 94–5
Ahsmann, M 162, 214
Aitken, R 87
Allan, J 232, 236
alternative (external) legal methodologies 125–6, 298
  see also theory and methodology, importance of
alternative teaching techniques, comparative legal education 182, 186, 195
alternative teaching venues *see* liberal arts and sciences education; prisons
'alternative truths' 25–6, 33, 132, 137, 297, 298
Althaus, C 146
Amaya, A 223, 224
Amis, K, *Lucky Jim* 86
Amsler, S 109
Ancient Greece, liberal arts tradition 203–4
Anderson, G 92, 94
anthropology of law 163–6, 178
  see also visuals for a critical legal profession
appraisals of academic performance 88–9, 91–2
Areeda, P 24
Arendt, H 46, 48–50, 54, 56–7, 291–2
arts resources *see* case reading, and resources from visual and dramatic arts
attention as virtue 226, 229–30, 241

Australia
Aborigines and Ayers Rock as place of law 163–5
empirical methodologies, use of 144–5, 154, 155, 156–8
policy research approach and reform options 146–7, 148
postgraduate Juris Doctor (JD) degrees 158
Youth Justice (Boot Camp Orders) Act (Queensland) 149–50
authority and education, relationship between 49–50

Baecker, D 51, 55
Baggen, P 45
Barber, B 210
Bargel, T 58
Baudrillard, J 165
Beck, U 54, 268, 285, 307
Becker, J 203, 207, 303
Bell, J 90
Berman, H 211, 212
Berman, S 210
Bickel, N 60, 63–4, 71, 72, 73, 74
Biesta, G 284, 313
Bildung ideal 35–57, 291–2
and academic education changes 43–6
education and authority, relationship between 49–50
history 37–43
and managerialism in universities (neoliberal approach) 44–5, 51–2, 54–5, 292
political dimension 42–3, 48–50
questioning oneself and one's own views 47–8, 53
Re-*Bildung* as contemporary reconceptualization 36–7, 46–50
Re-*Bildung* as ideal for legal education 50–57
Re-*Bildung*, and re-gaining authority of Academia 55–7
research and education, emphasising unity of 45–6, 55, 56–7
and self-formation 36, 37, 38, 39–40, 42–3, 48–9, 53–4
skeptical legal education (SLE) 32
and sociality 41–2, 54
state intervention, resistance to 40–42
technological innovations and information dissemination, effects of 45, 51, 53–4
see also interdisciplinary approach
black-letter law (legislation and case law) 6, 25, 116, 128–9, 162, 166–7, 186
Böcker, A 164, 173
Bohlin, H 47–8
Bolitho, J 147, 148
Bologna Process 77, 202, 214–15
Bourdieu, P 61–2, 63, 69, 70, 73, 74, 75–6, 292
Brecht, B, *In Praise of Learning* 119–20
Bridgman, P 146
Brockmann, J 58
Brown, LN 86
Buckel, S 62, 72, 77
Burchill, S 126, 140, 297
Burns, K 152, 153, 157
Burnyeat, M 24, 29
Bybee, K 211, 212, 213

Canaan, J 109, 111, 116, 296
Cane, P 153
canon, legal *see* legal canon
career, academic *see* legal academics
career prospect issues 130–31
and international law 101
labour market and liberal arts education 206
training for lawyers, need for enhanced 154–9
vocational training *see* vocational training
Carrington, P 16, 20
case law, black-letter law (legislation and case law) 6, 25, 116, 128–9, 162, 166–7, 186
case reading, and resources from visual and dramatic arts 244–66, 292, 304–6
Choose Your Island activity 256, 258, 259–61, 266
cognitive skills 246

comparing differences outcome 256
Cutting out the Ratio activity 256, 257, 265
Poster Session activity 256, 257, 265
precedent theory 247–9, 261–2
ratio decidendi (RD) determination example 247–9, 261–2, 300, 305
reading actively and imaginatively 247–50
see also visuals for a critical legal profession
case study method, criticism of 271
challenge and ability, finding balance between 271
see also ability
Christensen, S 157
Chui, W 124
Clinton, M 87, 88, 92
cognitive skills 246
see also ability; case reading, and resources from visual and dramatic arts
collegiate social controlling network 73–4
Collier, R 89, 165
Collini, S 205, 209
commercialised professionalism, emergence of 94–5
see also professionalism, legal academics
comparative legal cultures 166–70, 175–6, 178
comparative legal education 180–97, 300–302
alternative teaching techniques 186, 195
anecdotic exercises, use of 188–9
constructivist approach 187–90, 196
Cornell Prison Education Program (CPEP) 181–2, 301
crisis and revolution, current 181
Erasmus exchange programs 191, 194
importance of 183–7, 194–5
Inside-Out Program in prison environment 185–6
prison legal tradition 184–5
religious legal traditions, influence of 186–7
role-playing and critical legal thinking 189
students' prior knowledge, use of 187–8
teaching legal traditions in untraditional environment 182–90, 196–7
traditional comparative law teaching, defence of 193
traditional comparative law teaching, inadequacy 190–91, 193–5
traditional comparative law teaching, initial objectives and EU and US comparisons 191–3, 194
trans-systemic project, McGill University, Quebec 196
Western legal tradition focus 195
concepts, dealing with difficult 270, 278, 279, 280
constructivist approach 187–90, 196
conversation skills 19–20, 22, 32
dialogue, interpretation and understanding through 47–8
discourse and social engagement 111–12
liberal learning and 'free' conversation 18–19, 290
Cook, N 212
Cornelissen, W 35, 56
Cornell Prison Education Program (CPEP) 181–4, 301
corporate actors, portraying role of 175
see also visuals for a critical legal profession
Cotterell, R 194
Cownie, F 81, 91, 93
crime, government 'tough on crime' policies 147–50
critical attitude, methodology as 123
critical democratic citizenship 205–6, 209–10, 220–21
critical legal profession, visuals for *see* visuals for a critical legal profession
critical legal studies (CLS) movement 15–16, 21, 22, 25, 27, 32

critical legal thinking, and role-playing 189
critical pedagogy, and international law *see* interdisciplinary approach
critical thinking, stimulation of 208, 215, 216–19
Cross, R 151, 152
Cryer, R 126
Csikszentmihalyi's flow theory and ability to learn 271
cultural differences
  tolerance toward following legal rules 166–7, 169–70
  see also religious legal traditions, influence of
cultural hegemony
  Eurocentrism 106–7, 295–6
  global North dominance 100–101, 106–7
  and international law 100, 108–10, 296
curiosity and learning, stimulation of 207–8
curriculum limitations, dealing with 156, 157–8
Curry-Sumner, I 154

Davis, G 146
Davis, K 152
De Bono, E 26
De Mestral, A 191, 192, 194, 196
De Tocqueville, A 218
Dearlove, J 87
deconstruction techniques 25–6, 33, 297, 298
  see also skeptical legal education (SLE)
Dedek, H 191, 192, 194, 196
Deem, R 79, 92
delayed learning effect 278–9, 283
democratic citizenship 205–6, 209–10, 220–21
Devlin, R 133–4
Dewey, J 113, 183, 205
dialogue, interpretation and understanding through 47–8
  see also conversation skills
difficult texts and concepts, dealing with 270, 278, 279, 280
discourse and social engagement 111–12
  see also conversation skills
Dochy, F 77
doctrine and theory, relationship between 116–17
documentaries, impact of 175–6
  see also visuals for a critical legal profession
Dörpinghaus, A 111–12
Douzinas, C 125–6, 133
Drake, E 149
dual degree courses 158, 191
Duncan, N 145, 159
Dworkin, R 11, 84, 85, 135, 294, 312–13

eliticization and social climate 70–71, 77–8
  see also academic education, socialization
Ellickson, R 144
empathy development 219–20
  see also liberal arts and science education
empirical methodologies and evidence-based practice 142–59, 298–9
  anecdotal evidence 147–8, 298
  curriculum limitations, dealing with 156, 157–8
  evidence-based government policy, formulation skills 156
  evidence-based practice, concept of 143–6
  judicial process, importance of facts 150–54
  legal practice benefits 155, 298–9
  social evidence base in developing legislation 146–50
  social science research on law and justice system, increase in 153–4
  teaching methods and availability 156–7
  training for lawyers, need for enhanced 154–9

see also theory and methodology, importance of
epistemic injustice, reasons for 227–9
see also students' perception and seeing injustice
Erasmus exchange programs 191, 194
ethical awareness 230–33, 234, 235–7, 239–40, 304
see also students' perception and seeing injustice
ethical individualism 84, 294
see also legal academics
Eurocentrism 106–7, 295–6
see also cultural hegemony
Evans, T 79
Evetts, J 94
evidence-based practice *see* empirical methodologies and evidence-based practice
examination
apparatus, anonymized 66–9
dress requirements 68
integration of assessment paper 275–6
judicial examination office, effects on students 67–8
myths and stories, dealing with 68
oral examiners and impression management 65
organized psychological pressure during examination phase 64–5
stress, coping strategies 60, 68–9, 311
technology and its effects 63–75
see also grades
experiential learning *see* prisons

Fanghanel, J 87
Feminist Judgments Project 132
Ferall, V 205, 206
Fishwick, E 147, 148
Foucault, M 62, 63, 72, 105, 121, 123, 128, 129, 131, 138, 139–40, 141, 165, 232, 234, 292
Foucault's mirrors 235–7, 239, 240, 241, 242, 304
Francot, L 268–9, 283
Frankel, M 151
Freckleton, I 151
Freidson, E 80, 82
Freire, P 110–11, 116, 117, 118, 296
Fricker, M 227, 228, 231
Fuller, L 136
Furedi, F 3, 86

Gadamer, H 21, 25, 33, 34, 46–7, 53, 54, 290, 291
Galanter, M 173
Garrison, J 113
Geary, A 125–6, 133
Gee, E 211
Genn, H 145, 155
Gerlof, K 60
Germany, academic freedom (*Lehrfreiheit*), history of 82–3
Giamatti, AB 208, 213
Gill, R 44
Giroux, H 3
Glenn, P 183, 184
global citizenship 202, 212–13
global North dominance 100–101, 106–7
see also cultural hegemony
Goldhaber, M 220
Goodhart, A 247
Goodman, D 211, 212
Goodman, N 244
governance changes, resistance to 92, 94
government intervention, resistance to, and *Bildung* ideal 40–42
governmentality of legal education, concerns over 131–2
grades
competition for good 73–4, 76
nobility 72–3
see also examination
Gramsci, A 100, 106, 108, 112, 113–14
Greco, J 224
groups
discussion benefits 275
personal details, sharing, and group connections 188
supervision 272–3, 274, 280, 306–7
Guest, D 87, 88, 92

Hale, B 158
Halsey, A 89, 93
Hammersley, M 157
Hanlon, G 94
'hard' and 'soft' modules, distinction between 103–4
  see also legal education
Harvey, D 109
Hawkins, H 210
Hazard, J 180
Head, B 142
Hegel, G 46–7, 112
Heinrich, P 71
Henkel, M 92
Heyes, C 236
hierarchy in legal education, effects of 130
  see also legal education
Hjorland, B 143
Ho, H 224
Horlacher, R 37, 38, 39, 43
Horstkemper, M 59
Howieson, B 231
humanitarianism, international lawyers as agents of 106
Humboldt, W von 37, 39–43, 44, 47, 53, 83, 204, 291
Humphreys, D 206
Hunter, R 132
Husa, J 167, 187, 194

ILAC (Issue, Law, Apply, Conclusion) formula to ITAC (Issue, Theory, Apply, Conclusion) formula 137–40, 297
imagination
  narrative 202, 209, 212, 219–20
  reading actively and imaginatively 247–50
information dissemination and technological innovations 45, 51, 53–4
information and judgment skills 19–20, 28, 29–31
injustice, seeing *see* students' perception and seeing injustice
Inside-Out Program in prison environment 185–6
  see also prisons
institutional constraints on educators 108–10
institutional (faculty) management 24–6, 33
institutions, governance changes 85–9, 90–93
instrumental learning and applied education 18–19
  see also skeptical legal education (SLE)
intellectual inheritance and tradition, dealing with 32, 33, 312
intellectual integrity development 20–21
intellectual uncertainty 274, 283–4, 292
interdisciplinary approach 212–16, 218–19
  Bildung as complement to training 113–14, 296
  Bildung etymology 112–13
  career prospect issues 101
  critical pedagogy and *Bildung* 110–14
  critical pedagogy and *Bildung* in practice 114–19
  critical reflexivity 111–12
  cultural hegemony 100, 108–10, 296
  dialogical teaching 110–11
  discourse and social engagement 111–12
  indeterminacy, revealing 118
  labinar experiment 115–16
  neoliberalism effects 108–10, 111
  neutrality of law and case study approach 118–19
  passive attitude to learning 102–3, 107
  status quo reproduction 107
interpretation and understanding through dialogue 47–8
  see also conversation skills

Jackall, R 93
Jaschik, S 206
Jefferson, T 210
judgment and information skills 19–20, 28, 29–31

judicial examination office, effects on students 67–8
see also examination
judicial process, importance of facts 150–54
judicial reasoning perspectives, looking at different 132–3, 136–7, 139–40

Kamba, W 190, 194, 195
Kant, I 15, 16, 31
Karran, T 83
Katzenbach, J 94
Kelly, P 206
Kelman, M 15
Kennedy, D 15–16, 21, 22, 25, 27, 83, 101–4, 107, 113, 116, 119
Kift, S 157
Kivinch, O 82
Knight, P 90
knowledge assessment ability 19, 31, 45, 46–7, 54, 188, 190, 231, 291
see also ability
knowledge fallibility, understanding 24
see also skeptical legal education (SLE)
Koblik, S 204
Koehler, J 151
Kolsaker, A 91, 92
Krautz, J 39, 40, 53
Kronman, A 4, 17, 29, 32, 207
Kuleszka, E 202
Kutscha, G 42

labinar experiment 115–16
labour market and liberal arts education 206
see also career prospect issues
Lang, E 204, 210
Lang, J 216
Latour, B 30
law as academic discipline 3–7, 282–3
Law Benchmark 90–91
'law and film' movement 160–61
see also visuals for a critical legal profession
Law and Lounge experiment *see* student self-organization and critique as skeptical reflexivity experiment
law students, lack of research into 60–61
Lea, J 147
learning, passive attitude to 102–3, 107
learning by playing 244–7
see also case reading, and resources from visual and dramatic arts
learning through experience experiment (Dewey) 113
legal academic education debate 3–7, 282–3
legal academics 79–95, 293–5
academic freedom 82–5, 91–2
academic obligations 83–4, 94–5
benchmarking 90–91
commercialised professionalism, emergence of 94–5
ethical individualism 84, 294
human resource management funding increase (England and Wales) 87–8
institutions and governance changes 85–9, 90–93
law degrees 81
managerialism in universities, move towards 87–9, 94, 294
professionalism 80–82, 84–5, 94, 294
public and private life of universities, distinction between 89–93
resistance to governance changes 92, 94
as team players 79–80, 93
university privileges, history of 82–3
work appraisals of academic performance 88–9, 91–2
see also teaching methods
legal canon
absence of 124–7, 297
suggestion 128–9
legal education
and authority, relationship between 49–50
and Bologna Process 77, 202, 214–15
as commodity 130
grades *see* grades

'hard' and 'soft' modules, distinction between 103–4
hierarchy, effects of 130
institutional constraints on educators 108–10
skeptical *see* skeptical legal education (SLE)
teaching methods *see* teaching methods
Legge, K 88
legislation
black-letter law (legislation and case law) 6, 25, 116, 128–9, 162, 166–7, 186
social evidence base in developing 146–50
Legrand, P 168
liberal arts and sciences education
Ancient Greece, liberal arts tradition 203–4
critical democratic citizenship stimulation 220–21
critical thinking, stimulation of 208, 215, 216–19
curiosity and learning, stimulation of 207–8
and democratic citizenship 205–6, 209–10
empathy development 219–20
Four Freedoms Awards 220–21
global citizenship 202, 212–13
interdisciplinary approach, benefits of 212–16, 218–19
labour market and liberal arts education 206
legal education and Bologna process 214–15
liberal arts education, European expansion 206–7, 214–15
liberal arts and sciences programmes, similarities between 207
liberal arts teaching 210–16
liberal arts tradition 203–10
liberal arts tradition, US development 204–5, 208, 214
narrative imagination 202, 209, 212, 219–20
orchestrating encounters 217–18, 219–20
proposals for change 319
research skills 217–19
University College, Roosevelt 216–21
vocational training versus liberal arts 205–6, 211–12
liberal learning and 'free' conversation 18–19, 290
see also conversation skills
liberal learning (Oakeshott), and skeptical legal education (SLE) 16–20, 22, 32
Ligertwood, A 151
Llewellyn, K 248
Lock, G 35, 43–4, 51
Lorenz, C 35, 43–4, 51

McConville, M 124
McCoubrey, H 125
Macedo, D 114–15, 117
McNay, I 87
managerialism
and *Bildung* ideal 44–5, 51–2, 54–5, 292
effects 106, 108–10
move towards 87–9, 94, 294
market pressures 99–100, 108–10
Marquard, O 28, 33
Maurer, S 62
Menand, L 206
methodology and theory *see* theory and methodology, importance of
Metzger, W 83
Meyer, P 235
Michelon, C 225, 227
Minkkinen, P 123, 125
moral and intellectual integrity development 20–21
Mullane, G 152, 153
Murdoch, I 226, 229
Murphy, W 89

narrative imagination 202, 209, 212, 219–20
Nelken, D 167, 168, 193

neoliberalism effects 1–2, 3, 108–10, 111
Nesbit, J 149
Netherlands
function of academic legal training 161–3
Law and Lounge experiment *see* student self-organization and critique as skeptical reflexivity experiment
network, collegiate social controlling 73–4
neutrality of law 105, 118–19, 123–4, 134
Newell, H 93
Nietzsche, F 52
Norris, C 26
Nussbaum, M 4, 16, 21, 22, 27, 28, 31, 32, 205–6, 230
Nutley, S 146

Oakeshott, M 16–20, 22, 32, 290
Odgers, S 151
Oelkers, J 37, 38
oral examiners and impression management 65
see also examination
orchestrating encounters *see* liberal arts and sciences education
Orford, A 102, 104, 105–6, 120
organized psychological pressure during examination phase 64–5
see also examination
organized uncertainty 74–5
see also academic education, socialization

Pacaluk, M 231
Pantin, W 82
Paulsen, F 82–3
performance-related self-image 74–5
see also academic education, socialization
Perkins, H 80–81, 85
personal details, sharing, and group connections 188
see also groups
Peters, M 100
Pilniok, A 59
Plato, *The Republic* 232–3
plurality of teaching voices, dealing with 25
Poikus, P 82
political analysis, avoidance of 16, 21–2, 23, 25, 30
see also prejudices and biases, overcoming
Pompa, L 185
Prahl, H 59
Prange, K 37
precedent theory, and case reading 247–9, 261–2
prejudices and biases, overcoming 21, 27–9, 32–3, 225, 227, 228–9, 231–3, 234, 238–9, 241
see also political analysis, avoidance of
Presthus, R 71
prisons
Cornell Prison Education Program (CPEP) 181–4, 301
Inside-Out Program in prison environment 185–6
prison clinic course, and mirror experiment 233–4, 237–42, 304
prison legal tradition 184–5
private and public life of universities, distinction between 89–93
privileges, history of university 82–3
professional influence on courses 103–4, 109–10
professionalism, legal academics 80–82, 84–5, 94–5, 294
proposals for change 314–21
psychological pressure during examination phase 64–5
see also examination
public and private life of universities, distinction between 89–93
Pyke, J 158

questioning
metaphysics of 31–4
oneself and one's own views 47–8, 53
practices, questioning 26–31, 33

Rachlinski, J 145–6
Rathus, Z 153, 154
ratio decidendi (RD) determination example 247–9, 261–2, 300, 305
Ratner, S 127
Raz, J 23
Re-*Bildung see under Bildung* ideal
reading actively and imaginatively 247–50
see also imagination
real life portrayals 174–7
see also visuals for a critical legal profession
regionalism of international law 106–7
see also interdisciplinary approach
Reichberg, G 224
Reimann, M 180, 181, 192, 193, 194, 195
Reinalda, B 202
religious legal traditions, influence of 186–7
see also cultural differences
research and education, emphasising unity of 45–6, 55, 56–7
see also Bildung ideal
research skills 217–19
Richardson, J 151
Rijke, N 219
Riles, A 116
role-playing and critical legal thinking 189
Rosa, H 55
Rosen, L 168
Roth, M 205, 209
Rudd, K 147

Samaha, J 211
Samuel, G 167, 249
Sandel, M 209, 210
Scager, K 269, 271, 274
Schaeper, H 62
Schauer, F 46
Schilling, H 112–13
self-discipline efforts 65, 74–5
self-estrangement tactics 65, 73, 76–7
self-formation, and *Bildung* ideal 36, 37, 38, 39–40, 42–3, 48–9, 53–4
self-organization *see* student self-organization and critique as skeptical reflexivity experiment (Law and Lounge experiment, Utrecht University)
self-worth of academics, importance of 93–4
Sen, A 225
Shafron, P 151
Shaviro, D 151
Shay, G 185–6
Sheldon, K 77
Shore, C 108
Siems, M 181
Silbey, S 211, 212
Simpson, A 248
Simpson, G 119
skeptical legal education (SLE) 15–34, 290–91
Ancient Skepticism and Socratic dialogues 24, 27, 28, 290, 292
Bildung ideal 32
conversation skills 19–20, 22, 32
critical legal studies (CLS) movement 15–16, 21, 22, 25, 27, 32
deconstruction techniques 25–6, 33, 297, 298
information and judgment skills 19–20, 28, 29–31
institutional context (faculty management) 24–6, 33
instrumental learning and applied education 18–19
intellectual inheritance and tradition, dealing with 32, 33, 312
knowledge fallibility, understanding 24
liberal learning and ‘free’ conversation 18–19, 290
and liberal learning (Oakeshott) 16–20, 22, 32
metaphysics of questioning 31–4
moral and intellectual integrity development 20–21
plurality of teaching voices, dealing with 25
and political analysis, avoidance of 16, 21–2, 23, 25, 30

prejudices, dealing with own 21, 27–9, 32–3
proposals for change 314–15
questioning practices, questioning 26–31, 33
reasons for 29–31
student participation 22
suspension of judgment, applying 29
teaching mode 23–4, 28, 29, 31, 32–3
value judgments, controversial nature of 23, 27–9, 32–3
vocational education concerns 19, 29–30
skill, methodology as 123–4, 128, 139
Slaughter, A 127
Smith, D 94
Smits, J 55
Snow, CP, *The Masters* 86
social engagement and discourse 111–12
see also conversation skills
social evidence base in developing legislation 146–50
social science research on law and justice system, increase in 153–4
sociality, and *Bildung* ideal 41–2, 54
socialization *see* academic education, socialization
sociology of law 170–74, 175, 177–8
Socratic dialogues and Ancient Skepticism 24, 27, 28, 290, 292
Sorkin, D 38, 39, 40, 41, 42
Sosa, E 224, 228
South Africa, *Pistorius Trial* 134–6, 137, 138–9
Stolker, C 4–5, 79, 163, 282, 283, 308
Stone, J 248–9, 261–2
student feedback, case reading, and resources from visual and dramatic arts 263–6
student newcomers' status 70–71
see also academic education, socialization
student number increases 86
student participation, call for more room for 22
student prior knowledge, use of 187–8
student self-organization and critique as skeptical reflexivity experiment (Law and Lounge experiment, Utrecht University) 267–87, 291, 292, 306–7
academic education and development 282–6
blind spots, recognizing 285–6
case study method, criticism of 271
challenge and ability, finding balance between 271
chronological study questions 275
critical assessment, encouragement of 268, 270, 274–5, 277, 278, 306–7
Csikszentmihalyi's flow theory and ability to learn 271
delayed learning effect 278–9, 283
difficult texts and concepts, dealing with 270, 278, 279, 280
group discussion benefits 275
intellectual uncertainty concerns 274, 283–4, 292
law as academic discipline 282–3
primary sources, avoidance of 270
self-organization as pedagogical tool 273–4
skeptical legal education (SLE) 268, 269, 273, 283–4, 306
skeptical legal education (SLE) and intellectual uncertainty 283–4
teacher involvement concerns 279–80, 284
virtual learning environment (VLE) 277
students' perception and seeing injustice 223–43, 304
attention as virtue 226, 229–30, 241
cries of pain, recognizing 226, 229–30, 240
epistemic injustice, reasons for 227–9
ethical awareness 230–33, 234, 235–7, 239–40, 304
experiential learning 233–7
Foucault's mirrors 235–7, 239, 240, 241, 242, 304
injustice and virtues, seeing 225–30, 233

negative prejudices 231–2
prejudices and biases, overcoming 225, 227, 228–9, 231–3, 234, 238–9, 241
prison clinic course 233–4
prisoners, involvement with, and mirror experiment 237–42, 304
systematic injustice and prejudice, relationship between 229
teaching virtues to students 230–34
virtue definition 225–6
virtue of openness 230, 235
virtue's role in legal decision-making 223–4
supersession, ethics of 32, 34
supervision of groups 272–3, 274, 280, 306–7
see also groups
systematic injustice and prejudice, relationship between 229
see also students' perception and seeing injustice

Taekema, S 5, 11
teaching methods
alternative techniques 186, 195
international law 102–4, 105–8, 117–18
practice and uncertainty of the professional, *Bildung* ideal 45–6, 53, 54, 55
research methodologies 156–7
skeptical legal education (SLE) 23–4, 28, 29, 31, 32–3
teacher involvement concerns, Law and Lounge experiment, Utrecht University 279–80, 284
teacher/student hierarchy, dealing with 113, 115–16
teaching legal traditions in untraditional environment 182–90, 196–7
teaching of methodologies 129–33
teaching virtues to students 230–34
see also legal academics; legal education
team players, legal academics as 79–80, 93
technology
examination technology and its effects 63–75
innovations and information dissemination, effects of 45, 51, 53–4
Teubner, G 168
theory and doctrine, relationship between 116–17
theory and methodology, importance of 121–41, 296–8
alternative (external) legal methodologies 125–6, 128, 298
conservative content of law modules, concerns over 130–32
education as commodity 130
Feminist Judgments Project 132
governmentality of legal education, concerns over 131–2
hierarchy in legal education, effects of 130
ILAC (Issue, Law, Apply, Conclusion) formula to ITAC (Issue, Theory, Apply, Conclusion) formula 137–40, 297
interrogation and application skills 125, 133–7, 138–9
judicial reasoning perspectives, looking at different 132–3, 136–7, 139–40
legal canon suggestion 128–9
legal research methods and absence of canon 124–7, 297
methodology as critical attitude 123
methodology as skill 123–4, 128, 139
methodology as way of thinking 123
teaching methods versus teaching of methodologies 129–33
theoretical categorizations 126–7
theoretical character of other disciplines, borrowing 125
theory application, learning 128
theory aversion, reasons for 130
theory versus methodology, difference between 121–4
traditional legal theory 125

see also empirical methodologies and evidence-based practice
Thornton, M 78, 89
Threadgold, T 105, 108
Tillmann, K 59
tolerance toward following legal rules, cultural differences 166–7, 169–70
traditional comparative law teaching 190–95
see also comparative legal education
training for lawyers, need for enhanced 154–9
see also career prospect issues
trans-systemic project, McGill University, Quebec 196
Trow, M 90
Trowler, P 90, 93
Turkey, epistemic injustice 227–8, 229, 239
Twining, W 151

UK
academic freedom, history of 82
legal academics *see* legal academics
Nuffield Report and use empirical methodologies 145, 155
Universal Declaration of Human Rights, on education 44
university privileges, history of 82–3
US
Cornell Prison Education Program (CPEP) 181–4, 301
Society for Empirical Legal Studies 144

Vacca, J 183
value judgments, controversial nature of 23, 27–9, 32–3
see also skeptical legal education (SLE)
Van Aarsen, J 219
Van Dalm, L 218
Van der Burg, W 163
Van der Schaaf, M 154
Van Hoecke, M 124–5
Veitch, S 311
virtual learning environment (VLE), Law and Lounge experiment, Utrecht University 277
virtues
attention as virtue 226, 229–30, 241
definition 225–6
teaching virtues to students 230–34
virtue of openness 230, 235
see also students' perception and seeing injustice
visuals for a critical legal profession 160–79
anthropology of law 163–6, 178
Australian Aborigines and Ayers Rock as place of law 163–5
comparative legal cultures 166–70, 175–6, 178
comparative legal cultures, reasons for making comparisons 167–8, 175–6
corporate actors, portraying role of 175
documentaries, impact of 175–6
'law and film' movement 160–61
Netherlands, function of academic legal training 161–3
Netherlands, law school curriculum and civil effect, black-letter law versus other courses 162
as portrayals of real life 174–7
reasons for use of visuals 174–7
rule of law, use of 172–3
sociology of law 170–74, 175, 177–8
tolerance toward following legal rules, cultural differences 166–7, 169–70
see also case reading, and resources from visual and dramatic arts
vocational training
concerns 19, 29–30
versus liberal arts 205–6, 211–12
see also career prospect issues
Vogel, A 86
Von Hentig, H 112
Von Humboldt, W 36, 37, 204, 291

Walker, V 151
Watson, A 168

Watson, I 164
Waxman, M 181
Webber, B 211
Weber, M 16, 23, 33–4
Weber, S 62
Weijers, I 45
Weil, S 226, 229
Weinstein, J 151
Western legal tradition focus 195
  Eurocentrism 106–7, 295–6
  see also cultural hegemony
White, J 5, 271
White, N 125
Wilson, D 149
Wilson, F 88
Winterton, G 180
Witteveen, W 298, 312
Wittgenstein, L 27–8
Wittpoth, J 76
work appraisals of academic performance 88–9, 91–2
Wrase, M 58
Wright, S 108

Young, I 229
Youth Justice (Boot Camp Orders) Act (Queensland), Australia 149–50

Ziegler, P 146
Zimmermann, H 62
Zuckerman, A 151